NATURE AND TIME

Volume II

NATURE AND TIME

Volume II

Paths to Justice and Transformation

DONG IN BAEK

RESOURCE *Publications* • Eugene, Oregon

NATURE AND TIME, VOLUME II
Paths to Justice and Transformation

Copyright © 2025 Dong In Baek. All rights reserved. Except for brief quotations in critical publications or reviews, no part of this book may be reproduced in any manner without prior written permission from the publisher. Write: Permissions, Wipf and Stock Publishers, 199 W. 8th Ave., Suite 3, Eugene, OR 97401.

Resource Publications
An Imprint of Wipf and Stock Publishers
199 W. 8th Ave., Suite 3
Eugene, OR 97401

www.wipfandstock.com

PAPERBACK ISBN: 979-8-3852-3906-1
HARDCOVER ISBN: 979-8-3852-3907-8
EBOOK ISBN: 979-8-3852-3908-5
VERSION NUMBER 02/03/25

DEDICATION

TO THE HONORED MEMORIES of Professors Jürgen Moltmann, Yorick Spiegel, Albrecht Ulrich, and Klaus Otte.

With deepest gratitude and reverence, I lay this work at your feet—you, my esteemed mentors and spiritual fathers, whose teachings and steadfast examples have indelibly marked my journey.

To thee, Professor Jürgen Moltmann, whose theological voyage was forged amidst the crucible of war and captivity. Thy profound reflections turned personal anguish into a relentless pursuit of hope and reconciliation, guiding my soul through faith's intricate dance with humanity and nature. Thy works ever whisper of hope's boundless reach, even when night is darkest.

To thee, Professor Yorick Spiegel of Frankfurt University, my doctoral guide and chief examiner. Thy unwavering devotion to the call of teaching, despite thine own trials, has etched an enduring legacy upon my life and labor. Thine insights into ethics and the human psyche, coupled with thy personal fortitude, embody the resilience and commitment this tome seeks to explore. Thy counsel has been the compass shaping my grasp of man's condition and the tangled web of moral choice.

To thee, Professor Albrecht Ulrich of the Free University of Berlin, who steered me as I embarked upon a second scholarly odyssey in international relations. Thy profound and contemplative discourses on peace have deeply influenced my approach to reconciliation and the tapestry of global understanding. Though fate forbade thy return to the halls of learning, thy legacy lives in the principles of peace and conflict's resolution that thou didst so fervently champion. Thy impact profoundly shapes my toil in peacebuilding, in Korea's shadow and beyond.

To thee, the late Professor Klaus Otte of Basel University, my secondary examiner and a luminary in the studies of Karl Barth. Thy scholarly rigor and devotion to theological truth have carved deep furrows in my theological pursuits. The vastness of thy knowledge and thy unwavering commitment to academic excellence guided me through theology's labyrinthine passages; thy legacy yet inspires me as I grapple with faith's urgent questions in a world divided.

Each of you trod paths strewn with formidable trials, transmuting personal hardships into wells of wisdom and compassion. Your lives stand as monuments to resilience, courage, and adversity's transformative might. Through your teachings and the very fabric of your lives, you have shown that suffering may forge growth's crucible, leading to a richer, more nuanced grasp of both the human heart and the divine. Your legacies affirm that even in the depths of personal or collective sorrow, a beacon of renewal, a path toward peace and reconciliation, ever remains.

It is my fervent hope that this work mirrors the depth of your teachings and fuels the ceaseless dialogue on reconciliation—not solely upon the Korean Peninsula but wherever division and strife sow seeds of hatred and ruin. The themes herein are universal, touching upon ideological clashes, religious and political strife as in Palestine, and any realm where humanity aches for healing and restoration.

May this endeavor honor your memories and kindle in future generations the pursuit of peace with the passion and dedication you so luminously exemplified throughout your storied careers. Your legacies shall forever remind us that even amid suffering's grasp, hope, renewal, and reconciliation remain within reach.

CONTENTS

Preface | xi

Prologue: Bridging Nature, Time, and Reconciliation | xv

Introduction: Fusion of Horizons | 1

    Franz Rosenzweig's Perspective on Liberation | 3

    Gustavo Gutiérrez and Liberation Theology | 6

    Karl Barth and Natural Theology | 8

    Leonardo Boff's Ecological Liberation Theology | 10

    The Korean Demilitarized Zone and Ecological Peacebuilding | 13

    Reconciliation in Liberation and Peace Theology | 15

    Political Reconciliation and Power Dynamics | 17

    Desmond Tutu and Restorative Justice | 19

    James Cone's Black Liberation Theology | 21

    Dietrich Bonhoeffer on Ethical Action and Resistance | 23

Chapter One: Global Liberation: Theology in Action | 26

    1.1. Power, Ideology, and Resistance: Approaches to Liberation | 27

        1.1.1. Franz Rosenzweig on Liberation: Divine and Human Collaboration | 28

        1.1.2. Theological, Historical, and Practical Approaches to Oppression | 50

        1.1.3. Bultmann and Liberation Theology | 57

        1.1.4. Unraveling Power, Identity, and Resistance | 71

1.2. The Evolution of Theology in Social Justice | 78

    1.2.1. Merging Traditions for Justice | 78

    1.2.2. Integrating Secular Thought and Theology | 86

1.3. Justice and Redemption in Rosenzweig, Levinas, and Arendt | 93

1.4. Global Dialogues on Liberation | 102

1.5. Identity, Freedom, and Critical Voices | 115

1.6. Conclusion | 123

Chapter Two: New Concepts and Methods in Liberation Theology | 128

2.1. Theology and Social Justice | 129

    2.1.1. Making the Kingdom Real Through Action | 129

    2.1.2. Expanding Theological Justice | 138

    2.1.3. Authenticity, Society, and Justice | 145

2.2. Innovating Theology Education and Discourse | 156

    2.2.1. Addressing Ecology, Justice, and Suffering | 156

    2.2.2. Diverse Narratives in Theology | 166

    2.2.3. Rethinking Theology Education | 174

2.3. Conclusion: A Holistic Approach to Liberation | 182

Chapter Three: North Korea, Human Rights, and the Kingdom of God | 189

3.1. Justice, Human Rights, and Exclusion in Theology | 190

3.2. Ethics of the Kingdom: Justice, Peace, and Ecology | 198

    3.2.1. Justice and Human Dignity in the Kingdom of God | 198

    3.2.2. Relational Theologies for Reform | 207

3.3. Liberation Theology's Role in North Korean Justice | 215

    3.3.1. Dignity and Justice for North Korea's Oppressed | 216

    3.3.2. Educating for Human Rights | 226

    3.3.3. Embracing Suffering in Mission | 237

3.4. Jesus' Call to Justice | 249

   3.4.1. The Exodus and Liberation | 250

   3.4.2. Jesus and the Oppressed | 260

3.5. Challenging Power with Theology and Justice | 272

   3.5.1. Nonviolence and Prophetic Imagination | 273

   3.5.2. Theology and Justice in Modern Thought | 284

3.6. Approaching Human Rights in North Korea | 296

Chapter Four: Conclusion: A Framework for Sustainable Liberation | 302

   4.1. Franz Rosenzweig and the Collaborative Path to Liberation | 303

   4.2. Expanding Liberation Theology with Interdisciplinary Insights | 306

   4.3. A Multifaceted Framework for Addressing Human Rights Abuses in North Korea | 309

   4.4. Reimagining Theological Education through Praxis | 311

   4.5. The Kingdom of God as a Present Reality: A Call to Social Justice and Active Engagement | 313

   4.6. Environmental Justice within Liberation Theology | 316

   4.7. Reimagining the Church as a Countercultural Force | 318

   4.8. Historical Memory and Liberation | 320

   4.9. Integrating Theology and Practical Justice | 322

Epilogue | 325

About the Author | 329

Bibliography | 331

PREFACE

DEAR READER,

As you embark on the journey through *Nature and Time (Vol. II): Paths to Justice and Transformation*, you are invited into a rich dialogue that redefines traditional boundaries between nature, time, and history. This second volume in our series deepens the exploration of peace by presenting an integrated view where natural and historical forces interact dynamically. This interconnection offers fresh perspectives on peace, unity, and reconciliation, particularly within the complex context of the Korean Peninsula.

In this work, nature transcends its conventional scientific confines, and time is liberated from linear constraints. Together, they form a vibrant framework that influences human experience and societal development. By integrating the concept of natural revelation—the idea that nature itself is a profound source of insight—with historical narratives, we craft a unique lens to navigate the complexities and contradictions that define the Korean Peninsula.

Central to our discussion is how philosophical, theological, and socio-political paradigms can profoundly reshape our understanding of peace. Drawing upon the intellectual heritage of thinkers like Franz Rosenzweig, Rudolf Bultmann, and Eugen Rosenstock-Huessy, we explore revolutionary ideas about time, space, and relationality. Their perspectives encourage us to reexamine the enduring divisions and tensions on the Korean Peninsula, prompting us to envision history not merely as a series of events but as a living network of relationships and interactions that continuously shape our collective existence.

This volume challenges the perception of the Korean Peninsula as a static entity defined by past conflicts. Instead, it is portrayed as a dynamic and evolving space shaped by diverse historical, cultural, and ideological currents. Philosophical insights from Martin Heidegger, Immanuel Kant, and Friedrich Nietzsche delve into how deeply ingrained perceptions, cultural narratives, and historical memories influence the region's present and future. For instance, Nietzsche's concept of eternal recurrence invites us to consider the repetitive cycles of conflict and how these patterns might be broken. Heidegger's notions of existential spatiality and being-in-the-world help illuminate the lived experiences of division and the existential angst accompanying separation. These frameworks offer not just theoretical insights but practical avenues to reimagine policies and approaches that address deep-seated issues and promote genuine reconciliation.

Moreover, our discourse extends beyond theoretical analysis by incorporating theological insights that advocate for ethical engagement and action. The cyclical and relational concepts of time, as expressed by Rosenzweig, propose viewing peacebuilding not as a finite goal but as a continuous journey requiring enduring commitment and renewal. This understanding resonates with the natural cycles—the changing seasons, the ebb and flow of tides—suggesting that efforts toward reconciliation must be persistent, adaptive, and empathetic. Bultmann's reinterpretation of theological space enables us to address not only the physical divisions marked by borders and demilitarized zones but also the existential and spiritual separations between communities and individuals. By understanding these divides as both symbolic and relational, we encourage a more profound engagement with the human dimensions of conflict, urging us to heal not just the land but the hearts and minds of those who inhabit it.

In crafting this volume, I have been immensely fortunate to draw upon the support and wisdom of a diverse community spanning global divides. My deepest gratitude goes to esteemed colleagues, dedicated mentors, and the various communities of faith and scholarship who have been constant sources of strength, inspiration, and critical insight. From the warm and welcoming congregations in Portland and Vancouver, who provided a nurturing environment for dialogue and reflection, to the dynamic intellectual circles across Seoul, whose rigorous debates and rich cultural perspectives have significantly enriched this work, your contributions have been invaluable. Special thanks are due to my family, whose unwavering support, patience, and encouragement have been the foundation upon which this project rests.

Rather than offering simplistic solutions to complex problems, this book invites readers to engage deeply with the concepts of peace and unity. It challenges us to look beyond immediate conflicts and political divisions, exploring how the intertwined forces of nature and history can illuminate paths toward reconciliation. Through an interdisciplinary approach encompassing theology, philosophy, history, cultural studies, and social science, this work aims to foster a dialogue as varied and complex as the realities it seeks to address.

Ultimately, this volume is a call for renewed engagement with the world around us—a plea to transcend boundaries, whether physical, ideological, or emotional. It encourages us to see beyond entrenched narratives and explore how the interweaving of nature and time, of past and present, can offer transformative insights into reconciliation and unity. It is my sincere hope that this book serves as a catalyst for dialogue, reflection, and meaningful action, inspiring all who seek to build bridges across divides, heal wounds, and cultivate peace—not just on the Korean Peninsula but wherever division and conflict persist in our world.

Let us embark on this journey together, open to the possibilities that lie at the intersection of nature and time, ready to face the challenges ahead with wisdom, compassion, and a shared commitment to a more peaceful and unified world.

Warm regards,
Baek, Dong In
October 16, 2024

PROLOGUE

Bridging Nature, Time, and Reconciliation

NATURE AND TIME (VOL. II): Paths to Justice and Transformation invites readers into a rich dialogue that reinterprets traditional notions of nature, time, and history through the lens of natural theology, particularly within the context of the Korean Peninsula. This book is a continuation of our exploration of peace, where nature and time are not merely backdrops but are integrally involved in the divine narrative of reconciliation, rooted in a Trinitarian understanding. Here, nature serves not only as a creation of God but as an active participant in the ongoing work of peace, while time, shaped by the cyclical rhythms of creation, becomes a dynamic force that reflects divine order and grace.

This journey begins by acknowledging that nature and time are often perceived as passive elements in human endeavors. However, within the theological framework presented, they emerge as vital components actively contributing to the process of reconciliation. By reexamining these elements through the lens of natural theology, we uncover layers of meaning that connect the physical world with spiritual truths. The Korean Peninsula, with its unique historical and cultural landscape, provides a compelling backdrop for this exploration. The land itself, scarred by division yet resilient in its natural beauty, symbolizes the possibility of renewal and harmony. Time, often seen as a linear progression, is reimagined here as a cyclical and restorative force, mirroring the patterns found in nature and reflecting the continuous presence of the divine in the unfolding of history.

PROLOGUE

The integration of biblical themes, the activity of the Holy Spirit, and the unity of the Triune God forms the core of this work.[1] By engaging with the concept of natural revelation, we explore how God's creation—nature—provides a divine witness to the possibility of reconciliation. The natural cycles and rhythms of creation are not just metaphors but manifestations of God's sustaining power, demonstrating how reconciliation mirrors the ongoing creative work of the Trinity. This perspective encourages us to see peacebuilding as an endeavor that aligns with the divine act of creation, a continuous process that requires patience, empathy, and collaboration.

In delving deeper into the biblical narratives, we find that the Holy Spirit's movement within creation is a testament to God's desire for unity and harmony among all things. The Triune God's relational nature offers a model for human relationships, emphasizing interconnectedness and mutual indwelling. Natural revelation becomes a means through which we can perceive God's intentions for humanity and the world.[2] By observing the interdependence and balance within ecosystems, we gain a clearer understanding of how reconciliation can be pursued. The cyclical patterns of seasons, growth, decay, and renewal in nature reflect the spiritual journey toward healing and restoration. Peacebuilding, therefore, is not an isolated human effort but a participation in the divine rhythm, calling us to synchronize our actions with the greater cosmic order established by God.

The Korean Peninsula, divided for over seventy years, represents a striking example of how historical, cultural, and ideological differences can sustain division.[3] Yet, it also holds the potential for transformation

---

1. For theological reflections on Trinitarian concepts and their implications for peace and reconciliation, see Kang Wi Jo's exploration in "A Korean Theology and Praxis of Reconciliation for the Reunification of Korea," which discusses how the relational aspects of the Trinity can inform reconciliation efforts on the Korean Peninsula.

2. Discussions on natural theology and how it relates to peace can be enriched by considering perspectives that incorporate Korean spiritual concepts, such as the notion of **haewon-sangsaeng**, which focuses on resolving resentment and promoting life-sharing as a foundation for harmony. This is elaborated in the Park, "Notion of Reconciliation in Sangsaeng Theology for Korean Reunification," 94–114.

3. A detailed study on the missiological perspectives of peace and reconciliation between North and South Korea, discussing theological approaches like forgiveness, embrace, and the Kingdom of God, can be found in "Re-imagining Peace and Reconciliation between South and North Korea in the Missiological Perspective" by Joo Sang-Rak. This article addresses the complexities of peacebuilding amid ongoing tensions on the Peninsula.

through the interplay of divine and human actions. The Trinitarian framework helps us understand reconciliation not as a one-time event but as a persistent, evolving process that reflects the harmonious relationship within the Godhead. Just as the Father, Son, and Holy Spirit exist in perfect unity, so too can divided communities aspire to reflect this divine harmony through the pursuit of peace and unity.

The enduring division of the Korean Peninsula serves as a poignant illustration of the complexities inherent in human conflict. Generations have lived under the shadow of separation, affecting the social fabric and collective psyche of the people. However, by applying the Trinitarian model of relationship, we can envision a pathway toward healing that transcends political and ideological barriers. The mutual love and cooperation within the Trinity provide a blueprint for reconciliation efforts. This approach emphasizes that lasting peace requires ongoing commitment, open dialogue, and a willingness to embrace the other. It recognizes that transformation is possible when communities ground their efforts in principles that mirror divine relationships—self-giving love, mutual respect, and unity in diversity.

Philosophical perspectives from thinkers like Martin Heidegger, Immanuel Kant, and Franz Rosenzweig provide a deeper understanding of how our perception of time, space, and relationality influences our approach to reconciliation. Rosenzweig's reflections on the cyclical nature of time suggest that peace is an ongoing journey, echoing the unending movement of the Spirit within creation. Heidegger's concept of "being-in-the-world" emphasizes the existential reality of separation, while Kant's exploration of time invites us to rethink our temporal perceptions in light of divine revelation. These perspectives, integrated with theological reflections, offer a comprehensive approach to understanding peace on the Korean Peninsula.

By engaging in the philosophical works of Heidegger, we confront the notion of existence as fundamentally intertwined with the world around us. His idea of "Dasein" (being-there) highlights the inherent connectedness and the existential challenges that arise from our interactions with others and our environment. This perspective sheds light on the human condition within a divided land, where the sense of "being" is disrupted by separation. Kant's examination of time and space as forms of human intuition challenges us to consider how our understanding of these dimensions shapes our reality. By reorienting our perception of time through a theological lens, we open ourselves to experiencing history not just as a series of events but as part of a divine narrative. Rosenzweig's emphasis on the cyclical nature of time aligns with the biblical concept of seasons and the regenerative processes in nature, reinforcing the idea that reconciliation is a continual endeavor. Integrating these philosophical insights with theology enriches our comprehension of peace, allowing for a multidimensional approach that addresses both the metaphysical and practical aspects of reconciliation.

The theological concept of natural revelation plays a crucial role in this dialogue. Often seen as silent, nature speaks to us through its patterns and cycles, reminding us of God's continual presence and guidance. The renewal we observe in ecosystems, the balance and interdependence within nature, can serve as models for human communities striving for peace. This analogy suggests that reconciliation, like nature's cycles, is a process requiring continual renewal, where each step forward builds upon the previous, guided by the enduring presence of the Holy Spirit.

Natural revelation, as an expression of God's self-disclosure through creation, invites us to perceive the divine in the world around us. The rhythms of nature—the changing seasons, the lifecycle of plants and animals, the ebb and flow of tides—are more than mere physical phenomena; they are reflections of God's character and purposes. By attuning ourselves to these rhythms, we can gain an understanding of how reconciliation unfolds. Just as ecosystems thrive through diversity and interdependence, human societies can flourish when embracing these principles. The restoration of broken relationships parallels the regenerative processes in nature, suggesting that healing is both possible and integral to the fabric of creation. The Holy Spirit's role in sustaining and renewing creation underscores the importance of spiritual empowerment in peacebuilding efforts. Recognizing this connection encourages us to approach reconciliation with humility, acknowledging that it is ultimately rooted in divine grace and action.

Moreover, this volume emphasizes the need for a holistic approach that combines theological, philosophical, and socio-political perspectives. By drawing from biblical themes of creation, covenant, and redemption, we are reminded that reconciliation is not just a social or political endeavor but a spiritual journey that aligns with the divine purpose. The work of theologians such as Rudolf Bultmann and Eugen Rosenstock-Huessy underscores that true reconciliation addresses not only physical and political divisions but also the existential and spiritual separations that divide communities. The ethical imperatives drawn

PROLOGUE

from these reflections challenge us to engage deeply with the root causes of division, promoting healing and unity that resonate with the reconciling work of Christ.

In advocating for a holistic approach, this work recognizes that peacebuilding must transcend traditional boundaries between disciplines. Theological insights provide a foundation that grounds reconciliation in the character and actions of God. Philosophical perspectives offer tools for critically examining our assumptions about reality, time, and human relationships. Socio-political analysis addresses the structural and systemic factors that perpetuate division. By weaving these threads together, we can develop strategies that are both principled and pragmatic.

The biblical themes of creation, covenant, and redemption frame our understanding of God's interaction with humanity. Creation speaks to the inherent value and purpose imbued in all things. The covenant emphasizes relationship and commitment, highlighting God's desire for partnership with humanity. Redemption points to the possibility of restoration and new beginnings. These themes inform our approach to reconciliation, suggesting that it is a divine initiative that invites human participation.

The contributions of theologians like Bultmann, who emphasized demythologizing scripture to uncover existential truths, challenge us to confront the deeper meanings behind our narratives. Rosenstock-Huessy's focus on speech and dialogue underscores the importance of communication in bridging divides. Their work highlights that reconciliation must address the internal landscapes of individuals and communities—the fears, prejudices, and misunderstandings that hinder unity. Ethical imperatives arising from these reflections call us to act justly, love mercy, and walk humbly, echoing the prophetic traditions that advocate for social transformation rooted in spiritual renewal.

In conclusion, *Nature and Time (Vol. II): Paths to Justice and Transformation* calls us to reconsider how we approach peacebuilding by reflecting on the interwoven forces of nature, history, and divine action. It invites readers to move beyond immediate political concerns and engage with the broader, cyclical processes of creation that reveal God's ongoing work in the world. By fostering a dialogue that integrates the sacred rhythms of nature and the movement of time, this book encourages a deeper commitment to reconciliation, one that mirrors the eternal harmony of the Trinity and acknowledges the shared destiny of all creations.

PROLOGUE

This volume serves as a clarification call to reimagine peacebuilding not as a series of isolated initiatives but as a holistic engagement with the complexities of human existence. By situating our efforts within the context of nature's cycles and the unfolding of divine history, we align ourselves with forces that transcend individual agendas. Recognizing that political solutions alone are insufficient; we are urged to consider the spiritual dimensions of reconciliation. The interplay of nature, time, and divine action reveals patterns and possibilities that can inform and inspire our endeavors. Embracing the sacred rhythms of the natural world allows us to synchronize our efforts with a larger, divinely orchestrated movement toward unity and wholeness. This approach fosters hope and perseverance, reminding us that we are part of a grand narrative that is continually moving toward redemption. By mirroring the relational harmony of the Trinity, we affirm the interconnectedness of all creation and our shared responsibility in nurturing peace.

INTRODUCTION

Fusion of Horizons

THE CONCEPT OF "FUSION of horizons" plays an important role in theological discussions about oppression and liberation. It offers a framework for understanding how different perspectives can come together to form a more comprehensive approach.[1] Developed by Hans-Georg Gadamer and expanded by Paul Ricoeur, this idea centers on the notion that understanding is always a blend of present and historical contexts; neither exists independently. Instead, they interact and influence each other, allowing for a dynamic and evolving understanding.[2] This process is crucial when addressing societal challenges, particularly in the pursuit of justice, as it emphasizes the importance of dialogue and mutual understanding.

Gadamer argues that understanding isn't just about acquiring historical perspectives. It's the result of a dynamic interaction between the interpreter and the text, or between the interpreter and their broader context.[3] The fusion of horizons is thus not a static event, but an ongoing process shaped by the historical and linguistic contexts of both the

---

1. J. August Higgins's article in *Philosophy and Theology* explores how Gadamer's "fusion of horizons" can be applied to Christian spirituality, emphasizing the integration of experiences and perspectives within interpretive communities. This idea supports a framework where multiple viewpoints contribute to a more inclusive understanding, particularly in contexts of dialogue and reconciliation. Higgins, "Spirit and Truth," 469–90.

2. Gadamer, *Truth and Method*, 317.

3. Gadamer, *Truth and Method*, 350; Matthew W. Knotts provides insight into how Gadamer views horizons as dynamic, continually shaped by dialogue and critical engagement. This dialogical process is crucial in understanding and challenging preconceptions, which aligns well with discussions on social justice and addressing oppression (Knotts, "Readers, Texts, and the Fusion of Horizons," 233–46).

text and the interpreter.[4] This dialogical process allows new meanings to emerge, which is essential in tackling issues of oppression and injustice, where the voices of the marginalized must be brought into conversation with those of the dominant culture.

This merging of horizons doesn't aim to eliminate differences between perspectives but seeks to expand both present and historical contexts, so they overlap meaningfully.[5] Ricoeur adds that understanding isn't solely about empathy or agreement but involves confronting the differences between perspectives. This confrontation allows for critical engagement that goes beyond surface-level interpretations, providing a more thorough engagement with both divine action and human responsibility in the face of societal challenges.[6]

The fusion of horizons is closely linked to the concept of historically effected consciousness, which Gadamer describes as the awareness that our understanding is shaped by our historical context.[7] This awareness allows interpreters to recognize that their perspectives are influenced by their own traditions and biases, which can both help and limit their understanding. By acknowledging these limitations, interpreters are better equipped to engage in the dialogical process Gadamer advocates, where new meanings can emerge through the interaction of different perspectives.[8]

However, this process is not without challenges. Gadamer's hermeneutics has been critiqued for its idealism, particularly in cases where the fusion of horizons is difficult or impossible to achieve.[9] This critique highlights that understanding isn't always attainable, especially when the differences between perspectives are too great. Nevertheless, the fusion of horizons remains a valuable framework for engaging with societal challenges, as it encourages dialogue and the recognition of different perspectives, even when full understanding isn't possible.

---

4. Matthew W. Knotts discusses how Gadamer's concept emphasizes a continuous, evolving interaction between different contexts, allowing the process to remain open to new interpretations. This is particularly relevant when addressing complex issues like oppression and societal challenges (Knotts, "Readers, Texts, and the Fusion of Horizons," 233–46).

5. Mootz and Taylor, *Gadamer and Ricoeur*, 48.
6. Mootz and Taylor, *Gadamer and Ricoeur*, 4.
7. Gadamer, *Truth and Method*, 385.
8. Mootz and Taylor, *Gadamer and Ricoeur*, 3.
9. Mootz and Taylor, *Gadamer and Ricoeur*, 66.

Ricoeur's contribution to this discussion is particularly relevant when considering the tension between explanation and understanding. While Gadamer emphasizes the importance of dialogue, Ricoeur argues that explanation is a necessary part of interpretation because it allows for a more structured and critical engagement with the text or context.[10] This structured approach is essential in addressing issues of oppression, where the complexities of power dynamics and historical injustices must be carefully unpacked and analyzed.

In conclusion, the fusion of horizons provides a framework for understanding that is both dialogical and critical, allowing new meanings to emerge through the interaction of different perspectives. This process is essential in addressing societal challenges, particularly in the context of oppression and liberation, where understanding must be constantly negotiated and reinterpreted considering new contexts and voices.[11] By fostering dialogue and encouraging the recognition of different perspectives, the fusion of horizons offers a way forward in the ongoing struggle for justice and equality.

FRANZ ROSENZWEIG'S PERSPECTIVE ON LIBERATION

Franz Rosenzweig, an influential figure in theological discourse, emphasizes the interplay between divine action and human responsibility in the process of liberation. According to Rosenzweig, liberation isn't a one-time event but an ongoing journey unfolding through history.[12] This journey requires continuous alignment of human actions with the divine will, reflecting an evolving relationship between God and humanity.[13] This dynamic understanding of liberation mirrors Gadamer's idea of the "fusion of horizons," where the intersection of divine and human realms fosters a transformative approach to justice.

---

10. Mootz and Taylor, *Gadamer and Ricoeur*, 5.

11. Gadamer, *Truth and Method*, 601.

12. In discussing Rosenzweig's view of ongoing liberation, it's noted that he emphasizes a dynamic relationship between divine presence and human actions, which aligns with the continuous process of divine revelation and transformation. For further insight, refer to Berman's analysis of Rosenzweig's approach to divine love and its implications for human interaction with divine revelation (Berman, "Franz Rosenzweig on Divine Love," 806).

13. Rosenzweig, *Star of Redemption*, 32.

In this evolving process, Rosenzweig points out that the experience of liberation is deeply connected to moving away from nothingness. He describes the human condition as emerging from the "prison of nothingness," where the event of liberation defines human existence in its relationship to God.[14] This liberation isn't merely an escape but a continual process that shapes human identity in relation to the divine presence.

Rosenzweig further argues that human life is characterized by its temporality and individuality, with death serving as the ultimate boundary between the liberated self and nothingness. He suggests that death removes the last wall separating humanity from the void, challenging the permanence of liberation. Therefore, liberation must be constantly reaffirmed throughout life, as death robs individuals of the "character of liberation" they experience during their lifetime.[15]

This understanding of liberation extends beyond the individual to the collective experience of humanity. Rosenzweig's reflections on festivals of liberation, such as the Jewish pilgrimage festivals, illustrate how communal acts of remembrance play a crucial role in sustaining the collective memory of liberation.[16] He notes that these festivals symbolize the eternal journey of the people, reminding them of their shared history and destiny.[17] These communal practices ensure that the experience of liberation isn't confined to a single moment but remains an ongoing part of collective identity.

According to Rosenzweig, the process of liberation requires continuous creative action. He emphasizes that true liberation involves affirmation creative force that lifts individuals and communities out of the cycle of negation. This creative aspect demands that humans, in collaboration with the divine, participate in the ongoing creation of a liberated

---

14. Rosenzweig, *Star of Redemption*, 32.

15. Rosenzweig, *Star of Redemption*, 83.

16. The significance of ritual and communal memory in Rosenzweig's theology, especially within Jewish practices, can be examined through Joseph Turner's work in The Legacy of Franz Rosenzweig. Turner emphasizes how festivals play a key role in linking divine promises to communal life. This perspective is further explored in Herskowitz's analysis of Rosenzweig's understanding of revelation, where he discusses the theological interplay between divine self-disclosure and human response, framed within a Protestant context (Herskowitz, "Franz Rosenzweig's Account of Revelation," 583–606).

17. Rosenzweig, *Star of Redemption*, 335.

reality.[18] This perspective aligns liberation with a creative process rather than mere repetition of past experiences.[19]

Rosenzweig's view also acknowledges the role of revelation in this journey. He suggests that revelation serves as the foundation for the relationship between God, humanity, and the world.[20] Revelation connects the promise of redemption with the reality of human history, creating a bridge between divine action and human experience.[21] This bond offers hope, affirming that human actions are intertwined with the unfolding of God's redemptive plan.

Moreover, Rosenzweig incorporates a metaethical dimension, seeing the liberation of the human soul as an ongoing process that transcends physical and logical boundaries. He argues that humans, through their ethical choices and actions, contribute to breaking down the unity of the world and creating space for divine interaction.[22] This approach emphasizes the freedom of the human spirit to align with divine will, shaping the course of history through ethical living.

In his reflections on the relationship between revelation and redemption, Rosenzweig underscores the importance of maintaining the ethical connection between these two concepts. He suggests that revelation isn't a static event but one that continually influences human actions and ethical decisions. The hope for ultimate redemption is grounded in the present reality of ethical responsibility and human participation in divine action.[23] This connection reinforces the idea that liberation is an ongoing, ethical journey rather than a final, completed state.

Rosenzweig's thoughts offer a framework for understanding liberation as an evolving, collaborative process between the divine and human realms. He highlights the necessity of continuous ethical action, creative participation, and communal remembrance in the journey toward

18. Rosenzweig, *Star of Redemption*, 134.

19. Nadav S. Berman's recent article discusses Rosenzweig's theological approach to love, highlighting the dynamic and creative aspects of divine-human interaction, emphasizing the ongoing and transformative process of liberation (Berman, "Franz Rosenzweig on Divine Love").

20. Rosenzweig's understanding of revelation as a foundational element in divine-human relationships is explored through his concept of dialogical selfhood, where divine calls prompt human responses, creating a continuous relational dynamic (Fisher, "Divine Perfections at the Center of the Star," 188–212).

21. Rosenzweig, *Star of Redemption*, 113.

22. Rosenzweig, *Star of Redemption*, 24.

23. Rosenzweig, *Star of Redemption*, 113.

freedom. Through his exploration of the relationship between revelation and redemption, Rosenzweig invites us to consider liberation as both a present reality and a future hope, grounded in the active collaboration of human and divine will.[24]

GUSTAVO GUTIÉRREZ AND LIBERATION THEOLOGY

Gustavo Gutiérrez builds upon this understanding by emphasizing the necessity of confronting systemic oppression through both spiritual transformation and active social engagement. He insists that theology must directly engage with the historical realities that sustain injustice, advocating for a praxis rooted in the lived experiences of the oppressed.[25] To be a Christian, according to Gutiérrez, is "to accept and to live—in solidarity, in faith, hope, and charity—the meaning that the Word of the Lord and our encounter with that Word give to the historical becoming of humankind on the way toward total communion."[26] By regarding the unique and absolute relationship with God as the horizon of every human action, individuals place themselves within a wider context that encompasses the journey toward total communion.

He observes that Latin America is undergoing rapid transformation affecting every level of human activity, "from the economic to the religious," indicating that society is "on the threshold of a new epoch."[27] This profound societal change necessitates a theological response that addresses the complexities of such development. Gutiérrez acknowledges that this transformation isn't solely economic but also deeply human, asserting that "all this can be implemented if together with the transformation of the economic structure, the transformation of humanity is undertaken with equal enthusiasm."[28] Therefore, he emphasizes that spiritual and social transformation must occur simultaneously to effectively address systemic oppression.

Influenced by thinkers like Maurice Blondel and the impact of Marxist thought focusing on praxis, Gutiérrez contributes to developing a theology that emphasizes action geared toward transforming the world.

---

24. Rosenzweig, *Star of Redemption*, 98.
25. Gutiérrez, *Theology of Liberation*, 22.
26. Gutiérrez, *Theology of Liberation*, 32.
27. Gutiérrez, *Theology of Liberation*, xvii.
28. Gutiérrez, *Theology of Liberation*, 66.

He notes that "the influence of Marxist thought, focusing on praxis and geared to the transformation of the world," has added to the factors shaping contemporary theology.[29] This influence encourages a focus on practical action that emerges from the lived realities of those experiencing oppression, rather than relying solely on abstract theological constructs.

During the challenging decade of the 1970s, this attitude led to numerous experiences and theological reflections within the Latin American church. Formulas intended to express commitment to the poor and oppressed proliferated, as became clear at Puebla, which chose specific expressions to articulate this commitment.[30] This period highlighted the need for the church to reject any emphasis that sidelines the experiences of the marginalized. Gutiérrez points out that theological influences played a less significant role compared to the impetus provided by "a situation of fundamental oppression and marginalization that the Christian conscience" couldn't ignore.[31]

He emphasizes that theology must arise from lived faith expressed in prayer and commitment, stating that "the first stage or phase of theological work is the lived faith that finds expression in prayer and commitment."[32] To live the faith means putting into practice, in light of the demands of the reign of God, the fundamental elements of Christian existence. This faith is lived "in the church" and is oriented toward communal sharing and action, reinforcing the idea that theology must be grounded in the concrete experiences of the community.

Drawing on Ernst Bloch's distinction between affections of society and those of expectation, Gutiérrez highlights the role of hope as "the most important as well as the most positive and most liberating" emotion.[33] Hope anticipates the future and is "related to the broadest and most luminous horizon," serving as a driving force for collective efforts to overcome injustice.[34] This emphasis on hope underscores the belief that true liberation arises from a shared understanding that transcends individual and cultural boundaries.

Gutiérrez contends that addressing systemic oppression requires acknowledging the "horizon of political liberation," a task that remains

29. Gutiérrez, *Theology of Liberation*, 8.
30. Gutiérrez, *Theology of Liberation*, xxxvi.
31. Gutiérrez, *Theology of Liberation*, xix.
32. Gutiérrez, *Theology of Liberation*, xxxiv.
33. Gutiérrez, *Theology of Liberation*, 123.
34. Gutiérrez, *Theology of Liberation*, 123.

to be fully undertaken.³⁵ He refers to the texts of the magisterium of the Church, suggesting that further efforts are needed to engage with the political dimensions of liberation. This perspective calls for theology not only to interpret reality but also to actively participate in transforming it, aligning with the idea that liberation theology must be deeply connected to historical contexts.

In considering the concept of liberation theologically, he asserts the importance of initiating this examination "in the light of what we have just discussed."³⁶ He believes that theology must be intimately linked to the historical situations and lived experiences of people, particularly those who are oppressed. By engaging directly with these realities, theology can contribute to dismantling unjust social structures and promote a praxis that fosters total communion among humanity.

Ultimately, Gutiérrez's approach highlights that transformation and liberation aren't merely abstract concepts but are embedded in the practical actions and commitments of individuals and communities. By advocating for a theology that emerges from the lived experiences of the oppressed and actively seeks to transform both economic structures and human relationships, he provides a framework for understanding liberation as a collective endeavor. This perspective encourages a shared understanding that fosters collective efforts to dismantle systemic injustice.

KARL BARTH AND NATURAL THEOLOGY

The integration of natural theology within this framework introduces a complex relationship between creation and justice. Natural theology asserts that creation itself provides a foundation for justice, pointing to a divine order embedded in the natural world, which calls for an ethical response, particularly toward environmental concerns. Karl Barth, in his critique of the limitations of human reason in understanding God, doesn't dismiss the potential ethical influence of recognizing divine revelation within creation. Barth suggests that acknowledging God's presence in creation can lead to ethical actions that contribute to justice.³⁷

Barth's reflections build upon the idea that God's relationship with humanity through Christ is central. He emphasizes that any attempt to

---

35. Gutiérrez, *Theology of Liberation*, 100.
36. Gutiérrez, *Theology of Liberation*, 22.
37. Barth, *Church Dogmatics*, 153.

reduce the incarnation of God to mere human or heroic terms lowers it to the level of religious constructs, something that all religions might do but misses the essential nature of divine solidarity with humanity.[38] This solidarity isn't just a theological concept but a necessary association that holds implications for how humanity engages with both social and ecological justice.

In this context, Barth critiques early church theology for overextending its interpretations, especially concerning the sinlessness of Jesus. This overextension, according to Barth, could potentially obscure the liberative truth of Christ's nature, which is deeply connected to the liberation of both humanity and creation. In his view, any theology that overlooks the environmental or material aspects of this liberation fails to fully grasp the scope of Christ's redemptive work.[39]

Barth also touches on the limitations of modern theology, which, despite its advancements, has struggled to fully integrate these concepts into a holistic framework. He points to theologians like Gottfried Menken, who argued that Christ's assumption of human nature isn't just a return to an original state but is transformative, signifying a re-engagement with creation in its fallen state. This suggests that environmental justice isn't only an ethical necessity but is tied to the very nature of Christ's redemptive act.

The uniqueness of Jesus Christ, as Barth describes, brings with it liberation and purification, extending to both personal and communal dimensions of justice. The Church, by virtue of its connection to Christ, becomes the place where this liberation is made visible, not only in spiritual terms but also in tangible, historical actions that include stewardship of the earth.[40] This framework aligns with natural theology by expanding liberation beyond the human social sphere to include creation itself.

Barth's thoughts on mysticism further illuminate the ethical implications of recognizing divine presence in the world. Mysticism, which emphasizes a liberation from external religious forms, suggests that true liberation must also encompass a break from the exploitation of the natural world.[41] This underscores a form of environmental justice that is inherently linked to human liberation from structures that separate humanity from both God and creation.

38. Barth, *Church Dogmatics*, 153.
39. Barth, *Church Dogmatics*, 154.
40. Barth, *Church Dogmatics*, 214.
41. Barth, *Church Dogmatics*, 319.

In his broader theological framework, Barth argues that the negation of external forms, including religion and its constructs, can lead to an authentic freedom that integrates both human and environmental dimensions. Such freedom isn't merely a rejection of religious tradition but a deeper engagement with the divine order in the world, where justice for creation becomes a fundamental aspect of human ethical responsibility.[42]

Barth's exploration of time and temporality in relation to revelation also connects to the idea that the ethical responsibility toward creation isn't limited to a single moment in history but unfolds within the ongoing revelation of God in the world. Humanity's anxiety, rooted in the temporal nature of existence, must be met with an ethical response that includes care for creation.[43]

Finally, Barth's assertion that Christ's unity with humanity is also a unity with creation reinforces the idea that justice must be holistic. His theological reflections provide a framework where environmental and social justice aren't separate issues but are deeply interconnected within the broader scope of God's redemptive work.[44] This understanding aligns with natural theology by emphasizing that justice for creation reflects divine justice.

LEONARDO BOFF'S ECOLOGICAL LIBERATION THEOLOGY

The discussion of ecological justice within peacebuilding and reconciliation finds a robust foundation in Leonardo Boff's ecological liberation theology. Boff emphasizes the interconnectedness of all creations, highlighting that environmental stewardship isn't merely a supplementary concern but a core element of justice. This understanding is deeply connected to the notion that all beings, including humans, are part of a complex, interrelated system that can't be reduced to simple categories.[45] This view aligns with broader philosophical reflections on interconnectedness, where the ecological and social are inextricably linked.

Boff's exploration of complexity speaks to a fundamental truth: ecological systems operate through dynamic relationships involving both order and disorder, interaction, and organization. The ecological

---

42. Barth, *Church Dogmatics*, 323.
43. Barth, *Church Dogmatics*, 46.
44. Barth, *Church Dogmatics*, 163.
45. Boff, *Cry of the Earth*, 26.

perspective demands that we recognize these patterns, whether in the microcosmic realm of atoms or the macrocosmic domain of galaxies. The logic of complexity, which resists simplification, compels us to acknowledge that humans aren't external observers but participants in the unfolding of ecological realities.[46] This participatory role reflects the need for a holistic ethical framework that integrates both social and environmental concerns.

The relationship between subject and object, as Boff notes, can't be viewed in isolation. Humans are deeply embedded in the ecological systems they seek to understand, making the ideal of strict objectivity a fiction. Instead, Boff suggests a mode of thinking that is inclusive and multidimensional, recognizing that local ecosystems are connected to global realities. This interconnectedness extends to human social organizations, cultures, and even individual relationships, requiring an ethic that reflects the complexity of the world we inhabit.

Boff introduces the concept of dialogical, or perichoretic, logic, which emphasizes the importance of learning from diverse human experiences, especially in how they relate to nature. From ancient traditions to modern scientific discourse, all approaches contribute to a broader understanding of humanity's relationship with the environment. This dialogical approach reveals the diverse ways humans have communicated with nature, offering valuable perspectives for contemporary ecological ethics.

The ethic of care, particularly as exemplified by women in ecofeminist thought, becomes a crucial element in managing the complexity of everyday life. Boff highlights the importance of attention to detail and respect for life in all its stages. Women, through their relational approach to life, offer a model of care that goes beyond labor and touches on an ethic of respect and nurturing. This perspective on care becomes vital in understanding how to manage ecological complexity with sensitivity to the needs of both human and non-human life.[47]

Boff further argues that a new covenant with nature requires the integration of reason with intuition, heart, and emotion. This holistic approach, often associated with the feminine experience, challenges the dualisms of patriarchal culture that separate the human from the natural, the spiritual from the material. In overcoming these divisions, humans

---

46. Boff, *Cry of the Earth*, 26.
47. Boff, *Cry of the Earth*, 27.

can develop a consciousness that sees the sacredness of all life, fostering an ethic that's inclusive of ecological concerns. This approach not only redefines relationships with nature but also reshapes the broader understanding of justice.

The idea of self-organization, a central theme in Boff's ecological theology, offers a way of understanding life as an interplay of relationships and interactions. This process of self-organization, present in everything from atoms to stars, reveals the intrinsic connectedness of all things. Boff argues that this understanding must inform how humans view their role in the universe, recognizing that each action impacts the broader ecological system.[48] This perspective reinforces the need for an ethical approach that considers both human and environmental flourishing.

Boff also critiques current models of development and ecological management, arguing that they often prioritize short-term gains over long-term sustainability. Ecopolitics, as he describes it, should focus not only on balancing ecosystems but also on ensuring social justice, recognizing that environmental degradation disproportionately affects marginalized communities.[49] This dual focus on ecological and social justice highlights the inseparability of these issues in the pursuit of a just society.

In addressing the relationship between human and social ecology, Boff points out that humans are products of a long biological process, deeply connected to the elements of nature. Society's organization of its relationship with the environment must consider both the production of life and the preservation of ecological balance. This requires an ethical framework that considers not just economic or technological solutions but a fundamental shift in how humans relate to nature and to each other.[50] This shift is necessary for achieving a more sustainable and equitable world.

Finally, Boff calls for a reevaluation of mental ecology, suggesting that the state of the environment reflects the human psyche. The violence inflicted on nature stems from the internal violence within human minds, shaped by exclusionary and destructive worldviews. By addressing the internal ecology of human consciousness, Boff argues, we can begin to foster a gentler, more harmonious relationship with the natural world. This connection between inner and outer ecologies underscores

---

48. Boff, *Cry of the Earth*, 28.
49. Boff, *Cry of the Earth*, 5.
50. Boff, *Cry of the Earth*, 6.

the need for an integrated approach to justice that includes both mental and environmental well-being.

THE KOREAN DEMILITARIZED ZONE AND ECOLOGICAL PEACEBUILDING

The unique ecological context of the Korean Demilitarized Zone (DMZ) offers a rare opportunity to weave environmental conservation into broader peacebuilding initiatives. The absence of human interference over decades has allowed nature to thrive in this region, creating a potential space for cooperation in the context of North-South relations. Such collaboration would require both political and ecological efforts to converge, enabling shared stewardship over the environment. Gadamer's idea that understanding emerges through engagement with the other aligns with this situation, suggesting that through dialogical interaction, meaningful cooperation may develop.[51]

Gadamer's reflections on human existence highlight how rising above immediate environmental concerns involves developing a broader posture toward the world. This perspective implies not leaving our natural surroundings but adopting a more reflective stance toward them, recognizing our responsibilities within the ecological realm. Such an approach is essential when considering ecological collaboration in North-South relations, where joint efforts must stem from an acknowledgment of shared environmental dependencies.[52]

Drawing from the biological studies of Jakob von Uexküll, Gadamer discusses how the world of physics and the universe of life coexist. He emphasizes that understanding these various life-worlds, including those of plants, animals, and humans, requires a holistic view that transcends narrow scientific inquiry. This type of thinking is crucial in the DMZ context, where the flourishing ecosystems offer a model of cooperation that must consider the multifaceted lives present within the zone.[53] By viewing the environment not just in terms of physics but as a living universe, North and South Korea could approach conservation with a shared purpose that fosters both ecological and political trust.

---

51. Gadamer, *Truth and Method*, 461.
52. Gadamer, *Truth and Method*, 461.
53. Gadamer, *Truth and Method*, 467.

Moreover, Gadamer's concept of horizon relates directly to the possibility of peace through shared environmental stewardship. He argues that the horizon of time is often misunderstood; it's not merely something fleeting but a continual unfolding that shapes our understanding of the world. In the case of the DMZ, the horizon for North-South relations isn't simply the immediate future but a longer, shared history and potential future that could be shaped by collaborative ecological efforts.[54] Such a shared horizon can foster reconciliation by shifting focus from conflict to mutual care for the environment.

This engagement with the ecological horizon requires a shift in how both sides perceive their relationship with the land. According to Gadamer, the process of engaging with future possibilities involves encountering multiple, often conflicting expectations. These uncertainties need not prevent cooperation; rather, they can drive both parties toward common goals. The DMZ's ecological richness, coupled with the potential for political engagement, presents a scenario where initially conflicting expectations could gradually align through joint action.[55] This dialogical process would create a foundation for trust, built on the shared goal of preserving an invaluable environmental space.

Gadamer's idea of play as something not controlled by the players but as an event that unfolds independently of their individual will offers another useful metaphor for North-South cooperation in the DMZ. The cooperation required for environmental conservation isn't solely about the intentions of either side but about how their interactions manifest through shared experiences and actions.[56] This "play" of cooperation, rooted in ecological preservation, could help overcome the rigid subjectivities that have long defined the political divide in North-South relations.

In the broader sense of hermeneutics, Gadamer explains that understanding isn't simply about decoding the other's position but engaging with it in a meaningful and open-ended way. The environmental situation of the DMZ invites both sides to engage in such a hermeneutic process, where dialogue and cooperation become central to achieving a shared goal. This process requires acknowledging the complexity of the situation while remaining open to new interpretations and possibilities for cooperation.[57]

---

54. Gadamer, *Truth and Method*, 90.
55. Gadamer, *Truth and Method*, 117.
56. Gadamer, *Truth and Method*, 107.
57. Gadamer, *Truth and Method*, 164.

Finally, the concept of legal and moral frameworks that Gadamer discusses is also relevant to the DMZ's ecological potential. While political treaties often dictate the terms of peace, it's through broader ethical and moral engagement with shared spaces like the DMZ that deeper understanding and reconciliation can emerge. By focusing on the environmental well-being of the zone, North and South Korea may find a pathway to peace that's rooted not only in political agreements but also in a shared ecological ethic.[58] This shared responsibility toward the environment could serve as a model for future cooperation, fostering reconciliation through ecological justice.

RECONCILIATION IN LIBERATION AND PEACE THEOLOGY

Reconciliation plays a pivotal role in both liberation theology and peace theology, serving as a foundational concept that guides action toward justice and harmony. Jürgen Moltmann's theology of hope provides a framework where reconciliation isn't merely a future expectation but involves concrete, present actions directed toward the future of Christ in the world.[59] He emphasizes that the true mission of Christianity actively engages in reconciling those estranged from God, aligning with an eschatological vision that demands participation now rather than passively awaiting a future event.

Moltmann further argues that Christian thought should adjust not to human desires or arbitrary prescriptions but to the coming messianic reconciliation.[60] This means believers orient their actions and thinking toward this anticipated reconciliation, making it a guiding framework for engaging with the world. The goal of the Christian mission becomes clear in this context: it aims at reconciliation with God, which encompasses promoting eschatological freedom and human dignity.[61]

Participation in this process involves recognizing the sanctification of place, time, and humanity in acts that correspond with and partake in the eternal divine cosmos.[62] Moltmann highlights that in such acts, human culture—ever threatened by forces of chaos and annihilation—finds

---

58. Gadamer, *Truth and Method*, 128.
59. Moltmann, *Theology of Hope*, 284.
60. Moltmann, *Theology of Hope*, 290.
61. Moltmann, *Theology of Hope*, 329.
62. Moltmann, *Theology of Hope*, 99.

correspondence with the divine, suggesting that reconciliation is both a spiritual and cultural endeavor.

He contrasts this approach with other traditions, noting that while some seek unification with the divine in a mystical sense, Christianity asserts an eschatological distinction where baptism serves as a means of participating in the death and resurrection of Christ.[63] This participation isn't a passive experience but an active engagement that anticipates future fulfillment.

Moltmann observes that historical eschatology grapples with cosmology, much like the Israelite hope struggled with world history, understanding it as a function of the eschatological future of Yahweh.[64] This struggle reflects the tension between current realities and the anticipated future, reinforcing the need for active participation in working toward reconciliation.

Similarly, Paul Ricoeur's analysis of time and narrative supports the idea that our understanding of the future is shaped by how we interpret the present and the past. He suggests there's an interplay between our lived temporal experiences in both fictional and historical narratives, creating a "crossed reference" that influences action.[65] This concept implies that narratives have the power to reconfigure our perception of time, thereby motivating actions toward reconciliation.

Ricoeur further discusses the mediating role of "emplotment" in narrative, which serves as a bridge between the temporal aspects prefigured in practical life and the refiguration of our temporal experience.[66] By understanding how narratives shape our experience of time, we can see how they influence our actions toward future goals such as reconciliation.

Both Moltmann and Ricoeur emphasize that reconciliation and the shaping of the future aren't passive processes. They require active engagement with the present, informed by an understanding of the past, to work toward an anticipated future. This approach makes reconciliation an ongoing process embedded in our temporal experience rather than a distant, unattainable event.

---

63. Moltmann, *Theology of Hope*, 161.
64. Moltmann, *Theology of Hope*, 137.
65. Ricoeur, *Time and Narrative*, 32.
66. Ricoeur, *Time and Narrative*, 54.

INTRODUCTION

POLITICAL RECONCILIATION AND POWER DYNAMICS

Political reconciliation necessitates a reimagining of power dynamics, a theme explored by Reinhold Niebuhr through his concept of Christian realism. Niebuhr acknowledges the enduring presence of sin and self-interest in human affairs, arguing that the pursuit of justice must be tempered by an understanding of these limitations.[67] His framework contrasts with more idealistic approaches by suggesting that historical meaning is ultimately dependent on divine sovereignty, emphasizing the role of God's power and mercy in shaping justice, even within flawed human systems.

Niebuhr points out that ethical values often seem difficult, if not impossible, to implement in broader political and economic systems. He emphasizes that natural impulses in these spheres are often less restrained by reason and conscience than in private individual conduct.[68] This realism reflects a pragmatic approach, acknowledging the limits of human nature and the necessity of confronting these tendencies within political structures. Recognizing that achieving justice requires navigating complex motivations of self-interest and sin, Niebuhr's perspective offers a grounded approach to political reconciliation.

At the same time, Niebuhr doesn't abandon the pursuit of justice but advocates for a goal of equal justice that must be sought through political and economic means. He recognizes the inherent cynicism in choosing certain means to achieve these ends but also acknowledges the social significance of employing realistic strategies that align ethical ideals with the political realities of the day.[69] This balance between idealism and realism is crucial for understanding how to work toward justice in a world marked by power imbalances.

Niebuhr also reflects on the conditions under which revolutionary movements arise, noting that they're often driven more by hunger and desperation than by abstract ideals of justice.[70] His observations challenge middle-class assumptions about social change, highlighting the importance of understanding the material conditions that lead to upheaval. This perspective aligns with liberation theology's focus on

---

67. Niebuhr, *Moral Man and Immoral Society*, 25.
68. Niebuhr, *Moral Man and Immoral Society*, 78.
69. Niebuhr, *Moral Man and Immoral Society*, 165.
70. Niebuhr, *Moral Man and Immoral Society*, 186.

systemic oppression, where addressing economic and social inequalities is fundamental to any meaningful reconciliation.

Furthermore, Niebuhr emphasizes the difficulty of achieving objectivity in social situations where one's own interests are involved. He argues that while humans are capable of sympathy and a sense of justice, these qualities are often overshadowed by self-interest unless shaped by disciplined social education.[71] This understanding of human nature reinforces the need for power to be challenged by power in social conflicts, as purely rational or moral appeals often fail to account for the deeper motivations driving human behavior.[72]

Gadamer's hermeneutics complements Niebuhr's realism by providing a framework for understanding others through openness to their perspectives. Gadamer argues that true understanding requires engaging in a process where horizons merge, allowing for a deeper appreciation of the other's point of view.[73] This process of fusion helps mitigate power imbalances by fostering dialogue that doesn't seek to dominate but rather to understand. In the context of reconciliation, this dialogical approach allows for the transformation of relationships marked by inequality.

Gadamer's idea of openness also speaks to the necessity of mutual engagement in the process of understanding. He explains that understanding isn't about confirming preexisting beliefs but about allowing oneself to be addressed by the other, leading to a transformation of one's own horizon.[74] This approach is particularly relevant in contexts where power dynamics are at play, as it encourages both sides to engage with humility and openness, facilitating a more equitable reconciliation process.

Moreover, Gadamer emphasizes that mutual understanding isn't simply about reaching agreement but about participating in a process of reflection and openness where the past and present are brought into dialogue.[75] This idea can inform approaches to political reconciliation, where both parties must engage in a shared process of reflection that acknowledges historical injustices while remaining open to future possibilities for cooperation and understanding.

Ultimately, the fusion of Niebuhr's realism and Gadamer's hermeneutics provides a compelling framework for addressing the complexities

71. Niebuhr, *Moral Man and Immoral Society*, 29.
72. Niebuhr, *Moral Man and Immoral Society*, 31.
73. Gadamer, *Truth and Method*, 31.
74. Gadamer, *Truth and Method*, 281.
75. Gadamer, *Truth and Method*, 294.

of power dynamics in political reconciliation. Niebuhr's acknowledgment of human limitations and Gadamer's call for dialogical openness create a balanced approach that recognizes both the need for pragmatic strategies in confronting systemic injustices and the importance of fostering mutual understanding through dialogue. Together, these perspectives offer a way forward that's grounded in both ethical realism and a commitment to meaningful engagement with the other.

DESMOND TUTU AND RESTORATIVE JUSTICE

Desmond Tutu's leadership in South Africa's Truth and Reconciliation Commission offers a powerful example of how theological principles can be applied to the political process of reconciliation. His emphasis on restorative justice, rather than purely retributive justice, reflects a desire to heal divisions and restore relationships within a society torn apart by violence and oppression. Tutu made it clear that this approach wasn't meant to replace traditional justice systems forever but was a specific response to the unique circumstances of post-apartheid South Africa.[76]

Tutu argued that focusing solely on retributive justice could lead to ongoing cycles of resentment and vengeance. He feared that in situations like Rwanda, if punishment and retribution were seen as the final word, lasting peace would remain elusive.[77] His preference for restorative justice highlighted the need for a process that considered the broader goal of societal healing rather than simply punishing individuals for their past actions.

In his work, Tutu acknowledged the complexities of justice and the tensions between retribution and forgiveness. He pointed out that while many wanted tribunals to hold perpetrators accountable, the commission's aim wasn't to allow criminals to escape justice but to create a space where forgiveness could be part of the process of reconciliation.[78] This approach provided an alternative way of thinking about justice, one that sought to rebuild communities by addressing the underlying causes of division.

Tutu's emphasis on forgiveness didn't mean ignoring the atrocities committed under apartheid. Rather, it was about recognizing the

---

76. Tutu, *No Future Without Forgiveness*, 54.
77. Tutu, *No Future Without Forgiveness*, 260.
78. Tutu, *No Future Without Forgiveness*, 260.

humanity of both victims and perpetrators and finding a way to move forward without being trapped by the need for retribution. This approach was essential for the Truth and Reconciliation Commission, which sought to uncover the truth of what had happened in South Africa while also creating a path toward healing and unity.[79]

The process of reconciliation in South Africa was shaped by the recognition that past injustices couldn't simply be erased. Instead, the commission aimed to bring the truth to light in a way that allowed for acknowledgment of wrongdoing while also encouraging forgiveness and healing.[80] This approach resonates with Gadamer's concept of the fusion of horizons, where understanding emerges through dialogue and engagement with the other. In the context of reconciliation, this fusion allows for a shared vision of the future, despite the divisions of the past.

Tutu's work also involved confronting the power dynamics that had allowed apartheid to flourish. He noted that political leaders like F. W. de Klerk made courageous decisions to move the country toward democracy, but these decisions alone weren't enough to ensure lasting peace. The work of reconciliation required a broader engagement with society, where all voices could be heard and all experiences acknowledged.[81] This broader process of engagement reflects Gadamer's call for openness to the perspectives of others, fostering a dialogue that could bridge the gap between opposing sides.

The Truth and Reconciliation Commission, under Tutu's leadership, provided a space for South Africans to come together and share their often-painful stories in the pursuit of a more unified future. This process of storytelling, of listening to the experiences of both victims and perpetrators, was central to the commission's work. It allowed for a merging of narratives, where different perspectives could come together to form a more complete picture of the past.[82]

Tutu's model of reconciliation has important implications for other divided societies, including Korea, where longstanding mistrust continues to shape North-South relations. In the same way that South Africa's

---

79. Tutu, *No Future Without Forgiveness*, 181.

80. Tutu, *No Future Without Forgiveness*, 37.

81. Tutu, *No Future Without Forgiveness*, 250; P.G.J. Meiring discusses the integral role Desmond Tutu played in leading South Africa's Truth and Reconciliation Commission (TRC). The article highlights how the TRC, under Tutu's guidance, focused on broad engagement, encouraging dialogue between victims and perpetrators to work towards justice and healing (Meiring, "Forgiveness, Reconciliation, and Justice").

82. Tutu, *No Future Without Forgiveness*, 19.

INTRODUCTION

Truth and Reconciliation Commission sought to merge different historical and ethical horizons into a shared vision for the future, similar processes could help bridge the divide on the Korean Peninsula. By focusing on restorative justice and fostering dialogue, a path toward peace and unity could be forged.[83]

JAMES CONE'S BLACK LIBERATION THEOLOGY

James Cone's black liberation theology presents a compelling critique of traditional theological frameworks, particularly for their failure to address systemic oppression and racism. Cone argues that true reconciliation isn't simply the reconciliation of individuals but must involve a fundamental restructuring of societal systems. He highlights that without confronting the root causes of division, such as systemic racism and inequality, reconciliation becomes a mere capitulation to the status quo, benefiting those already in power.[84] His approach aligns with broader liberation theology, which seeks to address not just personal sins but also the social and structural dimensions of injustice.

Cone contends that reconciliation without justice is incomplete, emphasizing that rebellion against systemic injustice is the only authentic response to the absurdity of oppression.[85] This view critiques superficial reconciliatory efforts that fail to address the deeper social realities of racial and economic exploitation. For Cone, any meaningful reconciliation must begin by acknowledging and resisting these structures, which continue to dehumanize marginalized communities.

In describing the condition of black Americans, Cone reflects on the experience of alienation, noting that black individuals often live in a world that expects them to conform to certain standards of behavior that uphold white supremacy. True freedom, he argues, comes from rejecting these expectations and defining one's identity independently of oppressive structures.[86] This resonates with the broader liberationist perspective, which views freedom as inseparable from the struggle against injustice.

Cone also critiques the complicity of traditional Christian institutions in maintaining systems of oppression. He argues that sin warps not

---

83. Tutu, *No Future Without Forgiveness*, 45.
84. Cone, *Black Theology of Liberation*, xiii.
85. Cone, *Black Theology of Liberation*, 105.
86. Cone, *Black Theology of Liberation*, 108.

only individual relationships but also societal structures, particularly when religious leaders align oppressive powers rather than advocating for the liberation of the oppressed.[87] This critique challenges dominant narratives within Christian theology that have often ignored the political dimensions of sin and reconciliation.

This perspective on reconciliation requires a rethinking of historical narratives, particularly how they've been shaped by the perspectives of the oppressors. Cone argues that black theology must create new ways of looking at history that reflect the experiences and struggles of the oppressed.[88] This reordering of history is essential for the survival of black identity and the development of a theological framework that genuinely speaks to the experience of black liberation.

Gadamer's concept of the fusion of horizons aligns with Cone's view that understanding requires active engagement with the other. Gadamer emphasizes that understanding isn't a passive process but one that transforms both parties involved.[89] In the context of addressing systemic racism, this fusion of horizons can create a space where different historical and ethical perspectives come together, allowing for a more comprehensive approach to justice.

Gadamer's reflections on tradition and dialogue are also relevant to Cone's critique. He suggests that tradition isn't something static but is continually reinterpreted through dialogue.[90] For Cone, this reinterpretation is necessary to challenge dominant theological traditions that have justified racial oppression. By engaging in a dialogical process that reexamines historical narratives, communities can begin to address the structural dimensions of injustice.

In this way, both Cone and Gadamer provide frameworks for understanding how reconciliation must involve more than individual forgiveness. It must also involve a reimagining of the systems and traditions that have perpetuated inequality. Through active engagement and the fusion of differing perspectives, systemic injustices can be more effectively addressed, creating a pathway toward a more just and equitable reconciliation.

---

87. Cone, *Black Theology of Liberation*, 114.
88. Cone, *Black Theology of Liberation*, 14.
89. Gadamer, *Philosophical Hermeneutics*, 39.
90. Gadamer, *Philosophical Hermeneutics*, xvii.

INTRODUCTION

DIETRICH BONHOEFFER ON ETHICAL ACTION AND RESISTANCE

Dietrich Bonhoeffer's reflections offer valuable guidance on how the church can resist injustice without compromising its ethical integrity. He challenges the traditional aim of ethical reflection, which often seeks knowledge of good and evil, by suggesting that Christian ethics should invalidate this knowledge.[91] This perspective requires the church to reconsider its role in the world, not merely as an institution that dictates moral laws but as one that embodies a living example of ethical action in the face of oppression.

Bonhoeffer emphasizes that ethical reflection isn't just about personal goodness or making the world better through individual actions. He points out that both the self and the world aren't ultimate realities in themselves.[92] This understanding calls for a fusion of moral and practical horizons, where theological convictions are balanced with pragmatic actions that address the complexities of the political landscape.

He also discusses the importance of the church fulfilling its divine mandate by remedying injustices. The church's legitimate call for government action is grounded in its own adherence to this mandate.[93] By focusing on its essential mission, the church can maintain independence from state powers while standing in solidarity with the oppressed, thus contributing effectively to peacebuilding efforts.

Bonhoeffer introduces the concept of the four divine mandates—marriage and family, labor, government, and church—which possess concrete divine commissions and promises founded in revelation.[94] Recognizing these mandates helps the church navigate its relationship with secular institutions without subjecting them to alien laws but rather setting them free for genuine worldly service.[95] This framework allows the church to uphold ethical principles while engaging in political resistance.

He warns against the danger of the church reducing itself to a purely spiritual force, detached from visible action in the world. Doing so would render ineffective the revelation of God and transform Christ into merely a spirit.[96] Therefore, the church must embody its teachings through ac-

---

91. Bonhoeffer, *Ethics*, 21.
92. Bonhoeffer, *Ethics*, 186.
93. Bonhoeffer, *Ethics*, 291.
94. Bonhoeffer, *Ethics*, 325.
95. Bonhoeffer, *Ethics*, 326.
96. Bonhoeffer, *Ethics*, 199.

tive participation in addressing societal injustices, maintaining its integrity by aligning actions with theological convictions.

Bonhoeffer also critiques the reliance on knowledge of good and evil as the basis for ethical action. He suggests that Christian ethics should instead focus on the will of God as revealed in Jesus Christ.[97] This shift moves the church away from abstract moralizing toward concrete actions that reflect divine will, further reinforcing the need for a balance between moral convictions and practical engagement.

By adhering to this approach, the church can avoid becoming entangled in oppressive power structures. It maintains its independence by not aligning uncritically with state powers yet remains actively involved in societal transformation. This stance enables the church to contribute meaningfully to peacebuilding, as it addresses injustices without compromising its ethical framework.

Bonhoeffer's reflections thus provide a framework for the church to navigate political complexities. By integrating moral and practical considerations, the church can uphold its theological convictions while engaging in actions that promote justice and peace.[98] This balanced approach ensures that the church remains a steadfast advocate for the oppressed, effectively contributing to the transformation of society without losing its ethical grounding.

Conclusively, the fusion of horizons offers a critical framework for addressing the complexities of oppression and liberation. By fostering dialogue between different historical and cultural perspectives, it creates a space where diverse voices can contribute to a shared understanding of justice. This approach acknowledges that true understanding arises not from erasing differences but from engaging them constructively, allowing new meanings to emerge through interaction.

Moreover, thinkers like Franz Rosenzweig and Gustavo Gutiérrez expand this concept by emphasizing that liberation is an ongoing process, requiring continuous ethical action and active engagement with both divine and human responsibilities. Their perspectives highlight the importance of not only theoretical reflection but also practical commitment to justice.

Karl Barth and Leonardo Boff further broaden the discussion by integrating environmental concerns into the conversation. They argue

---

97. Bonhoeffer, *Ethics*, 21.
98. Bonhoeffer, *Ethics*, 186,

that true liberation includes ecological justice, as humans are deeply interconnected with the natural world. This ecological dimension of justice aligns with the idea of a holistic framework that incorporates both social and environmental well-being.

Additionally, the fusion of horizons proves essential in contexts of political reconciliation, as seen in the works of Reinhold Niebuhr and Desmond Tutu. Their focus on pragmatic realism and restorative justice demonstrates that addressing historical injustices requires both a commitment to dialogue and a readiness to act on ethical responsibilities.

In sum, the fusion of horizons provides a versatile and dynamic framework for understanding liberation and reconciliation. By encouraging continuous engagement with different perspectives, it offers a way forward in the pursuit of justice, grounded in ethical action and mutual understanding.

CHAPTER ONE

Global Liberation: Theology in Action

IN THE ONGOING STRUGGLE for global liberation, theological and philosophical frameworks have played a key role in shaping how societies understand oppression and envision pathways toward justice. The collaboration between human responsibility and divine action, as articulated by figures such as Franz Rosenzweig, offers a framework that emphasizes both historical development and spiritual engagement.[1] This approach highlights the necessity of recognizing liberation as a process requiring active participation, both in the spiritual and societal realms.

This chapter begins by examining various approaches to liberation, particularly through the lens of Rosenzweig's philosophy, which suggests that liberation is a continuous process of creation. His ideas, which focus on the collaboration between divine intervention and human action, are compared with thinkers like Marx, Freire, and Foucault, who provide more materialist or structural analyses of oppression. Together, these perspectives provide a more comprehensive understanding of how societal structures perpetuate oppression and how they can be challenged.

Theological discussions on liberation are further enriched by the contributions of liberation theologians such as Gustavo Gutiérrez, James Cone, and Leonardo Boff. Their engagement with existential theology, especially in dialogue with Rudolf Bultmann, emphasizes the importance

---

1. Rosenzweig's work offers a compelling integration of divine sovereignty and human agency, emphasizing that liberation is not a passive process but one requiring active human participation in historical change. His approach challenges reductionist materialist interpretations by underscoring the ongoing partnership between divine intervention and human responsibility, both of which play essential roles in achieving social and spiritual transformation (Rieger and Silva, *"Liberation Theologies and Their Future,"* 925.).

of addressing both personal and collective dimensions of oppression. These theologians argue for a faith that is not abstract but is actively lived out in solidarity with oppressed communities, engaging directly with historical realities.

The complexity of power, identity, and resistance is explored through the works of thinkers like Fanon, Butler, and Sen, who provide varied approaches to understanding how power shapes individual and collective identities. Their work highlights the importance of recognizing vulnerability and creating spaces for resistance within oppressive systems. These discussions invite ongoing reflection on the role of both theoretical and practical strategies in fostering liberation.

In integrating these diverse perspectives, this chapter aims to explore how theological and philosophical frameworks can inform real-world efforts toward liberation. By combining spiritual reflection with practical actions, it emphasizes the need for both immediate responses to oppression and long-term commitments to creating more just societies.

1.1. POWER, IDEOLOGY, AND RESISTANCE: APPROACHES TO LIBERATION

This section examines various perspectives on oppression and liberation, focusing on how power dynamics shape individual and collective identities. Beginning with Franz Rosenzweig's philosophy, we explore his emphasis on the collaboration between divine action and human responsibility. Rosenzweig views liberation as an ongoing process that unfolds through time, suggesting that both historical development and spiritual engagement are crucial in challenging oppression. His ideas set the foundation for understanding liberation as a collective journey that necessitates active participation.

We then delve into theological, historical, and practical approaches to oppression. By integrating Rosenzweig's theological perspectives with the practical strategies of thinkers like Marx, Freire, Foucault, Butler, and Sen, we gain a multifaceted understanding of how systemic issues of oppression can be addressed. These viewpoints highlight the importance of recognizing oppression as deeply embedded within societal structures, requiring both immediate action and long-term commitment to foster change.

The discussion continues with an analysis of how liberation theologians engage with Rudolf Bultmann's existential theology. Theologians such as Leonardo Boff, James Cone, Gustavo Gutiérrez, Jon Sobrino, José Míguez Bonino, Juan Luis Segundo, and Clodovis Boff argue for a theology that combines personal transformation with social liberation. They emphasize that faith must be lived out within historical reality, directly engaging with the struggles of oppressed communities. This approach connects personal faith with collective action, advocating for efforts to dismantle unjust social structures.

We also explore theories that unravel the complexities of power, identity, and resistance. Drawing from the works of Fanon, Foucault, Arendt, Butler, Gutiérrez, and Sen, we examine how oppressive structures influence identities and actions. These theorists provide frameworks that highlight both the challenges and potential pathways toward resistance and liberation. Their perspectives encourage ongoing dialogue about how individuals and communities can navigate and transform the oppressive systems that shape their realities.

By integrating these diverse viewpoints, this section aims to provide a comprehensive understanding of oppression and liberation. It underscores the necessity of combining philosophical reflections with practical strategies, emphasizing the need for collective efforts to build a just and equitable society. Through this exploration, we are invited to consider how theoretical frameworks can inform real-world actions toward social change.

1.1.1. Franz Rosenzweig on Liberation: Divine and Human Collaboration

Franz Rosenzweig's philosophy offers a significant framework for understanding the dynamics of oppression and liberation in human history. His perspective emphasizes the collaboration between divine action and human responsibility, portraying liberation as an ongoing process that unfolds through time. By introducing concepts like "Creation out of nothing," Rosenzweig suggests that each act of liberation is a new beginning, rendering previous forms of oppression obsolete and highlighting the continuous interplay between the divine and the human.

This section examines various scholars' interpretations of Rosenzweig's ideas, exploring how his thoughts have been understood, critiqued, and applied to contemporary social challenges. Peter Ochs and Leora Batnitzky discuss how Rosenzweig integrates philosophy and theology to create a framework that encourages active engagement with tradition and the world to overcome oppression. Robert Gibbs and Steven Kepnes focus

CHAPTER ONE

on his emphasis on ethical responsibility and communal practices, showing how his ideas promote practical actions rooted in community life.

Conversely, scholars like Benjamin Pollock and Aaron Hughes raise questions about the applicability of Rosenzweig's frameworks to modern forms of oppression. They suggest that while his emphasis on divine action is important, it may sometimes overshadow the urgency of human agency in addressing social injustices. By exploring these differing perspectives, this section aims to provide a comprehensive understanding of Rosenzweig's contributions to discussions on oppression and liberation, highlighting both the potential and the limitations of his thought in the context of contemporary issues.

Franz Rosenzweig presents a compelling framework for understanding oppression and liberation, emphasizing their roles in the historical and redemptive development of humanity. He views liberation as both a divine and human process, continuously evolving through different historical epochs. By incorporating the philosophical notion of "Creation out of nothing," Rosenzweig underscores the idea that liberation is not a one-time event but an ongoing act of creation, where previous forms of oppression are made irrelevant by the emergence of new realities. This continuous renewal highlights the dynamic interplay between divine intervention and human responsibility.

Peter Ochs elaborates on Rosenzweig's balanced view of divine sovereignty and human agency. Ochs suggests that, for Rosenzweig, liberation is a collaborative effort between God and humanity, where humans act as co-creators in the unfolding of redemptive history.[2] This shared responsibility underscores the idea that while divine action provides the framework for liberation, it is through human engagement with this framework that real change occurs.

Furthermore, Ochs examines Rosenzweig's critique of "supersessionism," particularly within Christian theological interpretations, which sometimes suggest that the Jewish covenant has been replaced or fulfilled entirely by the Christian one.[3] Rosenzweig rejects such notions, proposing instead that both Jewish and Christian traditions play ongoing roles in the redemptive process. He stresses the importance of understanding the continuity and coexistence of these religious traditions, rather than viewing one as having superseded the other.

2. Ochs, *Another Reformation*, 71.
3. Ochs, *Another Reformation*, 11.

In his discussion of postliberal theology, Ochs notes that thinkers like Max Kadushin and Eugene Borowitz also grappled with the question of how different religious traditions interact in the context of redemption.[4] According to Ochs, Rosenzweig's framework allows for a pluralistic view of religious participation in liberation, where each tradition contributes to a broader understanding of divine action and human responsibility.

Ochs continues to explore Rosenzweig's critique of supersessionism by addressing its practical implications in both Christian and Jewish contexts. He notes that Rosenzweig saw the concept as limiting the potential for collaboration between religious communities, particularly when it comes to addressing oppression and seeking liberation.[5] By rejecting supersessionism, Rosenzweig opens the door for a more cooperative and inclusive approach to liberation.

Ochs also highlights how Rosenzweig's theology aligns with the idea of continuous revelation, where divine action is not confined to a single historical event but unfolds over time, providing new opportunities for liberation in every generation.[6] This ongoing process allows each generation to reinterpret their role in the redemptive journey, emphasizing the necessity of active human participation in overcoming oppression.

In a further exploration of Rosenzweig's thoughts, Ochs addresses how the philosopher views suffering and redemption as interconnected. For Rosenzweig, the experience of suffering is not an isolated phenomenon but part of the larger process of redemption, where divine intervention transforms suffering into opportunities for growth and liberation.[7] This perspective encourages individuals to view their struggles within the broader context of a redemptive plan that is constantly evolving.

Ochs also reflects on Rosenzweig's view of Scripture as a tool for understanding the redemptive process. He suggests that for Rosenzweig, the reading of sacred texts is not merely a passive activity but an active engagement with divine wisdom that can guide individuals and communities toward liberation.[8] This view of Scripture reinforces the idea that divine action and human responsibility are intertwined in the pursuit of justice and freedom.

---

4. Ochs, *Another Reformation*, 82.
5. Ochs, *Another Reformation*, 12.
6. Ochs, *Another Reformation*, 7.
7. Ochs, *Another Reformation*, 187.
8. Ochs, *Another Reformation*, 57.

CHAPTER ONE

Finally, Ochs addresses how Rosenzweig's thoughts on redemption offer a corrective to Christian supersessionism, advocating for a renewed understanding of the relationship between Jews and Christians in the shared quest for liberation.[9] He argues that by reinterpreting traditional theological positions, both communities can engage in a more fruitful dialogue that acknowledges their distinct but complementary roles in the redemptive process.

In sum, Rosenzweig's perspective on oppression and liberation, as discussed by Peter Ochs, offers a balanced framework that emphasizes both divine action and human responsibility. It rejects the notion of supersessionism and encourages a collaborative and continuous engagement with the conditions of oppression, making liberation an ongoing act of creation that requires participation from all.

Franz Rosenzweig's exploration of oppression and liberation is deeply intertwined with his integration of philosophy and theology, as Leora Batnitzky discusses in her analysis of his work. She emphasizes that Rosenzweig's idea of "Creation out of nothing" serves as a powerful metaphor for the potential of radical transformation in the face of oppression. This notion allows for the possibility of liberation as an ongoing creative process, where previous oppressive structures can be made obsolete, thus offering a framework for societies to envision and enact new realities.[10]

Rosenzweig contends that idealism, as a philosophical system, cannot adequately account for certain fundamental aspects of human existence, such as death, language, or art. These limitations, he argues, open the door to the possibility of divine revelation, which has the transformative power to wholly reshape the human condition. In this context, revelation is not just an abstract concept but a lived experience that demands engagement with the world, thus linking theology directly to the practical matter of overcoming oppression.[11]

Leora Batnitzky further explores how Rosenzweig's shift from academic philosophy to Jewish education reflects his commitment to making theological ideas accessible and actionable in the real world. After completing The Star of Redemption, Rosenzweig turned his attention to projects such as the Freies Jüdisches Lehrhaus, an institution aimed at providing adult Jewish education. His focus on education underscores

9. Ochs, *Another Reformation*, 40.
10. Batnitzky, *How Judaism Became a Religion*, 80.
11. Batnitzky, *How Judaism Became a Religion*, 80.

his belief that liberation requires active participation from individuals, who must be equipped with the knowledge and tools to engage with both their tradition and the challenges of their time.[12]

Batnitzky points out that for Rosenzweig and Martin Buber, the act of translating the Bible was not merely a linguistic exercise but a theological one. By focusing on the literal meaning and the underlying themes of the text, their translation work sought to reorient the modern person's engagement with Scripture. This process of translation itself becomes a metaphor for liberation, as it disrupts familiar ways of thinking and forces individuals to confront the ethical demands of the text in new and challenging ways.[13]

In her analysis, Batnitzky also notes that Rosenzweig, like Buber, rejected the idea of religion as a static category. For Rosenzweig, God did not create religion, but rather relationships between human beings and the divine. This relational framework serves as the foundation for his understanding of liberation, where the act of revelation continuously renews and transforms the individual and collective human experience, encouraging a break from the constraints of oppression.[14]

Rosenzweig's critique of modern philosophical systems is also linked to his understanding of Zionism and the role of the Jewish people. Batnitzky explores how Rosenzweig's views differ from other Jewish thinkers such as Hermann Cohen, who opposed Jewish nationalism. While Cohen maintained that the Jewish mission was to model pure monotheism for the nations, Rosenzweig saw the Jewish people's role as more dynamic, involving active participation in the unfolding of history and redemption, which necessarily included the struggle against oppression.[15]

Batnitzky connects Rosenzweig's theological vision to broader philosophical discourses, showing how his rejection of supersessionism—particularly in relation to Christianity—reflects his commitment to pluralism and coexistence. For Rosenzweig, the relationship between Judaism and Christianity is not one of replacement but of mutual participation in the redemptive process. This perspective has direct implications for his understanding of liberation, as it underscores the need for

---

12. Batnitzky, *How Judaism Became a Religion*, 81.
13. Batnitzky, *How Judaism Became a Religion*, 82.
14. Batnitzky, *How Judaism Became a Religion*, 83.
15. Batnitzky, *How Judaism Became a Religion*, 55.

interreligious collaboration in the pursuit of justice and the dismantling of oppressive systems.[16]

In sum, Leora Batnitzky's examination of Rosenzweig's work reveals how his theological ideas offer a robust framework for addressing oppression. By integrating philosophy and theology, Rosenzweig provides a vision of liberation as an ongoing, creative process that requires active human participation alongside divine revelation. This perspective encourages individuals and communities to reimagine their roles in history, pushing them to confront and overcome the oppressive structures that limit human freedom.[17]

Franz Rosenzweig's understanding of oppression and liberation is intricately tied to the ethical framework that he develops in his theological work. Robert Gibbs emphasizes that, for Rosenzweig, the ongoing act of creation calls for moral accountability, demanding that individuals not only recognize but also actively oppose oppression in the world. This view places an ethical obligation on individuals to contribute to liberation through responsible actions and ethical living.[18]

Gibbs points out that Rosenzweig's interpretation of key Jewish prayers, particularly on Yom Kippur, reinforces the idea that individuals bear responsibility not just for themselves but for the entire world. This sense of universal responsibility is a defining characteristic of Jewish thought in Rosenzweig's framework. He contrasts this with the Christian approach, which, according to Rosenzweig, centers on cooperation, while the Jewish perspective is shaped through representation.[19] This distinction highlights the communal aspect of ethical responsibility in Rosenzweig's thought, where individuals act on behalf of their community and, by extension, humanity.

Gibbs further explores Rosenzweig's rejection of certain philosophical traditions, such as idealism, which tend to limit or reduce social responsibilities. Rosenzweig argues that such frameworks often fail to adequately address the need for self-critical judgment, a key element in resisting oppression and promoting liberation. According to Rosenzweig, idealism and paganism, as philosophical categories, diminish the

---

16. Batnitzky, *How Judaism Became a Religion*, 12.
17. Batnitzky, *How Judaism Became a Religion*, 80–83.
18. Gibbs, *Why Ethics?*, 18.
19. Gibbs, *Why Ethics?*, 18.

ethical demands placed on individuals and communities, leading to a neglect of broader social responsibilities.[20]

In contrast to these reductive approaches, Rosenzweig's ethical framework is grounded in the idea that responsive thinking—thinking that takes into account both the present and the future—is essential for meaningful ethical action. Gibbs notes that, for Rosenzweig, ethical responsibility is deeply tied to time, particularly the future, where the truth of ethical theories and actions will ultimately be verified. This future-oriented perspective on ethics encourages individuals to take responsibility not just for their current actions but for the long-term consequences of their decisions.[21]

Gibbs draws a connection between Rosenzweig's thought and the work of William James and Charles Peirce, particularly in their shared emphasis on empiricism. Rosenzweig, like James and Peirce, believes that ethical relations—whether between individuals or between humans and God—must be grounded in experience and verified over time. This approach allows for a practical application of ethical principles, as it requires individuals to continuously assess and respond to the needs of others in their community.[22]

Another key element of Rosenzweig's ethical philosophy, as Gibbs discusses, is the role of confession. In Rosenzweig's view, confession is not merely an acknowledgment of past wrongs but a transformative act that reorients the individual toward future responsibility. This transformation is essential in the context of ethical living, as it allows individuals to reconcile with their past while committing to more responsible actions moving forward.[23]

Gibbs also examines Rosenzweig's understanding of communal practices, particularly in the context of remembrance. For Rosenzweig, social practices such as observing the Sabbath or other Jewish holidays serve to anchor individuals in a collective memory, which in turn fosters a sense of ethical responsibility that extends beyond the individual. These practices remind individuals that they are part of a larger community, and that their ethical obligations are shaped by the needs and expectations of that community.[24]

20. Gibbs, *Why Ethics?*, 19.
21. Gibbs, *Why Ethics?*, 19.
22. Gibbs, *Why Ethics?*, 20.
23. Gibbs, *Why Ethics?*, 22.
24. Gibbs, *Why Ethics?*, 22.

CHAPTER ONE

Rosenzweig's approach to ethics is also informed by his understanding of language and communication. According to Gibbs, Rosenzweig believes that ethical responsibility arises from the interactions between individuals, particularly in the context of dialogue. In this framework, language is not just a means of communication but a tool for ethical engagement, as it binds individuals to one another and to their shared responsibilities.[25]

In a similar vein, Rosenzweig's focus on the communal use of the word "we" reflects his belief that ethical responsibility is inherently relational. The word "we" signifies a collective identity that is constantly evolving and must be judged by the ethical actions of the community. This dynamic view of communal identity reinforces the idea that ethical responsibility is never static but always subject to revision and reinterpretation as new challenges and opportunities for liberation arise.[26]

Overall, Gibbs highlights how Rosenzweig's ethical framework places a strong emphasis on the active role of individuals and communities in opposing oppression and fostering liberation. This framework is not merely theoretical but deeply practical, as it calls for continuous reflection, action, and re-engagement with the ethical demands of the present and the future.[27] By positioning ethical responsibility as a central element of his theological vision, Rosenzweig offers a compelling approach to confronting oppression and working toward a more just and liberated world.

Franz Rosenzweig's approach to liberation is deeply rooted in communal experience and shared traditions, as Steven Kepnes highlights in his exploration of Rosenzweig's work. Kepnes emphasizes that for Rosenzweig, liberation is not an isolated or individualistic experience but one that is realized within the context of community. The rituals and traditions of the Jewish community play a central role in guiding individuals and the collective toward justice and overcoming oppression.[28]

Kepnes points to Rosenzweig's allegorical interpretation of biblical texts, particularly the Song of Songs, where the divine-human relationship is portrayed as a journey of revelation. Rosenzweig's use of biblical passages underscores how communal rituals and liturgical readings serve as vehicles for experiencing divine revelation. This journey through

25. Gibbs, *Why Ethics?*, 115.
26. Gibbs, *Why Ethics?*, 184.
27. Gibbs, *Why Ethics?*, 19–22.
28. Kepnes, *Jewish Liturgical Reasoning*, 93.

revelation is communal in nature, as it unfolds within the shared practices of the Jewish community, linking the individual's experience of liberation to the broader community's engagement with tradition.[29]

The communal aspects of liberation are further emphasized in Rosenzweig's understanding of love as a commanded act. Kepnes discusses how Rosenzweig addresses the question of how love, often perceived as a free and personal emotion, can be commanded within a religious framework. Rosenzweig resolves this by pointing to the experience of love as something that is realized through communal obligations and responsibilities, suggesting that love, like liberation, is achieved through collective action and ethical engagement.[30]

In Rosenzweig's view, as explained by Kepnes, revelation is both a continuation of creation and a form of new creation. It builds upon the foundation of the original creation but introduces a transformative element that expands into the world as a redemptive force. This redemptive love, symbolized by the commandment to "Love your neighbor," highlights how revelation and liberation are deeply interconnected with communal ethics and responsibilities.[31]

Kepnes also draws attention to Rosenzweig's interpretation of communal rituals, such as the Shabbat and the reading of the Torah. For Rosenzweig, these rituals create a unique order of reality where the community is momentarily transported into a space where the divine can be directly encountered. These moments of communal liturgy provide a foretaste of liberation, as they offer an experience of redemption that transcends the limitations of everyday life, reinforcing the communal journey toward justice.[32]

The role of the Shabbat in Rosenzweig's thought is particularly significant, as Kepnes notes. Shabbat functions as a vehicle for social ethics, offering a communal space where the ideals of justice, peace, and liberation can be practiced. It serves as a reminder that liberation is not only a future goal but an ongoing process that can be experienced through the rhythms of communal life and ritual observance.[33]

Furthermore, Kepnes emphasizes that Rosenzweig sees communal rituals as moments that bridge the gap between the present and the

---

29. Kepnes, *Jewish Liturgical Reasoning*, 93.
30. Kepnes, *Jewish Liturgical Reasoning*, 94.
31. Kepnes, *Jewish Liturgical Reasoning*, 95–96.
32. Kepnes, *Jewish Liturgical Reasoning*, viii.
33. Kepnes, *Jewish Liturgical Reasoning*, 19.

CHAPTER ONE

anticipated future redemption. These rituals allow the community to participate in the redemptive process, even in a world where full redemption has not yet been realized. By engaging in these communal practices, individuals are reminded of their collective responsibility to work toward justice and to oppose oppression in their daily lives.[34]

Rosenzweig's focus on communal ethics extends to the role of repentance, or teshuvah, which he sees as a collective practice. Kepnes explains that for Rosenzweig, teshuvah is not just about individual repentance but about the renewal of the entire community. It is through this communal act of turning back to God and to each other that the community is strengthened and its efforts toward liberation are renewed.[35]

Kepnes also touches on Rosenzweig's reflections on the historical and existential challenges faced by the Jewish community, particularly in light of events like the Shoah and the establishment of the State of Israel. These events, while presenting new difficulties, also underscore the importance of communal memory and the collective effort to overcome oppression. Rosenzweig's thought offers a framework for understanding how the community can navigate these challenges while remaining committed to the pursuit of justice.[36]

Ultimately, Kepnes shows that Rosenzweig's vision of liberation is inseparable from the communal practices and traditions that sustain the Jewish people. It is through the collective engagement with these rituals, and the shared memory of the community, that liberation is both envisioned and enacted. This communal focus is central to Rosenzweig's ethical and theological framework, as it places the responsibility for justice and liberation not only on individuals but on the entire community.[37]

Benjamin Pollock offers a critical viewpoint on Franz Rosenzweig's emphasis on divine action, suggesting that such a focus might risk overshadowing the human effort required to confront oppression directly. Pollock raises the concern that Rosenzweig's theological framework, with its focus on divine intervention and revelation, could inadvertently reduce the urgency of human agency in addressing social injustices.[38] This critique prompts a reconsideration of the balance between divine sovereignty and human responsibility in Rosenzweig's thought.

34. Kepnes, *Jewish Liturgical Reasoning*, 20.
35. Kepnes, *Jewish Liturgical Reasoning*, 58.
36. Kepnes, *Jewish Liturgical Reasoning*, 131.
37. Kepnes, *Jewish Liturgical Reasoning*, 93–123.
38. Pollock, *Franz Rosenzweig and the Systematic Task of Philosophy*, 22.

Pollock highlights Rosenzweig's interpretation of philosophical systems, particularly his engagement with German Idealism. Rosenzweig critiques the tendency within Idealism to abstract human experience, often diminishing the particularity and lived reality of individuals. Pollock suggests that, while Rosenzweig is critical of these systems, his own focus on the divine could also lead to an abstraction that might undermine the practical engagement required to address oppression.[39] In this way, Pollock invites readers to consider whether Rosenzweig's theological vision sufficiently empowers human action.

In Pollock's analysis, Rosenzweig's framework is deeply rooted in the interplay between the divine and the human, but the question remains whether this balance adequately addresses the immediate need for human agency in overcoming social injustices. Pollock points to Rosenzweig's reflections on the philosophical history of systems, noting that while Rosenzweig critiques the systems of German Idealism for their universalizing tendencies, his own emphasis on the divine might introduce a different kind of universality that places too much reliance on divine action.[40] This concern is central to Pollock's critique of Rosenzweig's approach to oppression.

Pollock also explores the theological dimensions of Rosenzweig's thought, particularly the way he positions revelation as the key to understanding the human condition. While Rosenzweig argues that revelation allows individuals to see themselves as both whole and part of a greater whole, Pollock questions whether this theological framing might lead to a diminished sense of urgency in human efforts to confront and dismantle systems of oppression.[41] In this sense, Pollock is concerned that Rosenzweig's focus on the divine plan for redemption might detract from the pressing need for human-driven social change.

Additionally, Pollock draws attention to the eschatological aspects of Rosenzweig's theology, particularly his view that revelation and redemption are part of a historical process that will ultimately culminate in the end of time. Pollock argues that this future-oriented vision could potentially lessen the perceived importance of immediate human action in addressing present injustices.[42] This critique raises important questions about the role of human agency in Rosenzweig's vision of liberation

---

39. Pollock, *Franz Rosenzweig and the Systematic Task of Philosophy*, 24.
40. Pollock, *Franz Rosenzweig and the Systematic Task of Philosophy*, 42.
41. Pollock, *Franz Rosenzweig and the Systematic Task of Philosophy*, 79.
42. Pollock, *Franz Rosenzweig and the Systematic Task of Philosophy*, 81.

and whether it provides sufficient space for human efforts in the here and now.

Pollock contrasts Rosenzweig's approach with other philosophical traditions, such as those that place a stronger emphasis on human autonomy and responsibility. While Rosenzweig's work offers a rich theological framework for understanding the relationship between humanity and the divine, Pollock suggests that it might lack the tools necessary for fully empowering individuals and communities to take direct action against oppression.[43] This comparison underscores the tension between divine action and human responsibility in addressing social injustice.

Furthermore, Pollock engages with Rosenzweig's use of biblical figures and narratives, such as the relationship between God and Abraham, to illustrate the dynamic between divine promise and human action. While Rosenzweig portrays figures like Abraham as participants in the divine plan, Pollock questions whether this theological framing sufficiently encourages human initiative in the fight against oppression.[44] In this way, Pollock's critique highlights the potential limitations of Rosenzweig's theological approach in fostering human agency.

Ultimately, Pollock's critical analysis of Rosenzweig's focus on the divine invites a reevaluation of how theological frameworks can empower or hinder human action in the pursuit of justice. He raises important questions about whether Rosenzweig's theology provides enough emphasis on human responsibility in the face of oppression, suggesting that a more balanced approach might be necessary to ensure that divine action does not overshadow the role of human agency.[45] This critique encourages further exploration of how Rosenzweig's thought can be adapted to address the challenges of social injustice in a way that fully empowers human action.

David Novak's exploration of Franz Rosenzweig's theology emphasizes the crucial role of Jewish law and ethical commandments in the redemptive process. Novak argues that, for Rosenzweig, adhering to ethical commandments is not merely a ritualistic practice but a form of active participation in liberation. These concrete actions, guided by religious principles, serve as a direct response to oppression and help actualize the redemptive promise.[46]

43. Pollock, *Franz Rosenzweig and the Systematic Task of Philosophy*, 46.
44. Pollock, *Franz Rosenzweig and the Systematic Task of Philosophy*, 263.
45. Pollock, *Franz Rosenzweig and the Systematic Task of Philosophy*, 79–82.
46. Novak, *Jewish Social Contract*, 19.

Novak highlights the primacy of the Jewish community in this redemptive process, emphasizing that the community's historical and cultural identity is central to understanding the role of Jewish law. Unlike secular social contract theories, which often lack a real history or ontological foundation, the Jewish tradition draws from its historical past to sustain its hopes for a transcendent future. This historical and ontological connection, Novak suggests, allows the Jewish community to look beyond the present and anticipate a future that includes the messianic redemption.[47]

Novak also contrasts Rosenzweig's understanding of communal identity with modern social contract theories, noting that while secular society seeks to create neutral spaces for negotiation and cultural interaction, Jewish law remains deeply rooted in a religious framework that looks toward the culmination of history in divine redemption. For Jews, this connection to revelation and Torah provides a foundation for their social and cultural life, which transcends the secular aims of modern civil society.[48]

This orientation toward messianic redemption, Novak argues, is essential to understanding the Jewish community's participation in civil society. Jewish law and ethical commandments guide the community's actions in the present while pointing toward a future that is beyond human understanding. By living according to these commandments, Jews contribute to the ultimate fulfillment of history, even as they engage in the social and political realities of the present.[49]

Novak further examines how Rosenzweig's focus on ethical commandments aligns with the broader goals of a just society. He suggests that by adhering to the principles of Jewish law, the community does more than simply preserve its identity—it actively contributes to the common good of the larger society. This ethical framework provides a model for how religious traditions can engage with secular society while maintaining their cultural autonomy and contributing to social justice.[50]

In discussing the relationship between religious principles and civil society, Novak points out that Rosenzweig's framework does not call for the establishment of a religious state or the imposition of religious laws on others. Instead, it emphasizes that religious communities, including

---

47. Novak, *Jewish Social Contract*, 19.
48. Novak, *Jewish Social Contract*, 20.
49. Novak, *Jewish Social Contract*, 21.
50. Novak, *Jewish Social Contract*, 21.

the Jewish community, should negotiate their place within secular society through mutual respect and recognition of their cultural and religious contributions. This negotiation is ongoing and involves a balance between preserving communal identity and participating in the broader social contract.[51]

Novak also touches on the eschatological dimension of Rosenzweig's thought, noting that the ultimate goal of Jewish law and ethical living is not merely societal harmony but the eventual redemption of the world. This messianic hope, deeply embedded in Jewish law, provides the community with a long-term vision that shapes its actions in the present. By adhering to ethical commandments, Jews prepare themselves and the world for the eventual fulfillment of divine promises.[52]

In his analysis, Novak underscores the importance of maintaining a strong commitment to Jewish tradition and ethical commandments as a way of ensuring the community's ability to make meaningful claims within civil society. He suggests that the more deeply rooted the Jewish community is in its own tradition, the stronger its voice will be in negotiating its place within the larger social framework. This commitment to tradition, guided by ethical commandments, allows the Jewish community to contribute positively to the common good while maintaining its distinct identity.[53]

Through this lens, Novak presents Rosenzweig's theology as a framework for understanding how religious principles, particularly Jewish law, can serve as a response to oppression and as a path toward liberation. By participating in the redemptive process through adherence to ethical commandments, individuals and communities engage in concrete actions that address social injustices and contribute to the ultimate realization of redemption.[54]

George Y. Kohler provides a critical examination of Franz Rosenzweig's departure from traditional metaphysics, focusing on the implications of Rosenzweig's rethinking of creation. Kohler argues that Rosenzweig's radical shift in understanding creation might unsettle established philosophical foundations, raising concerns about the practical implications of such a framework for addressing real-world oppression. According to Kohler, Rosenzweig's approach, while intellectually bold,

---

51. Novak, *Jewish Social Contract*, 20.
52. Novak, *Jewish Social Contract*, 21.
53. Novak, *Jewish Social Contract*, 21.
54. Novak, *Jewish Social Contract*, 19–21.

may not offer the kind of immediate and actionable tools needed to confront social injustices effectively.[55]

In his analysis, Kohler points out that Rosenzweig's rejection of traditional metaphysical structures, particularly those rooted in German Idealism, is both innovative and disruptive. Rosenzweig seeks to move beyond the limitations of previous philosophical systems by proposing a dynamic and relational view of creation. However, Kohler questions whether this philosophical shift is practical for those seeking concrete solutions to oppression. He suggests that Rosenzweig's focus on the theological and metaphysical aspects of creation may overshadow more direct forms of human agency and social engagement.[56]

Kohler also explores the tension between Rosenzweig's theological innovations and their applicability to the lived experiences of individuals facing oppression. While Rosenzweig emphasizes the importance of divine action in the process of creation and redemption, Kohler argues that this focus might lead to a diminished sense of urgency in addressing social injustices. He contends that Rosenzweig's theological framework could risk placing too much emphasis on divine intervention, leaving less room for human responsibility in the fight against oppression.[57]

Furthermore, Kohler raises the question of whether Rosenzweig's rethinking of creation adequately accounts for the practical realities of social and political life. He notes that while Rosenzweig's ideas offer a fresh perspective on the relationship between humanity and the divine, they may lack the clarity needed to inspire direct action in the face of systemic injustice. Kohler suggests that a more grounded approach, which integrates both metaphysical insights and practical strategies for social engagement, might be necessary for Rosenzweig's framework to effectively address real-world challenges.[58]

Kohler acknowledges that Rosenzweig's critique of traditional metaphysics is significant in its own right, particularly in its challenge to the abstract and universalizing tendencies of German Idealism. However, he cautions that such a radical departure from established philosophical frameworks might not provide the necessary tools for confronting oppression in a meaningful and immediate way. Rosenzweig's reimagining

---

55. Kohler, *Reading Maimonides' Philosophy in 19th Century Germany*, 15.
56. Kohler, *Reading Maimonides' Philosophy in 19th Century Germany*, 22.
57. Kohler, *Reading Maimonides' Philosophy in 19th Century Germany*, 106.
58. Kohler, *Reading Maimonides' Philosophy in 19th Century Germany*, 140.

CHAPTER ONE

of creation, while offering a powerful theological vision, may not fully address the practical demands of social justice.[59]

Additionally, Kohler explores how Rosenzweig's theological innovations could be seen as both a strength and a limitation. On one hand, Rosenzweig's focus on the relational and dynamic aspects of creation provides a rich and complex understanding of the human-divine relationship. On the other hand, Kohler argues that this complexity might complicate efforts to mobilize communities toward collective action against oppression. He suggests that a more straightforward approach, which prioritizes human agency alongside divine action, could be more effective in achieving liberation.[60]

Kohler also discusses the broader philosophical implications of Rosenzweig's thought, particularly in relation to the role of metaphysics in addressing social and political issues. He notes that while Rosenzweig's work challenges many of the assumptions of traditional metaphysics, it may also leave certain gaps in terms of practical applicability. Kohler emphasizes the need for a balance between philosophical innovation and real-world relevance, arguing that Rosenzweig's theology might benefit from a more direct engagement with the practical concerns of social justice.[61]

In summary, Kohler's critique of Rosenzweig's departure from traditional metaphysics centers on the question of whether such a radical shift in perspective can effectively address the pressing issues of oppression and social injustice. While Kohler recognizes the intellectual and theological contributions of Rosenzweig's work, he raises concerns about its practicality in mobilizing human efforts to combat oppression. Kohler's analysis invites further reflection on how theological and philosophical frameworks can balance metaphysical depth with practical engagement in the pursuit of justice.[62]

Samuel Moyn examines the historical context surrounding Franz Rosenzweig's theological ideas, positioning them within broader movements for social change. He relates Rosenzweig's thought to contemporary struggles for liberation, showing how its emphasis on redemption and divine-human interaction resonates with modern social justice

---

59. Kohler, *Reading Maimonides' Philosophy in 19th Century Germany*, 30.
60. Kohler, *Reading Maimonides' Philosophy in 19th Century Germany*, 45.
61. Kohler, *Reading Maimonides' Philosophy in 19th Century Germany*, 48.
62. Kohler, *Reading Maimonides' Philosophy in 19th Century Germany*, 51.

movements.⁶³ Rosenzweig's focus on intersubjectivity and the importance of relationships between individuals offers a framework that aligns well with the collective aims of these movements.

Moyn connects Rosenzweig's ideas to the philosophical shift away from solipsism, as seen in thinkers like Heidegger. He notes that Rosenzweig's emphasis on human responsibility, in dialogue with the divine, provides an ethical foundation that can inspire collective action. This stands in contrast to more individualistic philosophical traditions that prioritize personal experience over communal engagement. Moyn suggests that Rosenzweig's approach, with its stress on shared responsibility, makes it particularly relevant to movements aiming for systemic change.⁶⁴

In exploring Rosenzweig's relevance to modern liberation efforts, Moyn points to the thinker's rejection of idealist metaphysics in favor of a more grounded, relational theology. Rosenzweig's focus on human agency within the redemptive process speaks to the need for active participation in the struggle against oppression. Moyn emphasizes that this framework does not leave change solely in the hands of divine intervention but calls for human action as a necessary component of the redemptive journey.⁶⁵

Moyn also draws attention to how Rosenzweig's work can be seen as a precursor to later philosophical movements that stress ethical intersubjectivity, such as the work of Emmanuel Levinas. Rosenzweig's exploration of the self in relation to others and the divine sets the stage for a more communal understanding of liberation, one that transcends the individual and addresses the collective experience of oppression. This relational dimension, according to Moyn, is central to understanding Rosenzweig's contributions to social justice discourse.⁶⁶

Furthermore, Moyn highlights how Rosenzweig's theological ideas are not confined to the religious sphere but have broader philosophical and political implications. By placing the individual within a network of responsibilities to others and to God, Rosenzweig provides a model that is particularly useful for addressing issues of social justice. Moyn argues that Rosenzweig's thought encourages a more inclusive approach to

---

63. Moyn, *Origins of the Other*, 71.
64. Moyn, *Origins of the Other*, 112.
65. Moyn, *Origins of the Other*, 113.
66. Moyn, *Origins of the Other*, 114.

liberation, one that considers the interconnectedness of all people within the framework of redemption.[67]

The historical context in which Rosenzweig developed his ideas also plays a critical role in their applicability to contemporary struggles. Moyn notes that Rosenzweig lived during a time of significant social upheaval, and his theology reflects a desire to address the moral and ethical challenges of his day. This historical perspective is essential for understanding how Rosenzweig's work can be applied to modern social movements, where the fight for justice continues to be an urgent concern.[68]

Moyn acknowledges the challenges of applying Rosenzweig's theology directly to political activism. While Rosenzweig provides a compelling vision of ethical responsibility, his ideas may not offer explicit strategies for addressing specific political injustices. However, Moyn suggests that the ethical framework Rosenzweig proposes can serve as a moral guide for those engaged in the fight against oppression, offering a way to think about justice that goes beyond immediate political concerns.[69]

In his assessment, Moyn also points out that Rosenzweig's rejection of abstract metaphysical systems in favor of a more concrete and relational theology makes his work particularly relevant to those seeking practical solutions to oppression. Rosenzweig's focus on the lived experience of redemption, rather than distant philosophical ideals, provides a framework that is more accessible to those working within social justice movements. This focus on the tangible aspects of human existence and the divine-human relationship makes Rosenzweig's theology adaptable to real-world applications.[70]

Ultimately, Moyn positions Rosenzweig as a thinker whose ideas continue to resonate with contemporary efforts to achieve liberation and justice. His emphasis on ethical responsibility, human agency, and the relational aspects of redemption offers a valuable framework for understanding and addressing modern forms of oppression. Moyn's analysis underscores the ongoing relevance of Rosenzweig's thought to both theological and social justice discourses.[71]

Paul Mendes-Flohr explores the implications of Franz Rosenzweig's thought for interfaith dialogue and cooperation, particularly in

---

67. Moyn, *Origins of the Other*, 83.
68. Moyn, *Origins of the Other*, 89.
69. Moyn, *Origins of the Other*, 121.
70. Moyn, *Origins of the Other*, 122.
71. Moyn, *Origins of the Other*, 123.

the context of addressing social injustices. Mendes-Flohr suggests that Rosenzweig's emphasis on shared human experience opens avenues for solidarity between different religious and cultural groups, fostering collaboration in the fight against oppression.[72] This shared experience is key to bridging divides and creating a collective effort toward justice.

Mendes-Flohr highlights how Rosenzweig's concept of the Zwischenmenschliche (the "in-between" or interhuman) underpins his belief in the potential for meaningful dialogue between people of different faiths. For Rosenzweig, the relationships between individuals and communities are not merely incidental but essential to understanding how humanity can unite in the pursuit of justice. This focus on relationality forms a foundation for interfaith cooperation, as it encourages diverse groups to engage with one another in their shared moral responsibilities.[73]

According to Mendes-Flohr, Rosenzweig's theology emphasizes the necessity of acknowledging the unique contributions of various religious traditions while recognizing the common human experience. This recognition helps to foster mutual respect and understanding, crucial components in forming alliances to combat oppression. By engaging in dialogue, religious communities can transcend differences and unite around shared ethical concerns, especially those related to justice and liberation.[74]

Mendes-Flohr also points to Rosenzweig's critique of abstract theological systems that ignore the practical, lived experiences of people. For Rosenzweig, it is not enough to discuss justice in theoretical terms; rather, real-world engagement is necessary. This perspective aligns well with efforts to create practical interfaith partnerships that address tangible issues of oppression, as these collaborations are grounded in shared experiences and commitments rather than abstract ideas.[75]

Rosenzweig's theology, as interpreted by Mendes-Flohr, calls for action that goes beyond religious boundaries, encouraging a collective effort toward a more just society. In this way, Rosenzweig provides a framework that invites diverse religious communities to participate in a shared mission of liberation. This framework is not limited to theological

---

72. Mendes-Flohr, *From Mysticism to Dialogue*, 180.
73. Mendes-Flohr, *From Mysticism to Dialogue*, 38.
74. Mendes-Flohr, *From Mysticism to Dialogue*, 41.
75. Mendes-Flohr, *From Mysticism to Dialogue*, 80.

CHAPTER ONE

discourse but extends to social and political realms, where concrete steps toward justice can be taken.[76]

One of the strengths of Rosenzweig's thought, as Mendes-Flohr notes, is its ability to engage with the complexities of modern social life without losing sight of religious values. This balance is particularly important in interfaith dialogues, where different communities come together to address common challenges while maintaining their distinct identities. By promoting solidarity without demanding uniformity, Rosenzweig's ideas encourage cooperative action that respects diversity.[77]

Mendes-Flohr underscores how Rosenzweig's focus on ethical responsibility extends to all people, regardless of their religious or cultural background. In this sense, Rosenzweig's thought is inclusive and expansive, making it a valuable resource for those seeking to build coalitions across religious lines in the pursuit of justice. The ethical imperatives that Rosenzweig outlines are not confined to any one tradition but are universal in their application.[78]

Finally, Mendes-Flohr suggests that Rosenzweig's approach to interfaith dialogue offers a model for how religious communities can come together in a world that is often divided by sectarianism. By focusing on what unites people rather than what separates them, Rosenzweig's thought provides a path forward for cooperation in the face of injustice. This approach invites religious communities to work together not only for the sake of their own members but also for the broader goal of achieving justice for all.[79]

Aaron Hughes offers a critical reflection on the impact of Franz Rosenzweig's thought on contemporary Jewish philosophy, focusing on the complexities involved in applying his frameworks to modern social challenges. According to Hughes, while Rosenzweig made significant contributions to Jewish thought, his ideas may not fully account for the intricacies of contemporary forms of oppression.[80] This observation raises important questions about the relevance of Rosenzweig's thought in addressing the realities of today's social injustices.

Hughes examines Rosenzweig's emphasis on translating the biblical narrative into modern philosophical frameworks. He acknowledges that

---

76. Mendes-Flohr, *From Mysticism to Dialogue*, 81.
77. Mendes-Flohr, *From Mysticism to Dialogue*, 39.
78. Mendes-Flohr, *From Mysticism to Dialogue*, 32.
79. Mendes-Flohr, *From Mysticism to Dialogue*, 42.
80. Hughes, *Invention of Jewish Identity*, 76.

Rosenzweig and his contemporaries, such as Martin Buber, were part of a larger intellectual movement that sought to reconnect Jewish tradition with modern philosophical thought. However, Hughes cautions that these efforts, while valuable, might not sufficiently address the unique challenges faced by marginalized communities in the current social context.[81]

Hughes suggests that the philosophical frameworks developed by Rosenzweig, which draw heavily on existential and dialogical thought, could fall short in offering practical solutions to systemic issues of oppression. While Rosenzweig's focus on human relationships and ethical responsibility provides a foundation for addressing social injustice, Hughes argues that this focus may not fully capture the structural nature of modern oppression, which often requires more direct forms of engagement and systemic change.[82]

Rosenzweig's critique of abstract philosophy and his turn towards a more concrete, relational understanding of human existence is central to his thought. However, Hughes questions whether this approach is adequate for engaging with the complexities of contemporary social movements, which often demand action on both individual and collective levels. The challenge, according to Hughes, lies in adapting Rosenzweig's frameworks to address these modern realities without losing the ethical depth of his ideas.[83]

Hughes highlights the tension between Rosenzweig's ideal of philosophical fidelity to Jewish tradition and the practical need for adaptation in the face of changing social conditions. Rosenzweig's emphasis on fidelity in translation, both literal and philosophical, reflects his desire to maintain the integrity of Jewish thought. Yet, Hughes suggests that this very commitment to tradition could limit the flexibility needed to respond to modern forms of social injustice, which often require more dynamic and innovative approaches.[84]

Moreover, Hughes explores the potential limitations of Rosenzweig's focus on relationality and dialogue as solutions to social injustice. While these concepts are central to Rosenzweig's vision of human responsibility, Hughes argues that they might not be sufficient when confronting systemic issues that require collective political action and structural reform. This critique invites readers to consider how Rosenzweig's ideas

---

81. Hughes, *Invention of Jewish Identity*, 78.
82. Hughes, *Invention of Jewish Identity*, 79.
83. Hughes, *Invention of Jewish Identity*, 80.
84. Hughes, *Invention of Jewish Identity*, 96.

might need to be expanded or reinterpreted to remain relevant in the context of contemporary social movements.[85]

Hughes acknowledges that Rosenzweig's contributions to Jewish philosophy remain significant, particularly in terms of his challenge to traditional metaphysical systems. However, he raises the concern that Rosenzweig's thought might not fully engage with the socio-political dimensions of oppression in the modern world. This critique underscores the need for further adaptation and reinterpretation of Rosenzweig's ideas to ensure their continued relevance in addressing the complexities of contemporary social justice efforts.[86]

In conclusion, Hughes calls for a critical reassessment of Rosenzweig's frameworks, suggesting that while they offer valuable insights into ethical responsibility and human relationships, they may require modification to effectively address modern forms of oppression. By inviting readers to consider the limitations of Rosenzweig's thought, Hughes opens a space for dialogue about how Jewish philosophy can evolve to meet the challenges of the present.[87]

In summary, the various scholars analyzed Franz Rosenzweig's approach to oppression and liberation, highlighting both its strengths and potential limitations. Rosenzweig emphasizes a collaborative relationship between divine action and human responsibility, suggesting that liberation is an ongoing process that requires active participation from individuals and communities. This perspective rejects notions like supersessionism and promotes interreligious dialogue and cooperation in the pursuit of justice.

Some scholars, like Peter Ochs and Leora Batnitzky, focus on how Rosenzweig integrates philosophy and theology to offer a framework for radical transformation. They point out that his ideas encourage individuals to engage with their traditions and the world in ways that can overcome oppression. Others, such as Robert Gibbs and Steven Kepnes, highlight Rosenzweig's emphasis on ethical responsibility and communal practices, showing how his thought calls for practical actions rooted in community and tradition.

At the same time, critics like Benjamin Pollock and Aaron Hughes question whether Rosenzweig's focus on divine action might overshadow the urgency of human agency in addressing social injustices. They raise

---

85. Hughes, *Invention of Jewish Identity*, 106.
86. Hughes, *Invention of Jewish Identity*, x.
87. Hughes, *Invention of Jewish Identity*, xiii.

concerns about the applicability of his frameworks to contemporary challenges, suggesting that further adaptation may be necessary to fully empower individuals and communities in the fight against oppression.

Scholars like David Novak and George Y. Kohler offer additional perspectives on Rosenzweig's thought. Novak emphasizes the role of Jewish law and ethical commandments as active participation in liberation, while Kohler raises questions about the practical implications of Rosenzweig's departure from traditional metaphysics. Their analyses contribute to a deeper understanding of how Rosenzweig's ideas can both inspire and challenge modern approaches to social justice.

Overall, the examination of Rosenzweig's work by these scholars reveals a complex interplay between divine sovereignty and human responsibility, tradition and innovation, communal practices and individual agency. Their discussions invite ongoing reflection on how theological and philosophical frameworks can be effectively applied to address the pressing issues of oppression and liberation in the modern world.

1.1.2. Theological, Historical, and Practical Approaches to Oppression

Franz Rosenzweig's insights into redemption and oppression provide a comprehensive understanding of these concepts as deeply intertwined with the historical process. He argues that the struggle against oppression is an integral part of a historical and redemptive journey, emphasizing that liberation involves both divine intervention and human action. Rosenzweig views historical development as a key medium through which humanity can recognize and continually challenge the enduring nature of oppression, suggesting that each epoch has its own unique battles and breakthroughs.[88]

To extend this view, Rosenzweig discusses the philosophical concept of "Creation out of nothing," positioning the idea as a radical reimagining of existence, where the historical creation of the world by God marks a fundamental break from any prior state of 'non-being.' This perspective is critical in understanding oppression, as it frames liberation not just as an act of transcending existing conditions but as an ongoing creation of new realities, where previous forms of existence—or oppression—become obsolete or transformed. Thus, for Rosenzweig, the act of divine creation at the beginning of time is not about bringing something into

---

88. Rosenzweig, *Star of Redemption*.

CHAPTER ONE

completion but about initiating an endless process of becoming, where the world continuously awakens to its created nature.

Further, Rosenzweig reflects on the dual nature of divine action and human responsibility in confronting oppression. He suggests that the divine act of creation sets the stage for a perpetual human recognition of our 'creatureliness'—a recognition that itself is a form of revelation. This revelation is not static but an active, ongoing process where humanity constantly realizes its state of being created. Such an understanding positions human existence within a framework of continuous creation, where our awareness of being perpetually created fosters a dynamic engagement with our conditions, including those of oppression.

This framework is contrasted with the idea of providence as viewed in Islamic theology, where Rosenzweig engages with the concept of 'particular providence'—the idea that God's care and intention reach into the minutiae of existence, challenging and reconfiguring our understanding of oppression and liberation. He points out that in Islamic thought, the continual re-creation of the world by God is seen not just as renewal but as an ongoing act of creation that impacts each moment and entity individually, thus reframing the universal experience of creation as a series of discrete, divine interventions. This notion extends the idea of redemption and liberation to encompass every aspect of existence, continuously redefined and governed by divine will.

By integrating these theological perspectives, Rosenzweig provides a framework for seeing oppression not merely as a human condition to be overcome but as a phenomenon deeply rooted in the existential dynamics between creation and providence. This offers a broader view where liberation is understood as a complex interplay of recognizing our ongoing creation as beings and engaging actively with the divine processes that shape our reality. Such a viewpoint encourages a more nuanced engagement with the historical and spiritual dimensions of fighting oppression, suggesting that every generation must reinterpret and act upon these divine and human responsibilities to move towards a more liberated and just society.

Rosenzweig's framework suggests that oppression is not merely a sequence of isolated incidents, but a recurrent theme deeply woven into the fabric of human history. This perspective encourages a recognition of oppression as a systemic issue that requires sustained and collective efforts to address. By viewing oppression as an enduring aspect of civilization, Rosenzweig aligns with the notion that history is not a series of disconnected events but a continuous process that shapes and is shaped by human actions.[89]

This understanding parallels Marx's materialistic interpretation of history, where all historical developments are seen as part of an economic process moving towards a final revolutionary transformation. Marx believed that the disintegration of bourgeois capitalist society was not just inevitable but necessary for the historical process to reach its culmination. He argued that this progression should be hastened, not hindered, to bring about a complete societal overhaul.[90]

Furthermore, Marx's emphasis on the proletariat as the key to societal transformation reflects a similar recognition of the need for collective action in addressing systemic oppression. Marx viewed the proletariat as the "chosen people" of historical materialism, uniquely positioned to lead the world towards a classless society due to their total alienation from the privileges of the bourgeoisie. This perspective underscores the idea that those most oppressed are often the ones who hold the potential for the most significant societal change.[91]

In conclusion, both Rosenzweig and Marx offer frameworks that highlight the importance of recognizing and addressing the deep-rooted nature of oppression within human history. Their approaches encourage an active engagement in the historical process, whether through theological reflection or revolutionary action, to move towards a more just and equitable society.[92]

In exploring the historical dimensions of oppression, Paulo Freire's emphasis on critical consciousness provides a vital educational framework for recognizing and dismantling the socio-political structures that perpetuate inequality. This process of "conscientization," as Freire outlines, is essential for individuals to become aware of their circumstances and to engage actively in transforming them.[93]

Freire's ideas have resonated globally, indicating the widespread relevance of his educational methods in various cultural contexts. His work began in the northeast of Brazil and expanded across continents, illustrating the universal applicability of his approaches to education and

---

89. Löwith, *Meaning in History*, 33.
90. Löwith, *Meaning in History*, 33.
91. Löwith, *Meaning in History*, 37.
92. Löwith, *Meaning in History*, 191.
93. Freire, *Pedagogy of the Oppressed*.

liberation.[94] This expansion underscores the pervasive nature of oppression and the global need for tools to recognize and combat it.

At the core of Freire's pedagogy is the belief that true education involves both reflection and action—what he terms praxis. Without this dual approach, efforts to change oppressive systems remain incomplete. This philosophy is grounded in the understanding that action without reflection leads to unguided efforts, while reflection without action fails to realize the potential for societal transformation.[95]

Freire also highlights the internal conflict within the oppressed between succumbing to the definitions of humanity imposed by oppressors or striving for a self-defined identity. This struggle is crucial for the oppressed as they work towards reclaiming their humanity and agency in a world structured to diminish it.[96] His pedagogical approach aims to transform oppression into a subject for reflection, enabling the oppressed to engage actively in their liberation journey.[97]

Foucault's analysis of power and its diffusion across social institutions provides a critical framework for understanding how oppression is maintained and perpetuated throughout history. He contends that power is not merely a matter of top-down control but is dispersed throughout society, embedded in institutions, discourses, and practices that shape and regulate behavior. This perspective emphasizes that oppression is a structural issue, deeply woven into the fabric of societal relations, rather than simply the result of individual actions.[98]

According to Foucault, power operates through a complex interplay of knowledge and authority, where each reinforces the other, creating systems that are difficult to dismantle. He argues that there is no knowledge without power relations and no exercise of power without the creation of knowledge. This relationship, which Foucault terms "power-knowledge," suggests that the structures of oppression are sustained by the very systems that produce and validate knowledge within society.[99]

Furthermore, Foucault points out that power is not just a force that represses but also one that produces reality, shaping individuals' identities and the social norms they adhere to. This means that power is not

94. Freire, *Pedagogy of the Oppressed*, 9.
95. Freire, *Pedagogy of the Oppressed*, 76.
96. Freire, *Pedagogy of the Oppressed*, 31.
97. Freire, *Pedagogy of the Oppressed*, 33.
98. Foucault, *Discipline and Punish*.
99. Foucault, *Discipline and Punish*, 27.

simply imposed from above; it is internalized and reproduced by those who are subjected to it. In this way, the oppressed are often complicit in their own subjugation, as they navigate and negotiate the power structures that define their existence.[100]

The pervasive nature of power, as described by Foucault, challenges the notion that oppression can be easily eradicated. Instead, it requires a thorough understanding of the complex and often hidden dynamics at play within society. Foucault's work underscores the need for a multifaceted approach to addressing oppression, one that considers the intricate ways in which power operates and is sustained over time.[101]

Rosenzweig's theological perspectives, when integrated with Foucault's theory of power, underscore the intricate process of redemption that necessitates active engagement with the entrenched structures fostering oppression. This alignment emphasizes the intersection of divine involvement and human agency in the pursuit of liberation, portraying the battle against oppression as a collective, enduring commitment that transcends time, cultural boundaries, and academic disciplines.[102]

Further elaborating on this notion, Rosenzweig discusses the shared experience of suffering and redemption, illustrating how collective narratives of oppression forge a communal path towards salvation. He reflects on the concept of shared suffering, where the oppressed identify with each other's pain, drawing a parallel to a divine sympathy that encompasses all human suffering. This shared experience not only deepens the understanding of oppression but also unites individuals in their quest for liberation.[103]

Moreover, Rosenzweig highlights the transformational potential of collective memory and tradition in sustaining hope and resilience among the oppressed. He connects the historical and religious celebrations, which commemorate past struggles and victories over oppression, to the ongoing journey towards redemption. These traditions serve as reminders that liberation is an ongoing process, deeply embedded in both cultural and spiritual practices.[104]

In these discussions, Rosenzweig brings to light the complex relationship between historical consciousness and spiritual redemption,

---

100. Foucault, *Discipline and Punish*, 185.
101. Foucault, *Discipline and Punish*, 205.
102. Galli and Rosenzweig, *Franz Rosenzweig and Jehuda Halevi*.
103. Galli and Rosenzweig, *Franz Rosenzweig and Jehuda Halevi*, 124.
104. Galli and Rosenzweig, *Franz Rosenzweig and Jehuda Halevi*, 236.

asserting that true liberation involves recognizing and transforming the oppressive structures that pervade society. This dual focus on spiritual renewal and practical action encapsulates the multifaceted approach required to address the deeply rooted nature of oppression.[105]

Judith Butler's perspective highlights the crucial necessity of immediate social and political actions to address and mitigate oppression, emphasizing the importance of recognizing life's precariousness and the urgent need to protect vulnerable populations. In her work, Butler argues for a politics deeply rooted in the recognition of human vulnerability, suggesting that by embracing our shared susceptibilities, we can foster a more humane international response to suffering. This approach demands not only awareness but also urgent and tangible actions that address the conditions of precarity experienced by many across the globe.[106]

Furthering this argument, Butler challenges the traditional views on grief, proposing that staying with grief can politically mobilize us by exposing the often-overlooked connections we share through human vulnerability. By understanding our collective exposures to harm and loss, we are impelled to act not out of isolation but through a shared ethical responsibility towards others. This stance contrasts with more abstract or delayed responses to injustice, pushing for an engagement with the immediate realities of suffering and the structural changes required to alleviate them.[107]

Moreover, Butler critiques the differential allocation of vulnerability and grief across global populations, stressing that the recognition of suffering must translate into protective actions for all lives, regardless of geographical or cultural divides. This critical view extends to challenging the norms that define whose lives are considered valuable and grievable within the international community. Her call to acknowledge and act against these disparities is a direct engagement with the practical needs of oppressed groups, aiming to transform the societal structures that perpetuate such inequalities.[108]

Butler's focus on immediate and actionable responses to oppression complements the broader theoretical frameworks by underscoring the importance of not only recognizing but also actively challenging the conditions that enable and maintain human suffering and inequality. This

---

105. Galli and Rosenzweig, *Franz Rosenzweig and Jehuda Halevi*, 272.
106. Butler, *Precarious Life*.
107. Butler, *Precarious Life*, 30.
108. Butler, *Precarious Life*, 31.

approach provides a necessary counterbalance to perspectives that may prioritize long-term philosophical or spiritual redemption over immediate material interventions.[109]

Amartya Sen's emphasis on freedom as a collective good that must be pursued through public reasoning and democratic engagement offers a practical approach to combating oppression. Sen argues that freedom involves not just the absence of constraints but also the presence of enabling conditions that allow all individuals to pursue a life they have reason to value. This perspective aligns with Rosenzweig's view on the importance of community and solidarity, emphasizing that liberation must be a collective endeavor supported by the active participation of diverse groups.[110]

Sen highlights the role of public reasoning in fostering these enabling conditions, suggesting that democratic engagement is crucial for the development of policies that can effectively address inequalities and enhance freedom. This approach corresponds with the communal aspects of Rosenzweig's theology, suggesting a synergy between individual capabilities and collective actions in the pursuit of societal well-being.[111]

Moreover, Sen's analysis extends to the specific mechanisms through which societies can improve their structural capacities to support freedom. He discusses the importance of education, equitable wealth distribution, and access to healthcare as foundational to enhancing freedoms and reducing inequalities. These ideas provide a framework for understanding how practical measures can support the philosophical and theological aspirations of communal liberation.[112]

In summary, the integration of Sen's pragmatic focus on public reasoning and policy with Rosenzweig's theological emphasis on collective action offers a comprehensive approach to understanding and addressing oppression. This combination underscores the necessity of both philosophical depth and practical application in crafting responses to the complex challenges of social inequality and oppression.[113]

In conclusion, the synthesis of Rosenzweig's theological framework with the practical approaches of thinkers like Marx, Freire, Foucault, Butler, and Sen offers a multi-dimensional understanding of oppression

---

109. Butler, *Precarious Life*.
110. Sen, *Development as Freedom*.
111. Sen, *Development as Freedom*, 333.
112. Sen, *Development as Freedom*, 333.
113. Sen, *Development as Freedom*.

and liberation. This perspective highlights the importance of recognizing oppression as a systemic issue that requires both immediate actions and long-term commitments. By integrating philosophical reflections on human responsibility and divine action with practical strategies for social change, this approach emphasizes the need for collective efforts to build a just and equitable society. The combined emphasis on community, democratic engagement, and the recognition of vulnerability underscores the essential role of both spiritual and material interventions in addressing the complexities of social inequality.

1.1.3. Bultmann and Liberation Theology

This section examines how liberation theologians engage with Rudolf Bultmann's existential theology, recognizing his emphasis on individual transformation while critiquing its focus on personal existence. Theologians like Leonardo Boff, James Cone, Gustavo Gutiérrez, Jon Sobrino, José Míguez Bonino, Juan Luis Segundo, and Clodovis Boff argue for a theology that addresses both personal and societal liberation. They emphasize that faith must be lived out within historical reality, engaging directly with the struggles of oppressed communities. By integrating Bultmann's framework with a commitment to social justice, these theologians develop a perspective that connects personal faith with collective action, advocating for existential authenticity that includes efforts to dismantle unjust social structures.

Leonardo Boff engages with Rudolf Bultmann's existential theology, incorporating its existential framework into his broader liberation theology. Boff appreciates Bultmann's emphasis on personal transformation but critiques its focus on individual existence, arguing that a comprehensive theology must address both personal and structural liberation. Boff sees in Bultmann's theology a valuable resource for emphasizing personal authenticity, but he insists that true liberation theology must also confront social and economic injustices that oppress communities.[114]

In Boff's view, liberation is not just a matter of personal existential decisions but must include a collective effort to dismantle the systems that perpetuate inequality. He notes that Bultmann's focus on individual decision-making can be limiting in the context of widespread structural oppression. For liberation theology, the concept of liberation must extend

---

114. Boff, *Trinity and Society*, 252.

beyond the personal and engage with broader societal transformations that enable collective freedom.[115]

Boff draws parallels between Bultmann's existential theology and the concept of "God of the poor," emphasizing that God's presence is realized not only in individual existential moments but also in the communal struggle for justice. He believes that the existential decision to live authentically, as Bultmann suggests, must also involve decisions that promote social justice and communal well-being.[116]

The theological framework Boff develops contrasts with Bultmann's by stressing that personal liberation is interconnected with the liberation of others. While Bultmann focuses on the individual's encounter with God through existential decisions, Boff insists that this encounter cannot be separated from the responsibility to fight for the rights and dignity of others, especially the marginalized.[117]

Boff critiques Bultmann's existential theology for not sufficiently addressing the communal aspects of faith and the importance of collective action in liberation. In Boff's view, theology must not only be about individual decisions but also about engaging with historical processes that contribute to social transformation and liberation for the oppressed.[118]

However, Boff does recognize that Bultmann's approach can serve as a catalyst for understanding the individual's role within the larger framework of societal change. He suggests that Bultmann's existential framework provides a starting point for individuals to recognize their own role in the liberation process, which can then extend into collective action.[119]

Through his theological work, Boff argues that existential authenticity must involve a commitment to solidarity with the poor and oppressed. This commitment, he contends, is not merely an abstract moral obligation but a tangible decision to participate in movements that promote justice and equality.[120]

Boff also addresses the Trinitarian aspect of liberation theology, which he sees as deeply communal and relational, in contrast to the more individualistic tendencies in Bultmann's thought. Boff argues that liberation is inherently communal, reflecting the relational nature of the

---

115. Boff, *Trinity and Society*, 235.
116. Boff, *Trinity and Society*, 86.
117. Boff, *Trinity and Society*, 159.
118. Boff, *Trinity and Society*, 104.
119. Boff, *Trinity and Society*, 135.
120. Boff, *Trinity and Society*, 51.

Trinity, where the persons of the Trinity exist in mutual self-giving and interpenetration.[121]

In conclusion, while Boff acknowledges the contributions of Bultmann's existential theology, he extends its framework to include a more robust emphasis on communal liberation. For Boff, true existential authenticity involves both personal transformation and active participation in the collective liberation of oppressed communities.[122]

James Cone engages deeply with Bultmann's concept of existential decision-making, integrating it into the African American struggle for liberation. While Cone values Bultmann's emphasis on personal authenticity, he critiques its limitations by expanding the idea to include the collective experience of racial oppression. Cone argues that existential decision-making must not only concern individual transformation but also address the broader, systemic realities of racism that African Americans face.[123]

Cone appreciates Bultmann's understanding of revelation as a personal, existential encounter but pushes further, stating that for the Black community, revelation is experienced in the shared struggle against racial oppression. Cone sees in Bultmann's theology a useful tool for interpreting the personal aspects of faith, but he insists that any authentic existential decision must also engage with the collective fight for justice. The lived experience of Black individuals and their communities is essential to understanding the nature of revelation and the divine.[124]

For Cone, the existential decision emphasized by Bultmann gains real significance when applied to the Black struggle for liberation. Cone critiques the abstract nature of existential decision-making in Bultmann's framework, arguing that it must be contextualized within the concrete realities of oppression. Authentic existence for Black individuals cannot be understood apart from their lived experiences of racial injustice and the call to resist that injustice.[125]

Bultmann's focus on personal transformation through existential decision is important to Cone, but he believes it must be coupled with a strong commitment to confronting systemic racism. Cone argues that existential authenticity is not just about self-transformation but also

121. Boff, *Trinity and Society*, 128.
122. Boff, *Trinity and Society*, xi.
123. Cone, *Black Theology of Liberation*, 32.
124. Cone, *Black Theology of Liberation*, 49.
125. Cone, *Black Theology of Liberation*, 55.

about participating in the liberation of the oppressed. For Black theology, revelation is not an individual, isolated experience but is intertwined with the collective liberation of the community.[126]

Cone critiques Bultmann for not sufficiently addressing the sociopolitical dimensions of revelation. While Bultmann emphasizes personal decision-making, Cone insists that revelation in the context of Black theology must involve a confrontation with the structural realities of white supremacy. Revelation is not just a personal spiritual experience but a call to action in the fight against racial oppression.[127]

Cone also draws on Bultmann's concept of existential decision to highlight the urgency of the Black liberation struggle. He argues that Black individuals must make existential decisions not only for their personal salvation but for the survival and liberation of their entire community. For Cone, these decisions are made in the face of a constant tension between life and death, as the Black community confronts systemic violence and dehumanization.[128]

The existential decision-making framework that Cone adopts from Bultmann is deeply connected to the broader reality of systemic racism. Cone argues that Black theology must interpret revelation as a call to resist oppression and pursue justice for the oppressed. This existential decision is not just about individual self-understanding but involves a radical commitment to the liberation of Black people from white supremacy.[129]

Cone extends Bultmann's existential framework by emphasizing the communal aspects of revelation. In contrast to Bultmann's more individualistic approach, Cone argues that revelation for the Black community is experienced collectively, through the shared struggle for freedom. This communal aspect of revelation is essential for understanding Black theology, which seeks to interpret God's will in the context of the fight against racism.[130]

For Cone, the personal existential decisions that Bultmann discusses must be understood within the context of communal liberation. Authenticity in Black theology means making decisions that not only transform the individual but also contribute to the collective liberation of the Black community. This interpretation of existential decision-making

---

126. Cone, *Black Theology of Liberation*, 56.
127. Cone, *Black Theology of Liberation*, 12.
128. Cone, *Black Theology of Liberation*, 13.
129. Cone, *Black Theology of Liberation*, 20.
130. Cone, *Black Theology of Liberation*, 31.

is central to Cone's theology of liberation, where faith and justice are inseparable.[131]

Cone acknowledges the strengths of Bultmann's existential theology but argues that it must be expanded to include a clear focus on social justice. Black theology, in Cone's view, cannot be content with personal authenticity alone but must engage with the realities of racism and seek to dismantle the structures that perpetuate oppression. This expanded framework makes existential decision-making relevant to the collective liberation struggle of African Americans.[132]

Gustavo Gutiérrez engages with Rudolf Bultmann's existential theology by acknowledging its significance in addressing personal faith but critiquing its individualistic focus. He argues that a true liberation theology must extend beyond personal existential concerns to address communal and societal dimensions, integrating faith with the historical realities of the poor and marginalized.[133]

Gutiérrez points out that Bultmann's perceived gap between the Old and New Testaments has led to a devaluation of Old Testament texts. He notes that contemporary theology is re-evaluating this stance, emphasizing the importance of the Old Testament in understanding the full narrative of salvation history.[134]

He discusses the political implications of Jesus's message, asserting that understanding Jesus requires acknowledging the inevitable political dimensions of his teachings. Gutiérrez references scholars like Augustin George to highlight that Jesus's mission cannot be separated from its political context.[135]

Gutiérrez critiques Bultmann's view that Jesus believed in the imminent end of time but considered this belief secondary. He argues that the expectation of the Kingdom of God was central to Jesus's message, emphasizing the present and historical dimensions rather than relegating it to a future event.[136]

He highlights a shift in Christian consciousness from an abstract approach to an existential, historical, and concrete view. This perspective

---

131. Cone, *Black Theology of Liberation*, ix.
132. Cone, *Black Theology of Liberation*, x.
133. Gutiérrez, *Theology of Liberation*, 223.
134. Gutiérrez, *Theology of Liberation*, 223
135. Gutiérrez, *Theology of Liberation*, 239.
136. Gutiérrez, *Theology of Liberation*, 240.

holds that human beings are called to a gratuitous fulfillment within history, integrating all dimensions of existence.[137]

Gutiérrez discusses the role of hope in Christian life and human existence. While theologians like Moltmann approached hope from a personal standpoint, Gutiérrez emphasizes its implications in historical and political reality. He references Ernst Bloch's focus on hope as a driving force for human beings, indicating a need to connect hope with concrete social transformation.[138]

He contrasts different positions on salvation and history, highlighting the importance of introducing absolute values into the historical and seemingly secular reality of human existence. Gutiérrez argues that Christianity differs from religions of otherworldly salvation by engaging directly with historical reality.[139]

Gutiérrez emphasizes the necessity for greater participation of all people in political activity, even within socialist societies. He references Herbert Marcuse's attempt to use psychoanalytical categories for social criticism, underlining the importance of integrating social analysis into theological reflection.[140]

He critiques approaches that fail to consider historical circumstances, such as those that anticipated industrialization would lead to independent societies without addressing underlying economic and social conditions. Gutiérrez stresses the need to base theological and social analysis on the actual historical context of Latin American countries.[141]

Gutiérrez argues that separating faith and political action into unrelated planes leads to an opportunistic coexistence of faith with any political option. He insists that faith and political action must enter into a correct and fruitful relationship to effectively address social injustices.[142]

He underscores the importance of evangelization focused on the poor, inspired by figures like John XXIII and decisions from the Vatican Council. Gutiérrez believes that the evangelization of the poor should be central to theological discussions and the mission of the Church.[143] Gutiérrez notes the urgent need for conscientizing evangelization, where

137. Gutiérrez, *Theology of Liberation*, 86.
138. Gutiérrez, *Theology of Liberation*, 123.
139. Gutiérrez, *Theology of Liberation*, 219.
140. Gutiérrez, *Theology of Liberation*, 21.
141. Gutiérrez, *Theology of Liberation*, 50.
142. Gutiérrez, *Theology of Liberation*, 138.
143. Gutiérrez, *Theology of Liberation*, xli.

the Church educates Christian conscience and stimulates initiatives that contribute to human formation. This awareness of being oppressed but not resigned is crucial for liberation.[144]

He emphasizes that evangelization must consider the personal and communal dimensions of Christianity, forming people committed to social transformation. Gutiérrez argues that preaching, liturgy, and catechesis should reflect this commitment to communal liberation.[145] By integrating these communal and societal dimensions into theology, Gutiérrez expands upon Bultmann's existential concerns. He contends that faith must be lived out in historical reality, engaging with the struggles of the poor and marginalized to achieve true liberation.

Jon Sobrino, in his book Jesus the Liberator: A Historical Theological Reading of Jesus of Nazareth, engages with Rudolf Bultmann's theology, particularly his method of demythologization. Sobrino appreciates Bultmann's effort to make the gospel more accessible to modern audiences by stripping away mythological elements, but he insists that Bultmann's approach overlooks key aspects of the historical Jesus. According to Sobrino, the life and teachings of Jesus must remain foundational for liberation theology. While Bultmann's existentialist interpretation serves a purpose, Sobrino emphasizes that Jesus' life cannot be disregarded if we are to understand liberation theology's aims.[146]

Sobrino critiques Bultmann's focus on the "Christ of faith," which he sees as a detachment from the historical reality of Jesus. Sobrino argues that liberation theology requires a connection to the historical Jesus, as it is through his life and teachings that the praxis of liberation emerges. For Sobrino, the historical Jesus grounds the movement towards liberation, and Bultmann's approach risks neglecting this critical aspect.[147]

In Sobrino's analysis, Bultmann's ethical-existential interpretation of the Kingdom of God as an inner, personal reality downplays its sociopolitical implications. Sobrino, by contrast, asserts that Jesus' proclamation of the Kingdom was not merely spiritual but had real implications for the world and called for a transformation of oppressive structures. Liberation theology, according to Sobrino, finds its roots in this aspect of Jesus' message—something Bultmann does not fully account for.[148]

144. Gutiérrez, *Theology of Liberation*, 69.
145. Gutiérrez, *Theology of Liberation*, 70.
146. Sobrino, *Jesus the Liberator*, 42.
147. Sobrino, *Jesus the Liberator*, 45.
148. Sobrino, *Jesus the Liberator*, 107.

Sobrino acknowledges Bultmann's contribution to eschatology but critiques his disconnection between eschatology and historical events. While Bultmann emphasizes the eschatological nature of the Christian message, he focuses on the resurrection and the paschal reality of Christ. Sobrino points out that this view abstracts from the historical actions and presence of Jesus, which are crucial for understanding how liberation takes place in real-world contexts.[149]

Further, Sobrino critiques the way Bultmann's eschatological focus centers on individual subjectivity. According to Sobrino, this approach limits the transformative potential of Christian eschatology, as it excludes the social and historical dimensions that are integral to liberation theology. In contrast, Sobrino asserts that the historical Jesus, with his engagement in the material realities of the poor and oppressed, brings eschatology into direct contact with history, calling for social transformation.[150]

Sobrino's perspective highlights the importance of the historical Jesus not just as a figure of faith but as a person whose life, actions, and teachings serve as a foundation for social justice. Bultmann's theology, while significant in some areas, is insufficient for Sobrino's liberation theology because it does not sufficiently account for the socio-political dimensions of Jesus' mission.[151]

For Sobrino, the historical context of Jesus, particularly his concern for the poor and oppressed, provides a lens through which liberation theology understands the call for justice. This contrasts with Bultmann's existentialist focus on personal salvation, which lacks the communal and historical engagement that Sobrino finds essential for a theology of liberation.[152]

Sobrino insists that any theological reflection must start with the reality of Jesus' life. He criticizes Bultmann's demythologization for undermining this foundation by focusing too heavily on the resurrection and neglecting the radical implications of Jesus' life and teachings for the present-day struggle against oppression.[153]

In sum, while Sobrino recognizes Bultmann's contributions to making Christian theology relevant to modern audiences, he argues that the

---

149. Sobrino, *Jesus the Liberator*, 110.
150. Sobrino, *Jesus the Liberator*, 111.
151. Sobrino, *Jesus the Liberator*, 7.
152. Sobrino, *Jesus the Liberator*, 35.
153. Sobrino, *Jesus the Liberator*, 36.

historical Jesus must remain central for a theology that seeks to liberate. For Sobrino, it is not enough to rely on faith in the Christ of the resurrection; the life and teachings of Jesus are crucial for understanding how Christians are called to engage with and transform the oppressive structures of the world.[154]

José Míguez Bonino engages with Rudolf Bultmann's existential theology, aiming to integrate it with the social and political dimensions of liberation theology. He argues that personal authenticity, as emphasized by Bultmann, must be connected to collective action that addresses systemic injustices.[155]

Bonino critiques the limitations he perceives in modern Protestant theologians like Barth and Bultmann, suggesting they did not fully recognize the importance of political engagement as a means of humanizing society. He believes that authentic human action unfolds within historical contexts and carries the potential for liberation through political processes.[156]

Emphasizing the historical reality of theological events, Bonino aligns with Barth in rejecting any reduction of these events to mere expressions of personal faith, as he feels Bultmann does. He insists that events like the resurrection hold full historical significance and should inform our understanding and practice of faith today.[157]

Bonino introduces the concept of a "hermeneutical circulation," contrasting it with the "hermeneutical circle" often associated with Bultmann's approach. He advocates for a critical use of interpretive tools to engage with the historicity of scriptural events, enabling a reflection on Christian obedience in contemporary contexts.[158]

Highlighting practical applications of this method, Bonino references the work of Argentine Old Testament scholar José Severino Croatto. Croatto's book, *Liberación y Libertad: Pautas Hermenéuticas*, exemplifies how hermeneutical methods can inform theological reflection that is deeply connected to the struggle for liberation.[159]

Bonino emphasizes that theology must not remain abstract but should address the material dimensions of human existence. He argues

---

154. Sobrino, *Jesus the Liberator*, 37.
155. Bonino, *Doing Theology in a Revolutionary Situation*, 77.
156. Bonino, *Doing Theology in a Revolutionary Situation*, 77.
157. Bonino, *Doing Theology in a Revolutionary Situation*, 101.
158. Bonino, *Doing Theology in a Revolutionary Situation*, 102.
159. Bonino, *Doing Theology in a Revolutionary Situation*, 105.

that while theological heritage provides valuable resources, it requires reinterpretation to remain relevant to current social struggles and to contribute to the transformation of society.[160]

He critiques the supposed neutrality of traditional sciences and theologies that, in practice, often support the preservation of the status quo. Bonino asserts that recognizing the conflictual nature of reality is more objective and truthful to the human situation, and thus theology should align with efforts aiming for social change.[161]

Authentic Christian existence, according to Bonino, involves a commitment to concrete historical projects and actions. He posits a direct relationship between the pursuit of God's Kingdom and active engagement in societal transformation, suggesting that faith should inspire participation in shaping a more just future.[162]

Bonino addresses the risk of using theology as a disguise for avoiding engagement with human, historical, and material realities. He believes that the tools provided by contemporary critiques can help purify theological hermeneutics, allowing for a re-conception of theological heritage that is responsive to present challenges.[163]

He underscores the necessity of connecting personal authenticity with collective action. Bonino argues that individual faith must be linked to communal efforts to address systemic injustices, thereby integrating personal and social dimensions of liberation.[164]

Through this synthesis, Bonino contributes to a theology that is both existentially authentic and socially transformative. By engaging critically with Bultmann's existential theology, he develops a framework that incorporates personal faith with active participation in the liberation of oppressed communities.[165]

Juan Luis Segundo engages with Rudolf Bultmann's hermeneutics by acknowledging his significant contributions to interpreting the Scriptures, particularly the New Testament. He notes that while his own use of the term hermeneutics might initially seem less rigorous, he aims to

---

160. Bonino, *Doing Theology in a Revolutionary Situation*, xiii.
161. Bonino, *Doing Theology in a Revolutionary Situation*, 35.
162. Bonino, *Doing Theology in a Revolutionary Situation*, 150.
163. Bonino, *Doing Theology in a Revolutionary Situation*, 92.
164. Bonino, *Doing Theology in a Revolutionary Situation*, 75.
165. Bonino, *Doing Theology in a Revolutionary Situation*, xiii.

demonstrate that his approach builds upon and addresses limitations in Bultmann's methodology.[166]

Segundo observes that Bultmann recognized how the early Christian community depicted Jesus within the methodological framework of their time, utilizing concepts such as heaven, hell, and miraculous divine interventions. This historical context, Segundo argues, necessitates that modern interpreters consider the socio-cultural backdrop of the scriptures to fully understand their message.[167]

He discusses Bultmann's concept of the hermeneutic circle, where understanding God's word to humanity begins with understanding one's own existence. According to Bultmann, God communicates through individual existence, making personal experience the starting point for interpretation.[168]

However, Segundo questions why one should not prioritize a specific political stance as a necessary precondition for interpreting God's message in the Scriptures. He suggests that, contrary to Bultmann's approach, incorporating socio-political commitments can enhance understanding and make the hermeneutic process more relevant to contemporary issues.[169]

Segundo points out that Bultmann's hermeneutics are connected to the philosophy of the early Heidegger, particularly his work in Being and Time. Heidegger's focus on existential analysis influenced Bultmann's emphasis on individual existence in interpreting scripture.[170]

Despite Bultmann's consistent refusal to admit reliance on a specific philosophy—maintaining that understanding God's word depends on an intellectual grasp of language in general—Segundo argues that underlying philosophical perspectives inevitably shape one's hermeneutical approach.[171]

He critiques Bultmann's assumption that any divine intervention in the physical world must be considered mythical. Segundo contends that this view limits the recognition of revelation as a historical and

---

166. Segundo, *Liberation of Theology*, 8.
167. Segundo, *Liberation of Theology*, 86.
168. Segundo, *Liberation of Theology*, 98.
169. Segundo, *Liberation of Theology*, 99.
170. Segundo, *Liberation of Theology*, 122.
171. Segundo, *Liberation of Theology*, 123.

transformative event, which is essential for a theology that seeks liberation and social change.[172]

Reflecting on the hermeneutic circle, Segundo emphasizes that theological interpretation always presupposes a deep engagement with reality. He suggests that revolutionizing theology involves adopting new hermeneutic codes that account for socio-political contexts, as evidenced in works like The Secular City.[173]

Segundo argues that employing theories such as historical materialism enables interpreters to uncover the authentic nature of reality aligned with their historical commitments. This approach allows theology to be more responsive to the needs of oppressed communities and to contribute to their liberation.[174]

He notes that when metaphysics and ideologies are critically examined, they lose their appearance of autonomous existence. By explaining the formation of ideas through practical engagement with the world, theology becomes more grounded in real-world experiences and less abstract.[175]

Segundo asserts that viewing religion through the lens of ideological suspicion reveals how certain scriptural interpretations are imposed by ruling classes to maintain exploitation. Recognizing this dynamic allows for a hermeneutic that challenges oppressive structures and advocates for social justice.[176]

He clarifies that his intention is not to dismiss religious forces but to determine the extent to which they have influenced the qualitative and quantitative shaping of the global spirit. This involves assessing the impact of religious beliefs on historical events and societal developments.[177]

Referencing thinkers like Max Weber, Segundo highlights the importance of analyzing religion's influence on society without prematurely dismissing its earthly core. This perspective aligns with his advocacy for a hermeneutic that considers socio-economic factors in religious interpretation.[178]

---

172. Segundo, Liberation of Theology, 151.
173. Segundo, Liberation of Theology, 13.
174. Segundo, Liberation of Theology, 14.
175. Segundo, Liberation of Theology, 15.
176. Segundo, Liberation of Theology, 16.
177. Segundo, Liberation of Theology, 20.
178. Segundo, Liberation of Theology, 21.

Segundo emphasizes that without engaging with historical reality, theological interpretation remains incomplete. He argues that human experience within history is essential for a full understanding of God's message. Citing James Cone as an example, he illustrates how integrating socio-political context enriches theological reflection and contributes to liberation praxis.[179]

Clodovis Boff engages deeply with Rudolf Bultmann's existential theology, emphasizing the necessity of connecting theological reflection with concrete praxis. Boff notes that "in and through the hermeneutic operation, interpreters are themselves interpreted," highlighting the dynamic relationship between understanding Scripture and personal transformation.[180] He appreciates Bultmann's focus on the present moment but critiques the lack of emphasis on social action.

Building on this, Boff argues that theology must move beyond individual existential authenticity to address societal injustices. He points out that Bultmann and his contemporaries, "all insisted on this primacy of the present, all historicism to the contrary notwithstanding."[181] However, Boff contends that this focus remains insufficient without linking it to efforts aimed at transforming unjust social structures.

Boff underscores the importance of incorporating political dimensions into theological discourse. Referencing Gustavo Gutiérrez and others, he states that liberation theology cannot ignore themes such as "the whole theology of liberation" and the need to engage with systemic oppression.[182] He believes that without this engagement, theology risks becoming disconnected from the realities faced by marginalized communities.

He further critiques the limitations of traditional hermeneutics, suggesting that they often fail to inspire tangible change. Boff mentions that certain methodological approaches are "too banal and are sufficiently operational" but lack the depth needed for effective praxis.[183] He advocates for a theology that not only interprets the world but actively participates in its transformation.

Drawing attention to the influence of socio-political contexts, Boff discusses the relevance of Marxism as a tool for socio-analytic mediation.

179. Segundo, *Liberation of Theology*, 25.
180. Boff, *Theology and Praxis*, 297.
181. Boff, *Theology and Praxis*, 297.
182. Boff, *Theology and Praxis*, 301.
183. Boff, *Theology and Praxis*, 260.

He acknowledges that "the most straightforward practices of socio-analytic mediation are connected" to Marxist thought, especially in efforts to address social injustices.[184] However, he cautions that Marxism must be applied critically within theological frameworks.

Boff also reflects on the epistemological challenges in theology. He notes that determining the "scientific status" of theology often depends on what Pierre Bourdieu calls "cultural arbitrariety," and suggests that more important is understanding theology's role in effecting change.[185] This perspective shifts the focus from abstract definitions to practical implications.

He emphasizes that theology should inspire a commitment to justice, stating that it must be "grounded in transformative praxis aimed at dismantling unjust social structures."[186] By doing so, theology becomes a living discipline that responds to the needs of the oppressed.

In discussing the relationship between theology and other bodies of knowledge, Boff observes that Thomas Aquinas sought to "define the regional rationality of theology" in relation to the sciences of his time.[187] Boff uses this historical perspective to argue for a theology that is both intellectually rigorous and socially engaged.

Finally, Boff asserts that without linking existential authenticity to concrete actions, theology remains incomplete. He stresses that "theology cannot be separated from the lived experiences of the poor and oppressed," and must actively engage with the socio-political context to effect real change.[188] This approach aligns with the core principles of liberation theology.

Conclusively, the engagement of liberation theologians with Rudolf Bultmann's existential theology underscores a significant dialogue between personal authenticity and social transformation. Leonardo Boff, James Cone, Gustavo Gutiérrez, Jon Sobrino, José Míguez Bonino, Juan Luis Segundo, and Clodovis Boff each interact with Bultmann's ideas, appreciating his emphasis on individual transformation while critiquing the limitations of his focus on personal existence.

These theologians argue that true liberation theology must extend beyond individual existential decisions to address communal and

---

184. Boff, *Theology and Praxis*, 55.
185. Boff, *Theology and Praxis*, xxvi.
186. Boff, *Theology and Praxis*, 297.
187. Boff, *Theology and Praxis*, 115.
188. Boff, *Theology and Praxis*, 358.

societal dimensions. They emphasize that faith must be lived out within historical reality, engaging directly with the struggles of oppressed communities to achieve genuine liberation. By integrating Bultmann's existential framework with a commitment to social justice, they develop a more comprehensive theological perspective that connects personal faith with collective action.

A common theme among them is the necessity of linking existential authenticity with concrete efforts to dismantle unjust social structures. They contend that theology should not remain an abstract or purely personal endeavor but must actively participate in the transformation of society. This involves a commitment to solidarity with the poor and marginalized, reflecting a communal understanding of faith that is essential for liberation.

Furthermore, they critique Bultmann's theology for not sufficiently addressing the socio-political dimensions of revelation and the importance of collective action. By expanding upon his ideas, they incorporate the historical Jesus, socio-economic analysis, and the need for praxis into their theological frameworks. This approach ensures that theology remains relevant and responsive to the realities of systemic oppression.

In summary, their dialogue with Bultmann's existential theology enriches liberation theology by providing a foundation for integrating personal authenticity with social responsibility. These theologians contribute to a theology that is both personally transformative and socially engaged, emphasizing that faith must inspire action toward justice and equality.

1.1.4. Unraveling Power, Identity, and Resistance

Fanon's exploration of the psychological effects of colonization reveals how the colonized individual internalizes oppression, often turning this suppressed aggression against their own community. He describes how, within the constraints of the colonial system, the native experiences a daily struggle for freedom, expressing their repressed anger during the night, only to be subdued again by the oppressive structures of the day.[189] This dynamic illustrates how colonialism embeds itself deeply within the psyche of the colonized, creating a cycle of violence that perpetuates the colonial order.

---

189. Fanon, *Wretched of the Earth*, 10:52.

Fanon further elaborates on how colonized peoples are not entirely isolated in their struggles, as the ideas and movements from the outside world infiltrate and influence their resistance efforts. Despite the efforts of colonial regimes to suppress and control, the borders of these regimes remain permeable, allowing new thoughts and revolutionary ideas to inspire and fuel the ongoing fight for liberation.[190] This interconnectedness challenges the colonial narrative of dominance and control, demonstrating the resilience and adaptability of oppressed communities.

He also discusses how colonization seeks to achieve success by completely dominating and eradicating the native's sense of self and agency, reducing them to mere tools within the colonial machinery. The construction of infrastructure, such as railways, and the transformation of the landscape serve not only to exploit resources but also to symbolize the total control and dehumanization of the colonized population, rendering them politically and economically invisible.[191] This analysis highlights the comprehensive nature of colonial oppression, which extends beyond physical domination to encompass psychological and symbolic dimensions as well.

In describing the process of decolonization, Fanon portrays it as a violent upheaval, a fundamental reordering of the world that cannot be achieved through gradual reforms or negotiations. He argues that decolonization is an act of complete disorder, a radical break from the colonial past that involves reclaiming not only territory but also the colonized people's identity and humanity.[192] This perspective emphasizes the transformative nature of decolonization, where the oppressed must actively dismantle the structures of their oppression to achieve true liberation.

Foucault's analysis of disciplinary mechanisms in Discipline and Punish reveals how modern institutions such as prisons and schools' function to control and regulate individuals by meticulously organizing space and behavior. He describes how disciplinary machinery operates on the principle of strict partitioning, where each person is assigned a specific place, and each place is designated for a particular individual, thereby preventing collective formations and enforcing a rigid, individualized structure.[193] This method of control highlights how power perme-

---

190. Fanon, *Wretched of the Earth*, 10:70.
191. Fanon, *Wretched of the Earth*, 10:250.
192. Fanon, *Wretched of the Earth*, 10:6.
193. Foucault, *Discipline and Punish*, 143.

ates every aspect of life, subtly shaping behavior and consciousness in a way that individuals often internalize, leading to a self-regulating society.

Moreover, Foucault discusses how disciplinary institutions enforce conformity by continuously monitoring and comparing behavior against established norms. This perpetual surveillance and assessment create a boundary between what is considered normal and abnormal, effectively marginalizing those who do not conform to societal expectations.[194] This system of constant scrutiny and judgment illustrates how power operates not just through overt force but through the subtle, pervasive mechanisms that govern everyday life.

Foucault also traces how the principles of discipline, initially developed in military and medical contexts, were extended to other areas, influencing the organization of institutions such as hospitals in the eighteenth century. This expansion of disciplinary techniques demonstrates the adaptability and pervasiveness of these methods across different sectors of society.[195] It shows how modern society is structured around these principles of order and control, which function to maintain existing power dynamics.

In his broader analysis, Foucault emphasizes that disciplinary power is not simply repressive but also productive, creating specific types of knowledge and truth that reinforce the structures of control. The examination, as a disciplinary tool, embodies this power-knowledge dynamic, where the act of observing and assessing individuals also produces the knowledge that justifies further control.[196] This concept challenges the traditional understanding of power, showing that it operates through complex networks that shape not only social structures but also individual identities and perceptions.

By examining how these disciplinary mechanisms function, Foucault provides a framework for understanding the subtle and pervasive nature of power in modern society, which aligns with Bultmann's focus on individual existence but extends the analysis to the societal structures that deeply influence personal agency.

Similarly, Hannah Arendt's exploration of totalitarianism in The Origins of Totalitarianism offers a critical examination of how ideology is manipulated to sustain oppressive regimes. Arendt highlights that totalitarian regimes utilize ideology to craft a fictitious reality, which serves to

---

194. Foucault, *Discipline and Punish*, 183.
195. Foucault, *Discipline and Punish*, 210.
196. Foucault, *Discipline and Punish*, 227.

justify their actions and suppress dissent. This construction of a fictional narrative can be understood as a form of mythmaking, a process that Bultmann's method of demythologization could help unravel. However, Arendt also warns against oversimplifying complex political phenomena by reducing them solely to existential terms. She argues that such reductions can obscure the specific historical and material conditions that lead to the rise of totalitarianism, making it crucial to maintain a clear focus on these broader contexts.[197]

Arendt points out that while antisemitism was prevalent in educated circles throughout the nineteenth century, it did not become a widespread ideology until it was co-opted by totalitarian movements. She suggests that the transformation of antisemitism into a central element of Nazi ideology illustrates how totalitarian regimes are able to expand narrow ideas into broader, more dangerous ideological frameworks. This shift is not merely a historical accident but a deliberate manipulation of existing prejudices to serve the aims of the regime, highlighting the importance of examining the interplay between ideology and political power.[198]

Furthermore, Arendt discusses how totalitarian regimes, such as those led by the Nazis, relied on ideology to mobilize the masses and legitimize the use of terror. She emphasizes that terror alone cannot sustain a totalitarian regime; it must be coupled with an ideology that has gained widespread acceptance. This ideology provides a framework within which the regime can operate, justifying its actions and enabling the maintenance of power. Arendt's analysis underscores the dangers of ideologies that gain mass appeal, as they can quickly become tools for justifying widespread oppression.[199]

In her examination of how totalitarian regimes manipulate ideology, Arendt also notes the role of propaganda in solidifying these ideologies within the public consciousness. She argues that propaganda, particularly when it employs fabricated documents like the "Protocols of the Elders of Zion," can effectively mobilize people by convincing them of a distorted version of reality. This process demonstrates the power of ideology in shaping political movements and the importance of critically analyzing the narratives that support such regimes.[200]

---

197. Arendt, *Origins of Totalitarianism*, xi.
198. Arendt, *Origins of Totalitarianism*, xiv.
199. Arendt, *Origins of Totalitarianism*, 6.
200. Arendt, *Origins of Totalitarianism*, 7.

Arendt's work offers a valuable perspective on the intersection of ideology, power, and oppression, providing a critical framework for understanding how totalitarian regimes sustain themselves through the manipulation of ideology. This perspective complements Bultmann's focus on demythologization by emphasizing the need to deconstruct the ideological narratives that underpin oppressive systems while also recognizing the broader historical and material conditions that contribute to their emergence.

Judith Butler's exploration in Gender Trouble challenges traditional notions of identity, proposing that gender is not an innate attribute but rather a performative act that sustains certain cultural and social norms.[201] This concept of performativity disrupts essentialist views of identity, which often underlie and reinforce oppressive structures. By examining gender as a series of performative acts, Butler suggests that all forms of identity—whether constructed through language, culture, or social interaction—are similarly performative and thus not fixed. This understanding allows for a reevaluation of how identities are formed and maintained and opens possibilities for resisting and redefining those identities in ways that challenge oppressive systems.[202]

Butler's critique extends to the way language shapes identity, arguing that the fluidity of language itself resists the static categorization of identities. This resistance offers a political challenge, particularly for women, to redefine their subjectivity outside traditional frameworks of identity. By deconstructing the notion of a stable 'speaking subject,' Butler's analysis invites a broader critique of how identities are constructed within power structures, offering a path towards liberation from restrictive norms.[203]

Moreover, Butler discusses the implications of such performative acts on social and political levels, suggesting that the disruption of expected identity performances can lead to a broader destabilization of oppressive structures. This view aligns with Bultmann's focus on individual agency and challenges the categorical limits imposed on individuals by society. Butler's perspective encourages a questioning of the very categories through which agency is expressed, thereby aligning with existential themes of individual authenticity and resistance.[204]

201. Butler, *Gender Trouble*.
202. Butler, *Gender Trouble*, 43.
203. Butler, *Gender Trouble*, 117.
204. Butler, *Gender Trouble*, 94.

In summary, Butler's concept of performativity provides a critical framework for examining how identities are not merely expressed but constructed and maintained through repetitive acts. This analysis not only aligns with Bultmann's existentialist concerns but also opens up avenues for challenging and transforming the oppressive structures that rely on fixed identities to sustain power.[205]

Gustavo Gutiérrez offers a more socially engaged critique of existentialist theology, particularly in his work A Theology of Liberation. He critiques the existentialist focus on individual salvation, arguing that it often neglects the broader social and structural factors that contribute to oppression. Gutiérrez emphasizes that true liberation must address not only personal spiritual freedom but also the material conditions that sustain poverty and inequality. He highlights that liberation theology insists on collective action and social justice, challenging the notion that personal reflection alone is sufficient to combat the complexities of systemic oppression.

Gutiérrez also critiques the existentialist tendency to prioritize individual or small-group spiritual experiences over broader social and political contexts. He argues that this approach can lead to a narrow, disembodied understanding of faith that fails to engage with the lived realities of marginalized communities. In his view, Christian theology should not only concern itself with personal salvation but must also engage with the historical and social dimensions of human existence, advocating for the liberation of those oppressed by unjust structures.[206]

Furthermore, Gutiérrez points out that the history of salvation, as understood within liberation theology, is deeply intertwined with the history of human struggles for justice. He contends that salvation cannot be separated from the concrete historical conditions in which people live, suggesting that the spiritual and the material are inseparable in the pursuit of true liberation.[207] This perspective challenges the existentialist focus on individual decision and highlights the need for a more comprehensive approach that includes social and economic justice as integral components of theological reflection.

By integrating these critiques, Gutiérrez's work suggests that while existentialist theology provides valuable insights into personal agency and spiritual development, it must be supplemented with a robust

---

205. Butler, *Gender Trouble*.
206. Gutiérrez, *Theology of Liberation*, xi.
207. Gutiérrez, *Theology of Liberation*, 86.

analysis of social structures to fully address the realities of oppression. This more holistic approach calls for a theology that is both spiritually and socially engaged, advocating for transformation at both the individual and societal levels.[208]

Amartya Sen's work in Development as Freedom offers a valuable perspective that complements and extends the existential focus of Bultmann by emphasizing the importance of both individual agency and social structures in achieving true freedom. Sen argues that development should be understood not merely as economic growth but as the expansion of real freedoms that people can enjoy. This approach shifts the focus from narrow measures of development, such as GDP or personal income, to a broader view that includes social, economic, and political arrangements that enable individuals to lead lives they have reason to value.[209]

Sen highlights the critical role of removing major sources of "unfreedom," such as poverty, tyranny, and social deprivation, in fostering a truly free society. He underscores that despite global increases in wealth, many people remain deprived of basic freedoms due to economic poverty, lack of access to healthcare and education, and political repression. This analysis reinforces the need to address both the existential and material conditions that underpin oppression, recognizing that true liberation requires more than just the absence of constraints—it requires the presence of enabling conditions that allow individuals to fully participate in society)[210]

Furthermore, Sen emphasizes the interconnectedness of different types of freedoms, arguing that individual agency is both a constitutive part of development and a means to achieve broader social goals. He points out that the expansion of one type of freedom often reinforces others, creating a virtuous cycle that drives development forward. This framework not only aligns with Bultmann's focus on personal decision and agency but also expands it to include the social and political conditions necessary for these freedoms to flourish.[211]

In summary, Sen's concept of development as the expansion of substantive freedoms provides a comprehensive framework that integrates the personal focus of existentialism with a robust analysis of social structures. This approach underscores the importance of public reasoning,

---

208. Gutiérrez, *Theology of Liberation*, 4.
209. Sen, *Development as Freedom*, 3.
210. Sen, *Development as Freedom*, 4.
211. Sen, *Development as Freedom*, 6.

democratic engagement, and the removal of systemic barriers to freedom, offering a more holistic understanding of what it means to achieve true liberation.[212]

In conclusion, the discussion across various theorists like Fanon, Foucault, Arendt, Butler, Gutiérrez, and Sen offers a broad understanding of how interconnected oppressive structures influence individual and collective identities and actions. Through their collective works, the intricate ways in which power, ideology, and social structures intertwine are explored, presenting frameworks that highlight both the challenges and potential pathways toward resistance and liberation. This exploration not only enriches our understanding of societal dynamics but also invites ongoing dialogue about how individuals and communities can navigate and possibly transform the oppressive systems that shape their realities.

1.2. THE EVOLUTION OF THEOLOGY IN SOCIAL JUSTICE

This section examines how integrating various theological perspectives can create a more comprehensive framework for addressing contemporary social justice issues. By drawing on historical and cultural contexts, the works of Rosenstock-Huessy and Kwok Pui-lan highlight how hybrid theologies—those that blend different theological traditions—can reinterpret traditional doctrines to better respond to current societal needs. These hybrid approaches, which incorporate indigenous ecological knowledge, feminist perspectives, and other culturally rooted frameworks, offer practical ways to engage with complex social challenges. This ensures that theological practices remain relevant and attuned to the diverse needs of modern communities.

1.2.1. Merging Traditions for Justice

This section explores how the integration of diverse theological perspectives can contribute to a more comprehensive approach to contemporary issues of liberation and social justice. Drawing from historical and cultural contexts, the works of Rosenstock-Huessy and Kwok Pui-lan illustrate how theological intersections, such as those found in hybrid theologies, can address modern challenges by reinterpreting traditional doctrines to meet current needs. By incorporating indigenous ecological

---

212. Sen, *Development as Freedom*, 8.

CHAPTER ONE

knowledge, feminist perspectives, and other culturally rooted frameworks, these hybrid theologies provide practical and inclusive ways to engage with complex societal issues, ensuring that theological practices remain relevant and responsive to diverse communities.

Rosenstock-Huessy's exploration of historical intersections, where cultural, social, and theological forces converge, illuminates how diverse theological traditions can inform and transform each other, creating innovative frameworks for addressing modern challenges. His analysis in 1938 highlights moments when religious movements and political dynamics informed significant historical shifts, such as the Reformation.[213] These historical observations are pivotal in understanding how contemporary intersections of liberation, feminist, and ecological theologies can enrich a collective approach to justice.

In drawing from Rosenstock-Huessy's discussion on the Crusades and the repositioning of religious fervor into new contexts, we can see parallels in how modern theological movements repurpose traditional doctrines to meet the needs of today's societal challenges.[214] This analogy supports the idea that as different theological and cultural movements meet at these 'social crossroads,' they create potent opportunities for developing comprehensive approaches to systemic inequalities, echoing Rosenstock-Huessy's narrative on the evolution of religious and political thought.

Further, his recounting of Luther's defiance of the papal authority by labeling the pope as the Anti-Christ exemplifies a profound shift in theological frames that disrupted the then-prevailing ecclesiastical paradigms.[215] This historical account serves as a metaphor for today's theological hybrids that challenge and reinterpret traditional doctrines to foster more inclusive and responsive theological practices, highlighting the transformative potential at the intersection of various theological reflections.

Moreover, Rosenstock-Huessy's reflections on the foundational roles of universities during the Reformation underscore the significance of academic and intellectual contributions to theological evolution.[216] These institutions acted as crossroads for scholarly and ecclesiastical debates which profoundly influenced theological development, similar to

213. Rosenstock-Huessy, *Out of Revolution*, 364.
214. Rosenstock-Huessy, *Out of Revolution*, 632.
215. Rosenstock-Huessy, *Out of Revolution*, 556.
216. Rosenstock-Huessy, *Out of Revolution*, 375.

how contemporary theological education can serve as a breeding ground for hybrid theologies that draw from diverse cultural and intellectual traditions.

Lastly, his critique of the idealization of historical figures and movements sheds light on the dangers of romanticizing theological and political leaders, reminding us of the necessity to critically evaluate the implications of theological doctrines in practical contexts.[217] This critique encourages a balanced view in the synthesis of theological perspectives, ensuring that they remain grounded in reality and responsive to the practical needs of the oppressed, aligning with his broader discussions on the impact of historical forces at social crossroads.

Kwok Pui-lan's work significantly expands on the notion of hybrid theological practices by examining how Asian cultural contexts and Western feminist theology can integrate to address the lived experiences of women globally. Her analysis underscores that Asian theologians should develop theologies rooted in their realities rather than reflecting distant theological concerns. She argues that authentic Asian theology emerges not by transplanting Western theological questions but by responding to the concrete situations of Asian societies.[218]

This perspective is particularly resonant in the context of creating a hybrid theology that reflects both the specificities of Asian cultures, and the universal challenges faced by women across different geographies. By navigating through the complexities of cultural, historical, and theological intersections, these theologians strive not to recreate an untouched "Asian" essence but to engage actively with living traditions and contemporary issues.[219] Kwok's insights challenge the construction of a binary "Asia" versus "West," instead advocating for a theological approach that is deeply rooted in dialogue with people's lived religiosity and the political and historical issues of Asian contexts.

Moreover, Kwok critiques the adequacy of Asian theologians in fully theorizing how colonial legacies have reshaped Asian cultures. She points out the necessity for a deeper analysis of how colonization has influenced and altered Asian societies, advocating for a more rigorous intellectual examination of these impacts.[220] This critique is essential for understanding how postcolonial contexts can influence the development

---

217. Rosenstock-Huessy, *Out of Revolution*, 552.
218. Kwok, *Postcolonial Imagination and Feminist Theology*, 41.
219. Kwok, *Postcolonial Imagination and Feminist Theology*, 375.
220. Kwok, *Postcolonial Imagination and Feminist Theology*, 126.

CHAPTER ONE

of hybrid theological frameworks that are better suited to address the realities of formerly colonized societies.

In sum, Kwok Pui-lan's scholarship provides a critical foundation for understanding how hybrid theological practices can be developed by integrating diverse cultural and feminist perspectives. Her call for a theology that is both responsive to Asian realities and informed by global feminist discourses illustrates the potential for a more inclusive and effective theological approach. This integration not only enriches the theological landscape but also ensures that it remains relevant to the challenges and complexities of our globalized world.

Critics argue that hybrid theologies, which blend various theological traditions, risk compromising the distinctiveness of traditional doctrines. Such a synthesis, they assert, may lead to a diluted theology that is less coherent and effective in addressing specific religious and ethical issues. This concern highlights a significant tension between maintaining theological integrity and pursuing inclusivity and diversity in theological perspectives.[221]

In his work, Smith proposes a rethinking of the relationship between worship and educational paradigms within Christian higher education.[222] He questions the traditional separation of liturgical practice and academic learning, suggesting that a more integrated approach could enhance the overall educational experience. By linking liturgy, learning, and formation, Smith argues for a model of education that not only imparts knowledge but also shapes the spiritual and communal life of students.

Smith extends his critique to the prevailing educational models that emphasize abstract cognitive processes at the expense of embodied practices.[223] He points out that this disconnection leads to an education that neglects the formation of the whole person—emotional, physical, and spiritual. Smith advocates for a more holistic educational approach that incorporates physical rituals and practices, which he argues are crucial for the deep formation of students' identities and desires.

Finally, Smith stresses the need for educational strategies that recognize the formative power of liturgical practices.[224] He criticizes the reductionist approach that views education merely as the transmission

---

221. Smith, *Desiring the Kingdom*, 39.
222. Smith, *Desiring the Kingdom*, 39.
223. Smith, *Desiring the Kingdom*, 40.
224. Smith, *Desiring the Kingdom*, 40.

of information and argues for a pedagogy that sees students as fundamentally relational beings, shaped by their practices and communities. This approach challenges the dominant cognitive-focused models in theological education and suggests a paradigm shift towards a more integrated and experiential learning environment that aligns with Christian liturgical life.

The potential benefits of hybrid theologies are not merely academic; they hold significant practical implications, especially in their ability to address complex and multifaceted forms of oppression. Hybrid theologies, by blending various religious traditions, offer new and nuanced approaches to theology that can be particularly effective in diverse cultural contexts.

For example, the integration of Christian liberation theology with African indigenous spiritual practices offers innovative frameworks for understanding and confronting social injustices, specifically within postcolonial contexts. This combination enables a theology that is not only contextually relevant but also profoundly connected to the lived experiences of the people it aims to serve. Mbiti explores how African spiritual traditions have historically intertwined with social and cultural identities, providing a robust base for such theological endeavors.

Mbiti notes the significant influence of African religious heritage not just on the continent itself but globally, indicating a universal relevance that transcends geographical and cultural boundaries. He details how elements like African music, dance, and art forms, deeply embedded with religious and spiritual significances, have shaped and enriched global cultural landscapes.[225] This global influence underscores the potential of hybrid theological approaches to speak across cultures and communities, offering insights that are both locally informed and universally resonant.

Furthermore, Mbiti highlights the enduring impact of these traditions in shaping the character and cultural practices of African societies through religious ceremonies, social life, and even political structures.[226] The deep integration of religion with daily life in African contexts exemplifies how theology, when interwoven with indigenous practices, can effectively address the spiritual, social, and cultural needs of a community.

Through such an integrated approach, hybrid theologies like those combining Christian and African indigenous elements offer powerful

---

225. Mbiti, *Introduction to African Religion*, 4–5.
226. Mbiti, *Introduction to African Religion*, 6.

tools for social transformation. These theologies provide not only a deeper understanding of oppression and justice but also practical pathways for empowerment and change, rooted in the rich spiritual and cultural heritages of the communities they are meant to serve.[227] This demonstrates the vital role that culturally embedded theologies can play in fostering resilience and advocating for social justice across diverse global contexts.

Rosenstock-Huessy's concept of social crossroads can be aptly extended to encompass interactions among diverse religious traditions, promoting what is now increasingly recognized as interfaith or interreligious theologies. These innovative theological approaches strive to forge connections across different faith traditions, fostering a milieu where dialogue and mutual comprehension can flourish, leading to the evolution of new, hybrid forms of spiritual practice.

As Cornille illustrates, such dialogical engagements between different religious traditions are not merely theoretical exercises but involve real-world implications and practices. For instance, the "United Religions Initiative," initiated by Anglican Bishop William Swing in 1995, aims to foster persistent interfaith cooperation to resolve religiously motivated conflicts and promote peace. This organization embodies the practical application of interreligious dialogue and cooperation emphasized in interfaith theologies.[228]

Cornille further argues that this process of interaction and negotiation among religious traditions necessitates a form of dialogue that is both humble and open to reinterpreting traditional doctrines through engagement with their original meanings. This approach leads to the development of new theological theories that may diverge significantly from traditional doctrinal interpretations but are essential for a genuine and transformative interfaith dialogue.[229]

Moreover, the dynamic interplay and exchange of religious experiences among different faiths lead to a deeper and more creative understanding. This process is described as a dialogical interaction where both self and other contribute to the creation of something new, thus challenging the conventional notions of empathy and understanding in religious contexts.[230] This transformative interaction points to the poten-

---

227. Mbiti, *Introduction to African Religion*, 30.
228. Cornille, *Im-possibility of Interreligious Dialogue*, 102.
229. Cornille, *Im-possibility of Interreligious Dialogue*, 35.
230. Cornille, *Im-possibility of Interreligious Dialogue*, 173.

tial of interreligious theologies to not only bridge doctrinal divides but also to enrich spiritual practices across religious boundaries.

While Rosenstock-Huessy's concept of social crossroads aptly extends to interactions among diverse religious traditions, critics like Jane I. Smith highlight the complexities of these dialogues. In her book, "Muslims, Christians, and the Challenge of Interfaith Dialogue," Smith underscores that interfaith engagements often struggle with profound differences between faith perspectives, which can pose significant barriers to understanding and reconciliation. These engagements, she notes, necessitate a deep appreciation and acknowledgment of distinct religious beliefs and practices.[231]

Furthering this discussion, Smith illustrates through dialogues she observed, noting how differences within and between faiths can complicate communication. For instance, during interfaith discussions, participants often grapple with varied understandings of their own faiths, which can lead to uneven dialogue dynamics. This variation sometimes results in participants feeling under-informed or overly reliant on religious leaders, complicating the dialogue process.[232]

Smith also highlights a common challenge in these dialogues: the balance between expressing religious convictions and maintaining respectful engagement. She observes that while some participants are eager to share their beliefs, others may feel that such openness can inadvertently lead to coercive attempts at conversion, straining the dialogue.[233]

These insights suggest that effective interfaith dialogue requires not only recognition of the profound differences between religious traditions but also an understanding of the internal diversity within each faith. Such recognition can help foster a more genuine and constructive dialogue, aimed at mutual respect rather than consensus.[234]

Despite these criticisms, the potential for hybrid theologies to address contemporary issues of liberation remains significant. By incorporating diverse voices and perspectives, these theologies can create a more inclusive and holistic approach to social justice. For instance, the integration of indigenous ecological knowledge with Christian stewardship concepts can offer new approaches to environmental ethics and sustainable living. As LaDuke illustrates, Indigenous communities

---

231. Smith, *Muslims, Christians, and the Challenge of Interfaith Dialogue*, 186.
232. Smith, *Muslims, Christians, and the Challenge of Interfaith Dialogue*, 6–9.
233. Smith, *Muslims, Christians, and the Challenge of Interfaith Dialogue*, 91–92.
234. Smith, *Muslims, Christians, and the Challenge of Interfaith Dialogue*.

CHAPTER ONE

have long struggled with the environmental degradation caused by resource extraction and development activities. She notes that Indigenous knowledge, deeply rooted in a relationship with the land, can provide essential guidance for creating more sustainable and just environmental practices.[235]

LaDuke further emphasizes the grassroots efforts of Native environmental groups, who, despite limited resources, have achieved significant victories in protecting sacred sites and natural resources. These efforts highlight the importance of integrating Indigenous perspectives into broader environmental and theological discussions, as they bring valuable understandings of the interconnectedness of all life and the need for responsible stewardship.[236]

Moreover, LaDuke points out that these struggles are not just about environmental preservation but are also deeply tied to cultural survival and self-determination. The commitment of Indigenous communities to defend their lands and ways of life underscores the need for hybrid theologies that honor these connections and advocate for environmental justice on a global scale.[237]

In conclusion, by blending Indigenous ecological knowledge with Christian stewardship, hybrid theologies can contribute to a more comprehensive and equitable approach to environmental ethics, addressing both the spiritual and practical aspects of sustainability and justice.[238]

In conclusion, hybrid theologies harness the potential to address current liberation issues by blending various theological and cultural perspectives. This approach not only enriches theological discussions but also ensures their relevance in addressing the complexities of today's global challenges. By integrating insights from historical, cultural, and feminist viewpoints, such as those presented by Rosenstock-Huessy and Kwok Pui-lan, hybrid theologies facilitate a multifaceted engagement with social justice issues, offering a versatile framework that remains sensitive to diverse community needs. This synthesis of perspectives promotes a theology that is grounded, capable of responding to and influencing the practical and spiritual dimensions of societal challenges.

---

235. LaDuke, *All Our Relations*, 3–4.
236. LaDuke, *All Our Relations*, 4.
237. LaDuke, *All Our Relations*, 200.
238. LaDuke, *All Our Relations*, 225.

1.2.2. Integrating Secular Thought and Theology

This section explores how integrating secular philosophies with existential theology can offer new perspectives on understanding human experience and societal structures. By examining the ideas of thinkers such as Maurice Merleau-Ponty, Frantz Fanon, Judith Butler, Hannah Arendt, Herbert Marcuse, Richard Rorty, and Slavoj Žižek, it highlights how these philosophies challenge and extend traditional existential and theological concepts. The discussion focuses on the interplay between individual existence and broader social, political, and economic forces, offering frameworks that address both personal identity and collective action in the context of contemporary challenges.

Maurice Merleau-Ponty, in his exploration of human experience, emphasizes that perception is fundamentally rooted in our bodily existence, shaping how we interact with the world and influencing our ethical responsibilities. This view aligns with Bultmann's existential theology by underscoring the significance of personal existence in shaping one's life and faith. Merleau-Ponty's analysis suggests that the act of attention is not merely a cause, but a motive rooted in the consciousness, bringing clarity and direction to our actions as we move from indifference to engagement with the present.[239]

Merleau-Ponty further challenges the traditional views of human psychology by integrating aspects of sexuality that were previously attributed solely to consciousness. His observations suggest a dialectical process within what might be considered 'purely bodily' functions, re-integrating sexuality into the broader human experience. This perspective enriches existential theology by highlighting the complex interplay between the physical and the psychological in forming human identity.[240]

He also elucidates the interconnectedness of sensory experiences, illustrating that our perception of the world is not limited to isolated senses but is a cohesive unity that our existence projects before us. This holistic view of perception underscores the existential notion that our engagement with the world is deeply intertwined with our bodily existence, challenging us to reconsider how we understand our interactions with the world.[241]

---

239. Merleau-Ponty, *Phenomenology of Perception*, C. 6.6.2.Trans., 31.
240. Merleau-Ponty, *Phenomenology of Perception*, 158.
241. Merleau-Ponty, *Phenomenology of Perception*, 319.

Discussing the intricacies of perception, Merleau-Ponty points to the difficulties in maintaining strict classifications in sensory experiences, such as colors. This reflects the existential challenge of adhering to rigid frameworks in understanding ourselves and the world, which Bultmann also addresses in his theological discussions.[242]

His reflections extend into the realm of spatiality, where he argues that one's body acts as a mediator in the figure-background structure of perception, emphasizing the inherent engagement of the body with the world. This integration of bodily space into our understanding of external spaces highlights the existential commitment to being-in-the-world, which is central to both Merleau-Ponty's philosophy and Bultmann's theology.[243]

Through these discussions, Merleau-Ponty offers critical perspectives that challenge and extend Bultmann's existential theology, promoting a deeper engagement with the existential conditions that shape our lives. His work not only complements but also deepens the theological exploration of personal existence, responsibility, and the transformative potential inherent in our engagement with the world.

Frantz Fanon's critical perspective delves into the psychological effects of colonization and emphasizes the essential role of collective action for decolonization, providing a contrast to Bultmann's focus on individual faith. Fanon articulates that overcoming systemic oppression often demands a unified response that confronts entrenched power structures.[244]

In his examination of the interplay between decolonization and globalization, Fanon reflects on the ironic search for links between these two phenomena, suggesting that while decolonization focused on liberating nations from colonial powers, globalization might be seen as a continuation of some forms of control, albeit in a different guise.[245] He argues that the future of decolonized societies hinges on resisting the limiting choices imposed by former colonial and current global powers, suggesting a new path for the Third World beyond the restrictive frameworks of the past.[246]

Fanon's narrative also addresses the complexities of post-colonial identities and the ongoing impact of colonial legacies. He discusses how

---

242. Merleau-Ponty, *Phenomenology of Perception*, 176,
243. Merleau-Ponty, *Phenomenology of Perception*, 101.
244. Fanon, *Wretched of the Earth* (2007).
245. Fanon, *Wretched of the Earth* (2007), xi.
246. Fanon, *Wretched of the Earth* (2007), xiv.

the Third World's emergence is intertwined with global political dynamics, specifically the bipolar tensions of the Cold War, which need to end for genuine decolonization to occur.[247] His vision extends to a critique of narrow-minded nationalism and advocates for a broader, more inclusive approach to post-colonial nation-building that avoids falling back into the patterns of exclusion and exploitation characteristic of colonial regimes.[248]

Furthermore, Fanon challenges the conventional approaches to nation-building that often follow decolonization, pointing out that a new, more humane society can only be achieved through continuous commitment to national liberation, beyond the initial euphoria of independence.[249] He emphasizes that this process involves not just political change but a transformation in how individuals see themselves and their communities, advocating for a profound reevaluation of identities and societal structures.[250]

This perspective enriches the existential theological discourse by highlighting the need for a collective reimagining of society's foundational structures, suggesting that personal transformation is deeply connected to societal change. Fanon's analysis invites a rethinking of how theological and existential philosophies can inform and support struggles against oppression, blending individual and collective efforts for a comprehensive approach to liberation.[251]

Judith Butler's exploration of gender performativity in Gender Trouble offers a critical perspective that both challenges and complements Bultmann's theological focus on individual faith. She argues that gender is not an inherent identity, but a performance shaped by societal norms, influencing how individuals experience and express their identities, thus complicating the existential pursuit of authentic selfhood.[252] This analysis highlights the limitations imposed by societal gender constructs on individual freedom and responsibility, adding depth to Bultmann's examination of existential agency.[253]

Butler's discussion extends to the strategic and sometimes subversive ways identities are performed, suggesting that these acts can

---

247. Fanon, *Wretched of the Earth* (2007), xv.
248. Fanon, *Wretched of the Earth* (2007), xvi.
249. Fanon, *Wretched of the Earth* (2007), xvii.
250. Fanon, *Wretched of the Earth* (2007), 2.
251. Fanon, *Wretched of the Earth* (2007), 9.
252. Butler, *Gender Trouble*, iii.
253. Butler, *Gender Trouble*, xii.

challenge and dismantle restrictive norms. She hopes for a coalition that acknowledges the complexity of identities and works against the erasure of marginalized ones, especially within the bisexual community.[254] Her critique of identity categories points out the dangers of identity becoming a tool for the power structures it aims to oppose, emphasizing the need for a political reevaluation of how identities are used and understood.[255]

Moreover, Butler explores the genealogy of identity, not as an origin to be uncovered but as a series of effects produced by institutions and social practices. This approach shifts the focus from defining identities to understanding their formation as political processes, urging a reconsideration of the political implications of identity categories.[256] She questions the traditional goals of identity politics, proposing instead that understanding the variable construction of identity could lead to a more effective form of political engagement.[257]

By integrating Butler's observations, the existential discourse can be expanded to consider how social constructs and performative acts influence not only individual identity but also collective political action. Her work underscores the need for a theological and philosophical understanding that considers the profound impact of societal norms on personal and collective liberation efforts.[258]

Hannah Arendt provides a critical viewpoint on power and authority in modern societies, which offers a significant contrast to Bultmann's focus on personal transformation. In her exploration of the nature of totalitarianism, Arendt argues that the rise of such regimes reveals the perils of reducing politics to mere administration or ideology, shedding light on the dynamics between power, authority, and the public sphere.[259] Her discussion raises crucial questions about the interaction between individual responsibility and collective political action, suggesting that personal transformation must consider broader political contexts.[260]

Arendt discusses how antisemitism, particularly in the context of Nazi ideology, highlights the complexities of modern political life where seemingly minor issues can trigger catastrophic events, challenging our

---

254. Butler, *Gender Trouble*, xxvii.
255. Butler, *Gender Trouble*, xxviii.
256. Butler, *Gender Trouble*, xxxi.
257. Butler, *Gender Trouble*, 8.
258. Butler, *Gender Trouble*, 4.
259. Arendt, *Origins of Totalitarianism*.
260. Arendt, *Origins of Totalitarianism*, 3.

understanding of cause and effect in historical processes. This discrepancy, she notes, often outrages common sense and challenges the historian's sense of balance and proportionality.[261] Her analysis extends to the decline of traditional nationalism and the peculiar rise of antisemitism, which reached its climax precisely when the nation-state system and its balance of power collapsed, suggesting a complex interplay of historical forces rather than a straightforward causality.[262]

Moreover, Arendt critiques the simplistic identification of antisemitism with nationalism, pointing out that modern antisemitism actually grew as traditional nationalism declined. She highlights that early antisemitic movements were international in their scope, challenging the conventional understanding of nationalism.[263] This complexity underscores the inadequacy of traditional historical explanations and the need for a deeper understanding of how ideologies like antisemitism function within and beyond national boundaries.

Arendt's analysis offers a framework for rethinking political ideologies and their impact on both individual and collective identities. By delving into the historical and ideological foundations of totalitarianism and antisemitism, she encourages a reassessment of the individual's role within these broader socio-political movements, pointing out the shortcomings of considering personal transformation as detached from political contexts.[264] This perspective is crucial for understanding how individual actions are shaped by and can shape political structures, broadening the discussion on personal responsibility and collective action.

Herbert Marcuse critiques existentialism from a Marxist viewpoint, emphasizing its shortcomings in addressing the material conditions influencing human existence. According to Marcuse, existentialist thought overlooks how capitalist societies engineer needs and perpetuate alienation, potentially rendering existentialist theology a theoretical abstraction detached from the underlying economic and social conditions.[265]

Marcuse's critique, grounded in examples from "One-Dimensional Man" and other works, challenges the existentialist focus by asserting the necessity of confronting the economic and social bases that sustain oppression. He warns of the risks involved if existentialist theology does

---

261. Arendt, *Origins of Totalitarianism*, 3.
262. Arendt, *Origins of Totalitarianism*, 4.
263. Arendt, *Origins of Totalitarianism*, 4.
264. Arendt, *Origins of Totalitarianism*, 5.
265. Marcuse, *One-Dimensional Man*.

CHAPTER ONE

not engage with these foundational issues, as it might fail to provide any substantial critique or alternative to the existing societal structure.[266]

Further, Marcuse argues that a failure to integrate a critique of social and economic conditions into existentialist frameworks could limit their effectiveness and relevance. By not addressing these critical factors, existentialist approaches may not achieve a meaningful impact on societal change or adequately challenge the structures that facilitate human oppression.[267]

Ultimately, Marcuse suggests that for existentialist theology to be more than an isolated intellectual exercise, it must incorporate a broader analysis that includes the critique of capitalist structures and their impact on human freedom and well-being. This integration is crucial for renewing critical thinking and fostering effective radical politics.[268]

Richard Rorty critically assesses existentialism from a pragmatic viewpoint, focusing on the doctrine's emphasis on individual authenticity and existential concern. He contends that this emphasis might detract from addressing broader issues such as social justice and communal welfare. Rorty advocates for redirecting efforts from exploring absolute truths to fostering solidarity and establishing a more equitable society. This shift implies a potential need to temper existentialist concerns with individual responsibility in favor of more collective initiatives.[269]

Rorty's pragmatic critique is rooted in a broader discourse that challenges the efficacy of existentialism in addressing urgent communal concerns. He underscores the practical limitations of existentialism when it focuses narrowly on individual dilemmas, potentially at the expense of broader societal issues. The critique suggests a reorientation of priorities from solitary existential exploration to communal engagement and action.[270]

This reevaluation of existential priorities, according to Rorty, is necessary for the development of a society that values justice and collective well-being over individual existential achievements. By advocating for a pragmatic approach, Rorty positions himself within a discourse that

---

266. Marcuse, *One-Dimensional Man*, xi, xxxiv.
267. Marcuse, *One-Dimensional Man*, xxxix, 78.
268. Marcuse, *One-Dimensional Man*, 100, 148, 234.
269. Rorty, *Contingency, Irony, and Solidarity*.
270. Rorty, *Contingency, Irony, and Solidarity*, 41.

values actionable outcomes and communal progress as fundamental to societal development.[271]

In summary, Rorty's critique calls for existentialism to evolve in ways that better accommodate the demands of social justice and community solidarity. His perspective points towards a pragmatic approach where the focus shifts from individual to collective concerns, aiming to foster a society that prioritizes equitable conditions and shared human experiences.[272]

Slavoj Žižek delivers a challenging critique of both existentialism and liberation theology, arguing that these perspectives often overlook the ideological structures underpinning capitalism and neoliberalism. Žižek emphasizes the need for a radical critique that moves beyond individual responsibility towards a systemic understanding of oppression's maintenance and avenues for resistance.[273]

In his exploration, Žižek delves into how capitalist societies—extending from Western economies to the Eastern bloc and the Third World—necessitate a reimagined socialist ideal that broadens and deepens democratic principles. He highlights the ongoing disagreements about how to achieve such reformulations effectively, which further complicates the path toward systemic change.[274]

Furthering his critique, Žižek discusses the transformation from feudal to capitalist societies, illustrating how ideological shifts have redefined social and economic interactions. He argues that while feudal relations were overtly oppressive, capitalist societies disguise these dynamics through a 'fetishization' of commodities, thus obscuring the continuing relations of domination and servitude under new forms. This fetishism, according to Žižek, shifts focus from interpersonal relationships to those between commodities, thereby masking the underlying structures of control and dependence.[275]

By examining the ideological mechanisms at play, Žižek posits that capitalism's transformation of social relations into relations between commodities reveals a deep-seated form of control and alienation. This perspective challenges both existentialists and liberation theologians to reconsider their approaches, suggesting that without addressing the

271. Rorty, *Contingency, Irony, and Solidarity*. 42.
272. Rorty, *Contingency, Irony, and Solidarity*. 43.
273. Žižek, *Sublime Object of Ideology*.
274. Žižek, *Sublime Object of Ideology*, ii.
275. Žižek, *Sublime Object of Ideology*, 26.

CHAPTER ONE

ideological underpinnings of capitalism, their critiques may fail to reach the root of contemporary socio-economic issues.[276]

In conclusion, this section reflects on the varied approaches to understanding and addressing the intersections of existential concerns and societal structures. By exploring diverse philosophies and critiques from thinkers like Merleau-Ponty, Fanon, Butler, Arendt, Marcuse, Rorty, and Žižek, we gain a broader understanding of how individual experiences and societal frameworks interact. These discussions highlight the complexity of integrating existential and theological perspectives with political and social realities, urging a reconsideration of traditional approaches in favor of more inclusive and socially engaged frameworks. This synthesis emphasizes the need for a comprehensive view that appreciates the dynamic interplay between personal identities and broader societal structures.

1.3. JUSTICE AND REDEMPTION IN ROSENZWEIG, LEVINAS, AND ARENDT

This section examines the relationship between Franz Rosenzweig's theological concepts and the ethical ideas of thinkers like Emmanuel Levinas, Hannah Arendt, and others. Rosenzweig's approach frames efforts towards justice within a broader divine narrative, suggesting that individual and collective actions are part of a continual process of creation, revelation, and redemption. Integrating the ethical perspectives of Levinas and Arendt, the discussion explores how these actions relate to the broader moral framework, emphasizing the importance of recognizing the interconnectedness and diversity of global justice movements within the context of divine redemption.

Franz Rosenzweig's concept of the Star of Redemption emphasizes the interconnected processes of creation, revelation, and redemption, framing local struggles for justice within a broader divine narrative. This understanding views every action toward justice as integral to a continual divine plan, embedding local efforts within global movements of the divine economy of salvation.[277]

Exploring Rosenzweig's philosophical ideas further, we find a detailed examination of the phenomenon of newness in the spiritual world,

---

276. Žižek, *Sublime Object of Ideology*, 34.
277. Rosenzweig, *Star of Redemption*.

where he challenges idealism's inability to recognize the "spontaneous" due to its allegiance to the omnipotence of the logos. Rosenzweig argues that this has led to a misrepresentation of the rich diversity of life, reducing it to a chaotic ensemble of static entities.[278] This critique extends to the ways traditional philosophies have depicted the world and its spiritual phenomena, pushing for a reevaluation that respects the vitality and diversity inherent in the world.

Rosenzweig's thought is particularly critical of the idealist tradition from Parmenides to Hegel, where the comprehension of the world has been dominated by a logic that denies the spontaneous vitality of life. He proposes a metalogical perspective that does not impose unity but finds it inherent within the world's multiplicity, supporting a view where the world is understood not as created by the spirit but as permeated with it.[279] This shift allows for a worldview where the logos serves not as the creator but as the soul of the world, enhancing the understanding of the world as a living body continuously renewed and interacting dynamically with the spiritual.

Moreover, Rosenzweig discusses the concept of generation, contrasting it with creation. He suggests that generation, rather than creation, provides a framework that recognizes the inherent multiplicity and unity of the world without imposing an external creator, thus respecting the world's autonomy and richness.[280] This approach challenges the traditional theological view and advocates for an understanding that sees the world not as a passive creation but as an active participant in its ongoing formation.

In his reflections on time and eternity, Rosenzweig highlights how the eternal people deny traditional temporal sequences, embodying an existence that anticipates the end as the beginning, thus living outside conventional time. This inversion emphasizes a life lived in constant anticipation of redemption, integrating the temporal with the eternal.[281]

These thoughts from Rosenzweig call for a deeper engagement with the multiplicity and spontaneity of life, advocating for a perspective that sees local and global struggles for justice as inherently connected within the divine narrative. By understanding these struggles through the lens of creation, revelation, and redemption, there is a richer framework for

---

278. Rosenzweig, *Star of Redemption*, 55.
279. Rosenzweig, *Star of Redemption*, 55.
280. Rosenzweig, *Star of Redemption*, 146.
281. Rosenzweig, *Star of Redemption*, 443.

engaging with issues of justice and liberation, recognizing the diverse and dynamic ways they manifest in the world.[282]

Integrating Franz Rosenzweig's ideas with those of Emmanuel Levinas can offer enriched perspectives on the ethical dimensions of justice. Levinas, influenced by Rosenzweig, delves deep into the ethical responsibility to the "Other," which he sees as fundamental to human existence. He suggests that ethical relations not only precede but also shape the social and political spheres, aligning with the view that local acts of justice are crucial components of a larger moral framework.[283]

Levinas provides a thorough critique of how traditional phenomenologists, including Heidegger, have often overlooked the importance of the 'Other' in their analyses. He emphasizes that human individuals and groups tend to maintain an egocentric attitude, perceiving other individuals either as extensions of themselves or as objects to be manipulated. This critique is significant as it calls for a shift in perspective that respects the original experience of encountering the 'Other,' which does not reduce others to mere extensions or adversaries but recognizes their distinct existence.[284]

Further, Levinas explores the dynamics of face-to-face encounters, where the other is not merely an alter ego but a unique entity with whom one must engage genuinely. He points out that real communication and community formation require a sincere and responsible response to the 'Other,' advocating for a dialogue that respects and acknowledges the distinctiveness of each individual.[285]

Moreover, Levinas argues for a new way of thinking that focuses less on self-centered perceptions and more on understanding beings in their "radical otherness." This approach is less about assimilating or changing the 'Other' to fit preconceived notions but about striving to engage with them without compromising one's integrity or that of the 'Other.'[286]

This perspective, as articulated by Levinas, aligns closely with Rosenzweig's views on justice and ethical responsibility within the divine plan, suggesting that every interaction with the 'Other' is a critical part of a larger moral and spiritual journey. Together, the thoughts of Rosenzweig and Levinas encourage a deeper engagement with the ethical

282. Rosenzweig, *Star of Redemption*.
283. Levinas, *Totality and Infinity*.
284. Levinas, *Totality and Infinity*, 12–13.
285. Levinas, *Totality and Infinity*, 14.
286. Levinas, *Totality and Infinity*, 16–17.

dimensions of justice, emphasizing the importance of recognizing and respecting the unique qualities of every individual within the broader context of divine redemption.[287]

Hannah Arendt's exploration of the "banality of evil" in Eichmann in Jerusalem introduces a critical perspective that challenges the notion that all actions contributing to justice are automatically recognized as part of a divine plan. Arendt suggests that ordinary individuals can participate in systemic injustice without realizing their role in a larger narrative, which complicates the understanding of the divine plan in daily actions.[288] This perspective questions whether all actions necessarily contribute to redemption or might unknowingly perpetuate injustice.

Arendt illustrates the difficulty of reconciling the mundane nature of the perpetrator with the horrific nature of the crimes, which led some to inaccurately dismiss Adolf Eichmann as merely a clever liar, underestimating the ordinariness that characterized his evil actions.[289] She describes how, in the last moments of his trial, Eichmann seemed to reflect on a lesson about the terrifyingly mundane nature of evil, suggesting that evil can manifest not through monstrous acts but through the failure to think and reflect critically.[290]

Moreover, Arendt delves into the broader societal reluctance to confront uncomfortable truths, such as the resistance in Israel to the idea of an international court, reflecting a broader discomfort with examining the implications of justice that might transcend national narratives.[291] She challenges the simplistic narratives that emerged post-war, highlighting how individuals like Eichmann justified their actions under the guise of bureaucratic duty, without the intention to destroy, as evident in the initial indictment counts during his trial.[292]

Arendt's analysis extends to how Eichmann's own perception of his life being under an "evil spell" reflected his detachment from the reality of his actions and their consequences, showcasing a disturbing disconnect between intention and outcome.[293] This detachment is further illustrated in his reflections on operational failures, like the Nisko

---

287. Levinas, *Totality and Infinity*.
288. Arendt, *Eichmann in Jerusalem*.
289. Arendt, *Eichmann in Jerusalem*, 49.
290. Arendt, *Eichmann in Jerusalem*, 231.
291. Arendt, *Eichmann in Jerusalem*, 5.
292. Arendt, *Eichmann in Jerusalem*, 223.
293. Arendt, *Eichmann in Jerusalem*, 45.

Plan, where he blamed external factors rather than acknowledging the inherent immorality of the objectives.[294]

In essence, Arendt's work underscores the need for a deeper understanding of how seemingly ordinary actions and administrative duties can contribute to systemic evils. Her examination reveals the complexities of recognizing and confronting evil, urging a more nuanced view of responsibility that goes beyond conventional moral and ethical frameworks.[295] This analysis enriches the discourse on the interplay between individual actions and broader societal structures, challenging us to reconsider the assumptions we hold about justice, redemption, and the role of the divine in historical and contemporary contexts.

Edward Said's Culture and Imperialism offers a critical perspective on the presumption that local struggles for justice universally align with a divine plan. Said contends that cultural narratives, especially in imperial contexts, often justify oppressive actions, suggesting that efforts deemed just in one setting might perpetuate oppression elsewhere.[296] This insight challenges the view that all local actions are inherently beneficial within a divine economy, underscoring the necessity for a thorough evaluation of each struggle's wider consequences.

In his work, Said discusses the historical backdrop of European nationalism and its impact on scholarly and cultural interpretations. He notes that the celebration of humanity and culture in Europe often served to elevate national or European ideals at the expense of non-European peoples, intertwining cultural studies with nationalistic agendas.[297] This Eurocentric focus in fields such as anthropology and comparative literature portrayed non-European societies as either lacking or transcendent, obscuring their actual value and complexity.[298]

Furthermore, Said highlights the development of comparative literature as a discipline that, while aspiring to a trans-national vision, often placed European literatures at its center. This approach not only established a hierarchy of literatures but also reinforced European cultural dominance, neglecting the rich literary contributions of other regions.[299] The concept of "Weltliteratur" (world literature), as advanced by scholars

294. Arendt, *Eichmann in Jerusalem*, 68.
295. Arendt, *Eichmann in Jerusalem*.
296. Said, *Culture and Imperialism*.
297. Said, *Culture and Imperialism*, 44.
298. Said, *Culture and Imperialism*, 44.
299. Said, *Culture and Imperialism*, 45.

like Goethe and later academics, inadvertently supported a worldview that prioritized European literary canon, marginalizing non-European texts and perspectives.[300]

Said's critique extends to the academic realm where comparative literature and other humanities disciplines were shaped by a fundamentally Eurocentric paradigm. This paradigm, while purporting to be universal, actually supported and perpetuated a narrow, culturally specific view that often overlooked or misrepresented non-Western literatures and histories.[301]

Through this examination, Said elucidates the complex interplay between culture, imperialism, and the construction of knowledge, urging a reconsideration of how narratives of justice and liberation are framed. His analysis compels us to question the assumed universality of certain cultural values and to recognize the potential for cultural narratives to serve imperialistic or oppressive ends. This reflection is crucial for understanding the broader implications of local struggles within global contexts and challenges us to think critically about the narratives we accept as universally valid.[302]

Similarly, Gayatri Chakravorty Spivak's exploration of the "subaltern" in Can the Subaltern Speak? adds complexity to Rosenzweig's framework by highlighting how marginalized voices are often excluded from dominant narratives of redemption and liberation. Spivak's analysis suggests that within global liberation movements, the voices and needs of the most oppressed can be overlooked, calling into question the universality of these efforts.[303]

Spivak emphasizes the importance of recognizing the agency of subalterns, her term for the indigenous dispossessed, to make their own decisions. This focus is crucial in understanding how subalterns are often silenced within broader discourses, preventing their true participation in movements purportedly aimed at their liberation.[304] Further, Spivak underscores the impact of colonial control on the formation of postcolonial studies, highlighting her own background in India and her

---

300. Said, *Culture and Imperialism*, 45.
301. Said, *Culture and Imperialism*, 46.
302. Said, *Culture and Imperialism*.
303. Riach, *Analysis of Gayatri Chakravorty Spivak's Can the Subaltern Speak?*
304. Riach, *Analysis of Gayatri Chakravorty Spivak's Can the Subaltern Speak?*, 5.

CHAPTER ONE

academic formation in both India and America, which informed her critical perspectives.[305]

Spivak's critique extends to how Western academic inquiries often carry ideological biases, particularly in the study of developing nations. These biases can distort understanding and perpetuate the marginalization of the subjects studied, complicating efforts toward genuine liberation.[306] Moreover, Spivak discusses the importance of critically examining the beliefs that scholars bring into their engagements with other cultures, advocating for a more reflective approach that acknowledges the complexities of intercultural understanding.[307]

Spivak's work also sheds light on the personal influences on her scholarship, including the decolonization of India and her early experiences of colonial and postcolonial life. These experiences deeply shaped her intellectual journey and her commitment to addressing systems of oppression through her scholarship.[308] By challenging the cultural imperialism embedded in traditional academic practices, Spivak seeks to reframe the discourse around subalternity and liberation, advocating for a deeper recognition of the subaltern as a subject capable of speaking and resisting oppression.[309]

In this way, Spivak's insights provide valuable perspectives that challenge and expand traditional understandings of liberation and justice, emphasizing the need to include the most marginalized voices in discussions of global and divine narratives of redemption. Her work compels us to reconsider the efficacy and inclusiveness of liberation movements and the narratives that shape them.

Jacques Derrida's concept of 'deconstruction' in Of Grammatology can be applied to further examine Rosenzweig's notion of a unified divine narrative. Derrida's approach challenges the stability and definitiveness of any text, including sacred ones, by arguing that texts and meanings are inherently unstable and subject to various interpretations. This implies that even foundational religious narratives of creation, revelation, and redemption might not be as clear or consistent as traditionally understood. Such a perspective from Derrida's methodology underscores the

---

305. Riach, *Analysis of Gayatri Chakravorty Spivak's Can the Subaltern Speak?*, 6.
306. Riach, *Analysis of Gayatri Chakravorty Spivak's Can the Subaltern Speak?*, 17.
307. Riach, *Analysis of Gayatri Chakravorty Spivak's Can the Subaltern Speak?*, 13.
308. Riach, *Analysis of Gayatri Chakravorty Spivak's Can the Subaltern Speak?*, 16.
309. Riach, *Analysis of Gayatri Chakravorty Spivak's Can the Subaltern Speak?*, 20.

potential for diverse and even conflicting interpretations of what might constitute a coherent divine plan.

Derrida highlights those texts, through the act of deconstruction, reveal that presence, including divine presence, does not guarantee clarity or purity in understanding. He discusses how the divine origin of concepts does not prevent these ideas from being ambiguous or open to multiple interpretations, which means that even foundational religious axioms are not exempt from questioning and reinterpretation.[310] This notion challenges the traditional view of a transparent self-relationship with the divine, suggesting instead a complex interaction where meanings are perpetually deferred and reconfigured.

Furthermore, Derrida's work discusses the philosophical shift necessary in deconstruction, where established hierarchies and terms must be reevaluated. This process involves displacing previously dominant ideas to make space for emerging concepts that challenge old regimes and interpretations, effectively transforming the framework within which these ideas operate.[311] This approach encourages a reconsideration of how divine plans and moral narratives are understood, emphasizing the fluidity of interpretation rather than fixed meanings.

Derrida also explores the role of "differance," a concept illustrating that meanings are delayed or differentiated through the play of differences in language, further complicating straightforward interpretations of texts and ideas. This view points to a more nuanced understanding of interpretation itself, suggesting that all discourse, including that on metaphysics and divine narratives, is trapped within this web of deferred meanings.[312]

By examining the implications of deconstruction, Derrida invites a rethinking of how religious and moral narratives are constructed and understood, highlighting the potential for ambiguity and conflict within what might seem like universal truths. This critical perspective adds depth to the discussion about the nature of divine plans and the role of human understanding in interpreting these narratives, suggesting that our engagement with sacred texts and moral frameworks must acknowledge the inherent complexities and instabilities of interpretation.[313]

---

310. Derrida, *Of Grammatology*, 98.
311. Derrida, *Of Grammatology*, lxxxvii.
312. Derrida, *Of Grammatology*, xxix.
313. Derrida, *Of Grammatology*.

CHAPTER ONE

In his Ethics of Liberation, Enrique Dussel builds upon the philosophical contributions of Franz Rosenzweig by integrating the tangible realities faced by marginalized groups, which he believes should form the cornerstone of theological inquiry and liberation efforts. As Dussel elucidates in his discussion, this approach emerges from a deep engagement with the struggles of the oppressed, who he describes as the "wretched" of the world. Dussel emphasizes that liberation theology should not only arise from but also address the suffering, dignity, and resilience of those living on the margins of society.[314]

Further exploring the fabric of ethics, Dussel criticizes simplistic ethical interpretations that overlook the complex motivations driving liberation movements. He points to a blend of emotional and cultural factors rooted in the lived experiences of the oppressed as essential drivers for change, suggesting that these elements are crucial in understanding and fostering ethical behavior.[315]

Amid a backdrop of geopolitical shifts and the end of the Cold War, Dussel notes a waning of critical thought and a rise in disenchantment among the oppressed. He argues that the historical conditions of the oppressed necessitate a renewed approach to liberation that considers the shifting dynamics of power and despair, which often hinder the development of alternative social structures and impede the realization of social justice.[316]

In his further writings, Dussel advocates for a theology that not only reflects upon but actively engages with the injustices faced by the oppressed. He insists on a praxis that places the immediate and practical needs of marginalized communities at the forefront of theological discourse, aiming for a transformative impact that aligns with the principles of justice.[317]

By weaving together, the voices and experiences of those most affected by systemic injustices, Dussel's work presents a critical examination and reformation of existing theological frameworks. His focus is on creating a theology that is not only reflective but also responsive to the myriad challenges faced by the oppressed, thus ensuring their struggles are central to the pursuit of ethical and liberatory practice.[318]

314. Dussel, *Ethics of Liberation*, xiii.
315. Dussel, *Ethics of Liberation*, xviii.
316. Dussel, *Ethics of Liberation*, xx.
317. Dussel, *Ethics of Liberation*, 8.
318. Dussel, *Ethics of Liberation*.

Concluding, the interplay between Franz Rosenzweig's theological concepts and the ethical ideas of thinkers like Emmanuel Levinas and Hannah Arendt offers a multifaceted view of justice and redemption. Rosenzweig's framework, which situates individual and collective efforts towards justice within a divine narrative, is enriched by Levinas's focus on ethical relations with the "Other" and Arendt's scrutiny of ordinary actions contributing to systemic evils. This combination of perspectives encourages a broader view that recognizes both the interconnectedness and individuality within global and divine narratives of justice, challenging us to appreciate the varied and dynamic manifestations of these concepts in real-world contexts.

1.4. GLOBAL DIALOGUES ON LIBERATION

This section explores the intricate dynamics of dialogue across cultural boundaries, emphasizing the transformative potential of speech and inclusive interactions as fundamental to constructing social realities that respect and incorporate diverse cultural perspectives. Discussions by thinkers like Rosenstock-Huessy and others address how global dialogues can sometimes struggle against the entrenched power structures and historical legacies that shape international relations. They point out the challenges in achieving true cultural understanding and cooperation, advocating for a critical examination of how power and history influence dialogue, suggesting that recognizing and navigating these complexities is crucial for fostering genuine global solidarity and change.

Rosenstock-Huessy underscores the transformative power of speech and the importance of fostering open and inclusive dialogues to build understanding and solidarity across cultures. He suggests that such interactions are essential in creating social realities that embrace diverse cultural perspectives.[319] Despite the potential for these dialogues to reshape international relationships, the complexity of global interactions often reveals a stark reality where individuals are sometimes reduced to mere participants in the global economy, rather than being engaged as active contributors in shaping a universally inclusive order.[320]

The vision of a society where dialogue leads to tangible changes in the geopolitical landscape can seem idealistic when contrasted with

---

319. Rosenstock-Huessy, *Out of Revolution*, 51.
320. Rosenstock-Huessy, *Out of Revolution*, 291.

CHAPTER ONE

historical shifts that reveal a persistent centrality of powerful nations. For instance, Rosenstock-Huessy discusses the emergence of 'Eurasia,' a concept that reflects Russia's evolution into a global force, illustrating the dramatic shifts in power that can redefine global order.[321] These shifts often disrupt established perceptions, challenging the once dogmatic views of European centrality, and suggesting a dynamic reconfiguration of power that acknowledges multiple centers of influence.[322]

Furthermore, Rosenstock-Huessy explores the role of the Church in societal transformations, highlighting its dual capacity to both inspire and constrain the development of civilizations. He points out that while the Church has historically provided a framework for societal order, it has also been a site of contention and revolution, influencing profound changes in social structures.[323] This dual role is exemplified in the context of the Renaissance and the Reformation, periods marked by significant cultural and religious upheaval that reshaped European societies.[324]

Moreover, Rosenstock-Huessy's analysis extends to the cultural and political implications of historical narratives and their reinterpretation. He critiques the simplistic historical narratives that flatten complex periods into monotonous plains, arguing for a more nuanced understanding of history that recognizes the peaks and valleys of human struggle and achievement.[325] His work emphasizes the importance of maintaining a critical perspective on the narratives that shape our understanding of history and their impact on current global dynamics.

In sum, while Rosenstock-Huessy advocates for the potential of dialogue to foster global understanding and solidarity, his work also acknowledges the challenges posed by entrenched power structures and historical legacies. His insights encourage a critical examination of how dialogue and power interact in the global arena, urging a thoughtful engagement with the complexities of cultural and political exchanges that shape our world.[326]

Homi K. Bhabha's critique underscores the complexities within dialogues that ostensibly aim to foster global liberation but are often embedded within entrenched power structures, potentially perpetuating

321. Rosenstock-Huessy, *Out of Revolution*, 139.
322. Rosenstock-Huessy, *Out of Revolution*, 257.
323. Rosenstock-Huessy, *Out of Revolution*, 561.
324. Rosenstock-Huessy, *Out of Revolution*, 563.
325. Rosenstock-Huessy, *Out of Revolution*, 342.
326. Rosenstock-Huessy, *Out of Revolution*, 718.

inequalities rather than resolving them. Bhabha highlights how dialogues, while essential, require vigilance to the power dynamics at play that may influence these interactions unfavorably.[327]

He specifically points to situations where discussions about race and ethnicity become charged with underlying tensions of historical violence and victimization, complicating the potential for genuine understanding and solidarity across cultural lines. For instance, Bhabha discusses the dynamics of disrespect in the interactions between different racial groups, where the term itself becomes a flashpoint that encapsulates experiences of racialized violence and social victimization.[328] This underscores the need for a careful examination of the language and concepts used in cross-cultural dialogues to ensure they do not inadvertently reinforce the very disparities they aim to overcome.

Furthermore, Bhabha's analysis extends to how historical narratives are constructed and the perspectives they include or omit. He critiques the dominant historiographical practices that often marginalize non-Western viewpoints, as illustrated by Salman Rushdie's literary works, which challenge the conventional histories of India and Pakistan. Bhabha uses Rushdie's "The Satanic Verses" to emphasize how Western narratives frequently overlook the internal complexities and historical experiences of other cultures, leading to a skewed understanding of global interactions.[329]

Additionally, Bhabha argues for a recognition of the "interstitial intimacy" that can exist between conflicting cultural and social experiences, suggesting that true dialogue requires acknowledging and engaging with these in-between spaces of interaction. This involves a temporality of negotiation that acknowledges the historical connectedness and the contradictions between different cultural elements without forcing a simplistic resolution.[330]

Overall, Bhabha's work provides a critical framework for understanding the nuances and challenges of intercultural dialogue, advocating for a deeper engagement with the underlying historical and power dynamics that shape these discussions. This perspective is crucial for

---

327. Bhabha, *Location of Culture*.
328. Bhabha, *Location of Culture*, 3.
329. Bhabha, *Location of Culture*, 9.
330. Bhabha, *Location of Culture*, 37.

moving beyond superficial dialogues that fail to address the root causes of cultural and racial disparities in the global context.[331]

Paulo Freire's philosophy advocates for the use of education as a means to empower the oppressed and to foster liberation through dialogue. He argues that through education, individuals can articulate their experiences, which promotes a critical awareness and builds solidarity among marginalized groups.[332] This approach is encapsulated in his critique of traditional education systems, which he contrasts with a more interactive and engaging learning process.

In his discussions, Freire highlights the limitations of a system where individuals are seen merely as receptacles of knowledge. He argues that this "banking" model of education stifles critical thinking and creativity, thereby maintaining existing power structures rather than challenging them. This is seen in his observation that "the more students work at storing the deposits entrusted to them, the less they develop the critical consciousness which would result from their intervention in the world."[333] By emphasizing the active role of the oppressed in their own liberation, Freire shifts the focus from education as a mere transmission of facts to education as a practice of freedom.

Furthermore, Freire addresses the fear that often accompanies the shift toward critical consciousness, noting that participants in educational programs sometimes perceive this awakening as a threat to their current understanding of the world, which he describes as a fear of freedom. He writes, "Critical consciousness, they say, is anarchic,"[334] reflecting the anxiety that comes with questioning long-held beliefs and systems.

The journey toward empowerment and liberation, according to Freire, involves not only the rejection of the oppressor's model but also a redefinition of self-awareness among the oppressed. He discusses the complex dynamics within revolutionary movements, where the oppressed must constantly navigate between being influenced by the oppressor and asserting their own agency. This is encapsulated in his analysis of the revolutionary process, "Even revolution, which transforms a concrete situation of oppression by establishing the process of liberation,"[335] underscoring the ongoing struggle within liberation move-

---

331. Bhabha, *Location of Culture*.
332. Freire, *Pedagogy of the Oppressed*.
333. Freire, *Pedagogy of the Oppressed*, 60.
334. Freire, *Pedagogy of the Oppressed*, 19.
335. Freire, *Pedagogy of the Oppressed*, 31.

ments to not only change external conditions but also internal perceptions of self and society.

In summary, Freire's work provides a framework for understanding education as a critical tool in the struggle for liberation. By fostering dialogue that encourages critical thinking and collective awareness, education can become a transformative force that not only informs but also empowers individuals to challenge and change oppressive structures in their lives and communities.

Gayatri Chakravorty Spivak's seminal question, "Can the Subaltern Speak?", highlights a critical challenge within dialogues intended to foster inclusivity and liberation. Spivak suggests that hegemonic structures often silence or marginalize the most oppressed voices, thereby questioning the effectiveness of these dialogues in achieving true inclusivity.[336] This concern is crucial in understanding the limitations of well-intentioned efforts to give voice to those at the margins of society.

Spivak's analysis emphasizes that the world's poorest and most marginalized populations often lack a voice in societal dialogues. She argues that local elites—such as officials, educators, and religious leaders—and even Western scholars are unable to authentically represent these silenced voices. This inability stems from the inherent power dynamics and cultural disconnects that skew the representation of subaltern perspectives.[337]

Moreover, Spivak's work is framed within a broader critique of postcolonial studies and its methodologies. She challenges the assumptions that underpin scholarly efforts to speak for the subaltern, thereby questioning the very framework that seeks to elevate these voices. Her critique extends to the ways in which academic and intellectual endeavors often reproduce the power structures they aim to dismantle.[338]

This critique is grounded in a deep understanding of the theoretical underpinnings provided by thinkers like Jacques Derrida and Michel Foucault, who influence Spivak's thoughts on the intersection of power, knowledge, and representation. Their theories inform her skepticism towards claims of objective reality outside of discourse, emphasizing instead that reality is constructed through language and that various power claims shape our understanding of truth.[339]

---

336. Riach, *Analysis of Gayatri Chakravorty Spivak's Can the Subaltern Speak?*.
337. Riach, *Analysis of Gayatri Chakravorty Spivak's Can the Subaltern Speak?*, 9.
338. Riach, *Analysis of Gayatri Chakravorty Spivak's Can the Subaltern Speak?*, 13.
339. Riach, *Analysis of Gayatri Chakravorty Spivak's Can the Subaltern Speak?*, 29.

Spivak's approach, deeply rooted in deconstructive analysis, not only challenges the ability of the subaltern to speak but also the capacity of the supposed intermediaries to listen and convey subaltern experiences without distortion. Her work compels a reevaluation of how narratives are constructed and whose voices are prioritized or suppressed in the quest for liberation and representation.[340]

Overall, Spivak's examination of postcolonial discourse and her questioning of the subaltern's ability to speak serve as a crucial reminder of the complexities involved in attempting to understand and represent oppressed populations. Her observations call for a more thoughtful and reflective approach to dialogue and liberation, one that critically assesses the roles of both speaker and listener within entrenched hegemonic structures.[341]

Jürgen Habermas emphasizes the importance of adhering to principles of communicative rationality to ensure that dialogues genuinely foster liberation. He posits that for discussions to be effective, all participants must have equal opportunities to contribute, and efforts should be made to reduce power imbalances that could skew communication.[342]

Habermas explores the complex dynamics between the rationalization of the lifeworld and the challenges this poses to the communicative infrastructure. He suggests that while attempts to apply various theoretical approaches such as genetic structuralism have enriched our understanding, they also highlight the burdens placed on communicative practices within societal frameworks.[343] This observation calls for a careful balance in dialogue that acknowledges the intricate interplay of sociological and psychological dimensions.

Furthermore, Habermas delves into the historical and philosophical underpinnings that have shaped critical theory, notably its Marxist roots. He discusses the evolution of critical theory, initially grounded in a belief in the revolutionary potential of production forces, pointing out that such frameworks must continually adapt to remain relevant in analyzing modern societal structures.[344]

In addressing the relationship between individual agency and societal structures, Habermas argues for a model of communication that

---

340. Riach, *Analysis of Gayatri Chakravorty Spivak's Can the Subaltern Speak?*, 34.
341. Riach, *Analysis of Gayatri Chakravorty Spivak's Can the Subaltern Speak?*, 12.
342. Habermas, *Theory of Communicative Action*.
343. Habermas, *Theory of Communicative Action*, 378.
344. Habermas, *Theory of Communicative Action*, 382.

acknowledges both the subjective and the intersubjective realms. He critiques earlier phenomenological approaches for their limited engagement with the communicative aspects of the lifeworld, advocating instead for a perspective that fully recognizes the role of language and interaction in shaping human experience.[345]

Moreover, Habermas's discussion extends to the material and symbolic dimensions of the lifeworld, emphasizing the necessity of understanding both the functional connections within societal structures and their implications for communication and understanding.[346]

Overall, Habermas advocates for a comprehensive approach to dialogue that not only considers the theoretical and practical aspects of communication but also actively works to mitigate the distortions introduced by existing power structures. This approach underscores the importance of maintaining a critical perspective on the process of dialogue itself, ensuring it remains a tool for genuine liberation rather than a perpetuator of existing inequalities.[347]

Addressing language barriers and cultural differences is crucial for creating effective international coalitions. Translation services and cultural exchange programs are commonly employed to bridge these gaps. However, Martha C. Nussbaum warns that translation is not a neutral process—it can sometimes distort the original meanings and intentions, which might complicate dialogues rather than facilitate them.[348]

Nussbaum further explains that even well-intentioned translation efforts can unintentionally alter messages, potentially leading to misunderstandings instead of clearer communication. She stresses the importance of careful translation processes to avoid inadvertently changing the fundamental meanings of dialogues or texts in cross-cultural interactions.[349] Moreover, she discusses the particular challenges in conveying complex global issues such as justice and fairness through translation, noting that these concepts often have deep cultural and philosophical bases that are difficult to capture in another language. This complexity calls for a meticulous and thoughtful approach to translation, aiming to

---

345. Habermas, *Theory of Communicative Action*, 131.
346. Habermas, *Theory of Communicative Action*, 256.
347. Habermas, *Theory of Communicative Action*, 378.
348. Nussbaum, *Frontiers of Justice*.
349. Nussbaum, *Frontiers of Justice*, 6.

preserve the integrity of the original content while making it accessible to a broader audience.[350]

Echoing Nussbaum's concerns, Walter Benjamin delves into the intrinsic limitations of translation, suggesting that it can never fully capture the essence of the original text. This has significant implications for cross-cultural communication, especially in the contexts of international coalitions and liberation movements.[351]

Benjamin contends that translation involves more than the mere transfer of words; it is an interaction between languages that can profoundly affect the translator's own linguistic framework. He argues that translators should not merely preserve the current state of their own language but allow it to be significantly influenced by the foreign text. This approach encourages a more dynamic and reflective engagement with the original material, potentially leading to a richer understanding.[352]

Moreover, Benjamin suggests that the ultimate goal of translation should not be seen as a direct reproduction of the source but as a form of interpretation that complements and enhances the understanding of the original. He advocates for translations that resonate with the original's intent, creating a harmonious relationship between the source and the translation, rather than a mere mimicry.[353]

This thoughtful understanding challenges the view of translation as a straightforward communicative act and underscores the complexity of conveying detailed meanings across different linguistic and cultural contexts. Benjamin's thoughts highlight the need for translators to engage deeply with both the source and target languages, encouraging a transformative rather than a transactional approach to translation.[354]

Overall, the reflections of both Nussbaum and Benjamin emphasize the need for sensitivity and adaptability in bridging linguistic divides. Their discussions prompt a reconsideration of how languages interact within the translation process, suggesting that this endeavor can significantly influence both the message conveyed and the languages involved.[355]

---

350. Nussbaum, *Frontiers of Justice*, 21.
351. Benjamin, *Illuminations*.
352. Benjamin, *Illuminations*, 81.
353. Benjamin, *Illuminations*, 79.
354. Benjamin, *Illuminations*, 77.
355. Benjamin, *Illuminations*, 47.

Incorporating educational programs that promote intercultural dialogue, as advocated by bell hooks, is essential for developing the skills needed for effective communication across cultural boundaries.[356] Hooks emphasizes that education can be liberating, offering a mentorship that understands learning as a transformative experience, fundamentally shifting the educational encounters from strictly institutional to personally and socially enlightening.[357]

Moreover, hooks explore the concept of pleasure in learning, advocating for an educational environment where learning is not only informative but also engaging and enjoyable. This approach challenges traditional views and emphasizes the need for an educational setting that fosters critical thinking and enjoyment as integral to effective learning.[358]

Furthermore, hooks note the limited diversity in discussions around critical and feminist pedagogies, which are often dominated by white individuals. She highlights her own efforts to bring diverse voices into these discussions, drawing on a blend of anticolonial, critical, and feminist pedagogies to enrich educational practices.[359]

hooks also address the challenges educators face in adapting to diverse educational environments, acknowledging that many lack the necessary skills to effectively engage in culturally varied settings. This gap underscores the importance of developing pedagogical strategies that are inclusive and responsive to diverse student backgrounds.[360]

In summary, hooks advocates for educational practices that not only address but embrace cultural differences, which is crucial for preparing students and educators alike to navigate and contribute to a globally interconnected world. Her work urges an ongoing reassessment of educational strategies to ensure they are inclusive, engaging, and effective in promoting genuine intercultural dialogue.[361]

Conversely, Henry A. Giroux critiques the notion that educational reforms alone can effectively dismantle systemic oppression. He argues that such reforms are insufficient unless they confront the foundational power structures, suggesting that without this confrontation, educational initiatives are likely to result in superficial changes that do not tackle the

---

356. hooks, *Teaching to Transgress*.
357. hooks, *Teaching to Transgress*, 6.
358. hooks, *Teaching to Transgress*, 7.
359. hooks, *Teaching to Transgress*, 10.
360. hooks, *Teaching to Transgress*, 41.
361. hooks, *Teaching to Transgress*, 129.

root causes of inequality.³⁶² Giroux emphasizes the importance of critically examining forms of knowledge and social practices, advocating for a pedagogy that situates knowledge within specific historical contexts and seeks to uncover the underlying human interests it serves. This approach aims to make educational engagements more relevant and enlightening, promoting a deeper understanding among students.³⁶³

Giroux further engages with the historical and philosophical underpinnings of his critique by referencing the Frankfurt School, which identified crises in reason linked to broader crises in science and society. This connection illustrates how societal pressures can transform rationality into irrationality, providing a deeper context for the challenges within the educational system.³⁶⁴

Moreover, Giroux explores the tension between individuals and societal structures through the lens of the Frankfurt School. Despite the school's criticisms of mainstream societal frameworks, it offers valuable tools for understanding the conflicts inherent in the educational system, particularly through its analysis of the 'hidden curriculum' that influences educational outcomes through implicit norms and values.³⁶⁵

In conclusion, Giroux calls for a comprehensive reevaluation of education that extends beyond mere curriculum changes. He advocates for challenging the underlying power dynamics and ideological assumptions that perpetuate inequalities, aiming for educational reforms that can genuinely contribute to transformative societal change.³⁶⁶

Interfaith dialogues serve as a crucial avenue for building international coalitions, a point underscored by Eboo Patel, who emphasizes the importance of pluralism and social justice in these interactions. Patel observes that the field of interfaith work is complex and often contentious, marked by diverse and sometimes hostile reactions to religious diversity. This complexity highlights the need for dialogues that do not occur on neutral ground but rather within a context where differences are openly acknowledged and addressed.³⁶⁷

Furthermore, Patel notes that when young people from various religious backgrounds collaborate on volunteer projects, they become not

---

362. Giroux, *Theory and Resistance in Education*.
363. Giroux, *Theory and Resistance in Education*, 161.
364. Giroux, *Theory and Resistance in Education*, 13.
365. Giroux, *Theory and Resistance in Education*, 48.
366. Giroux, *Theory and Resistance in Education*, 107.
367. Patel, *Sacred Ground*, xi.

only committed to the cause of interfaith cooperation but also ambassadors for its importance. However, he acknowledges that such activities, while crucial, are insufficient on their own. This realization has spurred the development of new strategies aimed at enhancing the effectiveness of interfaith efforts.[368]

Additionally, Patel shares his personal motivation for founding an interfaith organization, which was inspired by his studies in the sociology of religion and a trip to southern Spain to explore its rich religious history. This personal journey underscores the deep cultural and historical connections that can inspire contemporary interfaith initiatives.[369]

While Patel's reflections underscore the necessity of continuous innovation and personal commitment in fostering understanding and cooperation among different faith communities, Edward Said's critique in "Orientalism" offers a cautionary perspective. Said warns against the romanticization or oversimplification of religion's role in cultural interactions, noting that such approaches can inadvertently reinforce stereotypes and deepen divisions rather than fostering genuine understanding.[370] Said examines how Western perceptions of Islam and the Orient have often been shaped more by European academic and governmental institutions than by a true understanding of the cultures themselves.[371]

Said also discusses the aggressive nature of cultural interpretations under colonial enterprises, such as Napoleon's expedition in Egypt, which sought to reshape Egypt through a modern French lens rather than understanding its own historical and cultural context. This imposition of Western frameworks on Eastern cultures often distorts and oversimplifies complex civilizations.[372]

Moreover, Said highlights the analogical constraints faced by Christian thinkers when trying to understand Islam, leading to significant misconceptions and a reluctance in the West to accept Muslim accounts of their own faith.[373]

In summary, both Patel and Said highlight the complex dynamics involved in interfaith dialogues and cultural interactions. While Patel focuses on the need for practical engagement and a personal connection

368. Patel, *Sacred Ground*, xii.
369. Patel, *Sacred Ground*, xiii.
370. Said, *Orientalism*.
371. Said, *Orientalism*, 164.
372. Said, *Orientalism*, 84.
373. Said, *Orientalism*, 60.

CHAPTER ONE

to the principles of pluralism and social justice, Said emphasizes the importance of critical self-awareness and careful engagement to avoid perpetuating misunderstandings and biases. Together, their insights provide a comprehensive view of the challenges and opportunities in building effective international coalitions through interfaith dialogues.

Adding to the dialogue on global coalitions, Chandra Talpade Mohanty provides a critical feminist perspective. Mohanty critiques the tendency of Western feminist movements to impose their frameworks on women in the Global South, often leading to the erasure of local struggles and unique contexts. She advocates for a context-specific approach to building solidarity, emphasizing the importance of recognizing the diversity of women's experiences across different cultures.[374]

Mohanty argues that last century, while significant for the maturation of feminist ideas and movements, also witnessed the decolonization of the Third World, the rise of capitalism, and the splintering of the communist Second World. These historical contexts are crucial for understanding the intersections of feminist struggles with broader socioeconomic and political movements.[375]

Furthermore, Mohanty emphasizes the necessity of a feminist politics that not only challenges the status quo but also envisions transformative strategies. She advocates for an antiracist feminist framework that is deeply rooted in decolonization and committed to an anticapitalist critique, which she believes is essential for addressing contemporary global issues.[376]

In her work, Mohanty also highlights the influential role of feminists from the Third World/South, whose perspectives helped shape her understanding of the relationship between feminism and nationalism, and the centrality of decolonization in feminist thought. Figures like Kumari Jayawardena and Nawal el Saadawi have been pivotal in theorizing the specific positions of women from Asia, the Middle East, Latin America, and Africa within feminist discourse.[377]

Overall, Mohanty's critique underscores the need for global liberation movements to be highly attentive to the specific needs and contexts of different communities. By advocating for a nuanced approach that respects the diverse experiences of women worldwide, Mohanty's work

---

374. Mohanty, *Feminism Without Borders*.
375. Mohanty, *Feminism Without Borders*, 2.
376. Mohanty, *Feminism Without Borders*, 3.
377. Mohanty, *Feminism Without Borders*, 5.

challenges the one-size-fits-all approach often adopted in global feminist movements. Her analysis highlights the complexity of building effective and truly inclusive international coalitions.[378]

Kwame Anthony Appiah's exploration of cosmopolitanism adds a significant dimension to the discourse on global ethical commitments and cultural respect. Appiah argues that while building connections across cultures is essential, these connections must be rooted in mutual respect and understanding, challenging the notion of a homogenizing universalism.[379] He suggests that the idea of universal agreement, even if appealing, often overlooks cultural specificities and the real challenges of cross-cultural understanding.[380]

Appiah critically examines the historical consequences of enforcing universalism without toleration, citing the religious wars in Europe as a stark example of how such ideologies can lead to conflict rather than peace. He emphasizes that a universalist approach that lacks tolerance can easily turn destructive.[381]

Further, Appiah discusses the importance of recognizing and valuing the distinctiveness of various cultural practices and beliefs. He stresses that cosmopolitanism should not demand homogeneity but should celebrate differences, fostering an environment where diverse cultural expressions are not only acknowledged but also appreciated.[382]

Moreover, Appiah elaborates on the concept of cosmopolitanism, which he views as an ethos of global citizenship where individuals can appreciate and engage with cultural diversity without losing sight of their own identities. This perspective encourages a deeper engagement with the world that is both inclusive and respectful.[383]

Overall, Appiah's work underscores the need for a balance between global cooperation and the preservation of cultural diversity. He advocates for a cosmopolitanism that respects individual differences and supports the idea that true liberation and ethical global interaction are based on understanding and respecting the complex identities and beliefs of others.[384]

378. Mohanty, *Feminism Without Borders*, 7.
379. Appiah, *Cosmopolitanism*.
380. Appiah, *Cosmopolitanism*, 57.
381. Appiah, *Cosmopolitanism*, 140.
382. Appiah, *Cosmopolitanism*, xv.
383. Appiah, *Cosmopolitanism*, xiv.
384. Appiah, *Cosmopolitanism*, xv.

In conclusion, the discussions highlighted in this section reflect the complex interplay between cultural respect, historical awareness, and the pursuit of genuine dialogue in building effective global coalitions. The viewpoints from thinkers like Rosenstock-Huessy, Bhabha, Freire, Spivak, Habermas, Nussbaum, Benjamin, hooks, Giroux, Patel, Mohanty, and Appiah emphasize the necessity of engaging with both the opportunities and challenges presented by cross-cultural interactions. These perspectives collectively underscore the importance of fostering environments where diverse voices are not only heard but also integrated into the fabric of global dialogues and actions.

Moreover, the underlying theme across these discussions is the call for a deeper engagement with the specific contexts and experiences of different communities. This approach is crucial for avoiding the pitfalls of imposing overarching narratives or solutions that fail to address the detailed realities of global diversity. By advocating for an approach that respects and values the unique cultural, historical, and individual identities involved, these thinkers provide a roadmap for building more inclusive and responsive global frameworks. Their contributions highlight the critical need for ongoing vigilance, thoughtful interaction, and a commitment to justice that transcends traditional boundaries and assumptions, driving us towards a more equitable global society.

1.5. IDENTITY, FREEDOM, AND CRITICAL VOICES

In the exploration of liberation within this section, we introduce a spectrum of thoughts that push the boundaries of traditional conceptions of freedom. By engaging with the theories of Martha Nussbaum, Charles Taylor, and Judith Butler, the discussion transcends typical political and social frameworks to tackle broader questions of personal growth, cultural recognition, and economic involvement. Each thinker offers a unique perspective on achieving a more holistic freedom, suggesting that true liberation involves not only overcoming oppression but also the creation of spaces for authentic self-expression and meaningful societal contributions. This approach seeks to redefine freedom as an expansive, interactive process rather than a static state.

In exploring the concept of liberation, this section introduces a range of perspectives that collectively challenge and expand the traditional boundaries of what it means to be free. Drawing on the ideas of thinkers like Martha Nussbaum, Charles Taylor, and Judith Butler, the discussion moves beyond conventional political and social frameworks to incorporate deeper questions of personal development, cultural recognition, and economic participation. Each philosopher contributes a distinct viewpoint on how to achieve a more comprehensive form of freedom, suggesting that true liberation is not only about overcoming oppression but also about creating opportunities for genuine self-expression and societal contribution.

Martha Nussbaum's capabilities approach significantly redefines the traditional understanding of liberation, extending it beyond simple political or social freedoms. She argues that true liberation requires enabling individuals to develop and utilize essential capabilities, such as health, education, and personal autonomy, which are foundational for a fulfilling life. This is elaborated in her work where she emphasizes the role of these capabilities in ensuring individuals can live lives they value.[385]

Nussbaum's theory stresses that mere freedom from oppression is insufficient if individuals lack the practical means to utilize their freedoms. She points out that policies aimed at enhancing human capabilities necessarily contribute to real freedom, allowing individuals to lead lives characterized by choice and empowerment. This involves not only providing access to necessary resources but also ensuring that individuals have genuine opportunities to participate fully in economic, social, and political life.[386]

In her approach, Nussbaum also highlights the importance of government and societal structures in supporting the development of these capabilities. She advocates for a model of governance that actively addresses inequalities and supports the growth of essential human functions through thoughtful policies. These policies, according to Nussbaum, should be targeted at leveling the playing field in terms of access to necessary services and opportunities, thereby enhancing the overall capability of individuals to function as free and equal members of society.[387]

Ultimately, Nussbaum's capabilities approach broadens the scope of what it means to be truly liberated. It shifts the focus from an absence of restraint to a presence of enabling conditions that foster substantial freedom and personal growth. This comprehensive view of liberation

---

385. Nussbaum, *Creating Capabilities*, x.
386. Nussbaum, *Creating Capabilities*, xi.
387. Nussbaum, *Creating Capabilities*, xii.

not only calls for the removal of barriers but also the proactive creation of positive conditions that allow for the realization of human potential, making it a pivotal framework for understanding and achieving genuine liberation in contemporary society.[388]

Seyla Benhabib critically addresses the challenges of cultural integration and the concept of modernity through a feminist and multicultural lens in her book, "The Claims of Culture: Equality and Diversity in the Global Era." She argues against the conventional view that modernity is a singular, homogeneous phenomenon, instead proposing that modernity is experienced differently across various cultural contexts. Benhabib emphasizes the need for a more inclusive understanding that respects and integrates diverse cultural narratives, thus redefining modernity as a pluralistic and dynamic process.[389]

In discussing the interaction between cultural fragments and personal identity, Benhabib critiques social movements that adopt cultural elements without fully addressing the underlying identity dilemmas these elements represent. She points out that such approaches often fail to resolve the deeper issues of identity and difference, leading to a paradox where movements aim to preserve a notion of purity within fundamentally impure traditions.[390] This critical viewpoint highlights the complexities of cultural identity in the context of modernity and liberation.

Benhabib also delves into the role of discourse ethics in multicultural societies, arguing that it allows individuals to bring their personal and moral dilemmas into public discussions without the constraints of hypothetical ideals. This approach, she suggests, fosters a more genuine dialogue that reflects the real-world moral conflicts people face, thereby facilitating a more effective integration of diverse cultural perspectives into the mainstream discourse on modernity.[391]

Her concept of interactive universalism further extends the application of discourse ethics to address the challenges of multiculturalism directly. Benhabib posits that cultures provide not only narratives but also practices that shape our interactions and self-perceptions. This framework suggests that engaging with these cultural narratives and practices

---

388. Nussbaum, *Creating Capabilities*, xv.
389. Benhabib, *Claims of Culture*.
390. Benhabib, *Claims of Culture*, 11.
391. Benhabib, *Claims of Culture*, 13.

is essential for understanding and navigating the complexities of identity and modernity in a globally interconnected world.[392]

Furthermore, Benhabib addresses the practical implications of her theories in multicultural and pluralistic societies. She argues for the co-existence of multiple jurisdictional systems to accommodate cultural and religious diversity without compromising fundamental normative principles. This approach underscores her advocacy for a pluralistic model of democracy that respects and integrates diverse cultural traditions while maintaining a commitment to universalist ethical standards.[393]

By critically examining these themes, Benhabib contributes significantly to the discourse on modernity, culture, and liberation, challenging traditional views and advocating for a more inclusive and dynamically understood modernity that acknowledges the rich tapestry of global cultural diversity.

Nancy Fraser in her work "Justice Interruptus" critically examines the shift in social justice from a primarily economic to a cultural focus. She suggests that modern social movements have transitioned from class-based struggles centered on economic redistribution to ones more concerned with cultural recognition and identity.[394] This reflects a broader change in the political landscape from a redistribution-focused to a recognition-focused framework. Fraser argues that true social justice must address both the economic disparities and the cultural recognition to effectively combat systemic injustices, proposing a more integrated approach that considers both redistribution and recognition as essential to achieving justice.[395]

Further elaborating on this dual approach, Fraser highlights the limitations of focusing solely on cultural identity, which can neglect underlying economic inequalities. She stresses the importance of not letting the recognition of cultural diversity overshadow the crucial need for economic equity, which remains a pervasive issue across many societies.[396] According to Fraser, addressing these intertwined aspects requires a critical reassessment of how social policies and practices can more

---

392. Benhabib, *Claims of Culture*, 14.
393. Benhabib, *Claims of Culture*, 19.
394. Fraser, *Justice Interruptus*, 2.
395. Fraser, *Justice Interruptus*, 3.
396. Fraser, *Justice Interruptus*, 4.

holistically approach issues of justice to include both economic redistribution and cultural recognition.³⁹⁷

Fraser's critique extends to the theoretical frameworks used to understand justice, suggesting that neither redistribution nor recognition alone can adequately address the complexities of contemporary social injustices. Her work calls for a combined approach that incorporates both elements, thereby providing a more comprehensive solution to the challenges faced by diverse societies today.³⁹⁸ This holistic view is crucial for developing a more effective and inclusive social justice strategy that transcends traditional boundaries and addresses the multifaceted nature of oppression.³⁹⁹

Judith Butler's critique of gender norms and identity challenges traditional notions of liberation, emphasizing the performative nature of gender and advocating for a liberation that dismantles normative constraints, allowing for more fluid and diverse identity expressions.⁴⁰⁰ She builds upon Monique Wittig's assertions that challenging gender at its most fundamental levels involves contesting the very grammar that constructs gender identity. This demands a recognition of the complexities and ruses embedded within linguistic structures that define and confine gender norms, urging a reevaluation of clarity in the context of identity politics.⁴⁰¹

Butler further explores the intersection of heterosexuality and phallogocentrism, questioning where these frameworks converge and where they can be disrupted. She suggests that language itself manufactures the notion of "sex" as a binary, supporting a structural system that perpetuates gender distinctions and heteronormative assumptions.⁴⁰²

In her examination of multicultural societies, Butler proposes a concept of 'interactive universalism,' a reformulation of discourse ethics that acknowledges the roles narratives and practices play in shaping identities. This approach facilitates encounters where individuals can engage with each other's differences, thereby fostering a more inclusive

---

397. Fraser, *Justice Interruptus*, 5.
398. Fraser, *Justice Interruptus*, 6.
399. Fraser, *Justice Interruptus*, 12.
400. Butler, *Gender Trouble*.
401. Butler, *Gender Trouble*, xx.
402. Butler, *Gender Trouble*, xxxii.

understanding of identity that accommodates multiplicity within social frameworks.[403]

Moreover, Butler contends with the legal and institutional frameworks that govern cultural and religious diversity, arguing for a pluralistic approach to societal design. This design should accommodate various traditions without violating essential normative conditions, thus allowing for a more equitable integration of diverse cultural identities within a universal framework of justice.[404] Through these observations, Butler extends her critique of gender norms to a broader critique of the structural constraints that govern identity and expression, advocating for a transformative approach to liberation that encompasses both individual and collective dimensions of freedom.

Amartya Sen enriches the discourse on liberation by associating it with the ability to make meaningful choices and exert agency, critiquing the traditional view that equates liberation solely with economic wealth. He argues that true freedom involves enabling individuals to pursue a life they value through expanded capabilities, thereby emphasizing the critical role of agency and active participation in economic life beyond just acquiring material wealth.[405]

In his book, Sen explains that understanding freedom requires recognizing the diverse capabilities that contribute to a fulfilling life. This includes not just economic transactions but also social interactions, educational achievements, and political participation, which collectively enable a person to live with dignity and choice.[406] His approach critiques the reductionist view that limits freedom to economic prosperity and argues for a broader interpretation that acknowledges multiple dimensions of human development.

Moreover, Sen discusses the importance of public policy in enhancing individual capabilities. He suggests that effective policies should aim not only to alleviate poverty but also to expand the freedoms that people enjoy, thus fostering an environment where individuals can genuinely thrive. This shift from a mere economic focus to a broader developmental perspective underscores the interconnectedness of various freedoms—from political rights to social opportunities.[407]

403. Butler, *Gender Trouble*, xxxiii.
404. Butler, *Gender Trouble*, xix.
405. Sen, *Development as Freedom*.
406. Sen, *Development as Freedom*, 24, 58.
407. Sen, *Development as Freedom*, 63, 73.

CHAPTER ONE

Sen's ideas on the capability approach challenge the conventional metrics of development and liberation. He stresses that freedom is not just the absence of restraint but the presence of enabling conditions that empower individuals to lead the lives they choose. By advocating for a comprehensive framework that integrates economic, social, and political dimensions, Sen reshapes our understanding of what it means to be truly free, urging a focus on the substantive freedoms that define a dignified and fulfilling human existence.[408]

Slavoj Žižek, integrating psychoanalytic and Marxist analysis, critically examines the commodification of cultural rebellion within capitalist societies. He underscores the need for profound engagement with liberation movements and calls for a comprehensive reassessment of societal norms.[409]

Žižek draws attention to the plight of individuals who exist on the margins of society, akin to Giorgio Agamben›s concept of Homo sacer—people who are alive yet not fully recognized as part of the social order. He exemplifies this with the uncertain status of Afghan prisoners at Guantanamo Bay, highlighting how they illustrate the broader condition of those excluded from the protections afforded to full citizens.[410]

Further, he explores the roles of humanitarian aid and military intervention in defining these margins, questioning whether the international community's response to crises is one of aid or aggression, as seen in the ambiguous deliverances from American planes over Afghanistan—either bombs or food parcels.[411]

Žižek also critiques the conventional separation between human rights and citizens› rights, challenging the sufficiency of global human rights frameworks to protect those regarded as Homo sacer. He argues for a critical reevaluation of democracy itself, urging that the analysis of Homo sacer not be diluted but used to question the foundational principles of democratic societies.[412] Through this critical lens, Žižek not only calls for awareness but also advocates for actionable change in addressing the profound disparities and ideological manipulations within global politics.

Cornel West, drawing from critical race theory, focuses on the intricate relationships between race, power, and social justice. He critiques

408. Sen, *Development as Freedom*, 75, xi.
409. Žižek, *Welcome to the Desert of the Real!*
410. Žižek, *Welcome to the Desert of the Real!*, 91.
411. Žižek, *Welcome to the Desert of the Real!*, 94.
412. Žižek, *Welcome to the Desert of the Real!*, 97.

both structural and cultural forms of oppression and calls for a comprehensive approach to social change that integrates racial justice.[413]

West discusses the complex dynamics of racial authenticity and the ethical and political contexts that shape these identities. He emphasizes how racial reasoning often obscures deeper issues of interest and community alignment, leading to a superficial engagement with racial issues that fails to challenge entrenched structures.[414]

Highlighting the manipulation of racial discourse in politics, West critiques the superficial use of racial reasoning by political figures, which serves to maintain the status quo rather than addressing the root causes of racial injustice in American society.[415]

Moreover, West argues that the notion of "blackness" cannot be understood independently of a racialized society that perpetuates racist degradation and exploitation. This understanding challenges simplistic notions of racial identity and pushes for a deeper examination of how racial identities are constructed and used within broader socio-political frameworks.[416]

Additionally, West is critical of the weak efforts toward racial justice and substantive redistributive measures in society. He links attacks on policies like affirmative action directly to broader resistance against redistributive efforts, arguing that such resistance not only exacerbates black social misery but also stifles middle-class black efforts to promote social equity.[417] Through these insights, West advocates for a radical re-evaluation of societal norms to ensure racial justice is central to social transformation.

In conclusion, this section synthesizes a variety of perspectives on liberation that challenge traditional notions of freedom by integrating critical, cultural, and ethical dimensions. Martha Nussbaum's capabilities approach emphasizes the necessity of fostering individual potential through enhanced opportunities and support structures, focusing on personal development and societal participation. Seyla Benhabib critiques the narrow definitions of modernity and argues for a more inclusive view that accommodates the complexities of cultural diversity. Nancy Fraser's dual focus on economic redistribution and cultural recognition seeks a

---

413. West, Race Matters.
414. West, Race Matters, 40.
415. West, Race Matters, 48.
416. West, Race Matters, 39.
417. West, Race Matters, 96.

CHAPTER ONE

more balanced approach to social justice, highlighting the interconnected nature of these issues. Judith Butler challenges existing gender norms and advocates for a broader, more flexible understanding of identity, encouraging a dismantling of normative constraints. Amartya Sen shifts the dialogue on liberation towards a broader appreciation of human capabilities and the diverse elements that contribute to a life of dignity and choice. Slavoj Žižek emphasizes the need for a deep engagement with global societal issues, pushing for a critical reassessment of democracy and human rights. Cornel West brings a critical race theory perspective, stressing the importance of addressing both structural and cultural forms of racial oppression to achieve comprehensive social change. Together, these viewpoints offer a multifaceted framework for understanding and promoting liberation in a way that is responsive to both individual needs and societal dynamics.

1.6. CONCLUSION

The discussion in this chapter reveals that understanding liberation requires engaging with a broad range of theological, philosophical, and social perspectives. Franz Rosenzweig's approach to liberation, which emphasizes divine action and human responsibility, provides a foundational framework for considering how theology interacts with social justice. Rosenzweig's notion of "Creation out of nothing" suggests that liberation is an ongoing, unfolding process, requiring continuous human engagement in both spiritual and practical realms.[418] This perspective ties theological reflection directly to the real-world struggles against oppression, offering a vision of liberation that is not confined to religious or theoretical discourse but actively seeks transformation.

Rosenzweig's emphasis on the collaborative nature of liberation challenges individuals and communities to recognize their responsibility in shaping history. His ideas of ethical responsibility and communal practices, as explored by scholars like Robert Gibbs and Steven Kepnes, encourage a theological vision that integrates individual and collective efforts in addressing systemic injustices.[419] This theological framework creates a basis for engaging with contemporary issues of social justice, encouraging faith-based communities to take action in the face of oppression.

---

418. Ochs, *Another Reformation*.
419. Kepnes, *Jewish Liturgical Reasoning*.

At the same time, thinkers like Marx offer a more materialistic view of oppression, focusing on the structural and economic dimensions of social inequality. Marx's analysis of class struggle introduces a secular framework that emphasizes the role of systemic exploitation in maintaining power dynamics.[420] This view complements Rosenzweig's theological reflections, offering practical insights into how power operates within societal structures. By recognizing the importance of both spiritual and material dimensions of oppression, this chapter highlights the need for an integrated approach to liberation.

The contribution of Paulo Freire to the conversation on liberation is critical. His concept of praxis, which combines reflection and action, emphasizes the importance of education as a tool for social transformation.[421] Freire argues that oppressed communities must be empowered to recognize their own agency and take collective action to challenge the structures of domination. This idea resonates with Rosenzweig's emphasis on human responsibility and underscores the importance of practical engagement in the process of liberation.

Foucault's theories of power and resistance further enrich this conversation. Foucault's concept of "biopolitics" examines how power operates through societal institutions, shaping individual identities and actions.[422] His analysis of how power circulates within social systems provides a structural lens through which to view oppression, complementing the more existential and theological perspectives offered by thinkers like Rosenzweig and Bultmann. Foucault's work invites us to consider how resistance to oppression can be organized not only through direct action but also through challenging the knowledge systems that sustain power relations.

Judith Butler's exploration of vulnerability introduces another dimension to the discussion of liberation. Butler's work highlights how marginalized groups experience precarity, a condition that requires immediate attention to ensure their survival.[423] By emphasizing the material conditions of oppression, Butler aligns with Freire's emphasis on praxis and Rosenzweig's call for active engagement with tradition and the world. Her work also underscores the necessity of addressing the immediate

---

420. Löwith, *Meaning in History*.
421. Freire, *Pedagogy of the Oppressed*.
422. Foucault, *Discipline and Punish*.
423. Butler, *Precarious Life*.

CHAPTER ONE

needs of oppressed communities while working toward long-term structural change.

Amartya Sen's capabilities approach adds to the conversation by reframing liberation in terms of the opportunities available to individuals to lead lives they have reason to value.[424] Sen's focus on public reasoning and democratic engagement aligns with Rosenzweig's vision of communal responsibility. His work emphasizes the importance of creating conditions that allow individuals and communities to flourish, thereby offering a practical framework for thinking about liberation in both spiritual and societal terms.

Liberation theologians like Leonardo Boff and Gustavo Gutiérrez extend these philosophical and theological reflections by emphasizing the necessity of linking personal faith with collective action. Boff critiques Bultmann's focus on individual existential decisions, arguing that true liberation theology must confront the socio-political dimensions of oppression.[425] Gutiérrez similarly incorporates socio-economic analysis into his theological framework, advocating for a faith that is lived out in solidarity with the oppressed.[426]

James Cone, a key figure in black liberation theology, further expands the dialogue by focusing on the specific experiences of African Americans in their struggle against systemic racism. Cone's work critiques traditional theological frameworks for neglecting the realities of racial oppression, calling for a more engaged and relevant approach to theology.[427] His emphasis on the need for theology to address the lived experiences of oppressed communities offers a compelling argument for why liberation must be understood in both personal and social contexts.

In addition to these thinkers, Jon Sobrino provides a perspective rooted in the historical Jesus. Sobrino critiques Bultmann's demythologization, arguing that the socio-political realities of Jesus's life and mission are essential to any understanding of liberation.[428] By focusing on the historical Jesus, Sobrino reminds us that theological reflection must be grounded in the realities of human history and the material conditions of the oppressed.

424. Sen, *Development as Freedom*.
425. Boff, *Trinity and Society*.
426. Gutiérrez, *Theology of Liberation*.
427. Cone, *Black Theology of Liberation*.
428. Sobrino, *Jesus the Liberator*.

José Míguez Bonino's contribution to the discussion emphasizes the importance of hermeneutical circulation, which involves a continuous process of interpretation between theology and socio-political realities.[429] Bonino's approach ensures that theology remains relevant to contemporary social struggles, advocating for a dynamic and responsive engagement with both tradition and the present moment.

The integration of these diverse perspectives results in a comprehensive understanding of oppression and liberation. By combining theological reflections on divine action with philosophical analyses of power structures and practical strategies for social change, this chapter underscores the complexity of addressing systemic injustice. Liberation is not a one-dimensional process but rather a multifaceted endeavor that requires the integration of spiritual, social, and material efforts.

Furthermore, the role of interreligious dialogue in liberation cannot be overlooked. Rosenzweig's rejection of supersessionism encourages a collaborative approach to theology, where different religious traditions can work together toward common goals of justice and liberation.[430] This emphasis on dialogue is echoed in the works of scholars like David Novak and George Y. Kohler, who explore how Jewish law and ethical commandments can contribute to contemporary discussions on social justice.[431]

Benjamin Pollock and Aaron Hughes, however, raise important critiques of Rosenzweig's framework, questioning whether his focus on divine action might overshadow the urgency of human agency in addressing contemporary social injustices.[432] These critiques challenge us to reconsider how theological frameworks can be adapted to empower individuals and communities in their struggles for justice.

The engagement between existential theology and liberation theology reveals both the strengths and limitations of focusing on personal transformation. While thinkers like Bultmann provide valuable insights into individual authenticity, liberation theologians argue that theology must also address the collective dimensions of social change. By linking existential authenticity with efforts to dismantle unjust social structures,

---

429. Bonino, *Doing Theology in a Revolutionary Situation*.

430. Ochs, *Another Reformation*.

431. Novak, *Jewish Social Contract*; Kohler, *Reading Maimonides' Philosophy in 19th Century Germany*.

432. Pollock, *Franz Rosenzweig and the Systematic Task of Philosophy*; Hughes, *Invention of Jewish Identity*.

theologians like Boff and Cone develop a more comprehensive approach to liberation.[433]

In conclusion, the expanded exploration of power, ideology, and resistance in this chapter provides a thorough understanding of how systemic oppression operates and how liberation can be pursued through a combination of spiritual, philosophical, and practical efforts. By engaging with diverse thinkers and traditions, this chapter offers a framework that not only addresses the theological dimensions of liberation but also connects them to real-world struggles for justice. This holistic approach underscores the importance of collective efforts in building a more just and equitable society, while also acknowledging the ongoing need for reflection and adaptation in the face of new challenges.

---

433. Boff, *Trinity and Society*; Cone, *Black Theology of Liberation*.

CHAPTER TWO

New Concepts and Methods in Liberation Theology

IN THE CONTEMPORARY DISCOURSE of liberation theology, there is an increasing recognition of the need to integrate diverse theological traditions to address the multifaceted challenges of global injustice. This subchapter explores how different theological perspectives—ranging from social justice and ecological awareness to feminist and postcolonial critiques—can converge to form a more comprehensive and effective framework for global liberation. By drawing on these varied traditions, theologians are better equipped to address the complex and interconnected issues facing marginalized communities worldwide.

The integration of these theological perspectives also calls for a reassessment of traditional methodologies in theological education and practice. Theologians are urged to move beyond mere intellectual engagement and toward praxis-oriented approaches that emphasize lived experiences and the struggles of oppressed groups. This shift is essential for ensuring that theological reflection remains relevant and responsive to the pressing social and environmental issues of our time, fostering a more inclusive and transformative understanding of faith.

Ultimately, this chapter argues that the convergence of diverse theological traditions is not just an academic exercise but a necessary step toward realizing a more just and equitable world. By embracing a holistic approach that includes social, ecological, and cultural dimensions, liberation theology can better address the realities of global oppression and contribute to the ongoing struggle for human dignity and liberation.

CHAPTER TWO

2.1. THEOLOGY AND SOCIAL JUSTICE

This section delves into the evolving concept of existential authenticity, examining how contemporary thinkers such as Richard Sennett, Judith Butler, Slavoj Žižek, Charles Taylor, Alain Badiou, Roberto Unger, Wendy Brown, and Cornel West challenge and reinterpret it within the context of modern society. They argue that authenticity is not a fixed or purely individual state but rather a dynamic process influenced by external economic, social, and political forces. By emphasizing the interplay between the self and society, these thinkers suggest that the pursuit of authenticity must account for collective responsibilities and be integrated with broader social justice efforts.

2.1.1. Making the Kingdom Real Through Action

In the opening of this section, the various theological interpretations presented demonstrate that the Kingdom of God is profoundly intertwined with practical and ethical action in the world. Miroslav Volf and other theologians like Elaine Graham, Brian Bantum, Sarah Coakley, Kathryn Tanner, Amos Yong, and Gustavo Gutiérrez each provide a framework through which the Kingdom is understood not merely as a spiritual or future state but as a dynamic and present reality. These perspectives suggest that the Kingdom is actively realized through engagement with social issues, where acts of inclusion, justice, and reconciliation are not just ideals but essential practices that reflect the divine in daily life. Through their discussions, these theologians encourage a shift from theoretical discourse to tangible action, urging a reevaluation of traditional roles and beliefs to foster a more compassionate and equitable society.

Miroslav Volf's theological perspective brings a vibrant and actionable interpretation to the Kingdom of God, emphasizing it as a realm manifested through tangible acts of inclusion and reconciliation. According to Volf, the Kingdom materializes in the world whenever individuals engage in acts that bridge divides and welcome the marginalized. This perspective reshapes the concept of the Kingdom from a future hope to a present reality, directly influenced by human efforts to embody divine love and forgiveness in their community interactions.[1]

---

1. Volf, *Public Faith*, 52.

Volf suggests that such a Kingdom is not passive but requires active participation in the form of radical hospitality and forgiveness, which he identifies as the core activities of the Church in society. These actions are seen not just as moral goods but as the primary means through which God's presence and Kingdom become apparent and operational in the world. This redefinition extends the theological understanding of God's reign beyond traditional eschatological confines to the immediate and relational dynamics of everyday life.

Drawing from the scriptural narratives, especially from the New Testament, Volf aligns this view with Jesus' teachings on the Kingdom of God, where acts of kindness towards the needy are equated with service to God Himself. This interpretation is vividly expressed in Matthew 25, where Jesus identifies with the hungry, the thirsty, the stranger, and the naked, thereby defining the Kingdom in terms of ethical responsibility and care for one another (Matthew 25:35–36).

Volf's theology challenges believers to recognize that their actions towards others are fundamentally actions towards God, thus infusing divine significance into every act of kindness and reconciliation. This approach not only redefines the spatial and temporal dimensions of God's Kingdom but also calls for a reevaluation of how theology is lived out in the Christian community. It moves the discourse from a future-focused anticipation to an immediate, lived experience that reflects God's ongoing creation and redemptive activity in the world.

Finally, this interpretation encourages a communal and active faith that is continually realized through interactions within society. Volf's emphasis on living out the Kingdom through practices of inclusion and reconciliation offers a robust framework for understanding the role of the Church in the modern world. It suggests a model of discipleship that is dynamically engaged with the world's pain and brokenness, actively seeking to mend it through God's love, thereby making the Kingdom of God a palpable and transformative reality.[2]

Elaine Graham, in her seminal work Transforming Practice: Pastoral Theology in an Age of Uncertainty, articulates a vision of the Kingdom of God deeply rooted in the everyday practices of justice and community care.[3] She challenges traditional notions of pastoral theology by advocating for a dynamic engagement with the social realities of

---

2. Volf, *Public Faith*, 52.
3. Graham, *Transforming Practice*.

CHAPTER TWO

the 21st century. This vision emphasizes that the Kingdom is realized not through abstract theological discourse but through concrete actions that promote social justice and reconciliation.[4]

Graham posits that the role of Christian communities is to act as catalysts for transformation within society, actively participating in the creation of a more inclusive and compassionate world. This involves a shift from a solely spiritual focus to an integrated approach where spiritual and social concerns are inseparable. Her theology calls for a robust engagement with issues such as poverty, inequality, and environmental degradation, viewing these endeavors as central to the Christian mission.[5]

In her analysis, Graham also critiques the church's historical reluctance to engage fully with social issues, urging a reevaluation of pastoral roles to include advocacy and activism. By doing so, she believes that the church can better reflect the inclusive and healing nature of God's Kingdom, which she argues should be evident in the church's commitment to addressing the pressing needs of the world.[6]

Furthermore, Graham explores the implications of a postmodern approach to theology, which recognizes the fluidity of cultural and social contexts and calls for a theology that is responsive and adaptable to these changes. She advocates for a pastoral theology that is not only informed by, but also actively shapes, the cultural and social discourses, making the Christian faith a living, breathing force for societal well-being.[7]

Ultimately, Graham's work serves as a call to action for churches and believers to rethink the implications of their faith for social justice. By framing the Kingdom of God as a present and active reality that demands participation and not just contemplation, she provides a framework for a transformative pastoral practice that aligns closely with the needs and challenges of contemporary society.[8]

Brian Bantum's "Redeeming Mulatto: A Theology of Race and Christian Hybridity" offers a compelling reexamination of race and Christian identity through the lens of hybridity. Bantum employs the Chalcedonian definition of Christ to explore the complex nature of human identities, arguing that just as Christ is fully divine and fully human,

4. Graham, *Transforming Practice*, 5.
5. Graham, *Transforming Practice*, 6.
6. Graham, *Transforming Practice*, 14.
7. Graham, *Transforming Practice*, 23.
8. Graham, *Transforming Practice*, 44.

believers too embody multiple identities that reflect the diverse nature of God's creation. This perspective challenges traditional views that often categorize identities in rigid, exclusionary terms, instead promoting a vision of the Kingdom of God as a space where hybridity is embraced and celebrated.[9]

Bantum critiques the historical complicity of Christianity in maintaining racial divisions, emphasizing that the church has often failed to recognize the full humanity of all people. He argues that this failure is not just a social issue but a theological one, rooted in a misunderstanding of the nature of Christ and, by extension, humanity. The church's role, according to Bantum, should be to break down these barriers and reimagine its practices to reflect a more inclusive and just community that aligns with the vision of God's Kingdom.[10]

Central to Bantum's theology is the concept of hybridity, which he sees as a divine attribute that challenges the purity often associated with racial and ethnic categories. He contends that Christian identity should not be about conforming to a singular cultural norm but about embodying the diverse, multifaceted nature of God's creation. This theological approach calls for a radical rethinking of how identity is understood and lived out within Christian communities.[11]

Bantum further argues that the church must actively participate in societal transformation by advocating for justice and reconciliation. This involves not only addressing personal prejudices but also challenging systemic structures that perpetuate inequality. He believes that the Kingdom of God is realized through the active work of believers who seek to create communities that reflect the inclusivity and justice of God's reign.[12]

In conclusion, Bantum's work offers a powerful critique of racial and ethnic divisions within Christianity and presents a transformative vision of the Kingdom of God. By embracing hybridity and promoting justice, the church can better reflect the diversity and inclusivity that are central to God's Kingdom. Bantum's theology calls for a lived faith that actively engages with the challenges of race and identity, seeking to build a more just and inclusive world.[13]

9. Bantum, *Redeeming Mulatto*, 95.
10. Bantum, *Redeeming Mulatto*, 210.
11. Bantum, *Redeeming Mulatto*, 104.
12. Bantum, *Redeeming Mulatto*, 143.
13. Bantum, *Redeeming Mulatto*, 1.

Sarah Coakley offers a nuanced approach to understanding the Kingdom of God by integrating the practice of contemplative prayer with active social engagement. In her work God, Sexuality, and the Self: An Essay on the Trinity, Coakley argues that the Kingdom is not merely a distant, mystical reality but something encountered both in personal prayer and in the pursuit of justice and love in the world. She emphasizes that the contemplative life is not an escape from the world but a means of deepening one's participation in God's work, empowering believers to engage in both personal and social transformation.[14]

Coakley discusses how the act of prayer, particularly when understood in a Trinitarian framework, can lead to a profound reorientation of the self towards God's will. This reorientation is not just an inward, spiritual process but one that naturally extends outward, compelling the believer to act in ways that reflect God's Kingdom on earth. The Holy Spirit, in Coakley's view, plays a crucial role in this process by sustaining and guiding believers as they navigate the complexities of living out their faith in a world marked by injustice and suffering.[15]

The Kingdom of God, therefore, is experienced both in moments of silent communion with God and in the active pursuit of social justice. Coakley challenges the dichotomy often drawn between spirituality and action, suggesting that true Christian discipleship requires both. The contemplative practices foster a deeper connection with God, which in turn fuels the believer's commitment to justice, peace, and love in the broader community.[16]

Furthermore, Coakley's theology highlights the importance of vulnerability and surrender in the Christian life. She argues that true transformation, both personal and societal, begins with the willingness to relinquish control and trust in the power of the Holy Spirit. This surrender is not passive but involves a dynamic participation in God's ongoing work of redemption in the world. It is through this process that the Kingdom of God becomes a tangible reality, seen in the lives of those who embody its values through acts of love and justice.[17]

In sum, Coakley's vision of the Kingdom of God integrates the contemplative and the active, the mystical and the practical. By rooting her theology in both prayer and social action, she offers a comprehensive

---

14. Coakley, *God, Sexuality, and the Self*, 13.
15. Coakley, *God, Sexuality, and the Self*, 16.
16. Coakley, *God, Sexuality, and the Self*, 19.
17. Coakley, *God, Sexuality, and the Self*, 21.

framework for understanding how believers can participate in the ongoing realization of God's Kingdom here and now.[18]

Kathryn Tanner's theology emphasizes the Kingdom of God as a dynamic interplay between divine grace and human agency, where believers are empowered to participate in God's work of redemption through acts of love and justice. She asserts that the transformative power of God's grace is essential in enabling believers to embody Christ-like virtues within their communities, thus contributing to the realization of the Kingdom on earth. Tanner underscores that the Kingdom is not merely an eschatological promise but a present reality that unfolds through the self-giving actions of believers, particularly in their solidarity with the poor and oppressed. This perspective aligns with her broader theological vision, where the incarnation of Christ serves as the ultimate model of divine self-giving, calling Christians to mirror this in their lives by engaging in practices that reflect God's love and justice in the world.[19]

By highlighting the role of the Holy Spirit, Tanner suggests that believers are not left to their own devices but are continually supported and guided by divine grace in their pursuit of the Kingdom. The Spirit's work in the life of the believer fosters a deep connection with the divine, which in turn inspires and sustains their efforts toward social transformation. This understanding challenges any notion of passivity in the Christian life, instead calling for an active engagement in the world that reflects the self-emptying nature of Christ.[20]

Tanner also explores how the Kingdom is made manifest in the communal life of believers. She argues that Christian communities are called to be places where the values of the Kingdom—justice, peace, and love—are lived out in tangible ways. This communal aspect of the Kingdom reflects the Trinitarian nature of God, where the relationships within the Godhead serve as a model for the relationships within the Christian community. In this way, the Kingdom is not just a future hope but a lived reality, shaped by the everyday actions and relationships of believers.[21]

Furthermore, Tanner's theology critiques any form of Christianity that remains complicit in systems of oppression, calling instead for a radical reimagining of the Kingdom as a space where true equality

---

18. Coakley, *God, Sexuality, and the Self*, 33.
19. Tanner, *Christ the Key*, 25.
20. Tanner, *Christ the Key*, 26.
21. Tanner, *Christ the Key*, 27.

and justice are realized. She emphasizes that the work of the Kingdom involves both personal transformation and social change, with a particular focus on solidarity with the marginalized. This approach challenges believers to examine how their faith intersects with issues of power and privilege, encouraging them to take concrete steps towards creating a more just and inclusive world.[22]

In sum, Tanner presents the Kingdom of God as an active and ongoing reality that believers are called to participate in through their actions. Her emphasis on the transformative power of grace, the role of the Holy Spirit, and the communal nature of the Kingdom offers a comprehensive framework for understanding how Christians can live out their faith in a way that reflects God's love and justice in the world.[23]

Amos Yong's theological perspective highlights the role of the Holy Spirit in the manifestation of God's Kingdom, emphasizing that it is not merely a distant future hope but a present reality actively unfolding in the world. Yong contends that the Kingdom is realized through the Spirit's work, which empowers believers to engage in transformative actions that align with God's redemptive purposes. He critiques traditional interpretations that limit the Kingdom to the afterlife, arguing instead for an understanding that sees the Kingdom as a space of healing, liberation, and renewal available in the here and now. This approach challenges Pentecostals and other Christians to reconsider their focus on the future and instead recognize and participate in the Kingdom's present reality by living out the values of justice, love, and reconciliation in their communities.[24]

Yong also explores how Pentecostalism's emphasis on the Spirit can offer a unique contribution to political theology, particularly in contexts of social and economic marginalization. He argues that the Spirit's presence in the world compels believers to engage with the socio-political issues of their time, advocating for a political theology that is both deeply spiritual and actively engaged with the challenges of the modern world. This perspective pushes back against any notion of Christian faith as being solely concerned with personal salvation, instead positioning it as a force for social transformation.[25]

---

22. Tanner, *Christ the Key*, 13.
23. Tanner, *Christ the Key*, 15.
24. Yong, *In the Days of Caesar*, 5.
25. Yong, *In the Days of Caesar*, 26.

Furthermore, Yong addresses the intersection of eschatology and politics, particularly how Pentecostal eschatology, often focused on the coming Kingdom, can be reimagined to inspire current political and social engagement. He suggests that Pentecostal communities, through their lived experiences of the Spirit, can offer alternative visions of society that challenge the status quo and promote justice and equity. This view invites Pentecostals to see their faith as inherently linked to the pursuit of social justice, grounded in the active presence of the Spirit.[26]

In examining the global spread of Pentecostalism, Yong identifies how different cultural contexts shape the expression of the Kingdom. He highlights the adaptability of Pentecostal theology to various social and economic conditions, showing how the Spirit's work can manifest differently depending on the needs and challenges of each community. This adaptability underscores the dynamic nature of the Kingdom as it takes root in diverse settings, always reflecting the Spirit's work in addressing the specific injustices faced by believers.[27]

Yong's approach calls for a reexamination of how Pentecostals and other Christians understand the Kingdom of God, encouraging them to see it as both a present and active force in the world, brought to life through the Spirit's work in and through the church. This understanding challenges believers to engage more deeply with the social and political realities around them, recognizing that their faith is not separate from but integral to the pursuit of justice and liberation in the world.[28]

Gustavo Gutiérrez, a key proponent of Liberation Theology, offers a compelling vision of God's Kingdom that is firmly grounded in the principles of justice and solidarity with the marginalized. His theological framework insists that the Kingdom of God emerges in the everyday actions of the church as it stands alongside those who are oppressed. Gutiérrez emphasizes that this involvement in social and economic justice is not peripheral but central to the mission of the church, reflecting a deep commitment to transforming the lives of the poor and disenfranchised.[29]

This approach challenges believers to view the Kingdom of God as a present reality, one that compels a radical reevaluation of societal structures and personal commitments. According to Gutiérrez, the Kingdom

26. Yong, *In the Days of Caesar*, 14.
27. Yong, *In the Days of Caesar*, 34.
28. Yong, *In the Days of Caesar*, 49.
29. Gutiérrez, *Power of the Poor in History*.

CHAPTER TWO

is realized not only through individual acts of kindness but through a concerted effort to dismantle systemic injustices that perpetuate inequality and suffering. This theological stance posits that true discipleship involves gritty, real-world engagement with the most pressing issues of our time.[30]

Gutiérrez also critiques any spiritualization of the Kingdom that detaches it from social justice issues. He argues that the spiritual renewal of individuals must go hand in hand with the transformation of societal structures. This dual focus ensures that the church does not retreat from the world but actively participates in its redemption, embodying the hope and justice of God's Kingdom through its advocacy and actions.[31]

Moreover, Gutiérrez's theology holds that the Kingdom of God is fundamentally about relationships—relationships that reflect God's love for humanity by striving to rectify the inequalities and brokenness of the world. This vision expands the scope of salvation to include social salvation, where the liberation of the oppressed is seen as a foretaste of the eschatological fulfillment promised in Christian doctrine.[32]

Finally, Gutiérrez calls the church to a deeper fidelity to the gospel by aligning itself with the poor and oppressed. This alignment is not merely a strategic or ethical choice but a theological imperative that mirrors the ministry of Jesus Christ. By committing to this path, the church actualizes the Kingdom of God, making it a tangible reality in the world today.[33]

In conclusion, the various theological perspectives explored emphasize the Kingdom of God as an active and immediate reality, shaped through practices of justice, inclusion, and reconciliation. These theologians argue that the manifestation of the Kingdom is not confined to future eschatological hopes but is realized in the present through the church's engagement with societal issues. This engagement involves both individual transformation and collective action aimed at addressing systemic injustices. The call is clear: the church must embody the Kingdom of God through concrete actions that reflect God's love and justice, making it a living experience within the community. Each perspective, while unique in focus, converges on the idea that active participation in the

---

30. Gutiérrez, *Power of the Poor in History*, 19.
31. Gutiérrez, *Power of the Poor in History*, 30.
32. Gutiérrez, *Power of the Poor in History*, 32.
33. Gutiérrez, *Power of the Poor in History*, 18.

world's pain and brokenness is essential for realizing the transformative power of the Kingdom of God.

2.1.2. Expanding Theological Justice

This section explores the evolving understanding of liberation theology, emphasizing the interconnectedness of ecological, social, and economic justice. Theologians like Catherine Keller, M. Shawn Copeland, Kwok Pui-lan, Elaine Graham, Marcella Althaus-Reid, and James H. Cone challenge traditional frameworks by integrating perspectives on environmental sustainability, race, gender, sexuality, and postcolonialism. Their work advocates for a more comprehensive approach to liberation, recognizing that justice must encompass both human communities and the broader ecological system, while also addressing the diverse lived experiences of marginalized groups.

Catherine Keller's process theology, particularly in her book "Cloud of the Impossible: Negative Theology and Planetary Entanglement," introduces the concept of "deep relationality," emphasizing the intertwined nature of ecological, economic, and social justice. Keller critiques traditional liberation theology for its insufficient focus on environmental issues, arguing that any meaningful pursuit of liberation must encompass a commitment to ecological sustainability alongside human justice.[34] She suggests that liberation efforts cannot be fully realized if they do not address the broader ecological systems that sustain life, making a case for an expanded theological framework that integrates environmental concerns with social and economic justice.[35]

Keller explores how process theology, with its roots in relational cosmology, offers a valuable perspective for understanding the interconnectedness of all life. She posits that liberation is not merely a human endeavor but one that must include the non-human world, recognizing the interdependence of all creation. This holistic approach challenges the anthropocentric focus of much traditional theology, calling for a reimagining of liberation that includes the well-being of the planet as integral to human justice.[36]

---

34. Keller, *Cloud of the Impossible*, 7.
35. Keller, *Cloud of the Impossible*, 9.
36. Keller, *Cloud of the Impossible*, 122.

Further, Keller connects this relational view to the concept of "entanglement" from quantum physics, using it as a metaphor for the non-separability of all existence. She argues that just as quantum particles are entangled, so too are social, economic, and ecological realities intertwined. This perspective reinforces the need for a theology that is responsive to the complex interrelations of these different spheres, advocating for a justice that is both socially and ecologically engaged.[37]

Moreover, Keller's work critiques the often-compartmentalized approaches to liberation that separate environmental issues from social justice. She argues for a more integrated approach that sees environmental justice as an essential part of the broader struggle for liberation, suggesting that true justice must encompass the health and sustainability of the Earth itself.[38]

In conclusion, Keller's theology calls for a rethinking of liberation as a deeply interconnected process that includes not only human communities but also the entire ecological system. Her work challenges traditional liberation theology to broaden its scope, incorporating ecological sustainability as a fundamental aspect of its mission.[39]

M. Shawn Copeland, in Enfleshing Freedom: Body, Race, and Being, brings attention to the ways in which Christian theology must grapple with the physical and embodied aspects of oppression, particularly regarding race and gender. She argues that understanding liberation requires a focus on the suffering bodies, like those of Black women and Jesus of Nazareth, which reveal humanity's capacity for both cruelty and redemption.[40] This perspective challenges traditional theological frameworks by emphasizing the necessity of addressing the lived, bodily experiences of marginalized groups.[41]

Copeland critiques the ways in which theology has historically overlooked the significance of race and embodiment, urging for a theological anthropology that recognizes the marks of gender, race, and culture on the human body.[42] She highlights how these physical markers influence not only personal identity but also the broader social and religious

---

37. Keller, *Cloud of the Impossible*, 22.
38. Keller, *Cloud of the Impossible*, 20.
39. Keller, *Cloud of the Impossible*, 43.
40. Copeland, *Enfleshing Freedom*, xi.
41. Copeland, *Enfleshing Freedom*, xii.
42. Copeland, *Enfleshing Freedom*, xiv.

dynamics, making the case for a theology that truly embodies solidarity with the oppressed.[43]

The importance of reclaiming the Black female body within theological discourse is central to Copeland's argument, especially in light of historical abuses like lynching, which have left deep scars on the collective psyche of African American communities.[44] She points out that the recognition and reclamation of these bodies within the Christian tradition is essential for a genuine liberation theology that seeks to uplift all of humanity.

Moreover, Copeland draws on the critique by bell hooks of postmodernism, which often fails to fully account for the embodied experiences of race and class, further emphasizing the need for a theology that engages deeply with these realities.[45] This engagement, according to Copeland, should not only address the abstract notions of liberation but also involve a concrete, lived solidarity with those who suffer under systemic injustice.[46]

In sum, Copeland's work challenges the church and theologians to reconceptualize liberation theology by placing the physical and embodied experiences of race and gender at the center of their analysis. This approach calls for a faith that is deeply engaged with the realities of human suffering and committed to the full humanity of all people, advocating for a liberation that is both spiritual and physical.[47]

Kwok Pui-lan, in her book Postcolonial Imagination and Feminist Theology, offers a critical examination of traditional liberation theology, arguing that it often fails to fully address the complexities of race, gender, and class. Kwok emphasizes the need for a theology that is intersectional, taking into account the diverse experiences of marginalized women in postcolonial contexts. She critiques the Eurocentric and patriarchal biases in traditional theological frameworks, calling for a more inclusive approach that engages with global feminist movements.[48]

Kwok argues that liberation theology, while powerful, has historically been shaped by modernist thinking and has often neglected the voices of women, particularly those from non-Western contexts. She

43. Copeland, *Enfleshing Freedom*, xv.
44. Copeland, *Enfleshing Freedom*, xvi.
45. Copeland, *Enfleshing Freedom*, 12.
46. Copeland, *Enfleshing Freedom*, 14.
47. Copeland, *Enfleshing Freedom*, 113.
48. Kwok, *Postcolonial Imagination and Feminist Theology*, 20.

highlights how feminist theology has evolved into a multivocal and intercultural movement, reflecting the diverse experiences of women across the globe.[49] This movement, she contends, must continue to challenge colonial and patriarchal structures within religious discourse.

In her analysis, Kwok also addresses the importance of decolonizing the mind, illustrating how postcolonial feminist theologians must navigate complex identities formed by experiences of colonization, exile, and diaspora. This process broadens the horizons of feminist theology, making it more attuned to the realities of global injustice.[50]

Kwok critiques the traditional sources of theology, such as Scripture and tradition, for often marginalizing women's experiences. She argues that feminist theology has rightly placed women's lived experiences at the center of theological reflection, challenging the dominance of male perspectives in religious thought.[51]

Ultimately, Kwok's work calls for a postcolonial feminist theology that is not only multicultural but also deeply committed to addressing the intersecting oppressions faced by women around the world. This approach seeks to transform theological discourse by making it more inclusive and responsive to the needs of marginalized communities.[52]

Elaine Graham, in her work on practical theology, critiques the historical detachment of the church from social issues and emphasizes the need for a theology deeply rooted in praxis. She argues that true liberation involves an ongoing, dialogical process where theology must actively engage with the world. By addressing the intersections of poststructuralist thought and pastoral practice, Graham challenges traditional views and advocates for a theology that is responsive to the complexities of the 21st century. This approach seeks to integrate ethical action and theological reflection in a way that addresses contemporary social and cultural issues.[53]

Graham also explores the implications of poststructuralism for practical theology, suggesting that the dismantling of grand narratives opens up new possibilities for understanding human nature, ethics, and agency. She contends that feminist and poststructuralist critiques have exposed the limitations of traditional theological frameworks, which

---

49. Kwok, *Postcolonial Imagination and Feminist Theology*, 21.
50. Kwok, *Postcolonial Imagination and Feminist Theology*, 22.
51. Kwok, *Postcolonial Imagination and Feminist Theology*, 22.
52. Kwok, *Postcolonial Imagination and Feminist Theology*, 23.
53. Graham, *Transforming Practice*, 4.

often fail to account for the diverse experiences and identities of marginalized groups. By incorporating these perspectives, Graham seeks to develop a more inclusive and dynamic theological praxis that can better address the needs of diverse communities.[54]

Moreover, Graham argues that theology must move beyond mere theoretical discourse and become a living practice that engages with the real-world issues of justice and equality. She emphasizes the importance of pastoral care and practical theology in shaping ethical horizons and fostering a sense of obligation toward social transformation. This involves rethinking the role of the church and its mission in society, advocating for a more active and participatory approach to faith that is grounded in the lived realities of individuals and communities.[55]

In her analysis, Graham also highlights the need for a new understanding of power and difference within the pastoral encounter. She calls for greater equality in pastoral relationships, challenging the traditional power dynamics that often reinforce societal inequalities. By advocating for a more egalitarian approach to pastoral care, Graham seeks to create spaces where all voices are heard and valued, and where the transformative potential of theology can be fully realized.[56]

Ultimately, Graham's work serves as a call to action for the church to reengage with the world in a meaningful way. She emphasizes that theology must be both reflective and active, constantly evolving to meet the challenges of contemporary society. Through a commitment to justice-oriented practices, Graham envisions a theology that is not only relevant but also transformative, capable of contributing to the ongoing struggle for liberation and equality in the 21st century.[57]

Marcella Althaus-Reid, in Indecent Theology,[58] presents a provocative critique of traditional liberation theology by challenging established moral and sexual norms. She argues that authentic liberation must account for the complexities of human sexuality, which have often been overlooked or suppressed in theological discourse. Her work aims to create a more inclusive theology that recognizes diverse sexual identities and experiences.

---

54. Graham, *Transforming Practice*, 13.
55. Graham, *Transforming Practice*, 27.
56. Graham, *Transforming Practice*, 49.
57. Graham, *Transforming Practice*, 65.
58. Althaus-Reid, *Indecent Theology*.

In her analysis, Althaus-Reid particularly critiques conventional theological frameworks for their tendency to uphold patriarchal and heteronormative structures. These structures have historically marginalized individuals who do not conform to traditional norms, thereby limiting the scope of theological reflection.[59] By integrating sexual theory and post-Marxist analysis, she seeks to dismantle these oppressive frameworks and advocate for a theology that is truly liberative.

A poignant example Althaus-Reid discusses is the symbolism of a Drag Queen dressed as the Virgin Mary during a carnival procession.[60] She uses this image to question how traditional theology has rigidly imposed sexual and gender norms, suggesting that such subversive representations can open up new possibilities for theological reflection that embrace rather than reject the diversity of human sexuality.

Additionally, Althaus-Reid addresses the historical alliance between European patriarchy and the Christianization of Latin America, which she argues has resulted in a form of sexual and cultural colonization. This critique extends to how theological narratives have been constructed to exclude or repress non-heteronormative sexualities, reinforcing a narrow view of what is considered "decent" within religious contexts.[61]

Proposing a "sexual rereading" of Marxist theology in Latin America, Althaus-Reid calls for a liberation theology that is concerned not only with social and economic justice but also with sexual justice. This approach challenges the church to reconsider its teachings and practices in light of the lived realities of people who have been marginalized because of their sexuality.[62]

Overall, Althaus-Reid's Indecent Theology is a significant reimagining of liberation theology, insisting on the inclusion of sexual diversity as central to the pursuit of true liberation. Her work invites theologians and believers alike to rethink the boundaries of what is considered theologically acceptable, advocating for a broader and more inclusive understanding of human freedom and dignity.

James H. Cone's seminal work, The Cross and the Lynching Tree,[63] underscores the critical intersection of race and liberation theology. Cone critiques mainstream theology for its oversight of systemic racism,

---

59. Althaus-Reid, *Indecent Theology*, 12.
60. Althaus-Reid, *Indecent Theology*, 9.
61. Althaus-Reid, *Indecent Theology*, 12.
62. Althaus-Reid, *Indecent Theology*, 19.
63. Cone, *Cross and the Lynching Tree*.

asserting that a truly liberative theology must directly confront the harsh realities of racial oppression and align itself with the ongoing struggles of Black communities. He argues that understanding and justice in theological discourse are incomplete without addressing the entrenched racial inequalities that shape American society.

Cone draws a compelling parallel between the crucifixion of Jesus and the lynching of Black Americans, suggesting that the true significance of Christian identity in the United States can only be understood through this lens.[64] This analogy seeks to highlight the historical and ongoing implications of racial violence, viewing Christ's suffering in conjunction with the experiences of Black individuals subjected to lynching. By doing so, Cone positions these acts of violence as central to the theological reflection on suffering and redemption in America.

Additionally, Cone shares insights from his personal journey, describing how his writing on the subject of lynching offered him a form of liberation from its traumatic legacy.[65] He explores how the symbol of the cross has helped him address the brutality and historical trauma associated with lynching, providing a theological framework to interpret and resist these acts of injustice.

In his reflections, Cone emphasizes giving voice to Black victims, allowing their stories and experiences to inform and challenge theological understanding and practice.[66] He urges his audience to recognize the terror that Black Americans have historically faced under systemic racism, linking this recognition to broader discussions of terror and violence.

Ultimately, Cone's work is not meant to provide definitive answers but to spark a broader dialogue about race, suffering, and redemption.[67] He calls for a reevaluation of both societal structures and theological interpretations that perpetuate racial disparities, advocating for a shift towards a more just and inclusive theological practice. This work invites theologians and believers to rethink the implications of the gospel in the context of America's racial history, pushing for a theology that not only reflects on these issues but actively engages with them.

In conclusion, Catherine Keller, M. Shawn Copeland, Kwok Pui-lan, Elaine Graham, Marcella Althaus-Reid, and James H. Cone each

---

64. Cone, *Cross and the Lynching Tree*, xv.
65. Cone, *Cross and the Lynching Tree*, xvii.
66. Cone, *Cross and the Lynching Tree*, xix.
67. Cone, *Cross and the Lynching Tree*, 1.

challenge traditional approaches to liberation theology, urging a broader, more inclusive perspective that considers ecological, racial, gender, and sexual dimensions. Their works collectively argue for a revised theological framework that not only critiques established norms but also actively engages with the diverse and complex realities of contemporary societies. This call to action emphasizes the necessity of integrating practical, lived experiences with theological discourse, aiming to achieve a comprehensive understanding and application of justice that addresses the interconnectedness of all life and human experiences.

2.1.3. Authenticity, Society, and Justice

This section explores the concept of existential authenticity in the context of modern society, examining how thinkers such as Richard Sennett, Judith Butler, Slavoj Žižek, Charles Taylor, Alain Badiou, Roberto Unger, Wendy Brown, and Cornel West challenge and redefine it. They discuss how contemporary economic, social, and political conditions complicate the pursuit of a stable and authentic self, arguing that authenticity must be understood as a dynamic process shaped by external pressures and collective responsibilities, rather than as a fixed or purely individual state.

Richard Sennett, in The Corrosion of Character: The Personal Consequences of Work in the New Capitalism, explores how the flexible and unpredictable nature of modern capitalism complicates the pursuit of authentic existence. He argues that in a world where work demands constant adaptability and where long-term commitments are devalued, individuals find it increasingly difficult to maintain a stable sense of self. This instability challenges traditional notions of existential authenticity, as people are forced to continuously reshape their identities in response to external economic pressures. Sennett's perspective suggests that authenticity must be rethought as a process of ongoing adaptation rather than a fixed state, critiquing earlier existentialist frameworks that assumed more stable social and economic conditions.[68]

Sennett highlights the erosion of real connections in this new economic landscape, noting that the sense of community is often shallow and based on superficial affirmations of shared values. He references Hans-Georg Gadamer's philosophy, where the self is described as not fully possessing itself, existing instead as a "flickering in the closed circuit

---

68. Sennett, *Corrosion of Character*.

of historical life." Sennett points out that in modern capitalism, there is no shared narrative of difficulty or fate, leading to a corrosion of character and the loss of a meaningful answer to the question, "Who needs me?" This loss is further compounded by the disconnection fostered by modern work environments, where even communities like those of programmers cannot fully answer this question.[69]

Drawing on Adam Smith's critiques, Sennett discusses how routine, while often seen as deadening, once provided a stable structure within which people could construct a coherent narrative for their lives. Smith observed that the division of labor, which breaks down tasks into repetitive motions, could deaden the mind. However, Sennett notes that in the current economy, even the predictability of routine has been replaced by instability, leaving individuals without the protective structures that once allowed for the accumulation of personal and professional achievements over time.[70]

Sennett illustrates this shift by contrasting the lives of people in the past, like the janitor Enrico, who could build a linear and cumulative narrative of his life, with those in the modern flexible economy. Enrico, with the help of union rules and a predictable work life, was able to construct a clear story for himself, which provided him with a sense of self-respect and identity. In contrast, today's workers face a world marked by short-term flexibility and flux, where the possibility of constructing such a coherent narrative has significantly diminished.[71]

In discussing the implications of this new economic order, Sennett shares his observations from a visit to Davos, where he found that the leaders of the flexible economy, while comfortable with entrepreneurial disorder, are uncomfortable discussing the fate of those left behind. These leaders acknowledge the shortcomings of the flexible regime but offer no guidance on how to lead an ordinary life within it. Sennett reflects on how this detachment from the experiences of the majority might eventually erode the influence these leaders have over the imaginations of those who struggle within the system.[72]

Sennett's examination concludes by suggesting that the conditions of the new economy, characterized by episodic and fragmented experiences, prevent individuals from forming a stable narrative of identity

69. Sennett, *Corrosion of Character*, 147.
70. Sennett, *Corrosion of Character*, 32–39.
71. Sennett, *Corrosion of Character*, 76, 30.
72. Sennett, *Corrosion of Character*, 147.

CHAPTER TWO

and life history. This lack of continuity and coherence in personal and professional lives reflects the broader instability that modern capitalism imposes on the quest for existential authenticity.[73]

Judith Butler's work on performativity challenges the traditional notion of a "true self" that exists beneath social performances, arguing that identity, including gender, is constructed through repeated actions rather than as an expression of an inner truth. Butler critiques the idea that there is a singular, authentic self that can be revealed, pointing out that the very idea of a "true self" can serve to reinforce restrictive social norms. She suggests that what is often understood as unity or coherence in identity is instead a product of ongoing performative acts that are shaped by societal expectations.[74]

This performative view of identity raises significant questions about the feasibility of achieving existential authenticity, especially in the context of gender. If gender itself is the result of repeated performances rather than an innate characteristic, the pursuit of an "authentic" gender identity becomes problematic. Butler emphasizes that the concept of a true, stable gender identity is tied to the binary model of gender, which itself is a social construct rather than a natural fact. Thus, the search for authenticity within this framework may inadvertently uphold the very structures it seeks to transcend.[75]

Butler also critiques the notion that identity can be fully captured or expressed through any particular performance. She argues that the self is structured by repeated acts that aim to approximate societal ideals of what is "true" or "real." This performative process means that identity is always in flux, never fully achieving the ideal it strives for. The postulation of a true gender identity, then, is revealed as a regulatory fiction—one that maintains power structures by dictating what constitutes "normal" or "acceptable" expressions of gender.[76]

In discussing the implications of performativity, Butler challenges the ontological distinctions between mind and body, as well as between consciousness and social roles. She argues that these distinctions often support political and psychic hierarchies, where the mind is seen as superior to the body. By deconstructing these binaries, Butler seeks to expose how they contribute to systems of subordination, suggesting that

73. Sennett, *Corrosion of Character*, 26, 43.
74. Butler, *Gender Trouble*, 20.
75. Butler, *Gender Trouble*, 26.
76. Butler, *Gender Trouble*, 192, 31.

the very framework through which we understand identity and authenticity is itself complicit in maintaining inequality.[77]

Finally, Butler addresses the role of coalition-building in movements for social change. She cautions against insisting on a unified or coherent identity as the basis for political action, arguing that such demands can hinder the dynamic and self-reflective processes necessary for effective coalitions. Instead, she advocates for a more fluid understanding of identity that allows for the complexities and contradictions inherent in any social movement. This approach challenges the idea that political unity requires ontological unity, opening up space for diverse and intersectional forms of activism.[78]

Slavoj Žižek critiques the focus on individual authenticity by highlighting how it often overlooks the deeper ideological structures that shape our desires and choices. He argues that what we perceive as authentic decisions are frequently the result of ideological interpellation, where individuals misrecognize themselves as autonomous agents while their actions are shaped by underlying ideological forces. This misrecognition, Žižek suggests, is a necessary condition for historical activity, as individuals must accept certain delusions to assume their roles in the historical process.[79]

Žižek further elaborates on the process of ideological interpellation, drawing on Althusser's concept, to explain how individuals are «called» into specific roles within the ideological framework. This process creates an illusion of pre-existing identity, as though one was always meant to occupy a particular social or class position. This «short circuit,» as Žižek calls it, often produces a comical effect, where the subject's supposed authenticity is revealed to be a product of the very ideology that defines and constrains them.[80]

He also critiques Althusser's theory for not fully explaining how ideological state apparatuses internalize these ideologies within individuals. Žižek points out that this process of internalization, where ideology becomes part of the subject's self-conception, is crucial to understanding how individuals come to identify with the roles they are assigned. Without a clear understanding of this process, the critique of individual

---

77. Butler, *Gender Trouble*, 17, 18.
78. Butler, *Gender Trouble*, 20.
79. Žižek, *Sublime Object of Ideology*, 2.
80. Žižek, *Sublime Object of Ideology*, 3.

authenticity remains incomplete, as it fails to account for the mechanisms that produce the illusion of authenticity in the first place.[81]

Moreover, Žižek discusses how ideological interpellation operates without clear identification, using Kafka's characters as examples of subjects interpellated by mysterious bureaucratic entities. This "interpellation without identification" underscores the ambiguity and complexity of the ideological process, where subjects are called into existence by forces they cannot fully comprehend or identify with, further complicating the notion of authentic choice or identity.[82]

Through these analyses, Žižek emphasizes that any pursuit of authenticity that does not critically engage with these ideological underpinnings is likely to remain superficial. The concept of authenticity must be rethought in light of the ways in which ideology shapes and constrains our perceptions and choices, challenging the very possibility of achieving a truly authentic existence within the frameworks of capitalist ideology.[83]

Charles Taylor, in his exploration of the "ethics of authenticity," emphasizes the importance of individual self-realization but warns against the dangers of relativism and narcissism that can emerge in modern culture. Taylor argues that the pursuit of authenticity should not lead to the denial of responsibilities such as citizenship, solidarity, or environmental stewardship. He criticizes the notion that relationships should be seen as merely instrumental to individual self-fulfillment, suggesting that such a view is self-defeating and ultimately undermines the value of authenticity itself.[84]

Taylor also challenges the idea that the culture of authenticity should be explained solely through material or economic factors, such as changes in production methods or consumption patterns. He argues that reducing the culture of authenticity to these factors ignores the underlying moral ideals that drive people to pursue authenticity. Taylor asserts that authenticity is a valid ideal, and that it is possible to reason about the conformity of practices to this ideal, suggesting that these arguments can have a meaningful impact on how we understand and pursue authenticity in our lives.[85]

---

81. Žižek, *Sublime Object of Ideology*, 43.
82. Žižek, *Sublime Object of Ideology*, 44.
83. Žižek, *Sublime Object of Ideology*, 2–44.
84. Taylor, *Ethics of Authenticity*, 22.
85. Taylor, *Ethics of Authenticity*, 21, 23.

Furthermore, Taylor traces the origins of the ethics of authenticity to the end of the eighteenth century, linking it to earlier forms of individualism. He acknowledges that while cultural pessimism often criticizes the culture of authenticity as being shallow or narcissistic, such pessimism is counterproductive. Taylor believes that instead of dismissing authenticity, we should strive to realize higher and fuller modes of authenticity, even though this is a continuous struggle against flatter and shallower forms.[86]

Taylor argues that cultural pessimism, which sees the pursuit of authenticity as a sign of decline, is misguided. He suggests that authenticity, when understood correctly, can lead to a richer and more meaningful life. However, achieving this requires a balance between individual self-realization and communal values. Taylor's perspective integrates these elements, offering a more comprehensive approach to authenticity that considers both personal fulfillment and social responsibility.[87]

In addressing the contemporary challenges to authenticity, Taylor discusses how individualism can lead to a loss of meaning and a retreat into personal isolation. He notes that while the pursuit of authenticity is important, it must be tempered by a sense of responsibility to others and a commitment to shared moral frameworks. This balance is crucial for ensuring that authenticity does not become a selfish or isolating pursuit, but rather a path to personal and communal well-being.[88]

Finally, Taylor points out that the ideal of authenticity has been discredited in some circles, not necessarily because of its flaws, but because it is often misunderstood or misapplied. He argues that a proper understanding of authenticity should involve not only the pursuit of personal self-realization but also an engagement with the broader community. This approach can help mitigate the risks of relativism and narcissism, making authenticity a more robust and socially responsible ideal.[89]

Alain Badiou critiques the existential focus on individual authenticity by arguing that it risks becoming overly inward-looking, potentially disconnecting individuals from broader political and collective actions. He asserts that true liberation cannot be achieved through personal authenticity alone but requires a commitment to universal truths and political causes that transcend individual concerns. Badiou emphasizes

---

86. Taylor, *Ethics of Authenticity*, 25, 79, 94.
87. Taylor, *Ethics of Authenticity*, 78, 94.
88. Taylor, *Ethics of Authenticity*, 12, 15.
89. Taylor, *Ethics of Authenticity*, 16, 17.

CHAPTER TWO

the necessity of aligning one's actions with a more collective and universal framework, suggesting that personal authenticity, when disconnected from larger social movements, may fail to contribute meaningfully to true liberation.⁹⁰

Badiou's philosophy revolves around the idea that mathematics is ontology, and this forms the basis of his argument against the isolation of individual authenticity from collective action. He explores how set theory, in particular, provides a framework for understanding being as an "inconsistent multiplicity," where the reality of existence is not merely a singular, self-contained entity but rather a complex, interconnected web of relations. This perspective underscores the importance of engaging with collective movements and universal truths, rather than retreating into the solitude of individual authenticity.⁹¹

In Badiou's terms, the focus on individual authenticity alone can be seen as an "axiom of choice" in philosophy, where the selection of a path centered on personal fulfillment neglects the broader implications and responsibilities that come with being part of a collective whole. He suggests that this choice, while seemingly liberating, can lead to a form of existential myopia, where the larger, more significant struggles of society are overlooked in favor of personal satisfaction. Badiou argues for a reorientation towards an "ontology of immanence," where being is understood not as an isolated self but as something that unfolds within and through collective actions and truths.⁹²

Moreover, Badiou's critique extends to the way personal authenticity can be co-opted by ideological forces, becoming a tool for reinforcing the status quo rather than challenging it. He points out that without a connection to universal truths and political causes, the pursuit of authenticity can be manipulated by existing power structures, reducing it to a superficial form of self-expression rather than a genuine challenge to societal norms. In this way, Badiou advocates for an approach to authenticity that is deeply intertwined with political praxis and collective action, ensuring that personal liberation contributes to broader societal change.⁹³

Badiou's philosophy suggests that the true path to liberation lies not in the isolated pursuit of individual authenticity, but in the alignment of

90. Badiou, *Being and Event*.
91. Badiou, *Being and Event*, xxiii.
92. Badiou, *Being and Event*, xvii.
93. Badiou, *Being and Event*, xvii.

one's actions with universal principles that transcend personal desires. He calls for a commitment to collective movements and causes that address the fundamental structures of society, arguing that only through such an approach can true liberation be achieved. This perspective challenges the traditional existential focus on the individual, advocating instead for a more expansive and socially engaged understanding of authenticity.[94]

Roberto Unger advocates for a "prophetic" form of existentialism that not only encourages personal introspection but also calls for radical social transformation. Unger suggests that philosophy, like poetry and politics, must serve as a prophetic voice in an age were democracy and global interconnectedness demand new forms of engagement. He argues that this prophetic role involves a vision of how we can respond to the experience of being "lost in a void," using the tools and resources available to us to create meaningful change in the present.[95]

Unger's approach emphasizes that prophecy should focus on the future, driving us to live more freely and fully in the present by reimagining and reconstructing the structures of society. He suggests that this forward-looking perspective is crucial for organizing our social and economic systems in ways that better align with human potential and dignity. By placing emphasis on what can be achieved now, Unger challenges us to reject static and nostalgic views of the past, advocating instead for dynamic and transformative actions.[96]

He further contends that true authenticity is not just about personal fulfillment but must involve a commitment to social and institutional changes that can elevate human life. Unger criticizes any approach that dismisses the prophetic ambition of higher-order discourse—discourses that inform powerful proposals for change. He argues that these proposals should not be dismissed as lofty or impractical but rather embraced as necessary steps towards realizing a more just and humane society.[97]

Unger's prophetic existentialism also addresses the challenge of embracing the new and the transformative, despite the resistance that often accompanies change. He believes that by separating thought from the fear of the new, we can open ourselves up to the possibilities that lie beyond the current social and economic orders. This perspective highlights the importance of imagination and creativity in envisioning and

---

94. Badiou, *Being and Event*.
95. Unger, *Self Awakened*, 27.
96. Unger, *Self Awakened*, 28.
97. Unger, *Self Awakened*, 46.

implementing social transformations that resonate with the prophetic vision of a more equitable world.[98]

In this context, Unger's philosophy calls for an active engagement with the world, where the personal and social dimensions of authenticity are intertwined. He posits that our thinking about nature and humanity must evolve to reflect a commitment to the transformation of social and economic structures, recognizing that our current systems often constrain human potential. By advocating for this integrated approach, Unger expands the concept of authenticity to include a proactive stance toward social change, urging individuals to not only seek personal growth but also contribute to the collective reimagining of society.[99]

Wendy Brown critiques the neoliberal focus on individualism by highlighting how it undermines collective forms of authenticity and distorts the true meaning of personal fulfillment. Brown argues that neoliberalism's emphasis on competition and self-reliance reshapes individuals into "homo oeconomicus," a concept where human beings are primarily seen as economic agents, constantly engaging in self-investment and cost-benefit calculations in all aspects of life. This market-driven rationality reduces authenticity to a commodified and self-centered pursuit, stripping it of its deeper, more communal significance.[100]

Brown contends that under neoliberalism, the concept of human capital becomes both an identity and a normative expectation—what we are, and what we should strive to be. This redefinition of individuals as economic actors pervades all domains of life, extending beyond literal wealth generation to affect personal relationships, education, and even self-concept. By making competition a normative rather than a natural condition, neoliberalism imposes market logic on areas traditionally governed by different values, thereby distorting the essence of authenticity and reducing it to an economic calculus.[101]

Furthermore, Brown critiques how neoliberal rationality saturates everyday practices and institutions, turning all forms of conduct and concern into economic parameters. This shift extinguishes the classic liberal democratic concerns with justice and the balancing of diverse interests, as market values become the only measures of all actions. In this context, authenticity is no longer about genuine engagement with oneself

---

98. Unger, *Self Awakened*, 62.
99. Unger, *Self Awakened*, 75.
100. Brown, *Undoing the Demos*, 10, 32.
101. Brown, *Undoing the Demos*, 34–36.

or society but is instead about aligning one's life with the demands of market competition and economic efficiency.[102]

Brown's analysis suggests that true authenticity must resist this neoliberal reconfiguration and instead foster solidarity and collective well-being. She argues that authenticity, when stripped of its communal aspects and reduced to individual self-reliance, becomes a shallow and hollow pursuit. Instead of adhering to neoliberal values, she advocates for an understanding of authenticity that emphasizes shared human experiences and collective action, aiming to rebuild the social bonds that neoliberalism seeks to dissolve.[103]

By revisiting classical ideas from thinkers like Aristotle, Brown emphasizes the importance of political life and communal engagement as essential components of human freedom and fulfillment. She challenges the neoliberal paradigm by advocating for a return to these richer, more interconnected forms of life, where authenticity is understood not as a solitary endeavor but as a shared journey towards a more just and humane society.[104]

Cornel West's reflections on existentialism and liberation theology emphasize the vital role of prophetic pragmatism in achieving existential authenticity. West argues that authenticity should not be limited to personal fulfillment but must be rooted in a commitment to social justice and the well-being of the community. He critiques the individualistic tendencies of traditional existentialism, which often focuses narrowly on the self without adequately addressing the systemic injustices faced by marginalized communities. For West, true authenticity is deeply intertwined with the struggles for social and racial justice, making the pursuit of authenticity both a communal and ethical endeavor.[105]

West's prophetic pragmatism draws from the rich tradition of black Christian thought, which has long been engaged in the fight for liberation and justice. He points out that to be part of the black freedom movement is to be in close contact with prophetic figures who view the world through the eyes of its victims, particularly through the lens of the Cross. This perspective, informed by the suffering and resilience of oppressed

---

102. Brown, *Undoing the Demos*, 43–50.
103. Brown, *Undoing the Demos*, 19, 43.
104. Brown, *Undoing the Demos*, 87–89.
105. West, *Cornel West Reader*, 171.

communities, provides a critical framework for understanding the interconnectedness of personal and collective liberation.[106]

In his critique of pragmatism, West highlights the need for a more robust engagement with the tragic and comic dimensions of life, as well as the operations of institutional and structural power. He argues that pragmatism, at its best, encourages relentless critical consciousness and promotes the democratization of American intellectual life. However, it must also be self-critical and remain aware of the implications of power in shaping knowledge and societal norms.[107]

West also emphasizes the importance of viewing every individual as deserving of dignity, respect, and love, especially those who have been denied these basic rights by societal structures. This moral claim is central to his prophetic pragmatism, which combines courageous resistance with a critical analysis of the social causes of unnecessary suffering. West's approach advocates for a collective struggle against various forms of social misery, insisting that authenticity must be linked to the broader goals of social transformation and justice.[108]

Ultimately, West calls for an authentic existence that is not just about self-realization but is also deeply connected to the fight for justice and the dismantling of systems of oppression. He underscores the necessity of a communal approach to authenticity, one that actively engages with the challenges of racism, sexism, homophobia, and other forms of discrimination. In doing so, West presents a vision of authenticity that is both ethically grounded and socially engaged, offering a powerful critique of any approach that prioritizes personal over collective liberation.[109]

Conclusively, this section demonstrates how various thinkers address the complexities of existential authenticity in the context of modern society. They argue that authenticity must go beyond personal fulfillment and be understood in relation to social, political, and economic structures. From Richard Sennett's critique of the flexible economy to Judith Butler's exploration of performativity, and from Slavoj Žižek's focus on ideological influences to Charles Taylor's ethics of authenticity, each thinker challenges the traditional notion of a stable, individualistic authenticity. Instead, they advocate for a more dynamic and socially

---

106. West, *Cornel West Reader*, 172.
107. West, *Cornel West Reader*, 183, 186.
108. West, *Cornel West Reader*, 14.
109. West, *Cornel West Reader*, 270, 402.

engaged understanding of authenticity, one that is intertwined with collective action and social responsibility.

2.2. INNOVATING THEOLOGY EDUCATION AND DISCOURSE

This section delves into the various approaches to praxis-oriented theological education, examining how different theologians have integrated key concerns such as social justice, ecological awareness, prophetic witness, feminist critique, postcolonial perspectives, and eschatological hope into their educational frameworks. These perspectives challenge traditional theological education to go beyond mere intellectual study, emphasizing the importance of engaging with the lived realities and struggles of marginalized communities and the broader ecological crisis.

The theologians discussed in this section argue for a theological education that is not only academically rigorous but also practically engaged with the world. They highlight the interconnectedness of all creation, the need for solidarity with the oppressed, and the responsibility of theological education to foster a transformative, justice-oriented practice. By doing so, they offer a broader and more inclusive framework that encourages students and educators alike to rethink how theology can be applied in ways that promote social and environmental justice.

2.2.1. Addressing Ecology, Justice, and Suffering

In the exploration of contextual and comparative theology, recent theologians have broadened and critiqued the methodologies, contributing diverse perspectives that both enrich and challenge traditional approaches. These thinkers, including Elizabeth A. Johnson, M. Shawn Copeland, Jürgen Moltmann, Kathryn Tanner, Miroslav Volf, and Serene Jones, have each addressed pressing contemporary issues such as ecology, intersectionality, capitalism, identity, and trauma. Their work underscores the necessity of integrating these real-world concerns into theological reflection, ensuring that theology remains relevant and responsive to the complex realities of human life and the natural world. Through their contributions, these theologians encourage a rethinking of how theology interacts with and addresses the multifaceted challenges of the modern era.

Recent theologians have expanded and critiqued the methodology of contextual and comparative theology, contributing diverse perspectives that enrich and challenge this approach. Among these voices, Elizabeth A. Johnson has brought significant attention to the importance of ecological theology. She argues that theological reflection cannot be complete without a deep understanding of the interconnectedness of all creation[110], emphasizing that the natural world must be considered as an irreplaceable element within the broader theological discourse.[111]

Johnson's work underscores the need to integrate ecological concerns into theological discussions to foster a more holistic understanding of God's creation. She critiques traditional theologies that have often overlooked or marginalized the environmental crisis, advocating instead for an ecological ethic that recognizes the intrinsic value of Earth's community of life.[112] Her perspective challenges theologians to rethink the scope of their reflections, ensuring that the natural world is not merely a backdrop but a central focus of theological inquiry.

In her exploration, Johnson also engages in a dialogue with evolutionary theory, particularly Darwin's insights, to highlight how the ongoing process of creation reflects divine creativity. She suggests that this continuous unfolding of life points to a God who is actively involved in the world, not just at its inception but throughout its history, thereby calling for a theology that embraces the dynamic and evolving nature of the natural world.[113]

Through these contributions, Johnson advocates for a theological framework that is responsive to the ecological realities of our time, urging a shift from anthropocentric views to one that honors the broader ecological context of life on Earth. This approach invites a reimagining of

---

110. Johnson's perspective is further substantiated by discussions on eco-justice within Christian theology, emphasizing the necessity for a reformation that integrates ecological considerations with social justice principles. This integration advocates for a holistic approach, acknowledging the interdependence of environmental sustainability and social equity. The Yale Forum on Religion and Ecology provides an in-depth examination of eco-justice ethics, highlighting how sustainability and social justice can be harmoniously pursued within theological frameworks (Yale Forum on Religion and Ecology, 2023). Additionally, Hessel and Ruether offer a comprehensive introduction to current thought on Christianity and ecology, exploring how ecological concerns are deeply interconnected with ethical imperatives for justice (Hessel and Ruether, Christianity and Ecology).

111. Johnson, *Ask the Beasts*, xv.

112. Johnson, *Ask the Beasts*, xvi.

113. Johnson, *Ask the Beasts*, xiv.

theological concepts in ways that align with the need for environmental stewardship and respect for all forms of life.[114]

M. Shawn Copeland's work emphasizes the critical importance of intersectionality in theology, particularly in understanding how different forms of oppression intersect and create unique challenges for marginalized communities. She argues that these intersecting systems of power form a complex "matrix of intersecting power dynamics" that must be recognized and addressed within theological discourse.[115] This perspective urges theologians to consider how various forms of oppression, such as those based on race, gender, and class, interact and reinforce each other, thereby creating distinctive experiences of marginalization.

Copeland further argues that a true commitment to intersectionality requires openness, listening, and a willingness to engage in self-correction. This process involves closely listening to the voices and experiences of those who have been marginalized, particularly over centuries of systemic injustice. Copeland emphasizes that authentic theological reflection must begin with this deep listening, allowing for a genuine re-evaluation of traditional theological practices and beliefs.[116]

In examining the intersection of race and social policy, Copeland highlights the importance of movements like #SayHerName, which resist police brutality against Black women. She draws on the work of Crenshaw and Ritchie to illustrate how the resurgent racial justice movement in the United States has brought attention to the specific vulnerabilities of Black women within the broader struggle for racial justice. This focus on the intersection of race and gender underscores the need for a theology that is responsive to these particular experiences of oppression.[117]

Copeland also critiques the historical role of the Catholic Church in perpetuating systems of oppression, particularly through the ownership of enslaved people by Catholic clergy and religious orders. She notes the ambivalence within the Church's teachings on sex and sexuality, particularly regarding female, lesbian, gay, and transgender bodies. This ambivalence reflects a broader discomfort within the Church toward bodies that do not conform to traditional norms, further marginalizing those who do not fit within these rigid categories.[118]

114. Johnson, *Ask the Beasts*, viii.
115. Copeland, *Enfleshing Freedom*, 56.
116. Copeland, *Enfleshing Freedom*, 97.
117. Copeland, *Enfleshing Freedom*, 192.
118. Copeland, *Enfleshing Freedom*, 64.

Moreover, Copeland examines how the Catholic sacramental economy has historically pathologized certain bodily expressions, particularly those of lesbian, gay, and transgender persons, compelling them to view themselves as disordered within the framework of Catholic teaching. This critique is part of her broader call for a reimagining of theological practice that fully includes and affirms the diverse experiences of all people, particularly those who have been marginalized by the Church's teachings.[119]

In addressing the broader historical context, Copeland references the discriminatory practices faced by Catholics and Asians during the raids of the 1920s and the internment of Japanese Americans during World War II. These examples illustrate how the Church has been complicit in, or at least silent about, systemic injustices against marginalized groups. This historical complicity calls for a re-examination of the Church's role in perpetuating or challenging systems of power.[120]

Finally, Copeland advocates for a theology that privileges the experiences and bodies of Black women, not to exclude others, but to bring specificity and particularity to theological reflection. She emphasizes that by focusing on these specific experiences, theology can better address the unique challenges faced by marginalized communities and can contribute to a more just and inclusive understanding of faith.[121] Through these reflections, Copeland calls for a theology that is deeply rooted in the lived experiences of marginalized communities, particularly Black women, and that insists on the importance of embodiment in theological discourse.

Jürgen Moltmann has long advocated for a theology that actively engages with the world's pressing issues, emphasizing that Christian hope should not remain an abstract concept but should inspire concrete actions toward justice and reconciliation. He critiques theologies that are detached from the realities of suffering and insists that true Christian theology must be grounded in the anticipation of God's kingdom, where the renewal of creation becomes visible through human participation in God's work.[122]

Moltmann's theology of hope is deeply eschatological, focusing on the future completion of God's kingdom while urging believers to live

---

119. Copeland, *Enfleshing Freedom*, 65.
120. Copeland, *Enfleshing Freedom*, 58.
121. Copeland, *Enfleshing Freedom*, xi.
122. Moltmann, *Ethics of Hope*, xii.

in a way that reflects this hope in the present. He argues that the work done in the world should be viewed "sub specie aeternitatis," or in the light of God's eternal kingdom. This perspective awakens believers to the importance of being vigilant and proactive, preparing for what is to come by engaging in acts that mirror the kingdom of God.[123]

His critique extends to traditional distinctions within Christian eschatology, such as those between the kingdom of God and the kingdom of the devil. Moltmann stresses that the kingdom of God on earth is not merely an abstract spiritual concept but a reality that counters the chaos spread by evil. He calls for a theology that actively seeks to bring about better orders in the world, aligning earthly governance with the values of God's kingdom.[124]

Moltmann also engages with the relationship between human rights and ecological rights, arguing that these should be integrated within theological ethics. He contends that if ethics allow themselves to be shaped solely by dominant worldviews, they fail to innovate and address the real needs of the world, including the urgent need for ecological sustainability.[125] This critique challenges theologians to rethink their approaches to ethics, ensuring they are not simply reactive but are actively contributing to the anticipation of God's new creation.

In his discussion on the intersection of nature and grace, Moltmann reflects on the limitations of traditional Catholic liberation theology, which has often seen hope as a supernatural virtue, disconnected from God's future. He advocates for a theology that recognizes the birth of Christian hope out of God's promise for the future, thereby linking hope more closely with the practical realities of liberation and justice in the present.[126]

Moltmann's vision is one of active participation in the struggle between the kingdom of God and the forces of evil in the world. He asserts that Jesus Christ is already Lord over all sectors of human life, and therefore, Christians are called to engage with the world in ways that reflect Christ's lordship, working towards the realization of God's kingdom on earth.[127]

---

123. Moltmann, *Ethics of Hope*, 6.
124. Moltmann, *Ethics of Hope*, 11.
125. Moltmann, *Ethics of Hope*, viii.
126. Moltmann, *Ethics of Hope*, xiv.
127. Moltmann, *Ethics of Hope*, 20.

His theology challenges the historical detachment of Christian practice from worldly affairs, particularly criticizing the retreat from responsibility for the world seen in certain theological traditions. Moltmann calls for a re-engagement with the world, urging Christians to take responsibility for the earth and its future, as the world belongs to God and is the arena where God's kingdom is to be realized.[128]

Moltmann's reflections are a call to move beyond mere anticipation of the future kingdom and to embody that hope in tangible ways today. He emphasizes that the messianic hope presented by the prophets is not just a distant dream but a driving force that calls people out of apathy and into active participation in movements for liberation. This hope is meant to be lived out, inspiring action that aligns with the kingdom of God and its values of justice and reconciliation.[129]

Kathryn Tanner critically explores the dynamics of finance-dominated capitalism, emphasizing how this economic system profoundly influences contemporary life and diverges from Christian values. She argues that capitalism today is characterized by a focus on financial profit, which has increasingly overshadowed other forms of economic activity. In this system, finance is no longer merely a support for production but has taken on a life of its own, prioritizing profit generation above all else, often at the expense of broader social responsibilities.[130]

Tanner describes how finance-dominated capitalism has created a situation where profit is primarily generated within the financial sector, including banking, insurance, and real estate, rather than through traditional production. This shift means that financial activities are now central to the economy, dictating the behavior of corporations and governments alike. The drive for financial profits often leads to a narrowing of corporate responsibility, where the focus is on maximizing shareholder value rather than considering the welfare of employees or the broader community.[131]

In discussing the implications of this economic model, Tanner notes that the responsibilities of corporations have increasingly been transferred to individuals. This shift has resulted in individuals bearing the costs of economic activities, whether in terms of their health, employment stability, or financial security. Governments, under pressure to

---

128. Moltmann, *Ethics of Hope*, 29.
129. Moltmann, *Ethics of Hope*, 36.
130. Tanner, *Christianity and the New Spirit of Capitalism*, 9.
131. Tanner, *Christianity and the New Spirit of Capitalism*, 11.

attract private investment at minimal cost, have also adopted practices that discipline both corporations and individuals, further entrenching the power of finance.[132]

Tanner points out that this system prioritizes immediate financial returns over long-term investments in workers or communities. For example, practices like the rapid selling of mortgages allow financial institutions to offload risks, focusing on short-term profits rather than the long-term health of the economy. This approach reflects a broader trend within finance-dominated capitalism, where future considerations are often sacrificed for immediate financial gain.[133]

Furthermore, Tanner critiques how the emphasis on maximizing shareholder value leads to practices that prioritize efficiency and cost-cutting over the well-being of employees and communities. This shift marks a departure from previous business models that might have balanced profit-making with investments in people and local communities. In finance-dominated capitalism, the focus is on minimal expenditure and maximum profit, often resulting in the exploitation of workers and the erosion of community ties.[134]

Tanner's analysis extends to the theological implications of this economic system. She argues that contemporary capitalism often conflicts with Christian teachings, particularly those related to economic justice and the common good. The relentless pursuit of profit within finance-dominated capitalism undermines the ethical foundations of Christian theology, which emphasizes care for the marginalized and the responsible stewardship of resources.[135]

Tanner challenges theologians to critically engage with these economic structures, advocating for a theology that not only critiques the injustices inherent in finance-dominated capitalism but also offers alternative visions rooted in the values of the gospel. Her work calls for a reexamination of how theology can resist these economic practices and support a more just and equitable economic system, one that aligns more closely with Christian ethical principles.[136] Through this critique, Tanner urges a rethinking of the relationship between theology and economics,

---

132. Tanner, *Christianity and the New Spirit of Capitalism*, 23.
133. Tanner, *Christianity and the New Spirit of Capitalism*, 14.
134. Tanner, *Christianity and the New Spirit of Capitalism*, 20.
135. Tanner, *Christianity and the New Spirit of Capitalism*, 51.
136. Tanner, *Christianity and the New Spirit of Capitalism*, 55.

highlighting the need for a theology that actively supports economic justice and resists the exploitative tendencies of contemporary capitalism.

Miroslav Volf's exploration of theology emphasizes the critical role it plays in addressing issues of identity, exclusion, and reconciliation. He critiques the ways in which theology has sometimes contributed to division and exclusion, arguing that a theology that does not engage with the realities of human suffering and conflict is incomplete. Volf draws on thinkers like Friedrich Nietzsche, who viewed Christianity as promoting "active sympathy for the ill-constituted and weak," to illustrate how theological perspectives have been both critiqued and misunderstood by secular critics.[137]

Volf acknowledges that from the perspective of critics like Nietzsche, religion, and particularly Christianity, can appear as a force of oppressive irrationality, insisting on shaping the world according to the precepts of a God whom these critics believe does not exist. However, Volf's focus is not on debating the existence of God but on addressing the "malfunctions of religion"—the ways in which religious beliefs can sometimes go astray and contribute to harm rather than healing.[138]

In advocating for a theology that promotes reconciliation, Volf stresses the importance of engaging with the world in a way that reflects the transformative power of faith. He argues that true prophetic religion requires both "ascent" a connection with the divine—and "return"—a commitment to transforming the world. Without this dual focus, Volf suggests religion loses its prophetic edge and becomes either irrelevant or oppressive.[139]

Volf also discusses the importance of public engagement for people of faith, emphasizing that faith should guide how believers engage with the world, not only shaping their personal lives but also informing them of their contributions to the common good. He argues that faith provides a way of life that offers guidance on which paths to take and which to avoid, particularly in the context of public and social engagement.[140]

In his critique of the Stoic and Nietzschean views of human flourishing, Volf contrasts these with a Christian perspective that emphasizes love and care for others. He argues that if we believe in a God who is love and that we are created for love, then ideals like the Stoic pursuit of tranquil

137. Tanner, *Christianity and the New Spirit of Capitalism*, 22.
138. Volf, *Public Faith*, 23.
139. Volf, *Public Faith*, 27.
140. Volf, *Public Faith*, 34.

self-sufficiency are insufficient. Instead, a Christian understanding of flourishing involves active care and engagement with the needs of others.[141]

Volf's work consistently underscores the potential of theology to contribute positively to public life. He calls for a theology that not only avoids complicity in division and exclusion but actively works to bridge divides and promote peace. By engaging with the world in ways that reflect the transformative power of faith, theology can play a crucial role in fostering social reconciliation and addressing the injustices that divide communities.[142]

Serene Jones has critically engaged with the intersections of trauma, theology, and feminist theory, challenging traditional theological approaches that have often overlooked or minimized the experiences of trauma survivors. In her work, Jones shares a personal encounter with a young woman named Leah, whom she was mentoring toward baptism. Leah suffered from post-traumatic stress disorder (PTSD) due to early childhood trauma, leading Jones to wrestle with what it would take for the church to genuinely engage with such deep-seated trauma as a social and spiritual issue.[143]

Jones explains that PTSD is characterized by the lingering effects of violence long after the initial event has passed. This condition, marked by symptoms such as memory loss, dissociative episodes, and a profound sense of powerlessness, affects not just individuals but can also resonate within communities and societies that have undergone collective trauma. For instance, Jones reflects on how the traumatic events of 9/11 drew the entire nation into a shared experience of trauma, highlighting how PTSD symptoms can mirror the collective distress of such large-scale events.[144]

Through her interactions with Leah, Jones gained a deeper understanding of PTSD, learning about the profound isolation and disconnection that trauma survivors often experience. Leah's struggles revealed the insidious nature of PTSD, where survivors find themselves cut off from their communities and sources of support, exacerbating their sense of isolation and making recovery even more challenging.[145]

Jones advocates for a theology that is more attuned to the realities of suffering and trauma. She argues that Christianity, rooted in the story

---

141. Volf, *Public Faith*, 89.
142. Volf, *Public Faith*, 38.
143. Jones, *Trauma and Grace*, xi.
144. Jones, *Trauma and Grace*, 27.
145. Jones, *Trauma and Grace*, 18.

CHAPTER TWO

of the crucifixion and resurrection of Jesus, already contains within it the resources to address trauma and grace. However, the church must be willing to engage with these narratives in ways that speak directly to the experiences of those who have been undone by violence. By doing so, theology can offer hope and healing within a framework that recognizes the complexities of human experience, rather than glossing over them or offering superficial solutions.[146]

In her work, Jones also explores how trauma survivors often find themselves in a state of disordered thoughts, continually replaying the traumatic events in their minds. This repetition mirrors the ways in which trauma can distort one's sense of reality, making it difficult to move forward or find peace. By acknowledging this reality, Jones calls for a theology that not only recognizes the pervasive impact of trauma but also seeks to offer tangible forms of grace and support that can help survivors navigate their difficult journeys.[147]

Jones's theological reflection is deeply informed by her encounters with trauma survivors and her understanding of the ways trauma impacts both individuals and communities. She stresses the importance of a trauma-informed theology that can meet people where they are, offering a space for healing that honors their experiences and provides a path toward restoration and wholeness.[148] Through this approach, Jones invites theologians and religious communities to rethink how they address suffering, ensuring that their practices are grounded in a deep awareness of the realities of trauma and the need for compassionate, responsive care.

In summary, the theologians discussed in this section each contribute to a broader and more inclusive understanding of theology by engaging with contemporary issues such as ecology, intersectionality, capitalism, reconciliation, and trauma. Their work challenges traditional theological frameworks, urging a reimagining of how faith interacts with the world. By addressing these pressing concerns, they call for a theology that is not only reflective but also actively involved in promoting justice, healing, and a deeper awareness of the interconnectedness of all aspects of life. This approach underscores the importance of grounding theological reflection in the lived experiences of individuals and communities, ensuring that it remains relevant and responsive to the challenges of our time.

---

146. Jones, *Trauma and Grace*, 21.
147. Jones, *Trauma and Grace*, 38.
148. Jones, *Trauma and Grace*, xiii.

2.2.2. Diverse Narratives in Theology

This section explores the evolving role of narrative theology, examining how various thinkers have engaged with the concept and expanded its application. It considers how narratives shape theological understanding and practice, drawing on perspectives from historical, sociological, and feminist critiques. By addressing the intersection of narrative with lived experiences, cultural contexts, and power dynamics, this section highlights the ongoing development of narrative theology as a framework that seeks to include and empower marginalized voices while rethinking traditional theological categories.

Rosenstock-Huessy's work emphasizes the transformative power of narratives, especially within the context of theology. His application of the grammatical method across historical, sociological, and theological disciplines illustrates how different modes of speech have shaped human understanding and orientation throughout history. For instance, he shows that tribal speech connected humanity to its ancestors and past, while Templar speech, as seen in ancient civilizations like Egypt, oriented people toward the cosmos. Greek speech turned inward, engaging with the self through poetry and philosophy, and the speech of Israel directed humanity toward the future through prophecy.[149]

With the advent of Christianity, these four ancient modes of speech were integrated, allowing individuals to move beyond a singular focus. This integration reflects a rhythm in human experience—from heeding prophetic imperatives to reflecting inwardly, learning from historical narratives, and finally, expressing one's own response to the realities they have encountered. Rosenstock-Huessy argues that this pattern is evident not only in the history of Western revolutions but also in any significant human experience, suggesting that this framework is crucial for understanding the unfolding of God's Kingdom as expressed in narrative theology.[150]

Rosenstock-Huessy also discusses how individuals discover themselves through speech, as outlined in his sociological and psychological works. He contrasts this with Martin Buber's concept of a two-fold reality, instead proposing a four-fold reality in which a person hears themselves addressed as "Thou," leading to the discovery of the "I," their subjective self. This discovery then prompts the individual to contribute

---

149. Rosenstock-Huessy, *Speech and Reality*, 6.
150. Rosenstock-Huessy, *Speech and Reality*, 6–7.

CHAPTER TWO

creatively to the community, forming a "We" in relationships, and finally being recognized as a "He" within broader social groups. This process, which Rosenstock-Huessy terms the "Cross of Reality," aligns with the goals of narrative theology, which values personal and communal stories as essential to understanding theological truths.[151]

In his theological writings, Rosenstock-Huessy further connects the act of speaking and listening with the divine. He suggests that what the church identifies as the Holy Spirit can be understood as the "speech of mankind," where the flow of life-giving speech across generations is seen as a manifestation of the Holy Spirit. This perspective redefines concepts of divinity and resurrection, emphasizing the importance of being heard by future generations. Such an understanding resonates with narrative theology's focus on the power of stories from marginalized communities as key sources for articulating the nature of God and liberation.[152]

Recent scholars have continued to develop and critique narrative theology, adding new perspectives and raising challenges that deepen our understanding of its role in both theology and practice. James K. A. Smith, for example, has emphasized that narrative is not only crucial for theological understanding but also for shaping practices of worship and spiritual formation. He argues that stories are central to how individuals and communities inhabit their faith, suggesting that narrative theology must engage deeply with the liturgical and embodied practices that shape believers' lives.[153]

Smith highlights that our lives are fundamentally shaped by what we love and desire, which are often molded by the narratives and practices we participate in. He points out that these narratives are not isolated but are part of a communal and traditional framework that shapes our social imaginary—how we envision the world and our place in it. This communal aspect of narratives emphasizes that narrative theology must consider the broader context of these stories and how they influence our perception of reality and value.[154]

Furthermore, Smith critiques the tendency of narrative theology to become overly abstract if it does not remain connected to lived practices. He argues that without this connection to embodied practices, narrative theology risks losing its relevance to the daily lives of believers. Instead,

---

151. Rosenstock-Huessy, *Speech and Reality*, 7.
152. Rosenstock-Huessy, *Speech and Reality*, 7.
153. Smith, *Desiring the Kingdom*, 53.
154. Smith, *Desiring the Kingdom*, 66.

Smith advocates for a theology that is deeply connected to the rituals and liturgies that form our desires and loves, recognizing that these practices play a crucial role in shaping our theological understanding.[155]

Smith also emphasizes the importance of recognizing the competing narratives that influence our lives. He notes that Christians are often shaped by multiple communities and stories, not just those within the church. This complexity requires a more nuanced approach to narrative theology, one that acknowledges the various influences on our beliefs and values. Smith suggests that understanding this dynamic can help narrative theology address the challenges posed by the pluralistic contexts in which we live.[156]

In conclusion, Smith's contributions to narrative theology underscore the necessity of integrating narrative with practice, ensuring that theology remains connected to the lived experiences and embodied practices of faith. His work challenges narrative theologians to consider how stories and practices together shape our understanding of God and our engagement with the world.[157]

Richard Kearney introduces the concept of "anatheism," which he describes as a return to God after the experience of doubt or disbelief. This idea is closely connected to the role of narrative in understanding the dynamics of belief in a post-secular world. Kearney argues that narratives of faith and doubt are essential for grasping the complexities of belief today, particularly in a world where traditional religious frameworks are increasingly questioned. According to Kearney, narrative theology should engage with stories that reflect these contemporary challenges, exploring how belief can be reimagined in the context of modern experiences of doubt and rediscovery.[158]

Kearney further explains that anatheism is not about creating a new religion or merging theism and atheism into a final synthesis. Instead, it is a third way, a space where the decision to believe or not believe is both tolerated and cherished. This space allows for the possibility of rediscovering faith in a God after God—a faith that moves beyond rigid dogmatism or militant atheism, offering a renewed understanding of the sacred in a world that often oscillates between belief and disbelief.[159]

---

155. Smith, *Desiring the Kingdom*, 127.
156. Smith, *Desiring the Kingdom*, 55.
157. Smith, *Desiring the Kingdom*, 148.
158. Kearney, *Anatheism*, xiv.
159. Kearney, *Anatheism*, 6.

He emphasizes that anatheism involves a moment of reckoning where individuals are free to choose between faith and non-faith. This choice reflects the ongoing tension between theism and atheism, making both belief and non-belief possible. Kearney describes anatheism as an invitation to revisit the fundamental encounter with the divine, particularly through the figure of the radical Stranger—a theme that resonates deeply with narrative theology's focus on stories of encounter and transformation.[160]

Kearney also highlights that anatheism challenges the duality of the sacred and the profane by exploring narratives that blur these boundaries. He suggests that engaging with such stories can liberate individuals from rigid ideologies, allowing them to explore new possibilities for belief or non-belief. This approach aligns with narrative theology's emphasis on the power of stories to shape and reshape our understanding of the divine in a post-secular context.[161]

In sum, Kearney's concept of anatheism invites narrative theology to explore the complexities of faith in contemporary contexts. By engaging with stories that reflect the ongoing tension between belief and doubt, narrative theology can address the challenges of a post-secular world, offering a space for reimagining faith in a way that embraces both the sacred and the profane.[162]

Catherine Keller's work in process theology intersects with narrative theology, particularly through her exploration of apocalyptic narratives. Keller suggests that the stories we tell about the end times and ultimate reality have a significant impact on our present actions and ethical commitments. She argues that these narratives often carry certain ethical implications that are deeply intertwined with Western history, and that they must be critically examined to avoid reinforcing exclusionary and destructive worldviews.[163]

Keller calls for a reimagining of apocalyptic narratives to reflect more hopeful and inclusive visions of the future. She proposes that instead of accepting traditional apocalyptic stories at face value, which can sometimes support harmful ideologies, we should explore narrative resources that allow for a more compassionate and interconnected

---

160. Kearney, *Anatheism*, 7.
161. Kearney, *Anatheism*, 11.
162. Kearney, *Anatheism*, 18.
163. Keller, *Cloud of the Impossible*, 10.

cosmopolitics. By engaging with these reimagined narratives, theology can contribute to a more just and loving world.[164]

Keller also emphasizes the importance of understanding how narratives about ultimate reality influence not only our beliefs but also our social and political practices. She points out that these narratives are not merely theoretical constructs but are deeply embedded in the way we live and interact with others. Therefore, it is crucial to critically engage with these stories to ensure that they promote a vision of the world that is inclusive and life-affirming.[165]

Through her work, Keller invites theologians and scholars to consider how traditional narratives, especially those related to the apocalypse, can be transformed to foster ethical and sustainable futures. She highlights the need for a new kind of narrative entanglement—one that is interreligious, international, and interethnic—reflecting the complexities and interconnectedness of our globalized world.[166]

In summary, Keller's contributions to process theology and narrative theology emphasize the need to rethink the stories we tell about the end times. By reimagining these narratives, we can develop more hopeful and inclusive visions of the future that align with ethical and compassionate practices, ultimately contributing to a more just and equitable world.[167]

Kwok Pui-lan offers a postcolonial critique of narrative theology, urging that it must pay more attention to the stories of those who have been colonized and oppressed. She emphasizes that narrative theology cannot simply include these voices as an afterthought but must fundamentally rethink theological categories and assumptions. Kwok argues that narratives have often been used to justify imperialism and marginalization, and therefore, a decolonizing approach is necessary to develop a truly liberative narrative theology.[168]

In her analysis, Kwok highlights how traditional narratives, such as those found in the Bible, have been shaped by colonial forces. She points out that these texts were often written and redacted by male colonial elites, aiming to reconcile their histories and identities under the shadow of empires. This recognition leads Kwok to call for a postcolonial

---

164. Keller, *Cloud of the Impossible*, 11.
165. Keller, *Cloud of the Impossible*, 35.
166. Keller, *Cloud of the Impossible*, 53.
167. Keller, *Cloud of the Impossible*, 25.
168. Kwok, *Postcolonial Imagination and Feminist Theology*, 23.

feminist interpretation that investigates the role of gender and power in these narratives, seeking to uncover the ways they have reinforced colonial control and marginalization.[169]

Kwok also discusses the importance of reimagining these narratives to reflect the experiences and perspectives of women from the Global South. She notes that these women, often marginalized from national politics and religious discourse, have developed unique approaches to political theology that challenge both patriarchy and colonialism. By bringing these perspectives into the conversation, Kwok argues that narrative theology can be transformed into a more inclusive and liberative framework that genuinely addresses the needs and realities of the oppressed.[170]

Furthermore, Kwok emphasizes that this approach is not merely about expanding the scope of narrative theology but about fundamentally challenging the assumptions that have underpinned traditional theological discourse. She points out that many Asian people remain hostile to Christianity because it is still associated with the pain and suffering of colonial contact. Thus, a new narrative discourse must be developed—one that not only includes diverse voices but also critically examines the colonial history of these narratives.[171]

Through her postcolonial critique, Kwok Pui-lan challenges theologians to rethink how narratives have been used historically and to develop a narrative theology that is truly decolonizing and liberative. This involves not only incorporating the voices of the oppressed but also reexamining and reshaping the foundational categories and assumptions of theological discourse to reflect a more just and inclusive vision of faith.[172]

Amos Yong engages with narrative theology through the unique lens of Pentecostalism, arguing that the stories emerging from Pentecostal communities worldwide offer rich resources for theological reflection. He emphasizes that Pentecostal narratives, particularly those that highlight the active presence of the Holy Spirit, provide valuable perspectives on divine agency and human experience. However, Yong also critiques narrative theology for sometimes failing to fully engage

---

169. Kwok, *Postcolonial Imagination and Feminist Theology*, 8.
170. Kwok, *Postcolonial Imagination and Feminist Theology*, 24.
171. Kwok, *Postcolonial Imagination and Feminist Theology*, 43.
172. Kwok, *Postcolonial Imagination and Feminist Theology*, 7.

with the theological importance of these narratives, urging for a more robust integration of Pentecostal experiences into broader theological discussions.[173]

Yong points out that Pentecostalism, with its focus on the Holy Spirit's active role in the world, brings a distinctive understanding to theology that is grounded in lived experiences. These narratives are often conveyed through oral traditions, dreams, and visions, which are central to the spiritual lives of Pentecostal believers. This oral and experiential nature of Pentecostal theology challenges more abstract theological frameworks, calling for a narrative theology that is deeply connected to the lived realities of faith communities.[174]

Furthermore, Yong argues that Pentecostal narratives should be recognized for their contributions to the broader theological discourse, particularly in how they reframe traditional Christian doctrines such as the Trinity and the Incarnation. He suggests that these stories, which often emerge from the margins of the global church, offer fresh perspectives on how God is understood and experienced in different cultural contexts. This intercultural dimension of Pentecostalism highlights the need for narrative theology to be inclusive of diverse voices and experiences, particularly those from the Global South.[175]

Yong also addresses the challenges that Pentecostal theology faces in being integrated into the wider theological conversation. He notes that while Pentecostalism has often been marginalized in academic theology, its emphasis on the experiential and the practical offers a valuable corrective to more abstract approaches. By incorporating Pentecostal narratives, narrative theology can become more attuned to the realities of faith as lived by believers around the world, bridging the gap between theological reflection and everyday practice.[176]

In summary, Amos Yong's engagement with narrative theology through the lens of Pentecostalism highlights the importance of incorporating the stories and experiences of Pentecostal communities into the broader theological conversation. He calls for a narrative theology that fully acknowledges the theological relevance of these narratives, ensuring

---

173. Yong, *Spirit Poured Out on All Flesh*, 23.
174. Yong, *Spirit Poured Out on All Flesh*, 49.
175. Yong, *Spirit Poured Out on All Flesh*, 71.
176. Yong, *Spirit Poured Out on All Flesh*, 29.

that they are not only heard but also deeply integrated into the ongoing development of Christian theology.[177]

Elisabeth Schüssler Fiorenza has emphasized the significance of feminist critique within narrative theology, arguing that while narrative theology can be a powerful tool for bringing marginalized voices into the theological conversation, it must be vigilant to ensure that these narratives do not reinforce existing power structures. Schüssler Fiorenza advocates for a feminist narrative theology that not only tells the stories of women and other marginalized groups but also critically examines how these stories are told and whose interests they serve.[178]

Schüssler Fiorenza discusses the need to scrutinize the ways narratives are constructed and perpetuated, particularly within religious contexts. She warns that without critical examination, narrative theology runs the risk of perpetuating the very kyriarchal (hierarchical and oppressive) systems it seeks to challenge. To avoid this, Schüssler Fiorenza calls for a narrative theology that is aware of its own power dynamics and actively works to dismantle structures of domination.[179]

Furthermore, Schüssler Fiorenza points out that feminist narrative theology should not only focus on the inclusion of marginalized voices but also on how these voices are represented. This involves questioning traditional interpretations and challenging narratives that have historically silenced or misrepresented women and other marginalized groups. By doing so, feminist narrative theology can contribute to a more equitable and just theological discourse.[180]

In her critique, Schüssler Fiorenza also highlights the importance of intersectionality, noting that feminist narrative theology must consider the multiple and overlapping identities of individuals, such as race, class, and sexuality, and how these intersect with gender. She argues that a truly liberative narrative theology must address the complexities of these identities and the ways they interact with systems of power.[181]

Through her work, Schüssler Fiorenza challenges theologians to create a feminist narrative theology that goes beyond simply adding women's stories to the existing framework. Instead, she calls for a comprehensive rethinking of how narratives are constructed, who controls

177. Yong, *Spirit Poured Out on All Flesh*, 27.
178. Schüssler Fiorenza, *Transforming Vision*, 13.
179. Schüssler Fiorenza, *Transforming Vision*, 116.
180. Schüssler Fiorenza, *Transforming Vision*, 137.
181. Schüssler Fiorenza, *Transforming Vision*, 11.

them, and how they can be used to promote justice and equality in both religious and social contexts.[182]

In conclusion, this section highlights the diverse ways in which narrative theology is being developed and critiqued across various theological perspectives. From Rosenstock-Huessy's emphasis on the transformative role of speech in human history to James K. A. Smith's focus on the connection between narrative and practice, it becomes clear that stories play a crucial role in shaping theological understanding. Richard Kearney's concept of anatheism and Catherine Keller's exploration of apocalyptic narratives further illustrate the importance of reimagining traditional stories to reflect contemporary challenges and ethical considerations. Additionally, Kwok Pui-lan's postcolonial critique and Amos Yong's engagement with Pentecostal narratives emphasize the need to include marginalized voices and experiences in theological discourse. Elisabeth Schüssler Fiorenza's feminist critique serves as a reminder that narrative theology must be vigilant in questioning how stories are told and whose interests they serve, ensuring that it promotes justice and equality. Together, these perspectives demonstrate the evolving nature of narrative theology and its potential to foster a more inclusive and reflective approach to understanding faith.

2.2.3. Rethinking Theology Education

This section explores various approaches to praxis-oriented theological education, highlighting how different theologians have integrated social justice, ecological concerns, prophetic witness, feminist critique, postcolonial perspectives, and eschatological hope into their frameworks. Each perspective challenges traditional theological education to expand its focus beyond mere intellectual study, urging it to address the lived realities and struggles of marginalized communities, the ecological crisis, and the need for a distinctively Christian engagement with the world. These approaches emphasize the interconnectedness of creation, the importance of solidarity with the oppressed, and the responsibility of theological education to foster a transformative, justice-oriented practice.

Leonardo Boff's work expands the principles of Liberation Theology by integrating the ecological dimension into the broader framework of social justice. He argues that the struggle for liberation must encompass

---

182. Schüssler Fiorenza, *Transforming Vision*, 57.

not only human concerns but also the well-being of the planet, thus advocating for an ecological perspective within theological education. Boff emphasizes that the universe, in its constant state of creation and complexity, points toward a deeper understanding of God's relationship with creation. This ecological consciousness invites a new dialogue between theology and the natural world, encouraging a more holistic approach to understanding liberation.[183]

Boff highlights the importance of recognizing the interconnectedness of all creation, viewing the cosmos as a dynamic interplay of relationships, much like the relational nature of the Trinity. He suggests that the divine act of creation involves a continuous process of bringing forth new life and sustaining it, which mirrors the ongoing creative activity of God. This perspective challenges theological education to move beyond anthropocentric views and to consider the broader cosmic community as part of God's creation, thereby integrating ecological concerns into the core of theological reflection.[184]

Furthermore, Boff argues that ecological theology must address the limitations of modern cosmology, which often neglects the interiority and life inherent in all beings. He suggests that an ecology-based cosmology offers a way to overcome this impasse by recognizing the spiritual dimension of creation and its connection to the divine. This approach aligns with his call for a more inclusive and comprehensive understanding of the common good, one that extends beyond human interests to include the entire cosmic community.[185]

Boff's work also critiques the traditional understanding of creation as a static event, instead proposing that creation is an ongoing process in which all beings are participants. He emphasizes the role of human beings as co-creators with God, responsible for the care and preservation of the Earth. This conception of human practices as an extension of God's creative activity invites theological education to incorporate environmental stewardship as a fundamental aspect of its curriculum, reinforcing the idea that true liberation must involve the whole of creation.[186]

In summary, Leonardo Boff's integration of ecological concerns into Liberation Theology challenges theological education to broaden its scope, incorporating the well-being of the planet into its understanding

183. Boff, *Cry of the Earth*, 21.
184. Boff, *Cry of the Earth*, 167.
185. Boff, *Cry of the Earth*, 42.
186. Boff, *Cry of the Earth*, 197.

of social justice. By advocating for an ecological perspective that recognizes the interconnectedness of all creation, Boff calls for a more holistic approach to theology that aligns with the ongoing creative activity of God and the responsibility of humans as co-creators.[187]

Cornel West contributes significantly to the discourse on praxis-oriented theological education by underscoring the vital role of prophetic witness in theological training. He argues that meaningful theological education must tackle systemic injustices while simultaneously nurturing a prophetic voice that challenges power structures and advocates for justice. West highlights the need for theological education to combine critical reflection with active engagement in social justice, urging students to embody principles of love and justice within their communities. This approach, he contends, is crucial for cultivating not just intellectual understanding but also the moral resolve necessary to confront and transform injustices.[188]

West emphasizes that the prophetic tradition, deeply rooted in the teachings of Judaism, Christianity, and Islam, serves as a moral compass guiding this transformative education. He notes that this tradition calls for justice for all peoples, rejecting xenophobia, nationalism, and imperialism. In his view, prophetic witness transcends tribalism and nationalism, focusing instead on the broader pursuit of justice and compassion in the face of oppression.[189]

He further elaborates that the prophetic commitment to justice is not merely a historical legacy but a living, dynamic force that must be actively cultivated in theological education. By integrating this prophetic tradition into theological training, students are equipped to engage in the ongoing struggle for justice, armed with both the intellectual tools and the moral courage to advocate for the oppressed and marginalized.[190]

West also critiques contemporary religious and political practices that have strayed from this prophetic tradition. He argues that many religious and political leaders have diluted their commitment to justice, aligning themselves with power structures that perpetuate oppression rather than challenging them. This departure from prophetic witness, he suggests, undermines the moral authority of religious and political

---

187. Boff, *Cry of the Earth*, 215.
188. West, *Democracy Matters*, 16.
189. West, *Democracy Matters*, 17.
190. West, *Democracy Matters*, 18.

institutions, making it all the more crucial for theological education to reclaim and reinvigorate this tradition.[191]

In summary, Cornel West's perspective on praxis-oriented theological education highlights the necessity of integrating prophetic witness into the curriculum. He advocates for a form of theological education that not only addresses systemic injustices but also equips students with the moral and intellectual tools needed to challenge oppression and foster transformation in their communities.[192]

Ivone Gebara has significantly influenced the conversation around praxis-oriented theological education by introducing a feminist critique that challenges traditional, often patriarchal, approaches. Gebara advocates for an inclusive and intersectional framework in theological education that addresses the intersecting oppressions of gender, race, and class. She argues that theological education should not only educate but also empower marginalized voices, ensuring that the pursuit of justice is inclusive and addresses the needs of those often overlooked by traditional frameworks.[193]

Gebara emphasizes the importance of understanding and interpreting the complexities of evil, particularly as experienced by women and other marginalized groups. She highlights that traditional theological perspectives have often failed to consider these experiences fully, thus perpetuating structures of inequality. By employing a phenomenological approach, Gebara seeks to bring the lived experiences of marginalized women to the forefront, using their testimonies as a critical tool for understanding the broader implications of oppression.[194]

In her work, Gebara also critiques the way theological education has traditionally handled the concept of salvation, arguing that it must be redefined in a way that resonates with the concrete, everyday struggles of marginalized communities. She suggests that salvation should not only be understood in spiritual or eschatological terms but also as a present, lived reality that addresses the immediate needs and sufferings of oppressed individuals.[195]

Furthermore, Gebara's intersectional approach calls for a radical rethinking of the epistemological structures underlying theological

---

191. West, *Democracy Matters*, 124.
192. West, *Democracy Matters*, 50.
193. Gebara, *Out of the Depths*, 1.
194. Gebara, *Out of the Depths*, 14.
195. Gebara, *Out of the Depths*, 22.

education. She points out that traditional theological frameworks are often male-oriented and fail to capture the diverse perspectives necessary for a truly inclusive education. By incorporating gender as a critical lens, Gebara encourages a more nuanced understanding of theology that is sensitive to the different ways in which people experience and interpret their realities.[196]

Through her feminist critique, Gebara challenges the theological community to rethink its approaches to education, urging for a system that not only acknowledges but actively works to dismantle the structures of oppression that have long been embedded in theological discourse.[197]

Kwok Pui-lan has critically engaged with praxis-oriented theological education by incorporating postcolonial perspectives, arguing that it is essential for this education to confront the historical legacies of colonialism and imperialism. She emphasizes the need for a critical appropriation of the past, advocating for a continuous reinterpretation of history that acknowledges the complexities of identity formation, especially for those who have been colonized, exiled, or marginalized. This approach challenges the romanticization or idealization of heritage, urging a more nuanced understanding that remains open to new interpretations.[198]

In her work, Kwok highlights the importance of examining the relationship between women and nature in feminist religious discourse, noting that this connection should not be seen in a simplistic or essentialized way. She articulates the hopes of women who have struggled against patriarchal and colonial systems, emphasizing the need for theological education to address these intertwined oppressions critically.[199]

Kwok also explores the role of Asian feminist theologians who have redirected the focus of theology towards the lived experiences and popular cultures of women in Asia, moving away from the elitist and often patriarchal traditions that have dominated theological discourse. This shift reflects a broader commitment to engaging with the realities of marginalized communities, rather than constructing an idealized or monolithic view of "Asia" or "the West."[200]

Furthermore, Kwok advocates for a decolonizing approach to theology, one that challenges traditional theological puzzles and constructs by

---

196. Gebara, *Out of the Depths*, 66.
197. Gebara, *Out of the Depths*, 72.
198. Kwok, *Postcolonial Imagination and Feminist Theology*, 22.
199. Kwok, *Postcolonial Imagination and Feminist Theology*, 25.
200. Kwok, *Postcolonial Imagination and Feminist Theology*, 40.

engaging with the living traditions and emergent issues in Asian politics and history. This approach calls for an ongoing dialogue with cultural and religious pluralism, emphasizing the importance of postcolonial theories in rethinking theological education.[201]

Through her postcolonial critique, Kwok Pui-lan urges theologians to reconsider how theological education can be restructured to prioritize the voices and experiences of those historically marginalized by colonial structures. She calls for a theology that not only acknowledges but actively works to dismantle the lingering effects of colonialism within theological discourse.[202]

Jürgen Moltmann's work emphasizes the critical role of eschatology in shaping praxis-oriented theological education. He argues that such education must be rooted in a hopeful vision of the future, inspired by the Christian belief in the coming Kingdom of God. Moltmann suggests that theological education should not merely prepare students for ministry in the present but should also encourage them to envision and work towards a more just and compassionate world. This future-oriented perspective, grounded in hope, motivates students to actively participate in societal transformation, seeing their efforts as part of the broader divine plan for renewal and justice.[203]

Moltmann also critiques approaches that focus too narrowly on individual salvation or a passive acceptance of suffering in anticipation of the afterlife. He warns that such perspectives can lead to fatalism and disengagement from the world's challenges, rather than fostering the active hope that drives transformative action. For Moltmann, true eschatological hope does not retreat from the world but engages deeply with its struggles, empowering believers to confront injustice and work towards the realization of God's Kingdom here and now.[204]

In his broader theological framework, Moltmann connects this hope to the concept of the Kingdom of God, which he describes as an ongoing process of renewal that involves both the church and the world. This eschatological vision is not limited to a distant future but is seen as breaking into the present, challenging Christians to live out the values of the Kingdom in their everyday lives. For Moltmann, the task of theological education is to cultivate this dynamic hope, inspiring students to

---

201. Kwok, *Postcolonial Imagination and Feminist Theology*, 41.
202. Kwok, *Postcolonial Imagination and Feminist Theology*, 24.
203. Moltmann, *Coming of God*, 50.
204. Moltmann, *Coming of God*, 86.

become agents of change who embody the principles of justice, peace, and love in their communities.[205]

Through his focus on eschatology, Moltmann provides a compelling framework for praxis-oriented theological education that is both deeply rooted in Christian tradition and profoundly relevant to contemporary social issues. His work calls for a theology that is not content with the status quo but is always looking forward, driven by a vision of a better world that is possible through the active participation of believers in God's redemptive plan.[206]

Stanley Hauerwas offers a critical perspective on praxis-oriented theological education by highlighting the potential dangers of aligning too closely with secular social justice movements. He argues that while engagement with social justice is crucial, it is equally important for theological education to maintain its distinctively Christian character, grounded in the practices and traditions of the church. Hauerwas cautions against allowing theological education to be influenced by secular ideologies, which can dilute the theological foundations that should inform and guide Christian practice. He stresses that theological education should remain deeply rooted in the Christian narrative and ecclesial practices, ensuring that its engagement with social issues is shaped by a robust theological framework rather than by external, secular agendas.[207]

This perspective challenges the notion that theological education should be merely a tool for social activism, urging instead that it be a means of forming individuals who are deeply embedded in the life of the church. Hauerwas insists that the church's unique story and its communal practices should be the primary sources of wisdom and guidance for those engaged in theological education, rather than the shifting tides of secular social movements. This approach underscores the importance of a theology that is not only engaged with the world but also deeply connected to the Christian tradition.[208]

In advocating for a theology that is distinctively Christian, Hauerwas emphasizes the need for theological education to foster a critical engagement with the world, one that is informed by a Christian understanding of justice, community, and the good life. He warns that when theological education becomes too closely aligned with secular social

---

205. Moltmann, *Coming of God*, 316.
206. Moltmann, *Coming of God*, 6.
207. Hauerwas, *Community of Character*, 133.
208. Hauerwas, *Community of Character*, 39.

justice movements, it risks losing its ability to offer a truly transformative vision of society, one that is grounded in the hope and practices of the Christian faith.[209]

By focusing on the importance of maintaining a distinctively Christian approach to theological education, Hauerwas calls for a renewal of theological reflection that is deeply informed by the church's traditions and practices. This, he argues, is essential for ensuring that theological education remains a vital and transformative force within both the church and the wider society.[210]

Gustavo Gutierrez has profoundly shaped the discourse on praxis-oriented theological education by insisting that it must be deeply connected to the lived experiences of the poor and oppressed. He argues that theology should not be an abstract intellectual exercise but rather a practical endeavor that is informed by and contributes to the struggles of marginalized communities. Gutierrez emphasizes that the reality of the poor, marked by hunger, exploitation, inadequate healthcare, and lack of education, must be at the forefront of theological reflection. This connection to the poor is essential for any theology that seeks to be truly liberative and transformative, ensuring that theological education remains grounded in the real-world experiences of those who are most vulnerable.[211]

Furthermore, Gutierrez advocates for a theology that emerges from the context of those who live on the margins of society. He stresses that authentic theological reflection is deeply rooted in both contemplation and active commitment. This means that theology must be continually enriched by the experiences of those who are oppressed, allowing their voices and struggles to shape the discourse. For Gutierrez, true theological reflection involves not just talking about God, but doing so in a way that is intimately connected to the lived reality of faith within marginalized communities.[212]

In this light, Gutierrez's vision of theological education calls for a deep solidarity with the poor, where theological work is not separated from the community but is instead a product of shared struggle and hope. This approach highlights the necessity of integrating theological education with the practical efforts to address the systemic injustices

---

209. Hauerwas, *Community of Character*, 145.
210. Hauerwas, *Community of Character*, 54.
211. Gutiérrez, *We Drink from Our Own Wells*, 125.
212. Gutiérrez, *We Drink from Our Own Wells*, 136.

faced by the poor, ensuring that theology remains a force for genuine liberation and transformation.[213]

In conclusion, the discourse on praxis-oriented theological education as presented by Leonardo Boff, Cornel West, Ivone Gebara, Kwok Pui-lan, Jürgen Moltmann, Stanley Hauerwas, and Gustavo Gutierrez underscores a collective call to expand the scope and focus of theological studies. These thinkers advocate for a theology that actively engages with social, ecological, and global injustices while remaining deeply rooted in spiritual traditions and communal practices. They emphasize the necessity of incorporating real-world experiences, especially those of marginalized groups, into theological reflection and education. By doing so, they argue for a theological framework that not only understands but also addresses the complexities of human and ecological relationships, promoting a holistic and action-oriented approach to spirituality and social transformation.

2.3. CONCLUSION: A HOLISTIC APPROACH TO LIBERATION

In contemporary liberation theology, there is an increasing recognition of the necessity to integrate diverse theological traditions to address the multifaceted challenges of global injustice. This recognition stems from an understanding that no single theological tradition can fully capture the complexities and interconnectedness of modern global issues. By drawing on various perspectives, such as those related to social justice, ecological awareness, feminist critique, and postcolonial analysis, theologians aim to construct a more comprehensive framework that can address these diverse challenges more effectively. These theological perspectives are not merely additive but are seen as crucial in creating a holistic approach that better reflects the lived realities of marginalized communities worldwide. The integration of these varied traditions allows for a more nuanced understanding of the diverse forms of oppression and provides a more robust basis for a theology that seeks to be relevant and responsive in the face of global inequalities.[214]

The integration of these diverse theological perspectives necessitates a significant reassessment of traditional methodologies in both theological education and practice. Theologians are increasingly urged to

---

213. Gutiérrez, *We Drink from Our Own Wells*, 14.
214. Gutiérrez, *Power of the Poor in History*.

transcend the boundaries of intellectual engagement and to adopt praxis-oriented approaches that prioritize lived experiences and the struggles of oppressed groups. This shift is not merely a methodological change but represents a fundamental transformation in how theology is understood and practiced. By emphasizing praxis, theologians are encouraged to engage directly with the real-world challenges faced by marginalized communities, ensuring that theological reflection is grounded in the realities of those it seeks to serve. This practical approach is essential for maintaining the relevance of theological discourse in addressing contemporary social and environmental challenges. Moreover, by focusing on the intersection of lived experience and theological reflection, this approach promotes a more inclusive understanding of faith, one that is dynamic and capable of evolving in response to the changing needs of society.[215]

The Kingdom of God is increasingly understood not merely as a distant eschatological hope but as an active and present reality that is realized through engagement with social issues. Theologians such as Miroslav Volf and Gustavo Gutiérrez emphasize that the Kingdom is intertwined with practical and ethical action in the world, where justice, inclusion, and reconciliation are not just ideals but essential practices that manifest the divine in daily life. This perspective shifts the focus from passive anticipation of a future Kingdom to active participation in its realization here and now. It challenges traditional views that might limit the Kingdom to a spiritual or otherworldly domain, arguing instead that the Kingdom is actively being constructed through the church's engagement with societal issues. This understanding encourages a reevaluation of traditional roles and beliefs, urging theologians and believers alike to consider how their actions contribute to the realization of the Kingdom in the present. This shift from theoretical discourse to tangible action is seen as essential for fostering a more compassionate and equitable society, where the values of the Kingdom are made manifest in concrete ways.[216]

Liberation theology is undergoing an expansion that incorporates a broader range of concerns, including ecological, racial, gender, and sexual dimensions. This expanded focus reflects a growing awareness that liberation cannot be fully realized without addressing the interconnectedness of these various forms of justice. Theologians like Catherine Keller and

---

215. Tanner, *Christ the Key*.
216. Volf, *Public Faith*; Gutiérrez, *Power of the Poor in History*.

M. Shawn Copeland are at the forefront of this movement, challenging traditional frameworks that have often been too narrow in their focus. By integrating perspectives on environmental sustainability, race, gender, sexuality, and postcolonialism, these scholars advocate for a more comprehensive approach to liberation theology. This approach recognizes that justice must encompass not only human communities but also the broader ecological system, acknowledging that the well-being of the planet is intrinsically linked to the well-being of its inhabitants. Additionally, by addressing the diverse lived experiences of marginalized groups, these theologians argue for a liberation theology that is truly inclusive and responsive to the complex realities of contemporary societies.[217]

The concept of existential authenticity is being reexamined in light of contemporary social, political, and economic conditions, with a growing consensus that it cannot be understood as a fixed or purely individual state. Thinkers such as Richard Sennett, Judith Butler, and Slavoj Žižek challenge traditional notions of authenticity, arguing that it must be seen as a dynamic process shaped by external pressures and collective responsibilities. This shift in understanding reflects a broader critique of the idea that individuals can achieve a stable, authentic self in isolation from the broader social context. Instead, these thinkers emphasize the importance of understanding authenticity in relation to the social, political, and economic structures that influence individual identity. They argue that a truly authentic existence must account for the ways in which these external forces shape the self and must be integrated with broader social justice efforts. This perspective encourages a move away from a purely individualistic conception of authenticity toward a more socially engaged understanding, one that recognizes the interdependence of self and society.[218]

Praxis-oriented theological education is increasingly seen as crucial for preparing theologians to engage effectively with the world. This approach emphasizes the integration of key concerns such as social justice, ecological awareness, feminist critique, postcolonial perspectives, and eschatological hope into theological education frameworks. Theologians argue that traditional theological education, which often focuses on intellectual study, must evolve to include practical engagement with the lived realities and struggles of marginalized communities. This shift is seen as

---

217. Keller, *Cloud of the Impossible*; Copeland, *Enfleshing Freedom*.
218. Sennett, *Corrosion of Character*; Butler, *Gender Trouble*.

essential for fostering a theological practice that is not only academically rigorous but also relevant and impactful in addressing contemporary societal needs. By emphasizing the interconnectedness of all creation and the need for solidarity with the oppressed, this approach to theological education seeks to cultivate a transformative, justice-oriented practice. It challenges students and educators alike to rethink how theology can be applied in ways that promote both social and environmental justice, ensuring that theological education remains a vital force for positive change in the world.[219]

Theological reflection on contemporary issues such as ecology, capitalism, and human suffering is becoming increasingly important, as highlighted by the work of theologians like Elizabeth A. Johnson and Jürgen Moltmann. These scholars stress the necessity of integrating real-world concerns into theological discourse to ensure that theology remains relevant and responsive to the challenges of modern life. Their work represents a significant shift from traditional theological frameworks that may have overlooked these issues, urging a reimagining of how faith interacts with the world. By addressing these pressing concerns, they argue that theology can play a critical role in promoting justice, healing, and a broader awareness of the interconnectedness of all aspects of life. This approach emphasizes the importance of grounding theological reflection in the lived experiences of individuals and communities, ensuring that it remains responsive to the challenges of our time and capable of contributing to positive social change.[220]

Narrative theology continues to evolve, with a growing recognition of the importance of stories in shaping theological understanding and practice. Scholars like James K. A. Smith and Rosenstock-Huessy emphasize that narratives are not merely illustrative tools but are central to how individuals and communities understand and live out their faith. This perspective highlights the need for narrative theology to engage deeply with the lived experiences of marginalized groups, ensuring that their stories are included in theological discourse. By incorporating these voices, narrative theology can offer a more inclusive and reflective approach to understanding faith, one that is attuned to the diverse realities of human experience. This ongoing development of narrative theology also involves rethinking traditional theological categories, allowing for a

---

219. Moltmann, *Ethics of Hope*; Tanner, *Christianity and the New Spirit of Capitalism*.
220. Johnson, *Ask the Beasts*; Moltmann, *Ethics of Hope*.

more dynamic and contextually relevant approach to theology that resonates with the lived experiences of contemporary communities.[221]

The integration of diverse perspectives into theological education is increasingly viewed as not just beneficial but essential for addressing the complex challenges of global liberation. By embracing a holistic approach that includes social, ecological, and cultural dimensions, theologians can develop a more comprehensive framework that is capable of addressing the realities of global oppression. This approach recognizes that liberation cannot be achieved through a single lens but requires a multifaceted understanding that accounts for the various forms of oppression that intersect in the lives of marginalized communities. By integrating these diverse perspectives, theologians aim to create a more responsive and inclusive theological framework, one that is better equipped to contribute to the ongoing struggle for justice and human dignity.[222]

Feminist and postcolonial critiques are increasingly challenging traditional theological categories, calling for a reimagining of theology that is more inclusive and responsive to contemporary realities. Scholars like Kwok Pui-lan and Marcella Althaus-Reid argue that theology must move beyond its traditional boundaries to fully engage with the diverse and complex experiences of marginalized groups. This involves not only incorporating the voices of women, people of color, and other marginalized communities into theological discourse but also critically examining how these voices have been historically excluded or misrepresented. By doing so, feminist and postcolonial theologians advocate for a more just and equitable theological framework that is capable of addressing the diverse needs of contemporary societies. This reimagining of theology challenges established norms and seeks to create a more inclusive and responsive theological discourse that is attuned to the realities of all people.[223]

Intersectionality is increasingly recognized as a crucial concept in understanding how different forms of oppression intersect to create unique challenges for marginalized communities. Theologians like M. Shawn Copeland argue that a genuine commitment to intersectionality requires more than just acknowledging the existence of multiple forms of oppression; it requires a deep engagement with the lived experiences of those who are affected by these intersecting systems of power.

221. Smith, *Desiring the Kingdom*; Rosenstock-Huessy, *Speech and Reality*.

222. Graham, *Transforming Practice*.

223. Kwok, *Postcolonial Imagination and Feminist Theology*; Althaus-Reid, *Indecent Theology*.

CHAPTER TWO

This approach to theology emphasizes the importance of listening to and learning from the experiences of those who have been historically marginalized, particularly within religious and social institutions. By incorporating intersectionality into theological discourse, theologians can develop a more nuanced and responsive approach to addressing the complex realities of oppression, ensuring that their work is grounded in the lived experiences of those they seek to serve.[224]

The role of the church in global liberation is increasingly understood as requiring active engagement with the world's pain and brokenness. Theologians argue that the church must go beyond merely advocating for justice and must actively embody the values of the Kingdom of God through concrete actions that reflect God's love and justice. This perspective challenges traditional views of the church as a passive or reactive institution, urging instead a more proactive role in addressing the systemic injustices that contribute to global oppression. By engaging with the world in meaningful and transformative ways, the church can play a vital role in the realization of global liberation, contributing to the creation of a more just and equitable world.[225]

Theologians like Alain Badiou and Cornel West emphasize the importance of engaging with political and social realities as part of the theological task. Their work highlights the need for theology to be intertwined with collective action and social responsibility, challenging traditional existential focuses on individual authenticity. This perspective argues that theology cannot be separated from the broader social and political context in which it operates, and that authentic theological reflection must engage with the pressing issues of justice and equity in the world. By integrating political and social analysis into theological discourse, these scholars advocate for a theology that is not only reflective but also active in promoting social change and justice.[226]

The role of prophecy in theology is increasingly seen as crucial for inspiring social and institutional changes that align with human potential and dignity. Theologians like Roberto Unger argue for a prophetic existentialism that emphasizes the importance of imagination and creativity in envisioning and implementing social transformations. This perspective challenges traditional views of prophecy as merely foretelling the future, instead understanding it as a dynamic and creative force that

---

224. Copeland, *Enfleshing Freedom.*
225. Volf, *Public Faith;* Gutiérrez, *Power of the Poor in History.*
226. Badiou, *Being and Event;* West, *Cornel West Reader.*

inspires action in the present. By encouraging theologians and religious communities to engage with the world in imaginative and transformative ways, this approach seeks to harness the power of prophecy to drive social change and promote human dignity.[227]

The integration of diverse theological traditions and methodologies is increasingly viewed as essential for addressing the complex challenges of global liberation. By bringing together perspectives from various theological traditions, theologians can create a more comprehensive and responsive framework that is better equipped to address the realities of global oppression. This approach recognizes that no single tradition or methodology can fully capture the complexities of modern global issues, and that a multifaceted approach is necessary to develop effective solutions. By fostering a more inclusive and responsive theological framework, theologians aim to contribute to the ongoing struggle for human dignity and liberation, ensuring that their work remains relevant and impactful in today's world.[228]

---

227. Unger, *Self Awakened*.
228. Gutiérrez, *Power of the Poor in History*.

CHAPTER THREE

North Korea, Human Rights, and the Kingdom of God

THE KINGDOM OF GOD offers a foundational framework for addressing the intersection of justice, human dignity, and liberation. This theological vision emphasizes the need to challenge both social and political systems that perpetuate inequality, oppression, and exploitation. Thinkers like Cornel West, Judith Butler, Slavoj Žižek, Amartya Sen, Martha Nussbaum, and Giorgio Agamben contribute significantly to this discussion by highlighting how power structures and legal frameworks can either support or undermine the pursuit of true liberation. These scholars push for a reevaluation of human rights and justice, encouraging more inclusive approaches that consider the lived realities of marginalized communities.

Their perspectives challenge conventional notions of freedom and rights, urging us to critically assess the role of capitalism, state power, and legal systems in perpetuating or mitigating inequalities. For instance, Žižek critiques liberal approaches to human rights for often maintaining the status quo, while Butler's work emphasizes the interconnectedness of human vulnerability and recognition. These contributions broaden the theological dialogue, integrating insights from various disciplines to provide a more holistic view of justice.

By incorporating these interdisciplinary perspectives, the discussion of the Kingdom of God moves beyond abstract religious concepts to address real-world injustices. This approach highlights the urgency of systemic reform, whether in social, economic, or environmental contexts, as seen in the works of these scholars. Their collective call is for a transformation that prioritizes the dignity of every individual and challenges oppressive systems that hinder true liberation.

3.1. JUSTICE, HUMAN RIGHTS, AND EXCLUSION IN THEOLOGY

This section examines the relationship between the Kingdom of God as a framework for liberation and various contemporary perspectives on human rights and social justice. By engaging with the works of thinkers like Cornel West, Judith Butler, Slavoj Žižek, Amartya Sen, Martha Nussbaum, and Giorgio Agamben, the discussion highlights how these ideas challenge traditional views and encourage a more comprehensive understanding of justice. This includes addressing systemic inequalities, reconsidering human capabilities, and critically assessing the ways in which power and legal frameworks can either support or undermine true liberation and dignity for all individuals.

Building upon the foundational elements of liberation theology and the Kingdom of God, contemporary thinkers like Cornel West enhance the discourse surrounding human rights, with a particular focus on how these ideals intersect with global injustices, including the situation in North Korea. West stresses the importance of recognizing the interplay between race and poverty when addressing global injustices, critiquing the superficial engagement that often characterizes mainstream discussions. He calls for a more thoughtful and inclusive approach that does not perpetuate systemic inequalities.[1]

In his analysis, West points out the troubling trend of rewarding 'false prophets'—those who, through their alignment with profit-driven agendas, divert attention from essential societal functions like education, steering focus instead towards punitive systems such as prisons. This manipulation, he argues, drains democratic life from American society, suggesting a dangerous shift from constructive community engagement to a more repressive state approach.[2]

Further expanding on this theme, West criticizes the U.S. policies that not only seek to police the world according to American interests but also impose an imperialistic vision on an unsuspecting U.S. citizenry. He identifies a continuity in these policies with those of previous administrations, which rarely questioned the underpinning dogmas of

1. West, *Democracy Matters*.
2. West, *Democracy Matters*, 4.

free-market fundamentalism and aggressive militarism, thereby contributing to a global stance that often undermines genuine democratic values.[3]

Reflecting on the historical vision of the civil rights movement, West highlights the solidarity between Jews and Blacks, underscoring its foundational role in advancing that movement. He suggests that this historical alliance should inspire and rejuvenate our commitment to democratic principles today, especially in confronting and challenging prevailing cynicism and apathy.[4]

Addressing the pervasive nihilism within American society, West discusses how widespread psychic depression and feelings of worthlessness contribute to a broader social despair. This despair, he notes, is not confined to any single community but affects a vast majority of American citizens, indicating a deep-seated crisis of purpose and identity within the society.[5]

He also draws on historical examples, such as Franklin D. Roosevelt, whose vision and courage starkly contrast with the lack of such qualities in today's leaders, as perceived by West. This comparison is used to critique contemporary leaders who fail to demonstrate the foresight and bravery necessary to guide society through challenging times.[6]

Ultimately, West's reflections emphasize the critical need for a reinvigorated democratic ethos that resists the encroachments of elite power and champions the dignity of all individuals. He calls for a societal shift that prioritizes profound respect for human dignity and the nurturing of a democratic community capable of resisting authoritarian and elitist tendencies.[7] This broad analysis serves not only as a critique of current practices but also as a call to action for those committed to fostering a more just and equitable society.

Judith Butler's exploration of power and recognition emphasizes the importance of understanding the vulnerability and interdependency of all lives when framing human rights in a way that includes the most marginalized individuals. This perspective challenges the conventional categorization and exclusion of people based on arbitrary markers, which often leads to their dehumanization. Butler draws on Michel Foucault's

---

3. West, *Democracy Matters*, 9.
4. West, *Democracy Matters*, 19.
5. West, *Democracy Matters*, 26.
6. West, *Democracy Matters*, 33.
7. West, *Democracy Matters*, 98.

idea that societies are not simply shifting from one form of governance to another—such as from sovereignty to discipline, or from discipline to governmentality—but that these forms exist in a triangular relationship. This triangle targets populations and operates through mechanisms of security, highlighting how power is exercised in modern societies.[8]

Butler further delves into the experience of loss and mourning, suggesting that such experiences can lead to significant transformations that cannot be anticipated or controlled. She argues that mourning is not merely a privatizing force that isolates individuals; instead, it can lead to a recognition of our shared vulnerability and interconnectedness. This collective understanding of vulnerability can, in turn, foster a more inclusive sense of community and political solidarity.[9]

The notion of the body is central to Butler's discussion, where she highlights that our bodies expose us to both connection and violence, making us agents of action as well as subjects to external forces. The public dimension of our bodies, which are socially constituted, underscores the political implications of our physical existence. This concept challenges the idea that we can fully control our bodies or claim complete autonomy over them, as they are always situated within broader social and political contexts.[10]

Moreover, Butler emphasizes that our interactions and relationships with others are not always predictable or clearly defined, which further complicates the struggle for autonomy. Living in a world where we are physically dependent on and vulnerable to each other, she suggests, requires us to rethink traditional notions of independence and self-sufficiency. This interdependence should inform our understanding of political life and community, as it reveals the inherent connections between personal and collective well-being.[11]

In this light, Butler's work encourages us to reconsider the ways in which societies structure power and recognition, advocating for a framework that more accurately reflects the complex, interconnected realities of human existence. This approach is especially relevant in addressing human rights issues, where the inclusion of marginalized voices is crucial for fostering a more just and equitable world.[12]

8. Butler, *Precarious Life*, 156.
9. Butler, *Precarious Life*, 21.
10. Butler, *Precarious Life*, 26.
11. Butler, *Precarious Life*, 27.
12. Butler, *Precarious Life*, 101.

CHAPTER THREE

Slavoj Žižek challenges conventional liberal approaches to human rights, arguing that they often fall short of creating meaningful change. He asserts that real liberation requires not just reforming existing structures but radically altering the underlying systems and ideologies that sustain them.[13] Žižek's perspective prompts a reexamination of how rights are understood and promoted in international contexts, urging a shift away from superficial reforms toward more transformative action.

Žižek draws from Lacanian theory to highlight the «inhuman» dimension of ethics, where the subject is seen as detached from individual personality traits or human individuality. He illustrates this by referencing figures in popular culture, such as cyborgs or aliens, who demonstrate more commitment to their tasks and a greater sense of dignity and freedom than their human counterparts. This notion suggests that the pursuit of true liberation may require a shift away from traditional humanist values, which often constrain our understanding of freedom and dignity.[14]

Furthermore, Žižek critiques the idea that within capitalist societies, people are seen as equals in terms of dignity and freedom. He argues that while direct hierarchical relations among people may have been transposed into relations between commodities, the underlying structures of domination remain intact. This analysis leads him to question the effectiveness of traditional human rights discourses, which may obscure the deeper relations of power and inequality that persist in modern societies.[15]

Žižek also addresses the role of objects in ideological structures, drawing on the concept of «objet a" from Lacanian theory. He discusses how in hegemonic systems, certain objects are elevated to embody the impossible ideal of society, functioning as symbols that sustain ideological systems. This observation challenges the simplistic narratives often found in human rights advocacy, suggesting that a more nuanced understanding of how ideologies operate is necessary for achieving genuine liberation.[16]

In another critical reflection, Žižek contrasts the postmodern reluctance to fully engage with radical ideas with the necessity of embracing a more decisive stance. He critiques the postmodern tendency to avoid

13. Žižek, *In Defense of Lost Causes*.
14. Žižek, *In Defense of Lost Causes*, 166.
15. Žižek, *In Defense of Lost Causes*, 203.
16. Žižek, *In Defense of Lost Causes*, 328.

"going all the way" in scientific or ethical inquiries, arguing that such hesitation only perpetuates existing power structures. Žižek calls for a more courageous approach that does not shy away from confronting the difficult truths about society and the human condition.[17]

Through these arguments, Žižek encourages a reassessment of the foundational assumptions behind human rights, advocating for a more comprehensive and transformative approach that moves beyond the limitations of liberal reformism. His work challenges readers to consider the deeper implications of power, ideology, and human dignity in the pursuit of true social change.[18]

Amartya Sen's analysis of human rights and development closely intersects with the ideas of John Rawls, particularly regarding the role of justice and fairness in evaluating societal progress. Sen expands upon Rawls's concept of "justice as fairness," which emphasizes the importance of ensuring that all individuals have access to the basic goods necessary to pursue their own conception of a good life. Rawls argues that a just society is one where inequalities are arranged so that they are to the greatest benefit of the least advantaged, and where everyone has an equal opportunity to access primary goods, such as rights, liberties, and opportunities.[19]

Sen builds on this framework by proposing that development should be assessed not just by economic growth or income levels, but by the capabilities people have to achieve the lives they value. He aligns with Rawls's focus on the distribution of opportunities but extends this by emphasizing the actual freedoms and capabilities that people possess. Sen argues that these capabilities are crucial for determining whether individuals can genuinely exercise their rights and participate fully in society.[20]

Rawls's concept of primary goods, which include not just material wealth but also rights, liberties, and opportunities, complements Sen's emphasis on substantive freedoms. While Rawls focuses on the fair distribution of these goods, Sen highlights the importance of translating these goods into real opportunities for individuals to lead meaningful lives. This shared concern for justice underscores the need for a holistic

---

17. Žižek, *In Defense of Lost Causes*, 423.
18. Žižek, *In Defense of Lost Causes*, 7.
19. Rawls, *Theory of Justice*, 92.
20. Sen, *Development as Freedom*, 72.

approach to development that considers both the distribution of resources and the actual freedoms people have to use them.[21]

Furthermore, Sen's critique of utilitarian approaches to development, which prioritize economic outcomes over individual well-being, resonates with Rawls's rejection of utilitarianism in favor of a justice-based framework. Rawls argues that utilitarianism fails to respect the distinctness of individuals by aggregating preferences and benefits across society. Similarly, Sen advocates for an approach that values individual capabilities and freedoms, rather than merely maximizing overall utility or economic output.[22]

In summary, by integrating Rawls's theories of justice with his own focus on capabilities, Sen provides a robust framework for evaluating development that goes beyond traditional economic measures. This approach seeks to ensure that all individuals, especially the least advantaged, have the real freedom to pursue the lives they value, thereby promoting a more just and equitable society.[23]

Martha Nussbaum builds upon Amartya Sen's capability approach by placing a greater emphasis on the specific capabilities that individuals need to live meaningful lives. While Sen provides the foundational idea that development should be measured by the real freedoms people enjoy rather than just economic growth, Nussbaum expands this framework by proposing a list of core capabilities that any just society should foster.[24] She argues that these capabilities are essential for human dignity and must be supported to ensure that people can truly exercise their rights and freedoms.

Nussbaum highlights the significance of these capabilities by contrasting them with mere legal rights. She points out that legal rights alone are insufficient if people do not have the actual capabilities to make use of those rights. For example, the right to education is meaningless if an individual does not have access to schools, quality teaching, or the necessary resources to learn. Thus, Nussbaum's approach emphasizes the importance of ensuring that individuals have both the legal framework and the practical means to achieve their potential.[25]

---

21. Sen, *Development as Freedom*, 73; Rawls, *Theory of Justice*, 64.
22. Sen, *Development as Freedom*, 19; Rawls, *Theory of Justice*, 136.
23. Sen, *Development as Freedom*, 64; Rawls, *Theory of Justice*, 136.
24. Nussbaum, *Creating Capabilities*.
25. Nussbaum, *Creating Capabilities*, 19.

She also critiques the narrow focus of traditional development metrics that prioritize economic indicators over human capabilities. Nussbaum argues that this approach fails to capture the true essence of human development, which should be centered on what individuals are actually able to do and be. This broader perspective requires societies to pay attention not only to economic growth but also to the conditions that enable people to exercise their capabilities fully.[26]

Moreover, Nussbaum's approach extends beyond human beings to include non-human animals, reflecting her concern for the capabilities of all sentient beings. She prefers the term "Capabilities Approach" over "Human Development Approach" to underscore the inclusivity of her framework, which provides a basis for a comprehensive theory of justice that encompasses both humans and animals.[27]

In developing her version of the capability approach, Nussbaum integrates concepts such as human dignity, political liberalism, and a threshold of basic capabilities that all individuals should be entitled to. This approach offers a more detailed and structured way of thinking about social justice, where the focus is not just on economic outcomes but on the real opportunities people have to lead lives, they value.[28]

By advocating for the promotion of these core capabilities, Nussbaum challenges societies to move beyond superficial measures of success and to ensure that all individuals, particularly the most vulnerable, have the actual means to live dignified and fulfilling lives. This perspective aligns closely with the broader goals of human development while also pushing for a more nuanced understanding of what it means to support human well-being.[29]

Giorgio Agamben delves into the concept of the "state of exception," examining how it impacts individuals who are excluded from the protection of the law, such as refugees or stateless persons. Agamben highlights the inherent dangers in systems that can arbitrarily place certain individuals outside the scope of legal protections, effectively stripping them of their rights and rendering them vulnerable to oppression.[30]

Agamben builds on Carl Schmitt's definition of sovereignty, particularly the idea that the sovereign is the one who decides on the state

---

26. Nussbaum, *Creating Capabilities*, 3.
27. Nussbaum, *Creating Capabilities*, 18.
28. Nussbaum, *Creating Capabilities*, 19.
29. Nussbaum, *Creating Capabilities*, 20.
30. Agamben, *State of Exception*.

CHAPTER THREE

of exception. He explains that this concept has historically been difficult to define due to its close relationship with extraordinary situations like civil war, insurrection, and resistance, which exist outside the normal conditions of law and order.[31] This "state of exception" creates a gray area where the law is suspended, and normal legal protections do not apply, thus placing individuals in a precarious position where their rights can be easily ignored or violated.[32]

Agamben further critiques how the state of exception has been used throughout history, pointing out that it is often justified as a necessary response to emergencies but is, in fact, a tool that can be abused to maintain control over a population. He discusses the historical origins of this concept, noting that it was first formalized during the French Revolution with the decree of July 3, 1791, which established the state of siege, a form of martial law that allowed for extraordinary measures to be taken in times of crisis.[33]

Moreover, Agamben emphasizes that the state of exception is not just a theoretical or historical concept but has real and dangerous implications in modern times. He warns that the normalization of the state of exception can lead to a situation where the suspension of law becomes the norm rather than the exception, effectively creating a permanent state of emergency where certain groups are perpetually excluded from legal protection.[34]

This critique of the state of exception is crucial in understanding how legal systems can be manipulated to legitimize exclusion and oppression. Agamben calls attention to the ethical and political implications of this practice, urging a reevaluation of the mechanisms by which the law can be used to justify acts that undermine the very principles of justice and human rights.[35]

In conclusion, the discourse on human rights, as enhanced by theorists like Cornel West, Judith Butler, Slavoj Žižek, Amartya Sen, Martha Nussbaum, and Giorgio Agamben, offers a comprehensive understanding of how different frameworks can interact to address global injustices. These perspectives, ranging from the critique of capitalist structures to the exploration of power dynamics and the vulnerabilities

31. Agamben, *State of Exception*, 1–2.
32. Agamben, *State of Exception*, 3.
33. Agamben, *State of Exception*, 11.
34. Agamben, *State of Exception*, 18.
35. Agamben, *State of Exception*, 50.

of marginalized groups, advocate for a more inclusive and equitable approach to human rights. This array of views encourages a reevaluation of traditional notions and supports a shift towards a society that genuinely respects and upholds the dignity and welfare of all individuals.

3.2. ETHICS OF THE KINGDOM: JUSTICE, PEACE, AND ECOLOGY

This section examines various theological perspectives that link justice and peace to both social and ecological contexts. It focuses on the work of thinkers such as Elisabeth Schüssler Fiorenza, J. Kameron Carter, Catherine Keller, Birch and Cobb, Larry Rasmussen, and Denis Edwards, each of whom offers a framework that challenges traditional systems of oppression and exploitation. These theologians call for a reimagining of theology to address issues such as power, race, colonialism, and environmental care. Their collective approach urges a more responsible and inclusive understanding of justice that encompasses both human communities and the natural world.

The concept of justice within these theological frameworks is expanded beyond human interactions, incorporating ecological responsibility as an integral part of ethical reflection. For example, Schüssler Fiorenza critiques patriarchal structures, urging for a theology that addresses intersecting systems of oppression, while Keller explores the dynamic, interconnected nature of creation. These perspectives invite a broader conversation about how humans relate not only to each other but to the planet, emphasizing the need for holistic approaches to justice that consider the well-being of all life forms.

Additionally, these thinkers engage with the challenges posed by global capitalism, colonialism, and environmental degradation. They highlight the importance of systemic reform in addressing both social inequalities and ecological crises. By drawing on relational and ecological theologies, they call for a shift in how society understands and practices justice, advocating for changes that align with values of interdependence, care, and sustainability for all of creation.

3.2.1. Justice and Human Dignity in the Kingdom of God

This section explores how the concept of the Kingdom of God serves as a foundation for addressing issues of justice, peace, and human rights in contexts like North Korea. It delves into the perspectives of several theologians, each offering a unique approach to how the Kingdom can influence societal transformation. Stanley Hauerwas highlights the Church's role as a prophetic community, separate from state power, while John Milbank critiques liberal democracy's inability to realize the values of the Kingdom, advocating for a more communal and holistic social vision. Shane Claiborne emphasizes radical discipleship rooted in simplicity and solidarity with the poor, while Ched Myers frames the Kingdom as a force of resistance against imperial structures. Lastly, Sallie McFague and John D. Caputo expand the discussion by incorporating ecological responsibility and postmodern theology, presenting the Kingdom as a call to redefine societal norms and power structures. Through these diverse theological frameworks, the section argues for the Kingdom as a critical tool for challenging both political and religious systems that perpetuate injustice.

The Kingdom of God, as a theological framework for justice and peace, provides a crucial basis for addressing systemic injustices and advocating for human rights, particularly in challenging contexts such as North Korea. Stanley Hauerwas emphasizes the distinct role of the Church as an alternative community that embodies the ethics of the Kingdom of God. He argues that the Church must resist the temptation to be co-opted by the state and instead act as a prophetic witness to the justice and peace that characterize God's Kingdom. This requires the Church to prioritize radical discipleship over political allegiances, maintaining its focus on the transformative values of the Kingdom.[36]

Hauerwas critically engages with the social and political commitments of the Church, warning against the dangers of allowing these commitments to dilute the Church's mission. He critiques the tendency of many mainline Protestant churches to align themselves with the social class of well-educated members, who often presume they have the authority to define the Church's social ethics. This alignment, according to Hauerwas, undermines the Church's ability to serve as a genuine alternative to worldly power structures and compromises its prophetic role.[37]

Hauerwas also challenges the idea of "political theology," arguing that all theology is inherently social and political because it deals with the ways in which the Church embodies the Kingdom of God in the world. He resists using terms like "social ethics" because they can imply that

---

36. Hauerwas, *Work of Theology*, 37.
37. Hauerwas, *Work of Theology*, 107.

some ethics are not social, whereas in reality, every theological and ethical reflection must consider its social implications.[38]

Furthermore, Hauerwas draws attention to the historical Anabaptist tradition, which emphasizes the importance of the Church as a disciplined community distinct from the state. He argues that the Anabaptists' understanding of the Lord's Supper as a corporate act, rather than a private, individualistic ritual, exemplifies the kind of ecclesiology that supports the Kingdom's values of justice and peace. This communal understanding underscores the necessity for the Church to remain independent of state power and to maintain its identity as a community of radical discipleship.[39]

Through these reflections, Hauerwas critiques contemporary Christian complicity in nationalism and militarism, urging the Church to reclaim its role as a counter-cultural force that witnesses to the Kingdom of God. This requires a commitment to justice and peace that is not swayed by political allegiances or societal pressures but is rooted in the radical teachings of Jesus.[40]

By examining the complexities of how the Church navigates its relationship with the state and society, Hauerwas calls for a return to the core values of the Kingdom of God—values that prioritize the well-being of all people and resist the allure of power and control. This approach challenges the Church to engage in a more faithful and consistent witness to the justice and peace of God's Kingdom.[41]

John Milbank offers a critical perspective on liberal democracy, asserting that it often fails to realize the justice and peace that the Kingdom of God envisions. He argues that liberal democracy, with its emphasis on individual rights and market-driven policies, tends to overlook the broader concerns of mutuality and the common good. Milbank suggests that the Kingdom of God presents a more compelling vision for society, one where these values are prioritized over the fragmented individualism that characterizes modern political and economic systems. This vision challenges both secular and religious communities to rethink their approaches and engage in transformative work that aligns more closely with the values of the Kingdom.[42]

38. Hauerwas, *Work of Theology*, 171.
39. Hauerwas, *Work of Theology*, 62.
40. Hauerwas, *Work of Theology*, 176.
41. Hauerwas, *Work of Theology*, 50.
42. Milbank, *Theology and Social Theory*, xxiv.

CHAPTER THREE

Milbank's critique extends to the way modernity, influenced by thinkers like Machiavelli, has reshaped political virtues. He notes that the ancient political virtue, which once prioritized honor and civic excellence, has been replaced by a more bureaucratic and economic focus in modern democracies. This shift, he argues, represents a departure from the communal values of the Kingdom of God, where justice is not merely about maintaining order but about fostering genuine community and participation.[43]

Additionally, Milbank draws on the Augustinian-Thomist tradition to challenge the secular management of power, advocating for a return to a framework where metaphysically secured values guide social and political life. He suggests that modern political theory, with its roots in Enlightenment thinking, often fails to address the deeper, more existential needs of society, which can only be met by a vision grounded in the Kingdom of God.[44]

In discussing the implications of his critique, Milbank points to the limitations of postmodernity, particularly its skepticism towards grand narratives or "metanarratives." He argues that while postmodernity rejects these overarching stories, the Kingdom of God offers a coherent and compelling narrative that can unify and guide social and political life. This perspective calls for a re-engagement with theological principles in public discourse, challenging the dominance of secular liberalism.[45]

Milbank also addresses the tension between pre-modern and postmodern elements in his work, acknowledging the complexities of integrating these perspectives. He advocates for a synthesis that draws on the strengths of both, while remaining critical of the weaknesses inherent in modern political and economic systems. This approach seeks to offer a more holistic vision of society, one that is in harmony with the values of the Kingdom of God.[46]

In essence, Milbank's work challenges both secular and religious communities to reconsider their approaches to justice, politics, and economics, urging them to align more closely with the values of the Kingdom of God. His critique of liberal democracy and modernity is rooted

---

43. Milbank, *Theology and Social Theory*, 33.
44. Milbank, *Theology and Social Theory*, 5.
45. Milbank, *Theology and Social Theory*, xx.
46. Milbank, *Theology and Social Theory*, xxii.

in a desire to see a more just and peaceful society, one that reflects the mutuality and common good envisioned by the Kingdom.[47]

Shane Claiborne advocates for a radical reimagining of Christian life, centered on the values of simplicity, nonviolence, and communal living. He challenges the Church's entanglement with consumerism and militarism, urging believers to reflect on the teachings of Jesus and the practices of the early Christian communities. Claiborne's vision calls for a return to a form of discipleship that rejects the lure of wealth and power, instead embracing a life of service and solidarity with the poor.[48]

In critiquing the Church's complicity in supporting systems of economic and military power, Claiborne points out how the Church has often drifted away from its foundational values. He recalls the teachings of his mentor, Tony Campolo, who emphasized that Jesus did not instruct the poor to seek out the Church, but rather commanded the Church to go out and meet the poor where they are. This call-to-action underscores Claiborne's argument that the Church must be actively engaged in addressing social inequalities, rather than passively waiting for the marginalized to seek help.[49]

Furthermore, Claiborne challenges Christians to evaluate their commitment to Jesus' teachings, not just for the promise of eternal life, but for the transformative power of living according to those principles in the present world. His focus on the here and now is a reminder that following Jesus requires a radical shift in how we relate to others, particularly the vulnerable and oppressed, rather than simply waiting for rewards in the afterlife.[50]

Claiborne also critiques the historical relationship between the Church and political power, especially following the reign of Constantine, which he sees as the beginning of the Church's compromise with imperial authority. He argues that this alignment led to a dilution of Christian discipleship, where repentance and conversion became superficial gestures rather than genuine commitments to living out the radical values of the Kingdom.[51] This critique serves as a call for the Church to disentangle itself from systems of political power and instead align with the countercultural ethos of the early Christian movement.

47. Milbank, *Theology and Social Theory*, xix.
48. Claiborne, *Irresistible Revolution*, 46.
49. Claiborne, *Irresistible Revolution*, 102.
50. Claiborne, *Irresistible Revolution*, 117.
51. Claiborne, *Irresistible Revolution*, 106.

CHAPTER THREE

In essence, Claiborne's theology centers on a rejection of materialism, violence, and political compromise, advocating for a return to the subversive and revolutionary nature of the Kingdom of God, where love, justice, and communal solidarity take precedence over wealth, power, and individualism.[52]

Through these reflections, Claiborne invites the Church to a deeper understanding of its mission, not just to save souls but to care for the entire creation. He warns against the tendency to prioritize short-term human concerns over long-term ecological sustainability, calling instead for a broader commitment that sees environmental stewardship as integral to the Kingdom's work.[53]

Ched Myers offers a socio-political interpretation of the Kingdom of God, framing it as a direct opposition to imperial power structures. He argues that the Kingdom calls for active resistance against oppression and for solidarity with marginalized communities. Myers critiques both secular and religious institutions that perpetuate injustice, emphasizing that the Church must actively oppose these forces if it is to genuinely embody the Kingdom. He presents the Kingdom not as a metaphorical or distant ideal, but as a tangible reality that challenges established power and demands concrete actions.[54]

Myers draws upon the Gospel of Mark to highlight how Jesus' actions and teachings are situated within this framework of resistance. For instance, he points out that when Jesus calls his disciples to follow him across the sea during a storm, their panic and fear reflect a lack of understanding of Jesus' mission. The storm is symbolic of the challenges and threats posed by imperial power, and Jesus' calming of the storm represents the need for faith in the face of overwhelming oppression.[55] This moment becomes a key example of how the Kingdom of God is not passive but calls for an active stance against fear and domination.

Furthermore, Myers contrasts the stories of the rich man and Bartimaeus in the Gospel, showing how Jesus' mission appeals to those on the margins of society while challenging those entrenched in wealth and power. The rich man's inability to give up his possessions stands in stark contrast to Bartimaeus, who, despite his blindness and poverty, has the faith to follow Jesus. This juxtaposition underscores Myers' argument

52. Claiborne, *Irresistible Revolution*, 63.
53. Claiborne, *Irresistible Revolution*, 102.
54. Myers, *Binding the Strong Man*, 196.
55. Myers, *Binding the Strong Man*, 196.

that the Kingdom is fundamentally about lifting up the marginalized and rejecting the security offered by wealth and political influence.[56]

The political implications of discipleship are further explored in Myers' interpretation of Jesus' response to his challengers. Jesus speaks of an eschatological vision where worldly structures, including marriage and family, are no longer the central focus. This vision challenges the power dynamics of Jesus' time, asserting that the Kingdom of God redefines societal norms and relationships in a radical way.[57] By doing so, Myers emphasizes that the Kingdom is not just a personal spiritual journey but a social and political revolution that transforms relationships and power structures.

Myers also critiques how some interpretations of the Kingdom of God seek triumphalism, associating the Kingdom with earthly power and victory. Instead, he presents the Kingdom as rooted in suffering, tribulation, and nonviolence. Mark's narrative, according to Myers, does not promise political domination but invites followers into a paradox of life through death, reflecting the politics of nonviolence that stands in opposition to imperial rule.[58]

By calling attention to the imperial backdrop of the Gospel narrative, Myers challenges both secular and religious institutions that align themselves with systems of power and privilege. His interpretation of the Kingdom calls for the Church to take an active, countercultural stance, resisting complicity in oppression and instead advocating for justice and peace alongside the marginalized.[59]

Sallie McFague views the Kingdom of God as encompassing the well-being of all creation, not just human society. She critiques traditional Christian thought for being overly anthropocentric, arguing that humans have often assumed a position of superiority over the rest of creation, which has led to environmental neglect. McFague emphasizes that humans are stewards of the earth, entrusted with the care of God's creation, and this role involves ensuring the flourishing of all life, not just humanity. She suggests that this stewardship means understanding the difference between good and evil, with the responsibility to act in ways that sustain rather than destroy the planet.[60]

56. Myers, *Binding the Strong Man*, 287.
57. Myers, *Binding the Strong Man*, 316.
58. Myers, *Binding the Strong Man*, 333.
59. Myers, *Binding the Strong Man*, 445.
60. McFague, *New Climate for Theology*, 74.

McFague further critiques the dominant societal frameworks—religion, economics, and government—for promoting an individualistic worldview, which assumes that humans are isolated beings who engage in relationships only when it benefits them. She argues that an ecological understanding of creation challenges this view, presenting a new anthropology that sees humans as fundamentally interrelated and interdependent with the rest of creation.[61] This understanding of interdependence demands that Christians incorporate ecological awareness into their theology, recognizing that the well-being of the planet is crucial for the flourishing of all life.

In advocating for an ecological theology, McFague introduces the concept of "ecological literacy," suggesting that Christians need to develop a deeper understanding of what makes ecosystems thrive. She connects this to the broader vision of the Kingdom of God, where the flourishing of all creation is central. By learning how ecosystems function and what actions are necessary to sustain them, humans can better fulfill their role as caretakers of God's body, the earth.[62]

McFague's critique extends to the global economic systems, which she argues prioritize growth and individual wealth at the expense of both human and environmental health. She contrasts this with an ecological economic paradigm that values sustainability and justice for all creatures, pointing out that current economic models fail to address climate change or the degradation of natural resources.[63] This alternative economic vision, rooted in Christian values, challenges market capitalism and calls for a redistribution of resources that supports both human and nonhuman life.

Ultimately, McFague's ecological theology presents the Kingdom of God as a vision that integrates human well-being with the health of the planet, calling Christians to rethink their relationship with creation and to adopt practices that reflect this interconnectedness.[64] This theological framework challenges Christians to take seriously their role in addressing environmental issues, framing creation care as a fundamental aspect of Christian discipleship.

John D. Caputo approaches the Kingdom of God from a postmodern perspective, seeing it as a dynamic challenge to established religious

61. McFague, *New Climate for Theology*, 76.
62. McFague, *New Climate for Theology*, 113.
63. McFague, *New Climate for Theology*, 88.
64. McFague, *New Climate for Theology*, 79.

and social structures. He interprets the Kingdom not as a fixed state of power or authority, but as an ongoing event that resists rigid definitions and traditional hierarchies. Caputo argues that theology itself must be open to continual reinterpretation, a process that mirrors the uncertainty and fluidity of the Kingdom's coming. For Caputo, the Kingdom is a space where weakness, rather than strength, holds sway, making it a "sublime weakness" that defies conventional notions of power.[65]

In this vision, Caputo describes the Kingdom as mocking traditional systems of power, such as the Roman Empire's brutality, by presenting a form of divine madness. This "madness" contrasts sharply with the logic of the world, where everything is measured by success and strength. Instead, the Kingdom calls for a rethinking of what counts as power, urging believers to embrace vulnerability and the unpredictability of grace, much like the way Jesus' Kingdom challenged Roman authority.[66]

Caputo further elaborates that the Kingdom's truth does not conform to the usual standards of historical accuracy or conventional wisdom. Instead, the truth of the Kingdom is performative, something to be enacted or lived out through acts of justice, forgiveness, and hospitality. He contrasts the world's transactional and exclusionary systems with the Kingdom's openness, where everyone is welcomed, even strangers and outsiders, defying social norms.[67]

He also critiques the traditional interpretation of God as omnipotent and omniscient, proposing instead a "weak theology" that reflects a God who operates through subtlety and fragility. For Caputo, the name of God represents an event—a call to goodness and justice rather than a forceful assertion of divine power. This interpretation aligns with his broader critique of established religious doctrines, suggesting that theology should embrace the ambiguity and evolving nature of faith.[68]

Caputo's exploration of the Kingdom of God calls for a reimagining of both theology and Christian practice, encouraging believers to live with the tension between weakness and strength, certainty and doubt. His postmodern reading opens space for a theology that is continually unfolding, where the Kingdom remains an invitation to challenge the status quo and embrace the unknown.[69]

65. Caputo, *Weakness of God*, 14.
66. Caputo, *Weakness of God*, 15.
67. Caputo, *Weakness of God*, 17.
68. Caputo, *Weakness of God*, 53.
69. Caputo, *Weakness of God*, 2.

In conclusion, this exploration of the Kingdom of God reveals a rich tapestry of theological perspectives that challenge established structures and call for a rethinking of how justice, peace, and human rights are addressed. From Stanley Hauerwas's focus on the Church as a countercultural community resisting political co-option, to John Milbank's critique of liberal democracy and its failure to prioritize communal values, to Shane Claiborne's radical call for simplicity and solidarity with the marginalized, these thinkers offer frameworks for the Church's role in advocating for systemic change. Ched Myers and Sallie McFague add further dimensions, emphasizing resistance to imperial power and ecological responsibility, while John D. Caputo invites a postmodern reimagining of the Kingdom as an event that disrupts traditional norms.

3.2.2. Relational Theologies for Reform

This section explores various theological perspectives that emphasize justice and peace within both social and ecological contexts. Key figures such as Elisabeth Schüssler Fiorenza, J. Kameron Carter, Catherine Keller, Birch and Cobb, Larry Rasmussen, and Denis Edwards offer frameworks that challenge traditional structures of oppression and environmental exploitation. Each thinker proposes a reimagining of theology to address issues of power, race, colonialism, ecological interconnectedness, and the ethical responsibilities of humanity towards both people and the planet. These theologies collectively call for a shift in how we understand justice, urging a more inclusive and responsible approach to the world.

Elisabeth Schüssler Fiorenza introduces the term "kyriarchy" to articulate a framework that critiques intersecting systems of oppression, shifting the discourse from singular, often patriarchal, interpretations. She positions this term prominently to encourage a deeper exploration of power dynamics that transcend traditional patriarchal structures and encompass a broader spectrum of oppression, including those based on race, class, and gender. This broader scope aims to unveil and address the multiple layers of power that influence societal norms and religious interpretations.[70]

Schüssler Fiorenza emphasizes that the damage inflicted by these oppressive systems exists independently of individual actors, suggesting an entrenched structural issue. She argues that the mission of theology

---

70. Schüssler Fiorenza, *But She Said*, 34.

should be to foster an evolution both in humanity and in our relationship with the earth, advocating for a mutually supportive coexistence. This vision aligns with her broader ecological and ethical concerns, framing justice as inclusive of environmental stewardship.[71]

In her critique of modern theological perspectives, Schüssler Fiorenza highlights the influential yet ambiguous role of figures like Teilhard de Chardin, whose mystical and evolutionary views inspire many but also bear the marks of his time's colonial and progress-oriented ideologies. She uses these reflections to call for a more critical engagement with theological figures, urging a reassessment of their contributions in light of contemporary understandings of justice and cosmology.[72]

Addressing the need for a rhetorical-ethical shift in biblical studies, Schüssler Fiorenza argues for transforming the scientific-positivist ethos that has dominated biblical scholarship. By reorienting towards a rhetorical and ethical framework, she believes that feminist and other liberation theologies can move from the margins to the center of biblical interpretation, thus influencing the perceptions, values, and imaginations of wider cultures and societies.[73]

She also engages with the notion of a "Public Health Department" in biblical studies, a metaphorical suggestion that biblical scholarship should serve public, communal health by addressing and healing the societal ailments perpetuated by oppressive interpretations. This idea reinforces her commitment to a theology that is actively engaged with the world's needs and challenges.[74]

Schüssler Fiorenza critically addresses how traditional interpretations can serve to reinforce patriarchal structures, using the metaphor of the "biblical bedtime story" to illustrate how dominant readings soothe or suppress dissent and maintain oppressive systems. She challenges this by advocating for a feminist hermeneutic that recognizes and resists these dynamics, thus reclaiming the power to interpret texts in ways that foster liberation rather than oppression.[75]

Finally, she discusses the intersection of feminist biblical interpretation with postmodern approaches, specifically the "new historicism." This alignment highlights her commitment to understanding truth

71. Schüssler Fiorenza, *But She Said*, 52.
72. Schüssler Fiorenza, *But She Said*, 60.
73. Schüssler Fiorenza, *But She Said*, 47.
74. Schüssler Fiorenza, *But She Said*, 77.
75. Schüssler Fiorenza, *But She Said*, 5.

as a dynamic and historically situated construct, which is essential for developing a critical feminist biblical interpretation that acknowledges the complexities of history and culture in shaping religious texts and practices.[76]

J. Kameron Carter critiques the theological imagination shaped by modernity, specifically focusing on how it perpetuates racial and colonial structures. He argues that to address these injustices, theology must disrupt the racial logic embedded within the modern body politic, particularly as it has shaped religious discourse. Carter emphasizes that a radical rethinking of theology is necessary, one that is both decolonized and antiracist.[77]

In his critique, Carter explores the role of race in shaping theological identities, arguing that the dominant theological discourse historically lacked safeguards against the emergence of a racial hierarchy. This racialized understanding of humanity became embedded in theology, leading to the marginalization of Black people and other racialized groups. Carter insists that a proper theological response must reimagine freedom in a way that includes all people, rather than being complicit in their exclusion.[78]

Carter also addresses how Black religious traditions, especially those within the Afro-Christian faith, offer a significant counter-narrative to modern theological practices. He argues that Black religious expressions were not merely cultural or social practices but also embodied theological resistance to the racial and colonial structures that oppressed them. Through lived and performed theology, Black Christians resisted the theological frameworks that excluded them, offering a vision of faith deeply intertwined with the pursuit of justice and freedom.[79]

In addition, Carter connects his analysis to historical figures like Gregory of Nyssa, whom he presents as an abolitionist intellectual. Gregory's stance against slavery serves as a theological precursor to the kinds of freedom narratives found in early Afro-Christian thought. Carter emphasizes that rethinking Christian theology requires revisiting these early theological voices, which challenge both the racial and colonial foundations of modernity.[80]

76. Schüssler Fiorenza, *But She Said*, 87, 88.
77. Carter, *Race*, 6.
78. Carter, *Race*, 35.
79. Carter, *Race*, 52.
80. Carter, *Race*, 7.

Carter further elaborates that Christian theology must move beyond the racialized logic that has defined it. He critiques the ways in which race has been constructed within theology, arguing that both Black and white identities have been shaped by this flawed framework. For Carter, a true reconstitution of theology involves dismantling these racial categories and reimagining theology in a way that transcends them, grounded instead in the particularity of Christ's flesh, which he identifies as Jewish covenantal flesh, rather than a racialized identity.[81]

Ultimately, Carter's work calls for a theological reformation that addresses the racial and colonial structures embedded in Christian thought. He highlights how Afro-Christian narratives and practices have historically resisted these structures and offers a pathway toward a more inclusive and justice-oriented theological imagination.[82]

Catherine Keller's contribution to ecological theology is rooted in a vision of creation that emphasizes the interconnectedness of all life forms, rejecting the notion of a static, hierarchical order. In her theological work, Keller draws on process theology and emphasizes the idea of creation as an ongoing, dynamic process. She challenges traditional Christian understandings of creation, which have historically depicted the universe as emerging from a formless nothingness (creatio ex nihilo), suggesting instead that creation arises from chaos, a "tehomic" depth full of potential and relationality.[83]

Keller critiques the traditional Christian theology that has sought to erase the chaotic elements of creation in favor of a clear, hierarchical order. This erasure, she argues, has limited theological understandings of the world and of God, leading to a vision of divine power that prioritizes control over relationality. By contrast, Keller's theology of becoming, influenced by process thought, opens up a space for understanding God's relationship with the world as one of interdependence and mutuality, rather than dominance.[84] Some critics contend that Keller's emphasis on process and relationality diminishes more traditional views of divine sovereignty, presenting a more fluid, less authoritative understanding of God's role in creation.

In her exploration of chaos and creation, Keller revisits the biblical narrative of Genesis, arguing that the "darkness" and "deep" (tehom)

---

81. Carter, *Race*, 8.
82. Carter, *Race*.
83. Keller, *Face of the Deep*, 4.
84. Keller, *Face of the Deep*, 5.

mentioned in the early verses of the Bible have been historically overlooked. She posits that these elements represent an important theological topic, one that underscores the ongoing, unfinished nature of creation. This reinterpretation challenges the dominance of creatio ex nihilo and instead suggests that creation emerges out of the depths of chaos, offering a more dynamic and complex theological understanding of the beginning of the world.[85]

Keller's theology of the deep does not merely serve as an abstract metaphor but is also a critique of the dominant theological frameworks that have shaped Western thought, particularly in terms of power, hierarchy, and mastery. She argues that the suppression of chaos in Christian theology has mirrored the suppression of otherness, including ecological otherness, leading to exploitative relationships with the environment. By reclaiming chaos as a foundational element of creation, Keller advocates for a theological perspective that recognizes the intrinsic value and interrelatedness of all life forms.[86]

Critically, some argue that Keller's approach, while offering a fresh theological perspective, risks reducing the transcendence of God in favor of an immanent, relational framework. This concern is raised particularly by those who feel that the theological emphasis on chaos and relationality could weaken traditional doctrines of divine authority and providence. Nonetheless, Keller's constructive theology continues to challenge anthropocentric and hierarchical assumptions, advocating for a theology that better reflects the complexity and interdependence of creation.[87]

Birch and Cobb, in their process-oriented ecological theology, advocate for a model that emphasizes the interconnectedness of all life forms, challenging the reductionist and mechanistic models that have dominated scientific and theological discourse. They critique models like Jacques Monod's, which present life primarily in terms of molecular structures like DNA, arguing that such views are too narrow to capture the complexity of living systems.[88] Instead, Birch and Cobb offer an ecological model that integrates individual organisms within their environments, stressing that life cannot be understood in isolation but must be seen in relational and ecological terms.

85. Keller, *Face of the Deep*, 6.
86. Keller, *Face of the Deep*, 11.
87. Keller, *Face of the Deep*, 12.
88. Birch and Cobb, *Liberation of Life*, 70.

Their ecological model, which they believe better reflects the dynamic interactions in the natural world, suggests that living organisms exist not merely as isolated entities but as participants in complex webs of relationships that include other organisms and their environments. This understanding aligns with the principle of population ecology, where the interdependence of life forms is essential for the functioning and survival of ecosystems.[89] Birch and Cobb's process theology situates humanity as one part of a larger ecological community, challenging anthropocentric views that place humans above other forms of life.

In critiquing sociobiology and its deterministic approach to human behavior, Birch and Cobb argue that such theories reduce human life to biological functions and neglect the significant role of culture and environment in shaping behavior. For instance, they refer to the work of E.O. Wilson, whose sociobiological framework attempts to explain human nature in purely biological terms. Birch and Cobb resist this reductionism, emphasizing that humans are not only biological beings but are shaped by their ecological and cultural contexts as well.[90] They argue for a more holistic understanding of human life, where culture and environment play crucial roles alongside biology.

Their theological vision calls for an ecological ethic that recognizes the intrinsic value of all life forms. This ethic necessitates significant changes in both individual and corporate behavior to address environmental degradation and the global ecological crisis. Birch and Cobb emphasize the need for human responsibility in maintaining the health of the planet, advocating for systemic changes that can support both human and environmental flourishing.[91] However, critics of Birch and Cobb's framework argue that their emphasis on ecological interdependence lacks specificity in addressing the political and economic structures that perpetuate environmental exploitation, suggesting that a more focused critique of these systems is necessary for meaningful change.

Larry Rasmussen's theology, like that of Sallie McFague, brings critical ethical considerations to the issue of environmental responsibility. In his work, Rasmussen argues for an "earth ethics" that calls on humans to reimagine themselves not as separate from nature, but as an integral part of the natural world. This approach critiques modern economies that prioritize profit and human convenience over the well-being of the

---

89. Birch and Cobb, *Liberation of Life*, 42.
90. Birch and Cobb, *Liberation of Life*, 112.
91. Birch and Cobb, *Liberation of Life*, 25.

planet, suggesting that such systems must be rethought in order to foster ecological sustainability and social justice.[92]

Rasmussen draws on the Earth Charter, a global document that emphasizes respect for the community of life and ecological integrity as foundational to addressing both environmental and social issues. He highlights the Charter's call for systemic change that integrates ecological concerns with social and economic justice, pointing out that these principles are interconnected and cannot be addressed in isolation.[93] This holistic perspective is central to his vision of an ecological ethics that not only addresses environmental destruction but also seeks to remedy social inequalities, advocating for policies that promote fairness and sustainability.

Rasmussen also critiques the anthropocentric mindset that dominates much of Western thinking, particularly within industrial paradigms that treat nature as a resource to be exploited. He argues that this mindset has contributed to the degradation of the planet's ecosystems and has led to a disconnection between humans and the natural world. For Rasmussen, an Earth-friendly ethic would involve moving away from this anthropocentric view, embracing a more inclusive understanding of the world that sees all forms of life as inherently valuable and deserving of care.[94]

While Rasmussen's framework offers a broad and comprehensive ethical approach, critics have raised concerns that his theology does not fully engage with the complexities of global capitalism, which continues to drive much of the environmental crisis. The argument is that while Rasmussen advocates for systemic change, he may not sufficiently address how entrenched political and economic structures contribute to ongoing ecological harm.[95] This critique suggests that a more focused analysis of these systems is necessary to complement his call for ethical and theological reimagining.

Ultimately, Rasmussen's work invites a deeper reflection on how humans interact with the planet, urging for a radical shift in both thought and action. His vision of "earth ethics" seeks to integrate ecological sustainability with justice for all beings, calling for a renewed commitment

---

92. Rasmussen, *Earth-Honoring Faith*, 118.
93. Rasmussen, *Earth-Honoring Faith*, 119.
94. Rasmussen, *Earth-Honoring Faith*, 146.
95. Rasmussen, *Earth-Honoring Faith*, 58.

to care for both people and the environment.[96] However, the challenge remains in translating these theological and ethical ideas into concrete policies and practices that can counter the dominant economic systems that prioritize profit over planetary health.

Denis Edwards draws on the relational nature of the Trinity to offer a theological framework that connects ecological theology with Christian doctrine. He highlights the concept of perichoresis, a term used to describe the mutual indwelling and relational nature of the three Persons of the Trinity. In both Western and Eastern traditions, the Trinity is understood as inherently relational, with the divine Persons existing only in relation to one another. Edwards uses this relational model as a way to rethink how humans should relate to the natural world, emphasizing that creation, too, is relational and interconnected.[97]

The revival of trinitarian theology in recent decades, according to Edwards, has led to its rediscovery as a practical doctrine with implications for salvation and human life. This rediscovery opens the door for theology to engage with contemporary ecological concerns in meaningful ways. Edwards suggests that trinitarian theology, when applied to creation, provides a foundation for understanding how the natural world is not separate from God but is a part of the divine communion. All of creation, he argues, springs from this divine relationship and ultimately finds its fulfillment within it.[98]

In exploring the implications of this theology, Edwards emphasizes that ecological issues, such as global climate change, should be understood in light of humanity's relationship with all of God's creatures. This relational view calls for a rethinking of human actions and responsibilities toward the environment, seeing the natural world not as a resource to be exploited but as an integral part of God's ongoing creative work. Edwards encourages Christians to adopt a sacramental view of nature, recognizing the divine presence in all creation and fostering an attitude of care and respect.[99]

Furthermore, Edwards suggests that Christian practices, particularly the Eucharist, hold profound potential for fostering an ecological ethos. He points out that ancient eucharistic liturgies began with thanksgiving for creation before moving to redemption in Christ. This

---

96. Rasmussen, *Earth-Honoring Faith*, 266.
97. Edwards, *Ecology at the Heart of Faith*, 74.
98. Edwards, *Ecology at the Heart of Faith*, 121.
99. Edwards, *Ecology at the Heart of Faith*, 99.

CHAPTER THREE

connection between creation and redemption, Edwards argues, should inspire Christians to see their ecological commitments as integral to their faith, rooted in a theology that embraces the whole of God's creation.[100]

While Edwards offers a compelling theological framework for addressing ecological concerns, some critics argue that his approach may be too abstract for practical application, particularly in the face of the urgent challenges posed by climate change. These critiques suggest that while Edwards' theology provides valuable perspectives on the relationality of creation, more concrete actions and strategies are needed to address the political, economic, and social structures that contribute to environmental degradation.[101] Nonetheless, Edwards' work continues to offer a theological basis for environmental stewardship that emphasizes the sacredness of all life and the importance of protecting the natural world.

In conclusion, the thinkers discussed in this section offer a diverse range of theological approaches to justice, ecology, and human responsibility. From Elisabeth Schüssler Fiorenza's focus on dismantling kyriarchal structures and advocating for a theology that addresses intersecting oppressions, to J. Kameron Carter's call for a decolonized and antiracist theology, each perspective emphasizes the need for transformative thinking in both theology and practice. Catherine Keller's exploration of chaos and relationality in creation challenges hierarchical views, while Birch and Cobb advocate for an ecological model that stresses interdependence. Larry Rasmussen and Denis Edwards both push for an ethical framework that integrates ecological responsibility with a deeper understanding of human relationships within the natural world. These diverse theologies offer important frameworks for addressing the complexities of justice, power, and ecological care in a changing world.

3.3. LIBERATION THEOLOGY'S ROLE IN NORTH KOREAN JUSTICE

This section focuses on how engaging with the theology of the Kingdom of God encourages individuals to reflect on their roles in addressing systemic injustices, particularly in relation to environmental degradation and social inequality. Theologians such as Michael Northcott, Daniel Bell Jr., and William Cavanaugh offer perspectives on how Christians should integrate faith with ethical responsibilities, emphasizing the need

---

100. Edwards, *Ecology at the Heart of Faith*, 102.
101. Edwards, *Ecology at the Heart of Faith*, 105.

for justice, community, and responsible stewardship of creation. These reflections challenge believers to connect their personal actions with larger global concerns.

Northcott's focus on ecological justice highlights the responsibility that wealthier nations have in addressing climate change and its disproportionate impact on poorer nations. His emphasis on accountability calls Christians to examine the consequences of their environmental actions and to take steps that align with their ethical and spiritual beliefs. The Kingdom of God, in this view, demands a reevaluation of how individuals and communities contribute to global inequalities and environmental harm.

Bell and Cavanaugh further extend the discussion by critiquing capitalist structures and individualism, arguing that Christian discipleship requires resistance to systems that perpetuate inequality. Bell's concept of capitalism as a "discipline of desire" and Cavanaugh's focus on collective responsibility within the church point to the need for Christians to embody alternative values rooted in care, justice, and community. Together, these perspectives encourage an active engagement in social transformation that reflects the principles of the Kingdom of God.

3.3.1. Dignity and Justice for North Korea's Oppressed

This section explores how liberation theology can be applied to the context of North Korea, focusing on the dignity of the oppressed and the need to address systemic injustice. Drawing from the works of theologians like Jon Sobrino, Leonardo Boff, and Gustavo Gutiérrez, it emphasizes the importance of advocating for human rights and transformative change. Through solidarity with the marginalized, promoting transparency and accountability, and engaging in nonviolent advocacy, liberation theology offers a framework for addressing the social, political, and economic challenges faced by the people of North Korea.

In applying liberation theology to the context of North Korea, one essential aspect is highlighting the dignity of the oppressed, a concept deeply rooted in the teachings of liberation theologians like Jon Sobrino. Sobrino emphasizes the importance of acknowledging the inherent dignity of marginalized and suffering individuals, similar to the way Archbishop Romero and Ignacio Ellacuría recognized the scandalous situation of the oppressed in their own context. By giving dignity to those who have been massacred or disappeared, liberation theology offers a path to repair the sins of dishonesty and ingratitude that society perpetuates by neglecting the oppressed.[102]

A critical understanding of dignity is also present in Sobrino's reflection on the contrast between wealth and poverty. He draws from Kant's distinction between "worth" and "dignity" to illustrate how, in a world dominated by wealth, the culture of "worth" tends to prevail, often overshadowing the inherent dignity of the poor. In contexts of extreme poverty like North Korea, Sobrino asserts that dignity, rather than material worth, defines the value of the oppressed. This parallels Jesus' teaching about the poor widow who, despite her material poverty, gave more than anyone else because of her dignity.[103]

Sobrino further argues that merely human efforts, however idealistic, are insufficient for the full liberation of humanity. Drawing on St. Augustine's concept that to be human, one must be "more than human," Sobrino contends that human history, if left solely to human endeavors, will fail to achieve true justice and liberation. This idea challenges efforts to liberate North Korea solely through political or economic means, suggesting that a deeper, transcendent approach is required for genuine human liberation.[104]

Another significant point Sobrino makes is the role of the poor in shaping the Church and society. He reflects on Ellacuría's insistence that the poor have the potential to transform the Church evangelically. In this sense, a society or Church that truly aims to be democratic or egalitarian must be structured around the rights of the disadvantaged. This is particularly relevant in the context of North Korea, where the marginalized are excluded from both social and ecclesial spaces, and any attempt at justice must focus on their rights and inclusion.[105]

Sobrino also addresses the fundamental struggle of human rights, framing it as the fight for life against death. He emphasizes that to protect human rights effectively, society must vehemently oppose the conditions of weakness, slavery, and oppression that perpetuate inequality. In North Korea, where human rights are systematically violated, this struggle

---

102. Sobrino, *No Salvation Outside the Poor*, 28.
103. Sobrino, *No Salvation Outside the Poor*, 75.
104. Sobrino, *No Salvation Outside the Poor*, 118.
105. Sobrino, *No Salvation Outside the Poor*, 10.

becomes especially poignant, as the pursuit of justice requires the rejection of death-dealing systems and the upholding of life-giving dignity.[106]

In his theological reflection, Sobrino underscores the importance of giving existence to victims by naming the tortured, dead, and disappeared. This act, which may seem small, is a crucial step in recognizing their fundamental human right to be remembered as dignified individuals. Applying this to North Korea, the global community must not only document human rights abuses but also ensure that the victims' names and stories are preserved, giving them dignity in both life and death.[107]

Sobrino critiques the global structure that dehumanizes the poor through an unquestioning acceptance of empire and economic disparity. He points out that in a world where poverty exists alongside conspicuous abundance, the silence in the face of such misery is not just problematic but dehumanizing. The stark inequality between the rich and the poor, particularly in the global context, highlights the need for a theology that addresses both material and spiritual injustice.[108]

Ultimately, Sobrino argues that the growing inequality between the rich and poor is a dehumanizing force that must be confronted. His critique of the insensitivity of the wealthy living in proximity to the poor without acknowledging their suffering can be applied to the situation in North Korea. The failure to recognize and act against the disparities within North Korea and between North Korea and the rest of the world reflects a broader dehumanization that liberation theology seeks to address.[109]

In his discussion on the Christian experience, Boff emphasizes that faith is not merely intellectual but also existential, recognizing the mystery of divinity becoming human. He suggests that the Church, as the mystical body of Christ, must be understood as the People of God. This concept reflects the shared faith of the entire Church, not just an isolated experience.[110] Similarly, creating platforms for North Korean defectors and other survivors to share their stories humanizes abstract data, making their experiences accessible to a broader audience.

Boff also examines the two meanings of politics, focusing on the search for the common good and the promotion of justice. He underscores

---

106. Sobrino, *No Salvation Outside the Poor*, 11.
107. Sobrino, *No Salvation Outside the Poor*, 28.
108. Sobrino, *No Salvation Outside the Poor*, 45.
109. Sobrino, *No Salvation Outside the Poor*, 46.
110. Boff, *Church, Charism and Power*, 15.

the need for a community-oriented approach to politics that harmonizes equality with freedom.[111] This mirrors the call for international forums where survivors of oppression can share their experiences, contributing to the global dialogue on justice and human rights. By involving these voices, advocacy efforts can address issues such as corruption and violence against human dignity.

In discussing intolerance and dogmatism, Boff argues that claiming possession of absolute truth leads to intolerance, as those who believe they possess the truth cannot tolerate other perspectives.[112] This resonates with the importance of allowing survivors of human rights abuses to present their own narratives. The diversity of personal experiences enriches the global understanding of oppression and challenges dogmatic views that may oversimplify complex realities.

Boff further critiques the historical shift of the Church towards a hierarchical structure, which limited the participation of the broader community in church affairs. He sees the base ecclesial communities as a space for greater participation and balance.[113] Similarly, international forums that give space to oppressed individuals to voice their experiences foster greater participation in the global conversation on human rights. These forums provide a platform for grassroots voices, promoting a more inclusive dialogue.

Lastly, Boff highlights the role of authority within the community, which originally stemmed from exemplary living rather than from the sacred power bestowed upon leaders.[114] This reflection on authority aligns with the idea that survivors' testimonies should be central in human rights advocacy. Their lived experiences provide a legitimate foundation for understanding and addressing global injustices, rather than relying solely on abstract data or institutional authority.

Pressing for accountability is a key component of applying liberation theology, particularly when it comes to addressing human rights violations. Advocating for sanctions and legal actions against perpetrators aligns with the principles of justice and the rule of law, as reflected in Gutiérrez's interpretation of the Populorum Progressio encyclical. The encyclical calls for building a world where every person, regardless of race, religion, or nationality, can live a fully human life, free from the

---

111. Boff, *Church, Charism and Power*, 27.
112. Boff, *Church, Charism and Power*, 42.
113. Boff, *Church, Charism and Power*, 128.
114. Boff, *Church, Charism and Power*, 50.

oppressive forces of other men or uncontrollable natural forces.[115] This vision supports the necessity of holding violators accountable for their actions to ensure such freedom.

In Gutiérrez's view, integral development represents a transformation from less human to more human conditions, focusing on those who are deprived of even the most basic essentials.[116] Similarly, advocating for accountability ensures that those responsible for these inhuman conditions are brought to justice. By working with international bodies and leveraging legal frameworks, liberation theology calls for action that not only condemns injustice but also actively seeks to create a more human and dignified world.

The theological reflection on the process of human liberation demands that we scrutinize oppressive structures, which, as Gutiérrez argues, are often manifestations of sin.[117] This sin appears in the form of exploitation, domination, and systemic oppression, and pressing for accountability is a direct response to these injustices. In doing so, liberation theology connects faith with the concrete struggle against such exploitation.

Liberation theology also emphasizes the creation of a new society characterized by solidarity, where political liberation aligns with spiritual liberation from sin, the root cause of all injustice.[118] This process of humanization is inseparable from efforts to hold those who perpetuate exploitation and oppression accountable. Through such actions, liberation theology seeks to foster a new humanity rooted in justice and solidarity.

Furthermore, Gutiérrez highlights that liberation theology must be verified through praxis, involving active participation in the struggles of the oppressed.[119] This practice includes advocating for sanctions and legal measures against those responsible for violations, aligning with the broader goal of creating conditions for a dignified life free from oppression.

Finally, as Gutiérrez describes, theology linked to praxis fulfills a prophetic function by interpreting historical events and proclaiming their true meaning.[120] In the context of human rights advocacy, this

115. Gutiérrez, *Theology of Liberation*, 23.
116. Gutiérrez, *Theology of Liberation*, 100.
117. Gutiérrez, *Theology of Liberation*, 103.
118. Gutiérrez, *Theology of Liberation*, 139.
119. Gutiérrez, *Theology of Liberation*, 174.
120. Gutiérrez, *Theology of Liberation*, 10.

means that pressing for accountability is not only a legal or political action but also a moral imperative deeply embedded in the theological framework of liberation.

Liberation theology also calls for economic and social reforms to address the systemic causes of oppression. Brueggemann critiques systems that are built on rigid moral frameworks, like the one represented by the Deuteronomistic Historian, suggesting that life is filled with ambiguity and complexity that cannot be reduced to simple moral causes.[121] This idea parallels the need for reforms in North Korea, where oppressive structures perpetuate inequality, and where access to basic necessities such as education, healthcare, and economic opportunity is severely limited.

Brueggemann further argues that theodicy, or the justice of God, is not just a theoretical issue but a form of social criticism against systems that fail to function humanely.[122] In the context of North Korea, this critique applies to the current regime's failure to provide for the basic needs of its people. Liberation theology, through its call for economic justice, demands that such systems be reformed so that all individuals can live with dignity.

The prophetic tradition, as explained by Brueggemann, includes a call for rulers to be held accountable and for unjust systems to be dismantled.[123] This resonates with the need for international efforts to advocate for reforms in North Korea, focusing on dismantling oppressive structures that deny the population basic human rights. Addressing these root causes is key to creating a more equitable and just society.

Brueggemann also discusses the creation of a new community bound by the Torah, which he suggests should not be understood merely as law but as a broader guiding principle for justice and social equity.[124] In the case of North Korea, reforms aimed at improving living conditions, education, and healthcare can be seen as part of building such a community—one where every person is given the opportunity to thrive, free from the constraints of authoritarian rule.

Finally, Brueggemann's critique of the "deed-consequence" framework, which suggests that rigid systems of justice often fail those who are already marginalized,[125] underscores the need for a more flexible and

---

121. Brueggemann, *Social Reading of the Old Testament*, 31.
122. Brueggemann, *Social Reading of the Old Testament*, 178.
123. Brueggemann, *Social Reading of the Old Testament*, 27.
124. Brueggemann, *Social Reading of the Old Testament*, 48.
125. Brueggemann, *Social Reading of the Old Testament*, 87.

compassionate approach to reform. In North Korea, this means not only addressing the immediate needs of the people but also creating long-term systemic changes that promote social and economic justice for all.

Education and awareness-raising are vital tools in engaging the global community with human rights issues in North Korea. Waetjen emphasizes the importance of a collective moral order, as represented by the "son of a human being" in Jewish apocalypticism, which can be understood as a symbol of a community united in purpose.[126] In the context of North Korean human rights advocacy, this collective identity can serve as a model for building a global coalition dedicated to justice and change.

Waetjen also draws attention to the role of individuals like Elijah and John the Baptizer, who serve as forerunners in the establishment of a new moral order.[127] In a similar way, individuals and organizations that raise awareness about the plight of North Korean citizens play a crucial role in preparing the international community for collective action. By informing people of the realities on the ground, advocates act as moral leaders, guiding others toward meaningful engagement.

The potential for human transformation is a recurring theme in Waetjen's work, as seen in the portrayal of human beings striving to realize the potentiality of God.[128] This concept aligns with the goal of education and awareness campaigns, which aim to mobilize the global community toward greater understanding and action. By highlighting the human dignity of North Korean citizens, these efforts seek to galvanize a movement for change that goes beyond mere sympathy to active support.

In Waetjen's discussion of discipleship, he points out that following a moral leader requires immediate and committed action.[129] For those engaged in advocacy for North Korean human rights, this means not only becoming informed but also taking tangible steps to support reform efforts. Whether through public education campaigns, policy advocacy, or humanitarian assistance, a global coalition must be ready to act in response to the knowledge gained through awareness-raising initiatives.

Finally, Waetjen highlights the importance of understanding the broader purpose behind individual suffering and action, as shown in the narrative of the Human Being who is Lord of the Sabbath.[130] In the

---

126. Waetjen, *Reordering of Power*, xiii.
127. Waetjen, *Reordering of Power*, 22.
128. Waetjen, *Reordering of Power*, 24.
129. Waetjen, *Reordering of Power*, 28.
130. Waetjen, *Reordering of Power*, 31.

context of North Korea, raising awareness about human rights violations serves a larger goal of building a society where every person's dignity is respected. By educating the global community and encouraging collective action, advocates can help foster the conditions for long-term reform and justice.

Solidarity is a fundamental element in liberation theology, emphasizing the need to not only advocate for policy changes but also to stand with the oppressed in tangible ways. Cox points out that human communities evolve through different forms—tribal, town, and technopolitan—but these forms of society all share a collective identity and responsibility.[131] In the context of solidarity, this means that individuals and groups must come together, offering practical assistance and moral support to those in need, transcending differences in societal structures.

As Cox explains, the tribal mentality is rooted in familial solidarity, where people celebrate their common ancestors through shared rituals.[132] This sense of unity can be seen as a model for how solidarity should be practiced in modern times—by building relationships based on mutual respect and working collectively towards justice and liberation. Liberation theology calls for this kind of deep connection, where standing with the oppressed is not just a symbolic gesture but a commitment to shared action.

Cox also notes that religion and culture are deeply intertwined with the social and economic structures of a society, meaning that true solidarity requires engaging with these systems.[133] This is particularly important in liberation theology, where solidarity involves addressing the root causes of injustice, including economic inequality and political oppression. Working together to challenge these structures underscores the importance of collective responsibility in addressing systemic injustices.

Furthermore, Cox emphasizes the importance of political and social change, tracing the desacralization of politics to biblical roots, particularly the Exodus.[134] In liberation theology, solidarity is seen as an active participation in the struggle for such change. It involves not only standing with the oppressed but also engaging in the political processes that can lead to liberation.

---

131. Cox, *Secular City*, 7.
132. Cox, *Secular City*, 8.
133. Cox, *Secular City*, 9.
134. Cox, *Secular City*, 31.

Finally, Cox argues that mobility and openness to new ideas are key aspects of modern urban life, suggesting that those who have experienced change are more likely to embrace further transformation.[135] This concept resonates with the idea of solidarity in liberation theology, where building relationships and working together for justice requires a willingness to adapt, grow, and act in new ways.

While liberation theology provides a solid framework for advocating justice, critics like Carl Raschke raise concerns about the potential for over-politicization. Raschke argues that when theology becomes too intertwined with political activism, there is a risk of compromising its spiritual and moral foundations.[136] This is particularly relevant in contexts where the focus shifts from the theological core to political movements, potentially losing the balance between these essential elements.

Raschke's perspective is rooted in the broader postmodern critique of certain modern ideologies, particularly those that blur the lines between distinct disciplines.[137] He suggests that liberation theology, while vital in addressing systemic injustice, must be cautious not to dilute its theological essence by becoming solely a tool for political change. The challenge lies in maintaining the integrity of the theological message while also engaging effectively in social and political advocacy.

Further exploring the relationship between theology and social engagement, Raschke emphasizes that theology cannot be fully separated from its cultural and social context, but it must also retain its distinct identity.[138] In the case of liberation theology, this means that while it engages with real-world struggles, it must continue to prioritize its spiritual dimensions and not merely serve as a political framework.

Moreover, Raschke highlights the importance of balance, particularly in how theological movements navigate complex social issues.[139] For liberation theology to remain effective, it must balance its commitment to justice with a sustained focus on its theological underpinnings. This balance ensures that the movement does not lose sight of its spiritual mission while advocating for social change.

In his analysis, Raschke reminds us that maintaining the integrity of theology in political contexts requires careful reflection and a

---

135. Cox, *Secular City*, 62.
136. Raschke, *Fire and Roses*, 1.
137. Raschke, *Fire and Roses*, 2.
138. Raschke, *Fire and Roses*, 54.
139. Raschke, *Fire and Roses*, 110.

commitment to preserving its foundational principles.[140] For liberation theology, this involves continuously engaging with the spiritual and moral dimensions of the movement, ensuring that it remains grounded in its theological roots while pursuing justice and liberation.

John Cobb, in his ecological perspective, argues that liberation theology must broaden its scope to include environmental justice, recognizing the connection between human oppression and environmental degradation. He suggests that a more comprehensive theological framework is required to address both human and ecological injustices.[141] In this view, liberation theology cannot limit itself to social and economic liberation but must also consider the health of the environment as integral to the well-being of oppressed communities.

Cobb emphasizes that the liberation of Latin American peasants and workers from economic colonialism and class oppression, while crucial, must be expanded to include liberation from ecological destruction.[142] This expanded view recognizes that many of the most vulnerable communities are also the most affected by environmental harm, and thus, environmental justice is a necessary component of achieving true liberation.

Furthermore, Cobb discusses how process theology, a school of thought that responds to liberation theology, also addresses the need for a broader approach to justice that includes environmental concerns.[143] This perspective underscores the idea that liberation theology must evolve to tackle the interconnectedness of human and environmental struggles, providing a more holistic response to oppression in all its forms.

Cobb's argument is rooted in the notion that political theology, and by extension liberation theology, must address the broader social structures that contribute to both human and ecological suffering.[144] By doing so, liberation theology can more effectively advocate for a world where both people and the environment are treated with respect and care. This approach calls for a shift in theological thinking, where justice for the earth and justice for humanity are seen as inseparable.

---

140. Raschke, *Fire and Roses*, 133.
141. Cobb, *Process Theology as Political Theology*, vii.
142. Cobb, *Process Theology as Political Theology*, viii.
143. Cobb, *Process Theology as Political Theology*, ix.
144. Cobb, *Process Theology as Political Theology*, 7.

Lastly, Cobb points out that the political dimensions of theology must be intertwined with ecological concerns, as the future of humanity is closely linked to the health of the planet.[145] Through this broader lens, liberation theology can remain relevant in addressing contemporary issues, ensuring that it speaks not only to human liberation but also to the liberation of the earth itself from destructive practices.

Conclusively, liberation theology provides a practical and theological framework for addressing the complex social, political, and economic challenges in North Korea. By focusing on the inherent dignity of the oppressed, as highlighted by theologians such as Jon Sobrino, it calls for an approach that recognizes the value of individuals suffering under systemic injustice. This framework promotes the need for solidarity, accountability, and advocacy, urging the global community to support the marginalized through nonviolent means.

Moreover, the application of liberation theology to North Korea emphasizes the importance of structural reforms. The focus on transforming oppressive systems, as argued by Gustavo Gutiérrez and others, stresses the necessity of addressing the root causes of inequality and human rights violations. This approach calls for reforms in areas such as healthcare, education, and economic opportunity, ensuring that all people have access to basic rights and are able to live with dignity.

Lastly, the inclusion of environmental justice, as discussed by John Cobb, broadens the scope of liberation theology. It highlights the interconnectedness of human oppression and environmental degradation, particularly relevant in the context of North Korea, where resource shortages and deforestation exacerbate human suffering. By addressing both ecological and social justice, liberation theology offers a comprehensive path toward the liberation of both people and the environment.

3.3.2. Educating for Human Rights

Education is a crucial tool in raising awareness about human rights abuses in North Korea, particularly in exposing the complex structures of oppression that govern the country. Theological education has a role in helping students critically examine these systems and engage in both reflection and action. By drawing on perspectives from figures like Paulo Freire, Gustavo Gutiérrez, and others, educational efforts can encourage

---

145. Cobb, *Process Theology as Political Theology*, 12.

students to understand the psychological and structural aspects of oppression, as well as their own responsibility in advocating for justice and dignity. This approach fosters a commitment to both learning and active participation in human rights advocacy.

In promoting awareness and understanding of the human rights situation in North Korea, education plays a vital role in unveiling the complex systems of oppression. Theological education should focus on critically examining these oppressive structures. According to Paulo Freire, the process of unveiling oppression is the first stage in the journey toward liberation, where the oppressed not only recognize their condition but commit themselves to transforming it through praxis.[146] This stage is essential for students and scholars to engage in both reflection and action, applying their understanding of oppression to advocate for justice.

As these educational programs delve deeper into the historical and contemporary contexts of human rights violations, Freire suggests that the oppressed often view the oppressor as a model of "manhood" in the initial stages of their struggle.[147] This insight is crucial when analyzing the mindset of North Korean citizens who may have internalized the values of their oppressors. It emphasizes the importance of educational efforts that challenge this internalized oppression and offer new models of dignity and freedom.

Freire also highlights the internal conflict faced by the oppressed—whether to reject the influence of the oppressor or remain passive.[148] In the case of North Korea, educational efforts must address this psychological division, encouraging students to move beyond being mere spectators to becoming active participants in the struggle for human rights. Theological education can serve as a platform for such transformation by fostering an environment where students critically engage with their role in advocating for the oppressed.

Moreover, Freire stresses that the violence of the oppressors dehumanizes not only the oppressed but the oppressors themselves, as they strip away the humanity of others. In response, the oppressed seek to reclaim their humanity through the pursuit of justice and the right to be fully human.[149] Educational programs that highlight this dynamic

146. Freire, *Pedagogy of the Oppressed*, 40.
147. Freire, *Pedagogy of the Oppressed*, 31.
148. Freire, *Pedagogy of the Oppressed*, 33.
149. Freire, *Pedagogy of the Oppressed*, 42.

can inspire students to view their advocacy not just as a political or social obligation but as a moral responsibility to restore dignity to the oppressed.

Freire's critique of traditional education systems also applies to the need for more engaged and participatory learning methods in theological education. He criticizes the "banking" model of education, where students passively receive information without critically engaging with it.[150] In contrast, he advocates for a problem-posing method that encourages students to think critically about the world and their place within it, fostering a more authentic form of thought and action.[151] This approach is particularly relevant when teaching about the complexities of oppression in North Korea, as it encourages students to move from passive recipients of knowledge to active agents of change.

The role of revolutionary leaders in this educational process is also critical. Freire warns that if leaders become disconnected from the people, they lose their vitality and effectiveness. Revolutionary leaders must think with the people, not for them, to maintain their legitimacy and power.[152] In the context of North Korea, educators and advocates must remain grounded in the lived experiences of those they seek to support, ensuring that their efforts are truly representative and responsive to the needs of the oppressed.

Ultimately, Freire's framework for education emphasizes the inseparability of reflection and action. He argues that thought and action must be united to create genuine social change.[153] For students and scholars engaging with the human rights issues in North Korea, this means that theological education should not only provide knowledge but also empower them to act on that knowledge, whether through advocacy, solidarity, or direct support for the oppressed.

The curriculum that focuses on the human rights abuses in North Korea must involve a critical examination of specific cases, such as arbitrary detention, torture, and the lack of freedom of expression. By doing so, students can develop a comprehensive understanding of the systematic violations occurring within the regime. As Gustavo Gutiérrez highlights, the institutionalized violence perpetuated by oppressors to maintain "order" is often deemed acceptable by those in power, while

---

150. Freire, *Pedagogy of the Oppressed*, 58.
151. Freire, *Pedagogy of the Oppressed*, 71.
152. Freire, *Pedagogy of the Oppressed*, 127.
153. Freire, *Pedagogy of the Oppressed*, 71.

the oppressed are condemned when they challenge this unjust system.[154] This notion helps students grasp the double standards at play in authoritarian regimes like North Korea and prompts them to question the ethical frameworks that allow such systems to persist.

In addition to analyzing these cases, Gutiérrez points out that many oppressive systems are characterized by the exploitation of workers and the abuse of power. These practices create subhuman conditions marked by sin and injustice.[155] Incorporating these perspectives into the curriculum helps students understand that the systemic nature of oppression goes beyond individual abuses; it involves a broader social and economic structure that dehumanizes its citizens. This understanding is crucial for fostering a sense of empathy and responsibility in future advocates.

The curriculum should also explore how these injustices are not isolated to specific individuals but are part of a larger, entrenched system that requires a comprehensive challenge. Gutiérrez stresses that the critique of individual abuses must extend to a repudiation of the entire system, which often includes religious, political, and social institutions.[156] This approach encourages students to adopt a more holistic view of oppression and to engage with the systemic changes needed to dismantle these structures.

Furthermore, Gutiérrez draws parallels between the political and religious reasons behind oppressive actions, such as those witnessed in the condemnation of Jesus by both religious and political leaders. This dual condemnation reflects how systems of power often work together to suppress challenges to their authority.[157] Educators can use this comparison to help students recognize the intersection of political and religious forces in contemporary authoritarian contexts, such as North Korea, where power is tightly controlled by a small elite group.

Theological education must also involve a discussion of how religious authorities have at times used their influence to marginalize and exploit others. Gutiérrez highlights cases where Christian leaders, ignoring the ethical demands of the gospel, have contributed to the oppression of their own communities.[158] This critical examination allows students to reflect on the role of religious institutions in both perpetuating and

154. Gutiérrez, *Theology of Liberation*, 64.
155. Gutiérrez, *Theology of Liberation*, 100.
156. Gutiérrez, *Theology of Liberation*, 102.
157. Gutiérrez, *Theology of Liberation*, 133.
158. Gutiérrez, *Theology of Liberation*, 160.

challenging injustice, providing a balanced perspective on the complexities of advocacy work.

In studying these abuses, it is essential to acknowledge how poverty itself is a violation of human dignity, as Gutiérrez argues that poverty is inherently contrary to the will of God (.[159] Understanding poverty as a fundamental injustice helps students frame human rights abuses not just in terms of physical violence but also in terms of economic deprivation and exploitation. This broader understanding of human rights is crucial for addressing the systemic roots of oppression in contexts like North Korea.

In the theological context, Gutiérrez also emphasizes the need for democratic participation and the liberation of all individuals from oppressive structures.[160] This notion can guide students in exploring how active participation in political and social life is necessary for human rights advocacy, reinforcing the idea that systemic change requires engagement at both the grassroots and institutional levels.

Finally, Gutiérrez points out that violence in oppressive systems is often justified by the oppressors, who maintain that their use of force is necessary to preserve order. However, when the oppressed seek liberation, their actions are framed as unjust.[161] This double standard underscores the importance of questioning the narratives provided by those in power and advocating for the right of oppressed people to resist dehumanizing systems. By incorporating this critical perspective into the curriculum, educators can help students develop a more nuanced understanding of resistance and justice.

Engaging students in discussions about the moral and ethical implications of human rights abuses is essential to helping them recognize not only the injustices but also their roles in addressing these issues. As James Cone emphasizes, theology must speak to the suffering and resistance of marginalized groups; otherwise, it fails to fulfill its purpose. He recalls how his theological journey began with a recognition that theology must address the suffering of Black Americans, or it would not be relevant to their experience.[162] This perspective is crucial when educating students about the moral responsibility they hold in supporting oppressed groups, such as those in North Korea.

---

159. Gutiérrez, *Theology of Liberation*, 165.
160. Gutiérrez, *Theology of Liberation*, xxii.
161. Gutiérrez, *Theology of Liberation*, 64.
162. Cone, *Black Theology of Liberation*, xvi.

CHAPTER THREE

Cone's reflections also point to the interconnectedness of all struggles for liberation. He argues that Christian theology cannot ignore the global structures of oppression, including the exploitation of the Global South by wealthier nations. For Cone, no one is truly free until all are liberated.[163] This global view reinforces the idea that addressing human rights abuses in North Korea is part of a larger fight for justice, one that requires collective effort and solidarity across borders.

Further, Cone criticizes the narrow focus on specific forms of oppression, such as racism, without recognizing the broader socio-economic systems that sustain inequality. He reflects on his earlier naiveté in failing to analyze capitalism's role in perpetuating oppression.[164] This insight is crucial for students studying human rights in North Korea, as it encourages them to examine the systemic nature of oppression, going beyond individual cases to understand the larger structures at play.

In discussing the role of theology in liberation, Cone asserts that God is encountered in human suffering, not as an abstract concept but as a liberating force for the oppressed.[165] This theological framework can guide students to see human rights advocacy not only as a moral duty but also as a spiritual calling to support those who suffer under oppressive regimes.

Moreover, Cone's emphasis on the importance of liberation as the central content of theology[166] can inspire students to view their academic study of human rights as intrinsically tied to real-world struggles for freedom. This perspective encourages a practical and engaged approach to theology, where intellectual study is linked to activism and advocacy.

Lastly, Cone highlights the necessity of viewing Christian communities as communities of the oppressed, aligning themselves with Jesus in his mission to liberate humankind.[167] This view reinforces the idea that students and scholars must engage with human rights issues, such as those in North Korea, through both theological reflection and direct action to support the oppressed in their fight for justice.

Educational efforts that aim to provide a comprehensive understanding of human rights issues must promote interdisciplinary approaches, drawing on fields such as sociology, political science, and

163. Cone, *Black Theology of Liberation*, xxi.
164. Cone, *Black Theology of Liberation*, xxii.
165. Cone, *Black Theology of Liberation*, xxiii.
166. Cone, *Black Theology of Liberation*, 1.
167. Cone, *Black Theology of Liberation*, 3.

economics. This broad perspective helps students appreciate the multifaceted nature of oppression and the various elements that contribute to its continuation. As Amartya Sen notes, development is not just about economic growth but about removing major sources of unfreedom, including poverty, tyranny, and social deprivation.[168] This approach underscores the importance of integrating multiple disciplines to fully grasp the complexity of human rights challenges.

Sen emphasizes that the lack of substantive freedoms, such as access to food, healthcare, and adequate living conditions, is often directly linked to economic poverty.[169] In an educational context, exploring this relationship between economic deprivation and human rights violations enables students to see how different factors, including access to resources and state policies, shape the experiences of oppressed populations. This interdisciplinary understanding encourages a more holistic approach to addressing human rights issues.

By considering how economic unfreedom makes individuals vulnerable to other forms of exploitation, Sen provides a framework for understanding how interconnected various forms of oppression are.[170] For students, this reinforces the idea that solving human rights problems requires not only addressing political oppression but also tackling the economic conditions that contribute to such exploitation. This perspective helps students develop a broader view of the social structures that perpetuate injustice.

In discussing the concept of capability deprivation, Sen expands the idea of poverty to include a lack of freedom and opportunities.[171] This idea can be incorporated into educational programs to help students understand that human rights violations are not limited to physical violence or political repression but also include more subtle forms of deprivation that affect people's ability to lead fulfilling lives. This understanding encourages students to think critically about the various dimensions of human rights and their implications for advocacy.

Sen also highlights the importance of participation and democratic rights in development, noting that political freedoms are essential for preventing economic disasters, such as famines, and for ensuring that

---

168. Sen, *Development as Freedom*, 3.
169. Sen, *Development as Freedom*, 4.
170. Sen, *Development as Freedom*, 8.
171. Sen, *Development as Freedom*, 20.

CHAPTER THREE

public policies serve the needs of all citizens.[172] Educators can use this perspective to emphasize the role of political engagement in human rights work, encouraging students to see advocacy not only as a matter of legal or moral responsibility but also as a means of creating more inclusive and responsive political systems.

By promoting an interdisciplinary approach to human rights education, students are better equipped to analyze the wide-ranging factors that contribute to human suffering and inequality. Sen's work provides a solid foundation for this approach, highlighting the importance of understanding the links between economic, political, and social freedoms in the broader context of human rights.[173] Through this comprehensive perspective, students can more effectively engage in advocacy and contribute to meaningful change.

Encouraging critical thinking and independent research is a fundamental part of fostering a comprehensive understanding of complex issues such as the human rights situation in North Korea. John Creswell highlights the importance of providing a framework for research that includes both qualitative and quantitative methods, as well as mixed approaches. These methods allow students to explore different dimensions of a problem and offer flexibility in how they approach their research questions.[174] In the context of human rights education, encouraging students to critically examine existing narratives and engage in independent research projects enables them to question dominant perspectives and contribute new ideas to the discourse.

Creswell emphasizes the need for thorough and thoughtful research design, which is essential for students conducting independent studies. He notes that research should involve clear methods and procedures for data collection, analysis, and interpretation, tailored to the type of inquiry being undertaken.[175] In the case of investigating human rights abuses in North Korea, students might use a combination of qualitative case studies and quantitative data analysis to explore how these abuses affect different populations. This blend of methodologies allows for a more nuanced understanding of the issues.

Moreover, Creswell highlights the value of reflexivity in qualitative research, encouraging researchers to reflect on their role and the impact

172. Sen, *Development as Freedom*, 16.
173. Sen, *Development as Freedom*, 10.
174. Tarrow, *Power in Movement*, xix.
175. Creswell, *Research Design*, xix

of their findings on the communities they study.[176] When students engage in research on sensitive topics like human rights violations, it is crucial that they remain aware of their positionality and consider how their work might influence public perceptions or policy decisions. Reflexive practices can help students approach their research with greater ethical awareness and sensitivity to the experiences of those affected by human rights abuses.

Independent research also benefits from the integration of theoretical frameworks, which Creswell discusses as key to shaping the questions asked and the analysis conducted.[177] For students exploring human rights issues, incorporating theories from political science, sociology, and economics can provide a more well-rounded understanding of the root causes of oppression and the potential solutions. By drawing on multiple disciplines, students can form a more comprehensive view of the factors contributing to human rights violations and how they might be addressed.

Through independent research, students are encouraged to delve deeply into specific aspects of the North Korean human rights situation, contributing to the broader academic and advocacy discourse. Creswell's approach to mixed methods research underscores the importance of flexibility in inquiry, allowing students to combine qualitative insights with quantitative evidence to build a robust analysis.[178] This approach equips students with the tools needed to explore human rights issues in a way that is both rigorous and adaptable to the complexity of the subject matter.

The role of theological reflection in education serves to connect human rights issues with broader ethical and spiritual concerns. By integrating theological perspectives into the curriculum, students can explore the moral obligations behind advocating for justice and dignity. Brueggemann discusses the importance of covenant as a central theological concept, connecting this idea with ethical action. Covenant, in his view, represents not only a theological commitment but also a framework for understanding and confronting injustice.[179] This connection helps students see that their advocacy for human rights is not only a legal or political endeavor but also a moral and spiritual responsibility.

176. Creswell, *Research Design*, xxi.
177. Creswell, *Research Design*, xx.
178. Creswell, *Research Design*, xxii.
179. Brueggemann, *Social Reading of the Old Testament*, 6.

CHAPTER THREE

Brueggemann also explores how the concept of covenant has evolved, noting that while it has often been confined to theological interpretation, it has sociological implications as well. Covenant creates a framework for understanding social justice, rooted in the belief that communities are called to act justly and uphold the dignity of all individuals.[180] This approach can encourage students to view their engagement with human rights not only through the lens of law and politics but also as part of a broader theological call to action.

In his reflections on the relationship between theology and social structures, Brueggemann highlights the importance of critical engagement with tradition. He explains that theological interpretation is not just about abstract principles but about how those principles are applied in real-world contexts. This encourages students to think critically about how their faith intersects with their actions in the world, particularly when addressing issues of oppression and injustice.[181]

Theological reflection, according to Brueggemann, is not just a passive exercise but an active engagement with the world. He emphasizes that preaching, as a form of theological interpretation, convenes new communities and calls them to act ethically in response to injustice.[182] This perspective reinforces the idea that theological education should inspire students to connect their faith with real-world issues, motivating them to advocate for those who are marginalized or oppressed.

Furthermore, Brueggemann challenges students to reconsider the traditional interpretations of biblical texts, encouraging a reading that emphasizes liberation and justice. He argues that biblical narratives, such as the Exodus story, provide powerful models for understanding the struggle for freedom and the ethical responsibilities of those who follow a covenantal faith.[183] By studying these narratives, students can gain a more grounded understanding of how theology informs their approach to human rights advocacy.

In this way, theological reflection becomes a means of connecting ethical responsibility with spiritual practice. By framing human rights as a moral imperative rooted in faith, Brueggemann's work offers students a comprehensive framework for understanding their role in advocating for

---

180. Brueggemann, *Social Reading of the Old Testament*, 18.
181. Brueggemann, *Social Reading of the Old Testament*, 5.
182. Brueggemann, *Social Reading of the Old Testament*, 209.
183. Brueggemann, *Social Reading of the Old Testament*, 22.

justice and human dignity in contexts like North Korea.[184] This approach encourages a deeper exploration of how theological principles can be applied to the challenges of modern-day oppression and injustice.

Fostering a culture of solidarity within educational institutions is essential in promoting a collective commitment to advocacy for justice. Waetjen emphasizes that creating a community where individuals actively engage with one another strengthens the broader effort toward social transformation. In his work, he highlights how Jesus' selection of the twelve on the mountain in Mark's Gospel points to a new community formed with a shared purpose, even though it may not be explicitly conveyed.[185] This concept can be translated into the academic environment, where faculty and students collaborate on initiatives aimed at promoting human rights.

Solidarity within a learning community encourages sharing resources and knowledge, which Waetjen discusses through the lens of Jesus' ministry. He describes how Jesus' ministry is not merely for the benefit of those who follow him but calls them into active participation in the mission of justice.[186] Similarly, students and faculty working together in advocacy efforts foster a deeper sense of responsibility and connection to the broader goals of human rights education.

Waetjen also speaks to the creation of a new moral order, which he interprets as a terrestrial and corporate reality.[187] In an educational setting, this translates into building a space where solidarity is not an abstract concept but a lived experience. Through shared projects and collective actions, students and faculty embody this new moral order, aligning their academic pursuits with practical efforts to advocate for justice and human dignity.

Furthermore, the eschatological role of Jesus' disciples, as described by Waetjen, is not passive but requires active engagement in God's mission.[188] This mirrors the role of students and educators in advocacy: they are not merely learners or beneficiaries of knowledge but are called to actively participate in efforts that seek to dismantle injustice. By fostering this active solidarity, educational institutions can cultivate a generation

---

184. Brueggemann, *Social Reading of the Old Testament*, 83.
185. Waetjen, *Reordering of Power*, xiv.
186. Waetjen, *Reordering of Power*, 22.
187. Waetjen, *Reordering of Power*, xx.
188. Waetjen, *Reordering of Power*, 66.

of individuals committed to making tangible contributions to the fight for human rights.

In creating a supportive environment for solidarity, Waetjen's exploration of the eschatological significance of community building can inspire students and educators to see their advocacy work as part of a larger, transformative project.[189] Through mutual support and collaboration, they can strengthen the collective impact of their efforts and contribute to a more just world.

In conclusion, educational efforts that focus on the human rights situation in North Korea must prioritize the active participation of students and scholars in both learning and advocacy. By integrating theological reflection with interdisciplinary approaches, students are better equipped to critically assess the complex structures of oppression and engage meaningfully in the pursuit of justice. These programs emphasize the importance of action alongside reflection, encouraging students to use their education as a tool for change.

Additionally, fostering a culture of solidarity within educational institutions strengthens the collective effort to address human rights abuses. Through collaboration and mutual support, students and faculty can build a learning community that not only discusses ethical responsibilities but also participates in real-world advocacy. Solidarity, in this sense, becomes a practical and shared commitment to human dignity and justice.

Finally, the integration of moral and spiritual considerations with academic learning allows students to connect their advocacy work to broader ethical principles. By examining human rights issues through a theological lens, students gain a deeper understanding of their moral obligations to act against oppression. This holistic approach ensures that education is not only a path to knowledge but also a call to engage in transformative efforts for a more just world.

3.3.3. Embracing Suffering in Mission

This section explores how engagement with the theology of the Kingdom of God encourages spiritual and personal growth by urging individuals to critically assess their roles in oppressive systems and environmental harm. Theologians like Michael Northcott, Daniel Bell Jr., William T.

---

189. Waetjen, *Reordering of Power*, 22.

Cavanaugh, Amos Yong, and others offer various perspectives on how Christians should live out the values of the Kingdom, emphasizing justice, community, and responsibility in addressing global inequalities, environmental degradation, and capitalist exploitation. These approaches challenge believers to integrate their faith into their ethical actions, both personally and communally.

Engaging with the theology of the Kingdom of God encourages individuals to reflect critically on their actions and their participation in oppressive systems. Michael Northcott argues that the Kingdom of God demands a radical shift in how individuals relate to each other and the environment, emphasizing justice and ecological responsibility as central tenets of Christian discipleship. He highlights the stark reality that a billion people, primarily in the tropics and the Southern hemisphere, are at risk of displacement or severe threats to their wellbeing if greenhouse gas emissions continue unchecked.[190] This underscores the urgent need for individuals and communities to reassess their environmental impact in light of broader global inequalities.

Northcott contrasts the carbon emissions of richer Northern nations with those of poorer Southern countries, noting that while the average carbon use in the South is around 0.2 tonnes per person, Northern consumers are responsible for an average of 12 tonnes per person. This stark disparity in carbon footprints points to the significant ecological debt owed by wealthier nations, who bear the responsibility for much of the atmospheric pollution.[191] Northcott argues that wealthier countries must recognize the damage their emissions are causing and take steps to compensate poorer nations for the harm inflicted by climate change.[192]

In discussing the ethics of climate change, Northcott calls for truth-telling and accountability, emphasizing that responsible action begins with acknowledging the substantial and interdependent world from which all life derives. He asserts that Christians, in particular, are called to live in accordance with Creation, which means aligning words with deeds and addressing the environmental crisis with integrity.[193] This moral framework challenges individuals and communities to take concrete actions that reflect their ecological responsibilities.

---

190. Northcott, *Moral Climate*, 84.
191. Northcott, *Moral Climate*, 85.
192. Northcott, *Moral Climate*, 57.
193. Northcott, *Moral Climate*, 40.

Furthermore, Northcott highlights the disproportionate contribution of wealthier nations to global carbon emissions. Europe and America, which together account for only 10% of the global population, are responsible for over 90% of the historical carbon emissions that have driven climate change.[194] This places a moral burden on these nations to lead efforts in reducing emissions and addressing the environmental damage they have caused, especially in the Global South.

Northcott also addresses the social implications of environmental degradation, pointing out that local, sustainable forms of exchange are being eroded by globalized economic practices. This destruction of local communities and ecosystems not only harms the environment but also weakens social bonds, as seen in the decline of local associations in places like the United States and the rise of single-person households in the United Kingdom.[195] He suggests that this breakdown of community is intimately connected with the ecological crisis, as both are driven by unsustainable economic practices.

Finally, Northcott envisions a future where, if current environmental trends continue, tens of millions of people from Africa and other regions will be forced to migrate due to climate change-induced displacement. He criticizes wealthy European countries for resisting international migration while contributing disproportionately to the environmental damage that drives such migration.[196] This observation calls for a reevaluation of global policies on migration and climate justice, urging wealthier nations to take responsibility for their role in the environmental crisis and its human impacts.

Daniel Bell Jr. argues that the theology of the Kingdom of God demands resistance to capitalist structures, which perpetuate inequality. He suggests that Christianity should not be limited to personal salvation but must actively confront the systemic exploitation embedded in global capitalism. Bell refers to the "Church of the poor" that has emerged in Latin America, which contests capitalism's dominance and emphasizes a preferential option for the poor. This movement, with its roots in liberation theology, raises the critical question of how Christians can resist the capitalist order, offering an alternative vision of community and justice.[197]

---

194. Northcott, *Moral Climate*, 50.
195. Northcott, *Moral Climate*, 15.
196. Northcott, *Moral Climate*, 49.
197. Bell, *Liberation Theology After the End of History*, 2.

Bell further explains that capitalism operates as a "discipline of desire," shaping human desires in ways that prioritize consumption and acquisition. This system, he argues, leads to harmful consequences for the majority of humanity, especially in the Global South. He draws on the work of Franz Hinkelammert to describe "savage capitalism," highlighting that its impact is not just economic but also ontological, altering the very way people experience and understand their desires.[198] According to Bell, this distortion of desire under capitalism calls for a Christian response that seeks to heal and liberate desire from its bondage to consumption and materialism.

Bell's analysis goes deeper by reclaiming Christianity as a social, political, and economic force that stands in opposition to capitalist discipline. He envisions the Christian community as a unique public entity, capable of embodying a true form of human organization that revolves around worship and liturgy rather than the acquisitive logic of capitalism.[199] In this view, Christianity is not merely a passive moral authority but an active political and economic alternative, rooted in its theological vision of human flourishing.

Bell also critiques the assumption that all subjects of capitalism are equally complicit in its acquisitive logic. He argues that while capitalism celebrates consumption, not all who are subjected to its discipline are consumers. Many in the Global South, for example, are not accumulating wealth but struggling to survive under the harsh conditions imposed by global capitalism.[200] This differentiation highlights the unequal burden placed on the world's poor by a system that benefits a privileged few.

Drawing on the philosophies of Gilles Deleuze and Michel Foucault, Bell describes capitalism as a system that not only exploits labor but also captures human desire, reshaping it to serve the interests of capital. He argues that this process of capturing desire is more insidious than traditional economic exploitation because it distorts the fundamental human capacity for longing and fulfillment.[201] This understanding of capitalism as a "discipline of desire" frames it as a system that needs not only economic reform but also spiritual healing.

Bell then presents Christianity as a "therapy of desire," offering a way to liberate human desire from the grip of capitalism. He draws

---

198. Bell, *Liberation Theology After the End of History*, 3.
199. Bell, *Liberation Theology After the End of History*, 4.
200. Bell, *Liberation Theology After the End of History*, 7.
201. Bell, *Liberation Theology After the End of History*, 9.

on historical Christian practices, such as those of Bernard of Clairvaux and the twelfth-century Cistercians, to argue that Christianity has long functioned as a system that shapes desire in ways that promote human flourishing. Far from being an apolitical moral force, Christianity offers a counter-discipline to capitalism, shaping desires in a manner that reflects the values of the Kingdom of God.[202]

In the broader context of Christian resistance to capitalism, Bell also touches on the role of forgiveness. He suggests that forgiveness, as a theological concept, can serve as a form of healing for the distortions caused by capitalist discipline. This forgiveness is not merely personal but extends to the social and economic realms, where it can help repair relationships and communities harmed by the inequalities and exploitations of capitalism.[203]

William T. Cavanaugh critiques the emphasis on personal spiritual growth within some theological frameworks, cautioning that this focus may shift attention away from the structural changes required for real justice. He argues that while individual moral improvement is important, it should not be the primary goal of Christian resistance to systemic injustice.[204] For Cavanaugh, the church's mission is not solely about personal salvation but involves participating in the broader work of addressing societal sins, including those rooted in political and economic systems.

Cavanaugh introduces the concept of the church as "co-crucified" with Christ, emphasizing that the church, like Christ, suffers under the weight of humanity's sins. The church, therefore, cannot be seen as purely holy or blameless; rather, it embodies both sinfulness and the potential for redemption.[205] This paradoxical identity of the church challenges any simplistic view of Christian community as a haven of purity, suggesting instead that the church's holiness is found in its willingness to acknowledge its complicity in sin while simultaneously striving for repentance and renewal.

Cavanaugh uses the metaphor of the church as both "whore and bride," drawing from the biblical story of Hosea to illustrate the church's complex role in salvation history. Just as Hosea's wife is unfaithful yet redeemed, the church exists in a state of tension between sin and grace.[206]

202. Bell, *Liberation Theology After the End of History*, 4.
203. Bell, *Liberation Theology After the End of History*, 5.
204. Cavanaugh, *Migrations of the Holy*, 163.
205. Cavanaugh, *Migrations of the Holy*, 163.
206. Cavanaugh, *Migrations of the Holy*, 164.

This image reinforces the idea that the church's mission is not to present itself as morally superior but to embrace its imperfections while striving for sanctification.

Furthermore, Cavanaugh argues that this understanding of the church should not lead to resignation or complacency. Instead, he calls for a "Chalcedonian ecclesiology," where the church's sinfulness is acknowledged alongside its visible holiness. The church's holiness is not defined by its purity but by its repentance, making its witness to the world credible precisely because it admits its failings.[207] This perspective calls for a collective form of resistance that transcends individual moral efforts and seeks to reform unjust systems through both repentance and social action.

Amos Yong emphasizes the central role of the Holy Spirit in guiding both personal and communal transformation within the theology of the Kingdom of God. He argues that the Spirit empowers individuals and communities to work toward justice, unity, and reconciliation. According to Yong, the Spirit's role is not limited to individual empowerment but extends to forming and shaping communities that reflect the values of the Kingdom of God.[208] This pneumatological perspective is essential for understanding how personal ethics and social justice are intertwined in Christian life.

Yong highlights those Pentecostal practices, in particular, offer a distinctive contribution to political theology through what he terms a "pneumatological imagination." This imagination allows for a deeper engagement with political and social issues, where the work of the Spirit is seen not only in individual transformation but in the shaping of just and reconciled communities.[209] This approach encourages Christians to view their faith as a force for social change, led by the Spirit.

In his discussion of Pentecostal identity and theology, Yong stresses that the Holy Spirit plays a foundational role in both theological reflection and practical action. He suggests that the Spirit empowers Christians to engage with societal issues in a way that fosters justice and peace. This framework calls for a holistic understanding of Christian life, where the personal and communal aspects of faith are seen as inseparable.[210] By embracing the Spirit's role in shaping both personal and social ethics,

207. Cavanaugh, *Migrations of the Holy*, 165.
208. Yong, *In the Days of Caesar*, 40.
209. Yong, *In the Days of Caesar*, 40.
210. Yong, *In the Days of Caesar*, 88.

believers are better equipped to address the challenges of injustice and inequality.

Yong also underscores the diversity within the church and how the Spirit fosters unity across different voices and perspectives. He argues that the Spirit not only empowers individuals but also brings together diverse communities to work toward common goals, such as justice and reconciliation. This pluralism is essential for the church's mission, as it allows for a richer and more inclusive engagement with the world.[211] The Spirit, therefore, plays a vital role in uniting believers across social, cultural, and political divides.

Furthermore, Yong explains that the Spirit's anointing of Jesus, as described in the Gospel of Luke, demonstrates how the Spirit empowers the church to engage in liberation and social renewal. The Spirit's work in Jesus' ministry is a model for the church's mission, calling Christians to be agents of justice and liberation in their own communities.[212] This focus on the Spirit as a force for both personal and societal transformation highlights the connection between faith and action.

Yong suggests that the Spirit's role in forming communities is key to understanding the political dimensions of the Kingdom of God. In Acts, the Spirit not only empowers individuals but also creates a community of believers committed to justice, worship, and service. This community-forming role of the Spirit has significant implications for how Christians engage with political and social issues, offering a vision of the church as a community that challenges injustice and works for the common good.[213]

Richard Bauckham highlights the eschatological dimensions of the Kingdom of God, emphasizing that this concept offers both present hope and future restoration. He describes this dual focus as essential for motivating Christians to work toward justice now, while remaining rooted in the ultimate fulfillment of God's promises. Bauckham explains that eschatology is not merely about the end times but is central to understanding the whole of Christian theology, as seen in the works of theologians like Jürgen Moltmann.[214]

Bauckham discusses how Moltmann's Theology of Hope frames the resurrection of Christ as an eschatological event, linking it with themes of promise, hope, and mission. This perspective encourages believers to

---

211. Yong, *In the Days of Caesar*, 94.
212. Yong, *In the Days of Caesar*, 104.
213. Yong, *In the Days of Caesar*, 107.
214. Bauckham, *Theology of Jürgen Moltmann*, 3.

see the resurrection not only as a past event but as a call to active participation in God's ongoing work of redemption in the world.[215] By connecting the cross and the resurrection in an eschatological framework, Moltmann's theology urges Christians to live in a way that reflects both the present and future dimensions of the Kingdom of God.

Moreover, Bauckham notes that Moltmann's theology is characterized by its openness to dialogue with other disciplines, a feature that stems from its eschatological orientation. Theology, in this view, is not a closed system but is always in conversation with the broader world, including political, social, and ecological concerns.[216] This openness is key to understanding how theology can contribute to the church's mission in the world, as it continually engages with the realities of human experience while holding onto the hope of the Kingdom's future fulfillment.

Bauckham also emphasizes that Moltmann's trinitarian theology builds on this eschatological vision, showing how the relationships within the Trinity reflect the mutual, non-hierarchical relationships that should characterize the Christian community and its engagement with the world.[217] This understanding of God's relational nature reinforces the idea that the Kingdom of God is not only a future hope but a present reality that calls for justice, reconciliation, and peace in the here and now.

John Milbank offers a critique of certain modern theological approaches to the Kingdom of God, suggesting that they may align too closely with secular political ideologies, particularly those emerging from neoliberalism. He argues that Christian theology should provide a vision of justice that is distinct from and not simply borrowed from contemporary political movements. For Milbank, a truly Christian account of reality, especially within a Catholic framework, is persuasive in ways that transcend political concerns.[218] This theological approach seeks to address deeper philosophical and spiritual issues, offering a holistic alternative to secular ideologies.

Milbank highlights that theology, particularly within the Augustinian tradition, functions as a third term linking philosophy and history, integrating human understanding of reality with divine revelation. He argues that this theological framework allows Christians to interpret history and contemporary events in light of the Incarnation and the church's

---

215. Bauckham, *Theology of Jürgen Moltmann*, 5.
216. Bauckham, *Theology of Jürgen Moltmann*, 7.
217. Bauckham, *Theology of Jürgen Moltmann*, 7.
218. Milbank, *Theology and Social Theory*, xi.

mission.²¹⁹ In contrast to secular ideologies that may focus on political solutions, Milbank emphasizes that theology provides a deeper foundation for understanding justice and human flourishing.

Additionally, Milbank points to the challenges posed by contemporary political movements, particularly those influenced by Hegelian and Marxist ideas. He critiques the way these ideologies often promote narratives of progress and emancipation that, in his view, lead to a form of nihilism. For Milbank, the Christian vision of the Kingdom of God offers an alternative to these secular metanarratives, focusing instead on peace, order, and reason grounded in a theological understanding of creation.²²⁰

Milbank also argues that the Christian theological tradition, particularly its emphasis on peace and community, provides a way to resist the atomizing tendencies of modern secular politics. He suggests that the church, through its practices and teachings, should embody a different kind of social and political order—one that prioritizes relationships, community, and mutual flourishing, rather than individualism and competition.²²¹ This vision of the church's role contrasts with secular political approaches, which often emphasize individual rights or economic efficiency over communal well-being.

In sum, Milbank's critique of modern theological approaches to the Kingdom of God is rooted in his concern that Christian theology risks losing its distinct voice when it aligns too closely with secular political ideologies. He calls for a return to the church's tradition, particularly its vision of justice and peace, as a way to offer a more comprehensive and faithful response to the challenges of modern society.²²² This theological framework offers a distinct alternative to secular political solutions, emphasizing the role of the church in shaping a just and compassionate world.

John Caputo offers a postmodern critique of traditional theological understandings of the Kingdom of God, emphasizing that it should not be reduced to a concrete political agenda. Instead, Caputo suggests that the Kingdom represents an ongoing ethical openness to the future—something always "to come" and never fully realized in the present.²²³ This approach challenges the belief that the Kingdom can be achieved

---

219. Milbank, *Theology and Social Theory*, xxiii.
220. Milbank, *Theology and Social Theory*, xii.
221. Milbank, *Theology and Social Theory*, xvi.
222. Milbank, *Theology and Social Theory*, xvii.
223. Caputo, *What Would Jesus Deconstruct?*, 35.

through human efforts alone, promoting instead a posture of humility and anticipation.

Caputo critiques the idea that the Kingdom of God is a fixed or final reality that humans can control or bring about through specific actions. He emphasizes that the Kingdom is not something the church or society can construct definitively, as it transcends human boundaries and constructions.[224] This notion reshapes the understanding of Christian action, calling for an attitude that is constantly open to new possibilities and the unpredictable ways in which God's reign might manifest.

In this framework, the Kingdom of God is seen as fundamentally disruptive to human priorities, including those within religious institutions. Caputo highlights how the Kingdom overturns established power structures, even those within the church, and calls into question the ways in which human institutions, including the church, have often failed to embody the radical spirit of the gospel.[225] This critique underscores the need for the church to remain open to transformation and renewal, never assuming that it has fully aligned itself with God's purposes.

Caputo's postmodern approach also emphasizes that the Kingdom of God resists any attempt to reduce it to a particular cultural or political framework. He argues that the Kingdom is not aligned with any single ideology or movement but is instead characterized by an openness that allows it to challenge all forms of human authority, including those that claim to represent it.[226] This perspective calls for a continual re-evaluation of how Christians engage with political and social systems, ensuring that they remain open to the new and unexpected ways in which the Kingdom might emerge.

In this way, Caputo's critique of traditional concepts of the Kingdom emphasizes the importance of remaining open to the future. Rather than seeing the Kingdom as something that can be fully realized through human effort, he stresses the importance of waiting and expecting its continual coming, always aware that it exceeds human control and understanding.[227] This ethical openness invites Christians to live in a state of expectation, always prepared to respond to the new and surprising ways God's reign might unfold.

---

224. Caputo, *What Would Jesus Deconstruct?*, 35.
225. Caputo, *What Would Jesus Deconstruct?*, 105.
226. Caputo, *What Would Jesus Deconstruct?*, 106.
227. Caputo, *What Would Jesus Deconstruct?*, 103.

CHAPTER THREE

Stanley Grenz contributes to the discussion of the Kingdom of God by exploring how it shapes Christian ethics, with a particular focus on building community and fostering mutual care. He argues that Christian ethics must be rooted in the values of the Kingdom, which prioritize love, service, and the common good, rather than individual gain.[228] This perspective underscores that ethical living is not just about personal moral decisions but about contributing to the flourishing of the entire community.

Grenz emphasizes that the ethical teachings of Jesus are grounded in the proclamation of the Kingdom of God, which introduces an eschatological perspective into Christian ethics. This means that ethical behavior in the present is motivated by the anticipation of God's future reign. The prophets' call to "right living" was not simply for personal piety but was based on the promise of God's future actions, which shaped the moral obligations of individuals and communities.[229] In this view, ethical action is inherently communal, as it involves participating in God's ongoing work in the world.

Furthermore, Grenz explains that the ethic of the Kingdom of God, as taught by Jesus, focuses on love and service as central values. Jesus' ethical teachings encourage believers to embody these values in their interactions with others, emphasizing the need for mutual care within the community of faith.[230] This approach challenges individualism by promoting a collective responsibility for the well-being of others, reinforcing that personal growth is connected to the health and flourishing of the community as a whole.

Grenz also notes that the early Christian ethic, particularly as articulated by Paul, was centered on the belief that Christians were called to be God's covenant partners. This covenant relationship, grounded in God's saving work through Jesus Christ, required believers to live in a way that reflected their participation in the Kingdom.[231] Thus, Christian ethics is not merely about following rules but about embodying the values of the Kingdom, contributing to a community built on justice, love, and mutual support.

By framing Christian ethics within the context of the Kingdom of God, Grenz emphasizes that ethical living is always relational and

---

228. Grenz, *Moral Quest*, 24.
229. Grenz, *Moral Quest*, 105.
230. Grenz, *Moral Quest*, 110.
231. Grenz, *Moral Quest*, 118.

oriented toward the common good. It requires a commitment to building a community where all members are cared for and where the values of the Kingdom—love, service, and justice—are lived out in concrete ways.[232]

Douglas John Hall critiques triumphalist interpretations of the Kingdom of God, emphasizing that such views often neglect the realities of suffering and weakness that are central to Christian theology. He argues that the Kingdom should not be understood as a justification for power and control but as a call to solidarity with those who suffer. Hall suggests that triumphalism, which focuses on victory and dominance, misses the core of the gospel message, which is about identifying with the marginalized and oppressed.[233]

In contrast to views that present the Kingdom of God as a realization of power, Hall highlights the vulnerability that lies at the heart of Christian faith. He explains that God's self-revelation, particularly in the person of Christ, is not a display of domination but a demonstration of humility and suffering.[234] This emphasis on the suffering God invites Christians to rethink their understanding of power, moving away from triumphalist visions of the Kingdom and toward an ethic of compassion and solidarity.

Hall contends that Christian theology must prioritize the experiences of the vulnerable, arguing that the Kingdom of God calls believers to align themselves with those who are oppressed. This solidarity with the marginalized is not a secondary aspect of the gospel but is central to its message.[235] The Christian mission, therefore, is not about achieving control or success but about standing with the powerless and sharing in their struggles.

Furthermore, Hall critiques the way triumphalist interpretations often obscure the importance of suffering in the Christian narrative. He suggests that by focusing too much on victory, such theologies fail to engage with the realities of pain and hardship that are intrinsic to the human experience. For Hall, true Christian theology must take suffering seriously, recognizing that it is through suffering that believers participate in the life of Christ and the unfolding of the Kingdom of God.[236]

232. Grenz, *Moral Quest*, 99.
233. Hall, *Professing the Faith*, 45.
234. Hall, *Professing the Faith*, 73.
235. Hall, *Professing the Faith*, 149.
236. Hall, *Professing the Faith*, 426.

In this way, Hall's perspective urges Christians to adopt a posture of humility, acknowledging that the Kingdom of God is not about human power or achievement. Instead, it is about being present with those who suffer and working for justice in ways that reflect the vulnerability and love embodied by Christ.[237] This understanding of the Kingdom challenges believers to resist the allure of power and control and to embrace a mission rooted in service, compassion, and solidarity with the oppressed.

In conclusion, the theology of the Kingdom of God invites Christians to reexamine their personal and social responsibilities. Michael Northcott's emphasis on ecological justice and the disproportionate burden placed on poorer nations highlights the need for global awareness and collective action in addressing climate change. His call for truth-telling and accountability challenges Christians to align their actions with their beliefs, fostering a deeper connection between faith and environmental stewardship.

Furthermore, theologians like Daniel Bell Jr. and William Cavanaugh explore the systemic injustices embedded in capitalist structures and personal spiritual growth. Bell's critique of capitalism as a "discipline of desire" and Cavanaugh's focus on the church's collective responsibility point to the need for Christians to resist the values of consumerism and individualism. Both argue that the Christian community must embody an alternative vision of justice, rooted in mutual care, forgiveness, and social action.

Finally, theologians such as Amos Yong, Richard Bauckham, and Douglas John Hall underscore the importance of the Holy Spirit's role in shaping Christian communities and the broader call to solidarity with the suffering and oppressed. Their perspectives emphasize that the Kingdom of God is not about power or dominance but about justice, reconciliation, and humility. This understanding calls Christians to engage actively in social transformation while remaining open to the ongoing and unfinished nature of God's work in the world.

3.4. JESUS' CALL TO JUSTICE

This section emphasizes the need to view Jesus' ministry as a direct response to political, social, and economic injustices rather than simply as a spiritual or personal mission. Scholars like Dorothee Sölle and Ched

---

237. Hall, *Professing the Faith*, 193.

Myers argue that Jesus' teachings challenged the oppressive systems of his time, including the Roman Empire, and focused on empowering marginalized groups, particularly the poor. They present Jesus as a figure whose life and message called for social and systemic reform, urging his followers to engage in actions that promote justice and equality.

Sölle and Myers critique the modern tendency to focus on the spiritual aspects of Jesus' teachings, often overlooking their broader societal implications. According to these scholars, Jesus' critique of wealth and power structures is key to understanding the political nature of his ministry. They assert that Jesus' actions were part of a larger movement aimed at confronting unjust hierarchies, not merely offering personal salvation. This perspective reframes Jesus' ministry as a call to collective resistance against oppression.

In addition to addressing economic and social injustices, this approach also highlights Jesus' challenge to racial and cultural hierarchies. Thinkers like J. Kameron Carter and Miguel De La Torre argue that Jesus' life disrupted social norms related to race, inclusion, and belonging. They extend Jesus' message beyond personal spirituality to focus on issues like colonialism and economic inequality, making his ministry relevant to contemporary struggles for justice and liberation.

3.4.1. The Exodus and Liberation

In exploring the Exodus narrative, the text underscores God's dedication to freeing the oppressed, as highlighted by Christopher J.H. Wright. This narrative not only showcases divine power but also serves as a model for challenging contemporary forms of exploitation. Wright views Israel's liberation from Egypt as a pivotal event in theological history, emphasizing a monotheistic stance against polytheistic cultures and dictatorial rule. He connects the giving of the law to ethical living, reflecting divine justice. This story is seen not just as historical but as an ongoing divine mission, urging believers to perpetuate this legacy of liberation in their own contexts. Wright's discussion points to a God actively involved in human history, advocating a continuous stance against oppression and promoting a societal framework grounded in justice and ethical governance. This approach invites readers to consider their role in addressing and resisting systemic injustices today, fostering a commitment to societal change anchored in the values illustrated through the Exodus.

The Exodus narrative is crucial for understanding God's commitment to liberating the oppressed. Christopher J.H. Wright describes this story as a foundational element of God's mission to deliver the marginalized from their oppressive circumstances.[238] The liberation of Israel from Egypt not only demonstrates God's power but also sets a model for resisting contemporary systems of exploitation and tyranny. This narrative offers an important lens through which modern readers can view their responsibility to act against oppression.

In discussing how the Exodus relates to mission, Wright emphasizes that Israel's role was missional, reflecting God's broader purpose for the world.[239] This missional perspective invites a reflection on how communities of faith today can engage with the world by embodying justice and freedom. It frames Israel's story as not only a historical event but as part of God's continuing work in the world, calling on believers to carry forward the mission of liberation in various contexts.

The Torah records the Exodus as a divine act that directly confronts and defeats Pharaoh's power. This event is framed as a decisive moment in Israel's theological history, one that contrasts sharply with the polytheistic creation myths of the surrounding cultures.[240] In this way, the narrative affirms monotheism and positions the God of Israel as uniquely powerful and just, standing in opposition to other deities and oppressive rulers.

Wright also highlights the law as a response to God's redemptive actions, urging the people to live in a way that reflects their newfound freedom. The law becomes a covenantal response to God's saving work, emphasizing ethical behavior as a reflection of divine justice.[241] This view positions the law as not merely a set of rules but as a moral imperative that flows from the experience of liberation.

In the broader biblical narrative, Israel's identity is formed and sustained through its relationship with Yahweh, even as it interacts with surrounding nations. Despite varying degrees of tolerance or hostility from these empires, Israel remains defined by its covenant with God.[242] This identity is not static but develops through Israel's engagement with its theological understanding of God's actions in history, continually reshaping its role among the nations.

238. Wright, *Mission of God*, 24.
239. Wright, *Mission of God*, 25.
240. Wright, *Mission of God*, 50.
241. Wright, *Mission of God*, 59.
242. Wright, *Mission of God*, 50.

Wright underscores that the biblical God is not a generic deity but one with a distinct name and identity—Yahweh, the Holy One of Israel, whom Christians know as Father, Son, and Holy Spirit.[243] This specific identity of God is key to understanding the theological implications of the Exodus, as it reveals a God who is actively involved in the history of a particular people while also claiming authority over all nations.

The narrative of the Exodus teaches that liberation requires ongoing vigilance. Wright suggests that Israel's continued reflection on God's actions—such as the Exodus and the return from exile—helped them to understand God's redemptive grace and their role in the world.[244] The return from exile, much like the Exodus, is framed as a second act of divine deliverance, reinforcing the ongoing nature of God's mission.

Wright notes that the power and authority of Yahweh extend beyond Israel to the other nations, as God appoints kings and uses foreign nations to accomplish divine purposes.[245] This broader scope of God's sovereignty challenges the idea that national gods are limited to the fortunes of their people, presenting Yahweh as the ultimate ruler who works through history for the benefit of all creation.

Furthermore, Wright reflects on the political implications of the Exodus, explaining that Israel's deliverance demonstrates a rejection of coercive power in favor of the sustaining word and deed of Yahweh.[246] This alternative political vision, based on divine creativity rather than military might, underscores the theological message that true power resides in God's ability to maintain and sustain communities through justice and grace.

Ultimately, Wright presents the Exodus as a story that continually calls Israel and, by extension, modern readers to recognize the enduring truth about their God. Even when faced with challenges, this recognition forms the basis for understanding God's ongoing work in the world.[247]

Walter Brueggemann argues that the Exodus story reveals the deep-rooted societal structures of power and injustice, urging faith communities to become agents of change in the face of oppression. He highlights how, in the biblical narrative, Pharaoh is presented as a figure whose policies are driven by fear and anxiety, particularly regarding the scarcity

---

243. Wright, *Mission of God*, 54.
244. Wright, *Mission of God*, 74.
245. Wright, *Mission of God*, 85.
246. Wright, *Mission of God*, 87.
247. Wright, *Mission of God*, 78.

CHAPTER THREE

of resources. Pharaoh's dreams, which Joseph interprets, lead to an economic system designed to concentrate wealth and power, exacerbating the suffering of the people.[248] This narrative underscores how fear and control can drive exploitation, making the story relevant for modern believers who seek to confront systems that marginalize the vulnerable.

Brueggemann explains that Pharaoh's policies were not merely about exploitation; they were rooted in a deep fear of his own workforce. The narrative suggests that Pharaoh was "scared to death" of the people he controlled, leading to aggressive actions that further oppressed them.[249] This dynamic between fear and control serves as a warning against the destructive effects of governance that prioritizes authority over the common good.

A key turning point in the Exodus narrative, according to Brueggemann, is when the cries of the abused laborers reach Yahweh, even though the cry was not directly addressed to God. This emphasizes Yahweh's role as a central figure in the public drama of social power, a divine force that draws the cries of the oppressed.[250] Brueggemann points out that this aspect of the narrative illustrates the theological importance of recognizing God's involvement in social justice, particularly in hearing the cries of those who suffer.

The miraculous escape through the Red Sea is another pivotal moment in the Exodus story. Brueggemann describes how the Israelites, once slaves in Egypt, watched the waters part and, upon reaching the other side, danced and sang in praise of Yahweh for their deliverance.[251] This celebration not only marks their physical liberation but also serves as a symbolic departure from the oppressive system of Egypt. It highlights the importance of divine intervention in the struggle for freedom, offering hope for those engaged in modern movements for justice.

However, the journey to freedom was not without its challenges. Brueggemann notes that once the Israelites were in the wilderness, they began to complain, and their complaints reached both Moses and Yahweh. God's response was to provide manna, the "wonder bread" that redefined the wilderness as a place of viable life, sustained by divine grace.[252] This provision of manna symbolizes God's ongoing care for the liberated

---

248. Brueggemann, *Journey to the Common Good*, 4.
249. Brueggemann, *Journey to the Common Good*, 9.
250. Brueggemann, *Journey to the Common Good*, 10.
251. Brueggemann, *Journey to the Common Good*, 13.
252. Brueggemann, *Journey to the Common Good*, 15.

people, even in the most desolate circumstances, and reaffirms the belief that liberation requires both divine support and human perseverance.

Brueggemann also emphasizes that the theme of grace in the wilderness continues to resonate throughout the biblical narrative, representing the sustaining presence of God in difficult times. The Exodus narrative stands as a central piece of Israel's collective memory, where God's generosity is contrasted with Pharaoh's system of fear and scarcity.[253] This juxtaposition between divine grace and human oppression offers a framework for understanding how faith communities today can confront systems of exploitation and advocate for justice.

Through this narrative, Brueggemann encourages modern readers to see the Exodus story as more than a historical account; it is a model for active resistance to unjust systems. The themes of divine intervention, human courage, and the collective struggle for justice are relevant for contemporary faith communities seeking to embody the values of liberation in their own contexts.[254]

Terence E. Fretheim explores the role of leadership in the Exodus narrative by focusing on Moses as a central figure who stands against systemic oppression. Moses' actions, from his initial confrontation with Pharaoh to his leading of the Israelites out of bondage, demonstrate the critical need for leadership that is both courageous and morally grounded. Fretheim emphasizes that Moses embodies resistance to the oppressive structures of Egypt, showcasing the importance of leadership in guiding people toward liberation.[255]

Fretheim further argues that the Exodus narrative moves from a state of enforced labor under Pharaoh to a place where worship becomes central to the community's identity. The shift from constructing buildings for Pharaoh to the joyful offering of the people for the building of a sanctuary for God represents a broader theological movement from oppression to freedom.[256] This transformation highlights how leadership, as exemplified by Moses, is not only about political liberation but also about guiding the people toward a new spiritual and communal reality.

In discussing the broader themes of the Exodus story, Fretheim notes that it intertwines narrative and law, reflecting how the liberation from Egypt is deeply connected to the giving of the law at Sinai. Moses,

---

253. Brueggemann, *Journey to the Common Good*, 16.
254. Brueggemann, *Journey to the Common Good*, 7.
255. Fretheim, *Exodus*, 1.
256. Fretheim, *Exodus*, 1.

as the mediator of both the liberation and the law, plays a crucial role in shaping the identity of the newly freed people. His leadership is essential in helping the Israelites understand that their freedom is not simply from oppression but also for a new way of life defined by their relationship with God.[257]

Fretheim also points out that the book of Exodus is not purely historical but is shaped by theological concerns. The narrative serves to communicate divine actions on behalf of the Israelites, with Moses' role being central to this divine-human interaction.[258] The story reflects the broader theological message that God is present in the struggle against injustice, and Moses' leadership is a key vehicle through which this divine intervention is made manifest.

The journey from slavery to worship, as Fretheim describes it, is one in which Moses leads the people through physical liberation and into a covenantal relationship with God. His leadership not only challenges the existing power structures but also sets the stage for a new community centered on worship and obedience to divine law.[259] This shift underscores the theological significance of leadership in liberation movements, showing how it must encompass both social and spiritual dimensions to be effective.

Fretheim's analysis reveals that Moses' leadership, grounded in a deep commitment to justice and obedience to God, offers a model for contemporary movements against oppression. The story of the Exodus teaches that leadership is essential in both initiating and sustaining change, particularly when confronting entrenched systems of power.[260]

James H. Cone emphasizes how the Exodus narrative provided significant meaning for the African American community during the Civil Rights Movement, becoming a crucial symbol for the fight against racial oppression. Cone draws parallels between the Israelites' liberation from Egypt and the African American struggle for freedom from systemic racism, showing how this story resonates with the experience of oppression.[261] The themes of divine justice and deliverance in the Exodus account became a theological framework for understanding God's

---

257. Fretheim, *Exodus*, 6.
258. Fretheim, *Exodus*, 7.
259. Fretheim, *Exodus*, 22.
260. Fretheim, *Exodus*, 5.
261. Cone, *Black Theology of Liberation*, xv.

commitment to the liberation of the oppressed, reinforcing the idea that God stands with those who are marginalized.

Cone further elaborates that the Exodus narrative speaks directly to the condition of African Americans, as it reveals a God who actively participates in the struggle for justice. For Cone, God's liberation of the Israelites serves as a timeless model, showing that God's involvement in history is not confined to one specific people or time but extends to all who suffer under systems of oppression.[262] This understanding of God's justice provides African Americans with theological grounds to resist racial injustice and to seek freedom, just as the Israelites did.

The Exodus story, according to Cone, challenges the traditional views of theology that have often been used to justify the status quo. He critiques the way some theologians have historically overlooked the importance of liberation within the biblical narrative, and he emphasizes that the Exodus is a call to resist oppression and injustice in all its forms.[263] Cone argues that any theology that does not address the realities of oppression, particularly the experiences of African Americans, is disconnected from the true message of the gospel.

Cone also notes that the Exodus story provides hope for those facing racial discrimination by showing that liberation is not only a possibility but also a divine promise. He draws attention to the fact that the liberation of the Israelites was not merely a physical deliverance but also a spiritual and communal one. This multifaceted liberation serves as an inspiration for African Americans to continue their struggle for justice, knowing that God is on the side of the oppressed.[264]

In his work, Cone stresses that the message of the Exodus is not just relevant for ancient Israel but has practical implications for contemporary struggles against oppression. He asserts that the story's themes of courage, resistance, and divine intervention are essential for understanding how African Americans can engage in their fight for freedom, drawing strength from the belief that God's liberation extends to all who suffer under unjust systems.[265]

By linking the Exodus narrative to the African American experience, Cone provides a theological framework that empowers the oppressed to challenge their circumstances, drawing on the biblical promise

---

262. Cone, *Black Theology of Liberation*, xvii.
263. Cone, *Black Theology of Liberation*, xviii.
264. Cone, *Black Theology of Liberation*, 10.
265. Cone, *Black Theology of Liberation*, 11.

of liberation as a source of strength and hope. His interpretation of the Exodus demonstrates that the struggle for racial justice is not separate from the gospel but is central to its message.[266]

Gerald O. West discusses how the Exodus narrative has been appropriated by African liberation movements, serving as a tool for resisting colonialism and postcolonial forms of oppression. West emphasizes that the story of the Israelites' journey from slavery to freedom has offered a vision of hope for African communities fighting against the injustices imposed by colonial powers. This narrative, according to West, resonates deeply with those who have faced systemic exploitation and marginalization.[267] The themes of divine justice and perseverance within the Exodus account inspire oppressed groups to remain steadfast in their struggle for liberation.

West highlights that African theologians and activists have drawn on the Exodus story as a source of empowerment, using it to frame their own liberation struggles. The narrative's emphasis on God's intervention in history to free the oppressed provides a theological basis for resisting both colonial and neocolonial forces. West points out that African leaders have found in the Exodus story a call to action, one that aligns with their own efforts to overthrow oppressive regimes and achieve self-determination.[268] The appropriation of the Exodus by African liberation movements demonstrates the universality of its message, which extends beyond its original context to address contemporary struggles for justice.

In his analysis, West also explores how the Exodus narrative has been used in postcolonial contexts, where the fight for freedom continues in different forms. The story serves not only as a reminder of past victories over oppression but also as a guide for addressing ongoing issues related to inequality and exploitation. For West, the Exodus offers a theological framework for understanding the dynamics of power and resistance in African societies, where the legacy of colonialism still shapes the social and political landscape.[269]

Moreover, West discusses how the narrative's themes of perseverance and divine justice provide hope to those facing seemingly insurmountable challenges. The Israelites' eventual escape from Egypt, despite the overwhelming power of Pharaoh's regime, serves as a powerful

---

266. Cone, *Black Theology of Liberation*, 13.
267. West, *Stolen Bible*, 4.
268. West, *Stolen Bible*, 7.
269. West, *Stolen Bible*, 237.

reminder that liberation is possible even in the face of overwhelming odds. This aspect of the Exodus story has been particularly meaningful for African communities struggling against systemic oppression, as it reinforces the belief that their efforts are supported by a higher moral and divine order.[270]

West concludes that the enduring relevance of the Exodus narrative lies in its ability to speak to the experiences of oppressed peoples across time and space. Its themes of resistance, hope, and divine intervention continue to inspire African theologians and activists who seek to create a more just and equitable society in the aftermath of colonialism.[271]

Michael Walzer offers a compelling interpretation of the Exodus story as a political allegory, particularly relevant for revolutionary movements throughout history. In his analysis, Walzer suggests that while the Exodus narrative provides a model for liberation, it also serves as a cautionary tale about the potential for new forms of oppression to arise in the wake of revolution. He argues that the Israelites' initial liberation from Pharaoh's Egypt eventually led to the reemergence of oppressive structures, even within their own society, as seen in their interactions with the Moabites and Philistines.[272] This idea underscores the need for constant vigilance to ensure that revolutionary movements do not replicate the very injustices they seek to dismantle.

Walzer further explores how the narrative portrays the Israelites as initially reluctant to rise up against their oppressors, describing them as "crushed, frightened, and despondent."[273] This reluctance is a recurring theme in revolutionary contexts, where the oppressed may struggle to break free from the psychological and social bonds of tyranny. Walzer's secular interpretation of the Exodus highlights the universal challenges faced by oppressed peoples in overcoming both external and internal obstacles to liberation.

In his discussion of the Levites' violent suppression of idol worshippers, Walzer examines the moral and political complexities of revolutionary justice. He points to the episode of summary executions as a "crucial moment" in the transition from bondage to freedom, raising important questions about the role of political violence in securing liberation.[274]

270. West, *Stolen Bible*, 238.
271. West, *Stolen Bible*, 343.
272. Walzer, *Exodus and Revolution*, 114.
273. Walzer, *Exodus and Revolution*, 47.
274. Walzer, *Exodus and Revolution*, 59.

By invoking this incident, Walzer invites readers to reflect on the ethical dimensions of revolutionary action and the potential for power to be misused in the aftermath of a successful revolt.

Walzer's interpretation of the Exodus also emphasizes the tension between idealism and pragmatism in revolutionary movements. He contrasts the messianic visions of total transformation with more practical approaches that acknowledge the limitations of historical reality.[275] This distinction highlights the need for revolutionary movements to balance lofty ideals with the practicalities of governance, lest they fall into the same traps of oppression they once sought to escape.

In sum, Walzer's reading of the Exodus story offers a nuanced understanding of liberation as both a political and moral journey. While the narrative provides hope and inspiration for those seeking freedom, it also serves as a reminder that the struggle for justice does not end with the overthrow of tyranny but requires ongoing commitment to ethical governance and social responsibility.[276]

In conclusion, the Exodus narrative serves as a foundational framework for understanding both the divine commitment to justice and the responsibility of communities to challenge systems of oppression. Through the work of scholars such as Christopher J.H. Wright, Terence E. Fretheim, and Walter Brueggemann, it is clear that this story is not just a historical account but a continuous call for resistance to injustice and the building of a society grounded in freedom and responsibility. This narrative invites modern readers to reflect on their role in continuing this mission in the world today.

The leadership of Moses and the challenges faced by the Israelites highlight the importance of moral courage and communal responsibility. Scholars like Fretheim emphasize that leadership, as demonstrated by Moses, requires a commitment to justice and a vision for creating a community that reflects divine values. This story illustrates how liberation involves both the dismantling of oppressive systems and the creation of a new, just order where communities thrive under God's care.

Finally, the political and theological reflections from thinkers like Michael Walzer and James H. Cone show that the lessons of the Exodus are timeless and relevant across different contexts. Whether applied to the struggle for racial justice or revolutionary movements, the Exodus

---

275. Walzer, *Exodus and Revolution*, 141.
276. Walzer, *Exodus and Revolution*, 124.

narrative offers a reminder that liberation requires ongoing vigilance and commitment to ethical principles. It serves as a powerful reminder that true freedom is not merely the absence of oppression but the creation of a just and equitable society.

3.4.2. Jesus and the Oppressed

In this section, the emphasis is placed on viewing Jesus' ministry as a direct challenge to political, social, and economic structures, rather than merely a spiritual or personal mission. Scholars like Dorothee Sölle argue that Jesus' teachings confronted oppressive systems, such as the Roman Empire, and advocated for the empowerment of the marginalized, especially the poor. Sölle and Ched Myers highlight how Jesus gathered a community that challenged the societal hierarchies of the time, stressing the need to understand his ministry within its socio-political context. This approach suggests that Jesus' actions were not solely about individual spirituality but about transforming society through justice and equality.

Furthermore, these interpretations argue that modern readings of Jesus often neglect the radical call for societal reform embedded in his teachings. Sölle critiques the focus on individual spirituality that overlooks the communal and societal dimensions of Jesus' message. Myers, similarly, emphasizes the importance of recognizing Jesus' critique of wealth and power structures. By reframing Jesus' ministry as a political movement for justice, these thinkers present his life as a model for resisting oppression and advocating for a more just and equitable world.

Dorothee Sölle emphasizes the importance of recognizing Jesus' ministry as a challenge to political and social systems, rather than simply as a spiritual or personal message. She argues that institutionalized religion has often diluted the political force of Jesus' teachings, rendering them more about individual spirituality than societal reform. Sölle highlights that the early followers of Jesus were not merely concerned with inner peace or personal salvation but were part of a movement that confronted oppressive systems, including the Pax Romana.[277] This context, she suggests, is crucial for understanding the political significance of Jesus' ministry.

In her analysis, Sölle points to how Jesus gathered the poor, including many women, to travel with him, forming a community that directly

---

277. Sölle, *Thinking About God*, 8.

challenged the social hierarchies of their time.[278] She emphasizes that the socio-economic conditions of Jesus' time were similar to those in many parts of the modern Third World, where extreme poverty and inequality prevail. By situating Jesus' actions in this context, Sölle argues that his ministry was not merely a spiritual mission but a political one, aimed at empowering the marginalized and critiquing the structures that oppressed them.

Sölle also critiques how modern interpretations often fail to grasp the radical equality present in the Jesus movement. She highlights how feminist readings of the Bible, like those in In Memory of Her, stress the importance of reading biblical texts creatively and critically to understand how Jesus' message of equality and justice was lived out in his time.[279] She critiques the tendency of traditional theology to prioritize male experiences, pointing out that Jesus' movement was one of inclusion and equality for all.

Drawing parallels between the ministry of Jesus and modern figures like Martin Luther King Jr., Sölle argues that the Civil Rights movement and Jesus' teachings share a common goal of societal transformation through nonviolent resistance to injustice.[280] King, she notes, saw in Jesus' message a challenge to all Americans to build a new society grounded in equality and justice. This comparison emphasizes the continued relevance of Jesus' political message in contemporary struggles for justice.

Furthermore, Sölle critiques individualistic spirituality, suggesting that Jesus' message calls for collective action. She argues that modern liberal spirituality, which focuses on the individual's relationship with God, neglects the communal and societal dimensions of Jesus' teachings.[281] Sölle stresses that Jesus' message was not about private spiritual comfort but about transforming society through collective engagement with the poor and oppressed.

In her discussion of the Pax Romana, Sölle highlights how the peace and order imposed by Rome were based on the subjugation and exploitation of other peoples. She contrasts this with the peace of Christ, which stands in opposition to imperial domination and reflects a radical alternative to the power structures of Jesus' time.[282] This distinction

---

278. Sölle, *Thinking About God*, 39.
279. Sölle, *Thinking About God*, 71.
280. Sölle, *Thinking About God*, 98.
281. Sölle, *Thinking About God*, 109.
282. Sölle, *Thinking About God*, 158.

between the Pax Romana and the Pax Christi, she argues, underscores the resistance inherent in Jesus' ministry, as his followers rejected the emperor's claim to divinity and refused to participate in the oppressive practices of the empire.[283]

Sölle also emphasizes God's preference for the poor, arguing that Jesus' teachings make it clear that God stands with the oppressed and marginalized in every situation. This "preferential option for the poor" is a central element of Jesus' message and serves as a moral imperative for Christians to align themselves with the suffering and the dispossessed.[284] She critiques interpretations of Christianity that neglect this focus on social justice, arguing that any theology that ignores the poor is disconnected from the heart of Jesus' message.

In discussing the Roman political system, Sölle critiques how early liberalism distanced itself from the moral and religious dimensions of human existence, promoting a free-market economy that prioritized wealth and power over the well-being of the poor. She connects this critique to Jesus' teachings, which she sees as a direct challenge to systems that exploit the vulnerable for economic gain.[285] Jesus' message, she argues, calls for an economic and political system that prioritizes the needs of the poor over the accumulation of wealth.

Finally, Sölle presents Jesus' life and ministry as a call to live in a way that reflects God's work of liberation. She emphasizes that faith is not about passive acceptance of suffering but about active engagement in creating a more just and equitable world. Jesus' teachings, she argues, represent a revolutionary way of living those challenges both personal and societal injustices.[286] This understanding of faith as a form of resistance highlights the transformative power of Jesus' message in both personal and political spheres.

Ched Myers provides a thorough political reading of the Gospel of Mark, emphasizing that Jesus' ministry was a direct confrontation with the social and economic hierarchies of his time. Myers points out that in ancient Palestine, powerful groups such as politicians and lawyers, much like their modern counterparts, held significant social power. The scribal class, which controlled the interpretation of the Torah, played a similar

---

283. Sölle, *Thinking About God*, 161.
284. Sölle, *Thinking About God*, 19.
285. Sölle, *Thinking About God*, 16.
286. Sölle, *Thinking About God*, 18.

role in shaping societal norms.[287] This concentration of power was a key target of Jesus' mission, as he sought to challenge the status quo and advocate for a new social order based on equality and justice.

Myers stresses that Mark's Gospel should not be interpreted solely through a literary lens but also within its socio-historical context. He argues that both the literary structure and the socio-political setting of the text are essential for a full understanding of its message. This "socio-literary" approach, as Myers calls it, allows readers to appreciate how the Gospel engages with the power dynamics of its time, particularly in relation to economic and social justice.[288] By using this method, Myers encourages readers to consider how the Gospel of Mark speaks to modern issues of inequality and oppression.

One of the key themes in Myers' reading is the rejection of wealth and the call for its redistribution. He highlights that Jesus' teachings consistently challenge the economic structures that favored the wealthy at the expense of the poor. Myers draws attention to how Mark's Gospel portrays the accumulation of wealth as a form of oppression, particularly in its connection to debt and purity codes. These cultural norms were used to maintain social hierarchies, and Jesus' ministry sought to overturn them, advocating instead for a system of justice where resources were shared equitably.[289]

In addition to his critique of wealth, Myers explores how the process of state formation in ancient Israel contributed to the establishment of oppressive political and economic systems. He notes that the completion of the temple in Jerusalem marked the final stage of Israel's transformation into a state like other imperial nations. This development brought with it a kingship ideology that legitimized social and economic inequality, and Jesus' ministry was a response to this imperial system.[290] Myers' analysis invites readers to reflect on how modern states continue to perpetuate similar forms of inequality and oppression.

Myers also discusses how prophetic movements in first-century Palestine anticipated new acts of redemption, drawing symbolic parallels between historical events and eschatological expectations. These movements, which often clashed with Roman authorities, reflected the broader social discontent of the time, as the common people sought liberation

---

287. Myers, *Binding the Strong Man*, 71.
288. Myers, *Binding the Strong Man*, xxviii.
289. Myers, *Binding the Strong Man*, 44.
290. Myers, *Binding the Strong Man*, 294.

from both political and economic oppression. Myers links Jesus' ministry to these prophetic traditions, emphasizing that Jesus' message was not merely spiritual but also deeply political, aimed at transforming the structures of power that oppressed the poor.[291]

Throughout his work, Myers underscores that Jesus' mission was about more than individual salvation; it was about creating a new social order rooted in justice and equality. The "triumphal entry" into Jerusalem, often misinterpreted as a simple messianic celebration, is described by Myers as a form of street theater designed to send conflicting signals to both the Roman and Jewish authorities.[292] This act, like much of Jesus' ministry, challenged the power structures of the time and pointed to an alternative vision of the Kingdom of God, one where wealth and power were redistributed, and the marginalized were lifted up.

J. Kameron Carter offers a framework for understanding Jesus' ministry through the lens of race and colonialism, emphasizing how Jesus' actions disrupted the racial and cultural hierarchies of his time. Carter argues that Jesus' radical inclusion of marginalized groups, such as Samaritans and tax collectors, was a direct challenge to the ethnocentric and exclusionary practices of first-century Palestine. These groups, often viewed as outsiders, were embraced by Jesus in a way that subverted societal norms, calling into question the boundaries of belonging and identity.[293]

Carter connects this to broader themes in Christian theology, suggesting that modernity's racial imagination is intertwined with religious ideologies. He critiques how Enlightenment thinking, which shaped much of modern Western discourse, has racialized the concept of humanity, creating divisions that are deeply rooted in both religious and political frameworks.[294] By bringing attention to this, Carter invites readers to reconsider how theology has historically been complicit in constructing racial hierarchies.

In examining early Christian theology, Carter refers to the work of Irenaeus of Lyons, particularly his opposition to Gnosticism, which denigrated the material world, including Christ's flesh. Irenaeus' defense of the incarnation, according to Carter, is significant because it affirms the material and embodied nature of Christ's humanity, which disrupts

---

291. Myers, *Binding the Strong Man*, 62.
292. Myers, *Binding the Strong Man*, 336.
293. Carter, *Race*, 5.
294. Carter, *Race*, 5.

the racial logic that later developed in modernity. Jesus' Jewish identity, in this reading, is critical for understanding how his life challenges the racialized notions of purity and superiority that were prevalent in both ancient and modern contexts.[295]

Carter also explores how Jesus' inclusion of Gentiles into the people of God can be seen as a further rejection of racial and cultural exclusivity. He argues that Jesus' flesh, in its Jewish constitution, symbolizes the blending of identities and the breaking down of barriers between different ethnic groups. This blending disrupts the structures of dominance and slavery that have historically defined social hierarchies.[296] By affirming the mixed nature of Jesus' identity, Carter presents a vision of Christianity that opposes the racial distinctions that have often been used to justify oppression.

Moreover, Carter critiques the way modernity's racial imagination has been framed by thinkers like Michel Foucault, who examined how race became a central organizing principle in modern societies. Carter draws on Foucault's analysis to show how the invention of race was not just a social or political phenomenon but also a theological one, deeply embedded in the ways that Western Christianity developed its understanding of humanity and difference.[297]

In this context, Carter challenges traditional theological interpretations that ignore the political dimensions of Jesus' ministry. He argues that by failing to address how Jesus actively worked against the racial and colonial structures of his time, these interpretations miss a crucial aspect of his mission. For Carter, Jesus' ministry was not only about individual spiritual transformation but also about reshaping the social and political realities that oppressed marginalized groups.[298]

Through this analysis, Carter calls for a reimagining of Christian theology, one that acknowledges the racial and colonial legacies that continue to influence how Jesus' life and teachings are understood today. His critique extends to modern Christian communities, urging them to confront these legacies and to align themselves with the inclusive and liberative aspects of Jesus' ministry.[299] This approach challenges readers

---

295. Carter, *Race*, 7.
296. Carter, *Race*, 30.
297. Carter, *Race*, 39.
298. Carter, *Race*, 44.
299. Carter, *Race*, 46.

to see Jesus' ministry as a force for dismantling racial hierarchies and creating a more just and equitable world.

Miguel De La Torre presents Jesus as a figure deeply connected to the marginalized and oppressed, particularly in Latin American contexts where colonialism and economic exploitation have left enduring scars. De La Torre draws attention to the fact that Jesus came from a humble, marginalized background. He likens Jesus' origins to coming from "the wrong side of the tracks," noting how this experience shaped Jesus' understanding of cultural bias and social exclusion.[300] By emphasizing Jesus' identification with those who are marginalized, De La Torre invites readers to see his ministry as a model for resisting the forces of oppression that continue to affect marginalized communities today.

De La Torre critiques interpretations of the Gospel that focus narrowly on individual salvation, arguing that such readings ignore the broader implications of Jesus' teachings for social justice. He stresses that the Gospel is not merely about personal morality but about organizing social life according to God's commandments and purposes. In this framework, labor and work are elevated from mundane activities to a divine calling, a theme also expressed by reformers like Martin Luther.[301] This understanding of labor ties into the larger theme of economic justice, as Jesus' ministry challenged the structures that exploited the poor and vulnerable.

Furthermore, De La Torre explores the connection between salvation and liberation, especially for those on the margins of society. He argues that salvation cannot be separated from the struggle for justice. Salvation arises when the quest for liberation intersects with the praxis of Christ, who willingly chose the cross as a form of solidarity with the oppressed.[302] For De La Torre, faith is not simply a spiritual endeavor but a call to action alongside those who are marginalized, a theme that challenges more traditional, individualistic understandings of salvation.

De La Torre also critiques how contemporary interpretations of the Gospel often fail to address the obligation of converts toward the oppressed. He suggests that privileged groups within society continue their pursuit of power and wealth without concern for how their actions affect the marginalized, all while feeling secure in their salvation.[303]

300. De La Torre, *Reading the Bible from the Margins*, 111.
301. De La Torre, *Reading the Bible from the Margins*, 73.
302. De La Torre, *Reading the Bible from the Margins*, 148.
303. De La Torre, *Reading the Bible from the Margins*, 138.

This disconnect between personal salvation and social responsibility is a major critique in his work, as he emphasizes that Jesus' teachings were deeply concerned with systemic injustice.

The example of the poor widow in Mark 12:41–44 illustrates, according to De La Torre, how Jesus highlighted the condition of the oppressed as a model for understanding the broader issues of racism, classism, and economic exploitation.[304] The widow's sacrificial giving, despite her poverty, serves as a critique of a system that takes from those who have little, rather than supporting and uplifting them.

In sum, De La Torre presents Jesus' life and ministry as a call to resist oppressive systems and to advocate for the liberation of the marginalized. He argues that interpretations of the Gospel that focus solely on individual salvation fail to engage with the broader themes of justice that are central to Jesus' message.[305] Through this lens, Jesus becomes not just a spiritual savior, but a revolutionary figure whose life and death symbolize resistance to imperial powers and economic injustice.

R.S. Sugirtharajah emphasizes that Jesus' ministry must be understood in light of the political and economic realities of first-century Palestine, particularly in relation to the imperial domination of Rome. He critiques Western interpretations of Jesus that often spiritualize his teachings, neglecting the fact that many of Jesus' actions were acts of resistance against the imperial powers of his time.[306] By focusing on the postcolonial dimensions of Jesus' ministry, Sugirtharajah encourages readers to explore how Jesus' message would have resonated with those living under colonial rule, such as the Jewish people under Roman occupation.

Sugirtharajah points out that Western exegetical traditions, influenced by an orientalist mindset, have often portrayed non-Christian religions like Hinduism as lacking a sense of historical and eschatological purpose, while emphasizing the linear, purpose-driven nature of biblical faith.[307] This perspective, he argues, mirrors the colonial mindset that seeks to elevate Western religious and cultural practices over those of colonized peoples. By critiquing this approach, Sugirtharajah calls for a more nuanced understanding of biblical texts, one that recognizes the political and historical contexts in which they were written.

304. De La Torre, *Reading the Bible from the Margins*, 120.
305. De La Torre, *Reading the Bible from the Margins*, 160.
306. Sugirtharajah, *Bible and the Third World*, 70.
307. Sugirtharajah, *Bible and the Third World*, 71.

In examining the resistance movements within colonized cultures, Sugirtharajah highlights how figures such as K.M. Banerjea in India appropriated Christianity in ways that were compatible with their own religious traditions, thus resisting the complete domination of colonial powers.[308] This historical example illustrates how the teachings of Jesus, when understood through a postcolonial lens, offer a framework for resisting imperialism and affirming the dignity of colonized peoples.

Sugirtharajah also addresses how early Christian communities, particularly those in Asia Minor, were shaped by the socio-political realities of the Roman Empire. He notes that many letters in the New Testament were written in or addressed to these communities, which were directly affected by the oppressive structures of imperial rule.[309] This context is crucial for understanding how Jesus' teachings, particularly his message of liberation, would have been received by those living under colonial domination.

In his critique of Western biblical scholarship, Sugirtharajah emphasizes the importance of recognizing indigenous interpretative practices, such as dhvani and rasa in India, which have been sidelined by the historical-critical method dominant in Western theology.[310] These indigenous approaches, he argues, offer valuable perspectives that can illuminate the liberationist themes within the Gospels, particularly for those living under the shadow of colonialism.

Overall, Sugirtharajah's reading of the Gospels encourages a deeper engagement with the political dimensions of Jesus' ministry. He critiques interpretations that reduce Jesus' teachings to personal spiritual matters and instead emphasizes the liberationist themes that are especially relevant to those living under oppressive systems of power.[311] Through this postcolonial lens, Jesus' actions can be seen as not only spiritually significant but also as acts of resistance against imperialism and exploitation.

Allan Boesak emphasizes that Jesus' ministry must be understood as a direct challenge to systems of racial and economic oppression, particularly in the context of apartheid in South Africa. Boesak critiques readings of Jesus that fail to engage with the realities of racial injustice, arguing that Jesus' life and death demonstrate a profound commitment

---

308. Sugirtharajah, *Bible and the Third World*, 90.
309. Sugirtharajah, *Bible and the Third World*, 14.
310. Sugirtharajah, *Bible and the Third World*, 72.
311. Sugirtharajah, *Bible and the Third World*, 87.

to standing in solidarity with those who are marginalized.[312] He frames apartheid as not just a political system but as a theological crisis, where Christians are called to resist the dehumanizing forces at play.

Boesak points to the South African government's use of emergency measures and violent repression during apartheid, noting that the state granted its soldiers and police officers the power to kill with impunity.[313] For Boesak, this brutality underscores the need for the church to speak out against such systemic violence. He argues that Jesus' ministry compels Christians to reject the complicity that many religious institutions have shown toward oppressive regimes.

In his discussion of apartheid as a crime against humanity, Boesak draws a parallel between the injustices of South Africa and the broader global systems of oppression. He argues that apartheid is not just a South African issue but a cancer in the body politic of the world, likening its effects to those of the nuclear arms race in its ability to harm humanity as a whole.[314] This global perspective reflects Boesak's belief that the liberationist message of Jesus has universal relevance for resisting all forms of oppression.

Boesak also critiques the apartheid government's policies, such as the forced relocations and the creation of "homelands" for Black South Africans, which he describes as a form of subtle genocide.[315] He sees in Jesus' ministry a model for resisting these dehumanizing policies, emphasizing that Christians must stand with the oppressed and work to dismantle the systems that perpetuate their suffering.

In reflecting on his own experience, Boesak connects the book of Revelation to the context of South Africa, arguing that John of Patmos, like the persecuted church under apartheid, wrote from a place of resistance against imperial power.[316] Boesak identifies with John's apocalyptic vision, seeing in it a call for God's final judgment on corrupt political and religious systems of oppression. This reading of Revelation underscores Boesak's belief that Christian faith is inherently subversive, aimed at challenging the status quo and advocating for justice.[317]

---

312. Boesak, *Comfort and Protest*, 10.
313. Boesak, *Comfort and Protest*, 48.
314. Boesak, *Comfort and Protest*, 66.
315. Boesak, *Comfort and Protest*, 68.
316. Boesak, *Comfort and Protest*, 13.
317. Boesak, *Comfort and Protest*, 29.

Boesak's understanding of Jesus' ministry is rooted in the conviction that Christian faith cannot be separated from the struggle for racial justice. He argues that any interpretation of the Gospel that ignores the political and social realities of oppression is incomplete. For Boesak, Jesus' solidarity with the marginalized is a central aspect of his message, and it calls for active resistance to all forms of injustice, particularly those rooted in racial discrimination and economic exploitation.[318] This emphasis on solidarity reflects Boesak's broader theological framework, which places the struggle for justice at the heart of Christian discipleship.

Jon Sobrino presents Jesus' life as a model for understanding God's preferential option for the poor. He emphasizes that those who are marginalized offer a unique perspective on theological concepts such as grace, justice, and the Kingdom of God. Sobrino believes that while the poor may not traditionally engage in theology as it has been understood, their experience and suffering provide a distinct lens through which these theological ideas can be understood and lived out.[319] He argues that the perspective of the poor brings something more valuable to theology than abstract content—it offers a way to see God and the world through the eyes of the oppressed.

Sobrino critiques the idea that Christian theology can be fully undertaken by those who are not poor or victims of oppression. He notes that while the poor themselves may not engage in theology as conventionally defined, their lived experiences are crucial for shaping a theology that addresses the real injustices of the world. This perspective challenges traditional theological frameworks that often separate spiritual salvation from social justice.[320] By engaging with the experiences of the poor, Sobrino calls for a more integrated approach that recognizes the holistic nature of Jesus' message, where salvation and justice are deeply interconnected.

Sobrino further explores the concept of the Kingdom of God, arguing that it cannot be reduced to an individual or collective utopia. Instead, the Kingdom must be seen as a transformed social reality that is rooted in justice for the poor. He asserts that the struggles for dignity, freedom, and life are central to the vision of the Kingdom, and these are the same struggles that the poor face in their everyday lives.[321] This

---

318. Boesak, *Comfort and Protest*, 37.
319. Sobrino, *Christ the Liberator*, 8.
320. Sobrino, *Christ the Liberator*, 270.
321. Sobrino, *Christ the Liberator*, 336.

vision of the Kingdom contrasts with the "light" utopias tolerated by the world, which do not adequately address the real oppression and injustice faced by the marginalized.

By focusing on Jesus' public life, from his baptism to the cross, Sobrino highlights that the entire narrative of Jesus is a testimony to God's solidarity with the oppressed. He compares this narrative to the theological process of the New Testament, where the memory of Jesus is handed down not as a mere theological abstraction but in the form of narratives that speak directly to the lived experiences of suffering and hope.[322] Through this comparison, Sobrino calls for a return to a more narrative-based theology that takes seriously the social and political dimensions of Jesus' life.

In conclusion, Sobrino challenges traditional interpretations that focus exclusively on spiritual aspects of salvation, arguing that Jesus' message cannot be separated from the realities of oppression and inequality. The Kingdom of God, as understood through the lens of the poor, is not a distant, abstract idea but a call for radical transformation in the here and now, one that prioritizes justice and dignity for the marginalized.[323] This integrated approach to theology invites Christians to actively engage in the struggle for justice as part of their faith, following the example set by Jesus.

Conclusively, this section underscores that Jesus' ministry went beyond individual spiritual teachings, positioning it as a direct challenge to political, social, and economic oppression. Dorothee Sölle and Ched Myers emphasize that Jesus' actions were rooted in confronting unjust systems, critiquing institutionalized religion's tendency to downplay the political force of his message. They argue that Jesus' ministry was aimed at empowering the poor and marginalized, calling for systemic reform and resisting oppressive structures like the Pax Romana.

In addition, thinkers such as J. Kameron Carter and Miguel De La Torre explore how Jesus' life disrupted social and racial hierarchies. Jesus' radical inclusion of marginalized groups challenged societal norms and called for a rethinking of identity and belonging. De La Torre further connects Jesus' ministry to modern issues of economic justice, critiquing interpretations that focus solely on personal salvation while neglecting the social implications of his teachings.

---

322. Sobrino, *Christ the Liberator*, 228.
323. Sobrino, *Christ the Liberator*, 335.

Finally, scholars like R.S. Sugirtharajah, Allan Boesak, and Jon Sobrino highlight how Jesus' message resonates with struggles against colonialism, apartheid, and global inequality. They argue that understanding Jesus' ministry through the lens of the oppressed reveals a vision for a new social order based on justice, solidarity, and liberation. This broader framework calls Christians to actively resist oppression and work towards a more equitable world, following the example of Jesus.

3.5. CHALLENGING POWER WITH THEOLOGY AND JUSTICE

In this section, several theologians bring distinct approaches to understanding the relationship between theology and social justice. The scholars discussed, including Herman Waetjen, Catherine Keller, John Caputo, Mark C. Taylor, Peter Rollins, Serene Jones, and Richard Kearney, explore ways in which theology can respond to societal challenges, focusing on how religious thought can be applied to contemporary issues of justice, power, and trauma. Their frameworks often reject rigid theological constructs in favor of more dynamic, relational approaches that encourage engagement with both historical and present realities.

Waetjen emphasizes the socio-political dimensions of scripture, presenting a dialectical method that connects the biblical text with modern issues of justice and inequality. Keller and Caputo explore how relationality and weakness can reshape traditional notions of divine power and human interaction, offering perspectives that invite theological inquiry into spaces of uncertainty and vulnerability. These approaches challenge static religious understandings, advocating for a theology that engages deeply with the complexities of life and society.

The section highlights how these thinkers deconstruct established theological models to address contemporary concerns. By focusing on relational and dynamic perspectives, their work opens pathways for reinterpreting faith in ways that are responsive to issues such as ecological crisis, social inequality, and personal trauma. Their collective efforts provide frameworks that allow theology to remain relevant in addressing the evolving challenges of modern society.

3.5.1. Nonviolence and Prophetic Imagination

This section explores the theological perspectives of Walter Brueggemann, James Cone, Jon Sobrino, and others on the relationship between prophetic imagination, nonviolence, and justice. Through a focus on scripture and the lived experiences of marginalized communities, these theologians provide frameworks for understanding how faith can be a powerful tool for confronting societal oppression and promoting transformation. Their work emphasizes the importance of narrating experiences of suffering, engaging in nonviolent resistance, and imagining alternative possibilities for justice that challenge the dominant systems of power and control.

Walter Brueggemann's work centers on the role of prophetic imagination in confronting societal oppression. His framework emphasizes how the act of narrating grief and suffering serves a political purpose, inviting communities to recognize injustice and challenge the systems that uphold it. Through biblical stories, particularly those addressing suffering and liberation, Brueggemann encourages readers to see how scripture can be a tool for critiquing oppressive structures and promoting social transformation.

James Cone's theology, particularly in the context of Black liberation, aligns with Brueggemann's prophetic imagination. Cone argues that theology must directly engage with the lived experiences of marginalized communities, interpreting their struggles for justice as central to faith. Both theologians see the act of narrating experiences of oppression as essential in advocating for societal change, linking theology with active resistance to injustice.

Walter Brueggemann emphasizes that the act of narrating painful experiences and expressing grief holds political significance. By recounting stories of oppression, individuals can draw attention to the suffering that fuels such grief, encouraging others to confront these realities. He asserts that, beginning in the late 1970s, these themes have become increasingly evident in discussions around societal and systemic oppression.[324] This perspective encourages readers to see how biblical texts, particularly those addressing suffering, align with contemporary challenges of exploitation and injustice.

Brueggemann explores how Moses dismantled the religious ideology of static triumphalism, which upheld oppressive systems. In its place,

---

324. Brueggemann, *Prophetic Imagination*, xvi.

Moses presented a vision of justice and compassion. This new framework not only exposed the flawed politics of oppression but also offered an alternative community grounded in fairness and care.[325] This approach challenges readers to understand how faith traditions can play a role in critiquing and dismantling oppressive structures, similar to the function of the Exodus narrative.

Brueggemann notes that Karl Marx observed a key connection between the criticism of religion and the broader critique of law, economics, and politics. This observation parallels Brueggemann's own understanding that the gods of oppression, exemplified in the Egyptian regime, represent ideologies that uphold injustice. The criticism of these systems is a necessary first step in moving toward a more just society.[326] Here, Brueggemann's work highlights the intersection of religious and political critique as a tool for confronting injustice.

Brueggemann also reflects on the importance of recognizing a God who is free from the constraints of oppressive power structures. He contrasts this vision with those that uphold order without justice, arguing that a truly free God calls for a politics of justice and compassion.[327] This understanding reinforces the idea that theology and social action are connected, and that religious beliefs should promote justice, rather than support the status quo.

In the Exodus narrative, the practice of justice and compassion emerges as a central theme, with the plagues serving as a pivotal moment of dismantling oppressive power. Brueggemann suggests that this story should be revisited frequently because it affirms a crucial reality—one that defies the logic of empire and asserts the possibility of a just community.[328] These narrative invites readers to see how acts of disruption can lead to the establishment of more compassionate systems.

The freedom that comes from a relationship with God, according to Brueggemann, is tied to the community's willingness to challenge the regime of oppression. He points out that Israel's complaints and grief during the Exodus are not acts of resignation, but expressions of trust in God's justice.[329] This highlights the role of lament in the prophetic

---

325. Brueggemann, *Prophetic Imagination*, 6.
326. Brueggemann, *Prophetic Imagination*, 7.
327. Brueggemann, *Prophetic Imagination*, 8.
328. Brueggemann, *Prophetic Imagination*, 10.
329. Brueggemann, *Prophetic Imagination*, 12.

tradition, a theme Brueggemann often revisits in his exploration of how communities process suffering.

Brueggemann describes how the gods of injustice, those who perpetuate order at the expense of equity, have reached their end. The criticism inherent in prophetic traditions has succeeded in exposing these false idols, paving the way for a new consciousness rooted in freedom.[330] This concept reflects Brueggemann's broader emphasis on the power of prophetic imagination, which energizes communities to envision alternative possibilities.

In discussing Jeremiah, Brueggemann portrays the prophet as embodying an alternative consciousness that counters the denial and numbness of the ruling powers. Jeremiah's grief over Judah's destruction is a clear expression of this alternative vision, one that refuses to accept the false security of unjust systems.[331] Jeremiah's example serves as a model for how contemporary communities might respond to the denial of injustice with lament and truth-telling.

Brueggemann ultimately asserts that justice and compassion are inseparable from the freedom of God. He argues that the emergence of a new social community, as exemplified by the Exodus, represents more than just a religious idea—it is the creation of a historical reality that embodies the ethics of justice.[332] This vision calls for communities to actively engage in the practice of justice, shaped by a deep understanding of divine freedom.

James H. Cone explores how Black theology serves as a vital framework for understanding the struggle for liberation among Black Americans. He emphasizes that Black theology is particularly relevant in America because of its symbolic power in representing both the reality of oppression and the divine character of the fight for justice. For Cone, the interpretation of Black theology revolves around recognizing the ongoing struggles of marginalized communities and highlighting their theological significance.[333] This perspective aligns with Brueggemann's understanding of prophetic imagination, as both theologians underscore the power of narrating painful experiences to bring about social transformation.

---

330. Brueggemann, *Prophetic Imagination*, 14.
331. Brueggemann, *Prophetic Imagination*, 47.
332. Brueggemann, *Prophetic Imagination*, 6.
333. Cone, *Black Theology of Liberation*, ix.

Cone argues that Black theology seeks to interpret the meaning of God's liberation in the context of the oppressed community. He acknowledges that many individuals have supported and encouraged this theological project, contributing to its development and relevance.[334] This focus on interpreting liberation through the lens of community echoes Brueggemann's emphasis on scripture as a tool for social critique, particularly in challenging oppressive structures and imagining new possibilities for justice.

In his critique of mainstream American theology, Cone asserts that white theology has often failed to engage with the struggles for Black liberation. He critiques it for being a theology of oppression rather than liberation, positioning Black theology as a corrective force that addresses the religious dimensions of revolutionary struggle.[335] This resonates with Brueggemann's discussion of how religious frameworks can support or challenge power structures, encouraging readers to recognize the political dimensions of theology.

Cone also notes that Black theology actively analyzes the oppressive nature of whiteness, seeking to dismantle the ideologies that perpetuate racism and inequality. By critiquing whiteness, Black theology aims to prepare marginalized communities for revolutionary action, much in the way that Brueggemann's prophetic imagination seeks to dismantle systems of injustice through a framework of compassion and justice.[336] This call to action reflects the political potential of both theologians' work in addressing systemic injustice.

In discussing the broader implications of Black theology, Cone points out that it encourages the Black community to reclaim their identity by rewriting history from their perspective. By challenging the oppressor's narrative, Black theology becomes an instrument of liberation, allowing the oppressed to construct a new understanding of their place in history.[337] This mirrors Brueggemann's view of prophetic imagination as a tool for envisioning alternative realities that challenge dominant ideologies.

Cone asserts that Black theology is inherently about survival, as it provides theological dimensions for the struggle for Black identity. It reorders religious language to expose the anti-Christian nature of forces

---

334. Cone, *Black Theology of Liberation*, x.
335. Cone, *Black Theology of Liberation*, 4.
336. Cone, *Black Theology of Liberation*, 8.
337. Cone, *Black Theology of Liberation*, 14.

CHAPTER THREE

that support white oppression, emphasizing that the search for Black identity is also a search for God's presence in the fight for freedom.[338] This reflects a similar understanding to Brueggemann's, where theology is not static but is actively involved in critiquing and transforming societal norms.

Throughout his work, Cone maintains that Black theology is a rebellion against the structures of white power. It encourages Black communities to resist the limitations placed upon them by society and to reject the definitions imposed by white supremacy.[339] This rejection of oppressive structures parallels Brueggemann's emphasis on the role of faith in confronting and dismantling unjust power systems.

Jon Sobrino emphasizes the centrality of praxis in theology, particularly in the context of solidarity with the poor and oppressed. He argues that a theology which does not engage with the suffering of marginalized communities lacks relevance and effectiveness. This mirrors Brueggemann's framework of societal transformation through scripture, where faith actively challenges unjust systems.[340] Sobrino insists that Christology must be understood not only in terms of theological reflection but also through its historical relevance to the realities of the oppressed, particularly in Latin America.[341]

Sobrino further explains that the historicity of Christology must be grounded in the life of Jesus of Nazareth, whose praxis is foundational for understanding the kingdom of God. He calls for a hermeneutics of praxis that prioritizes the practical outworking of Jesus' mission in the face of oppression, making theology relevant to the socio-political realities of the time.[342] This approach aligns closely with Brueggemann's idea that prophetic imagination engages with contemporary issues, bringing about transformation through action.

Sobrino's interpretation of the kingdom of God emphasizes its relationship with human liberation. He discusses how Jesus' mission centered around building the kingdom in the face of captivity, presenting it as both a theological and practical challenge.[343] By focusing on the kingdom of God as a framework for addressing both historical and

338. Cone, *Black Theology of Liberation*, 15.
339. Cone, *Black Theology of Liberation*, 18.
340. Sobrino, *Christology at the Crossroads*, ix.
341. Sobrino, *Christology at the Crossroads*, xv.
342. Sobrino, *Christology at the Crossroads*, xvii.
343. Sobrino, *Christology at the Crossroads*, 36.

anthropological realities, Sobrino draws a connection between faith and the lived experiences of the oppressed. This understanding resonates with Brueggemann's focus on the intersection of theology and social critique.

Sobrino highlights the tension within liberation theology between proclaiming the kingdom of God and addressing the socio-economic conditions of the poor. He critiques approaches that restrict the focus solely to the socio-economic dimension, arguing that the ranks of the oppressed include more than just the economically poor.[344] This broader view of oppression reflects Brueggemann's critique of societal power structures that sustain injustice, demonstrating the necessity of a comprehensive approach to theology and justice.

Leonardo Boff echoes Sobrino's emphasis on the need for liberation theology to emerge from the lived experiences of the poor. He insists that any meaningful theological reflection must be rooted in the "examination hall" of the humble, where theologians sit with the oppressed to understand their realities.[345] Critics of this approach, however, argue that focusing on socio-political issues may neglect other theological dimensions, much like the concerns raised regarding Sobrino's focus on praxis.[346] Nonetheless, Boff and Sobrino both advocate for a theology that challenges the status quo and calls for transformative action.

Ultimately, Sobrino's theology is centered on the belief that faith must engage with the suffering of the marginalized in a way that reflects the mission of Jesus. His call for a practical and actionable theology aligns with Brueggemann's emphasis on the prophetic role of scripture in addressing systemic injustice.[347]

Stanley Hauerwas places significant emphasis on the role of the Christian community in shaping ethical practices. For Hauerwas, ethics is not just about individual behavior but about the formation of a distinct community whose practices stand in contrast to the broader societal norms. Much like Walter Brueggemann's prophetic imagination, Hauerwas believes that Christian ethics should challenge the prevailing values of the larger culture. However, Hauerwas particularly highlights the importance of the church as the primary context in which these ethics are developed and lived out.[348]

---

344. Sobrino, *Christology at the Crossroads*, 37.
345. Boff and Boff, *Introducing Liberation Theology*, 24.
346. Boff and Boff, *Introducing Liberation Theology*, 29.
347. Sobrino, *Christology at the Crossroads*, 41.
348. Hauerwas, *Community of Character*, 54.

CHAPTER THREE

Hauerwas argues that Christian ethics cannot be detached from the communal practices of the church, which embodies a different way of being in the world. This perspective contrasts with approaches that primarily focus on societal critique without attending to the character of the community itself. For Hauerwas, it is through the church's practices—such as hospitality, service, and worship—that an alternative moral vision is cultivated and sustained.[349] This framework complements Brueggemann's vision of scripture as a tool for societal transformation, though Hauerwas places a more concentrated emphasis on the church as the agent of that transformation.

In developing his ethical framework, Hauerwas also critiques approaches to ethics that focus too narrowly on abstract moral principles or individual behavior. He insists that ethics must be embodied in communal practices, where members learn to live in ways that reflect the values of the gospel. This communal focus provides a model for how Christians can resist the dominant cultural values of consumerism, individualism, and power.[350] This approach aligns with Brueggemann's idea that the prophetic imagination requires active engagement with the world, but Hauerwas grounds this engagement in the practices of the Christian community.

Hauerwas further argues that the church should not simply reflect societal values but should embody an alternative vision of human flourishing. He contends that the church's practices are what make Christian ethics distinct from secular moral frameworks, and that these practices are essential for the formation of Christian character. This emphasis on the distinctiveness of the church's ethical vision reinforces his broader argument that Christian ethics is inherently communal and cannot be separated from the life of the church.[351] This complements Brueggemann's call for the church to engage with issues of justice, but with a particular focus on the formation of character through the practices of the faith community.

For Hauerwas, the ethical life of the church is not just about moral behavior but about embodying a way of life that contrasts with the world's values. The church, in his view, must cultivate practices that demonstrate the possibility of a different kind of community—one based on love, justice, and peace. This perspective resonates with Brueggemann's call for

---

349. Hauerwas, *Community of Character*, 219.
350. Hauerwas, *Community of Character*, 64.
351. Hauerwas, *Community of Character*, 76.

societal transformation through scripture but emphasizes the church as the primary locus of ethical formation and action.[352]

Dorothee Sölle emphasizes that theology must engage actively with political realities, particularly when addressing economic injustice and war. She critiques the tendency of certain theologies to reduce their message to mere propaganda against subversion and communism, arguing that such approaches fail to address the deeper roots of oppression and the urgent need for social transformation.[353] This resonates with Brueggemann's critique of power structures, but Sölle's focus is particularly on how faith must be tied to activism and resistance against unjust political systems.

Sölle identifies political apathy, especially in the context of the Vietnam War, as one of the most harmful forms of disengagement. She argues that while personal apathy seeks to minimize pain, political apathy represents a refusal to confront the suffering caused by systemic violence and injustice.[354] This critique aligns with Brueggemann's call for the prophetic imagination to awaken communities from complacency, urging them to engage meaningfully with the world's pressing issues.

In discussing suffering, Sölle explores the social dimensions of affliction, arguing that suffering is often tied to social degradation and fear. She contends that true affliction is not just a personal experience but one that is deeply embedded in unjust social conditions.[355] This echoes Brueggemann's understanding of lament as a communal act, one that acknowledges both personal and societal suffering while refusing to accept the status quo.

Sölle further critiques the notion that suffering is natural or neutral. She insists that suffering, especially that inflicted by human systems, must be recognized as something that can be resisted and transformed.[356] This perspective challenges the passive acceptance of suffering and encourages communities to actively resist the structures that perpetuate pain and injustice, much like Brueggemann's vision of scripture as a tool for challenging dominant power structures.

Sölle also emphasizes the role of faith communities in moving from passive endurance of suffering to active engagement with the world's

---

352. Hauerwas, *Community of Character*, 125.
353. Sölle, *Suffering*, 35.
354. Sölle, *Suffering*, 45.
355. Sölle, *Suffering*, 14.
356. Sölle, *Suffering*, 133.

CHAPTER THREE

pain. She argues that people must become attuned to the suffering of others and respond in ways that promote justice and healing.[357] This vision complements Brueggema

nn's prophetic imagination, where the act of recognizing and addressing suffering is central to the work of societal transformation.

Ultimately, Sölle's politically engaged theology insists that faith cannot remain disconnected from social action. She argues that theological reflection must be accompanied by concrete efforts to resist oppression and promote justice, particularly in the realms of economic inequality and war.[358] This activism-driven approach aligns closely with Brueggemann's emphasis on the necessity of challenging power structures, though Sölle's focus is explicitly tied to direct political engagement and resistance.

Jacques Ellul critiques the overwhelming reliance on technology in modern society, arguing that it dehumanizes individuals by subordinating them to a system driven by efficiency and control. He contends that the increasing dominance of technological systems leads to a society where human actions and values are shaped entirely by technique, often to the detriment of individuality and humanity.[359] This view aligns with Walter Brueggemann's critique of power structures but places particular emphasis on how technology contributes to societal control and alienation.

Ellul explores how the application of method to various phenomena, such as economics, creates a system in which technique becomes the organizing principle of society. He explains that the transition from doctrine to technique represents a critical shift where methods of control replace more human-centered approaches.[360] This critique of the technicalization of all aspects of life echoes Brueggemann's concern for the ways in which dominant ideologies shape societal norms, though Ellul focuses on technology as a key driver of these shifts.

Ellul acknowledges that many of the problems he identifies—such as the alienation caused by technological systems—have no easy solutions. He explains that his work is not prescriptive but rather an analysis of how these systems have developed and taken root in modern society.[361] This

357. Sölle, *Suffering*, 75.
358. Sölle, *Suffering*, 168.
359. Ellul, *Technological Society*, xxx, vol. 10.
360. Ellul, *Technological Society*, 161.
361. Ellul, *Technological Society*, xxviii.

reflective approach is similar to Brueggemann's emphasis on the need for theological reflection to address societal issues, though Ellul's focus remains on the pervasive influence of technology.

In critiquing the integration of natural and human processes into technological systems, Ellul points out that techniques, rather than eliminating natural elements, incorporate and control them, turning them into components of a larger, more rationalized system.[362] This mirrors Brueggemann's understanding of how dominant power structures seek to absorb and neutralize any elements that could challenge their control, though Ellul applies this specifically to the integration of human and natural systems into the technological order.

Ellul describes how modern cities, driven by technological imperatives, have eradicated the natural rhythms of day and night, heat and cold, and replaced them with an artificial environment characterized by overpopulation, media saturation, and a sense of purposelessness.[363] This critique parallels Brueggemann's concerns about the ways in which societal structures can suppress human creativity and community, though Ellul's focus is on the physical and psychological effects of a technologically dominated society.

Ellul further argues that primitive techniques were merely intermediaries between humans and their environment, allowing for individual and subjective experiences. However, modern technique, by contrast, eliminates subjectivity and individual differences, creating a uniform system of control that governs human interactions with the world.[364] This resonates with Brueggemann's critique of how societal systems can strip away the uniqueness of individual and communal experiences in favor of uniformity and control.

In summarizing his argument, Ellul notes that the terrifying reality of modern technological society is often too overwhelming for individuals to confront. As a result, many people adopt an attitude of denial or distraction, ignoring the ways in which technological systems shape their lives and limit their freedom.[365] This sense of denial is comparable to Brueggemann's description of the numbing effects of societal power structures, though Ellul emphasizes the specific role of technology in this process.

362. Ellul, *Technological Society*, 217.
363. Ellul, *Technological Society*, 429.
364. Ellul, *Technological Society*, 63.
365. Ellul, *Technological Society*, 149.

CHAPTER THREE

John Howard Yoder's theology emphasizes the nonviolent ethic of Jesus, positioning pacifism as central to Christian practice. Yoder argues that the teachings of Jesus, particularly those related to peace and resistance to violence, should shape how Christians engage with the world. This aligns with Brueggemann's focus on justice and societal transformation but places nonviolence as the primary means of addressing injustice.[366]

In discussing the challenges pacifism faces in modern times, Yoder notes that nonviolence is often viewed with skepticism, especially because it seems to contradict the more practical approaches of contemporary democratic humanism. Yoder acknowledges that some pacifists, such as the Jehovah's Witnesses, hold an extreme view, but he insists that nonviolence is deeply rooted in the biblical tradition and the teachings of the early church.[367]

Yoder also addresses how the Gospels consistently reflect the same nonviolent message, regardless of which Gospel is studied. He argues that the message of peace and resistance to violence is not limited to one interpretation or one Gospel writer but is a common thread throughout all of the Gospels.[368] This consistency reinforces his view that nonviolence is not a peripheral teaching but a core part of Jesus' message.

Additionally, Yoder notes that recent scholarship, particularly in the field of biblical studies, has further emphasized the importance of understanding Jesus' teachings on nonviolence. For instance, Robert Sloan's work on Luke's eschatology highlights how Jesus' message is as much about societal transformation as it is about personal faithfulness.[369] This suggests that the teachings of Jesus were meant to have a tangible impact on how individuals and communities engage with systems of power and violence.

Yoder's pacifism also draws from the idea that personal faithfulness should not be separated from social responsibility. He contends that being faithful to Jesus' teachings on peace necessarily involves challenging systems of violence and injustice in the world. Some pacifists, Yoder explains, have argued that personal faithfulness is more

---

366. Yoder, *Politics of Jesus*, 19.
367. Yoder, *Politics of Jesus*, 195.
368. Yoder, *Politics of Jesus*, 54.
369. Yoder, *Politics of Jesus*, 72.

important than broader societal obligations, but he believes that the two are interconnected.[370]

In conclusion, Yoder's theology centers on the conviction that non-violence is not only a personal ethic but a framework for engaging with societal issues. His work builds on the biblical foundations of peace and challenges Christians to actively resist violence in all its forms, drawing a strong parallel with Brueggemann's concern for justice, but with an emphasis on peace as the fundamental Christian response to injustice.

Conclusively, Walter Brueggemann's theological framework, which emphasizes the role of prophetic imagination, underscores the need for society to confront oppression by telling stories of suffering. This act of narrating grief, as seen in the biblical texts, is vital in bringing attention to injustice and calling for transformation. Brueggemann's view challenges individuals and communities to recognize how faith can critique and dismantle systems of power, offering a vision of a just and compassionate society.

Similarly, James Cone's Black theology operates within a framework that focuses on the liberation of oppressed communities. Cone argues that theology must actively engage with the lived experiences of marginalized people, emphasizing that the struggle for justice is central to faith. Both Cone and Brueggemann see the telling of these stories—whether through biblical narratives or contemporary experiences—as essential to promoting societal change and addressing systemic injustice.

Jon Sobrino's theology adds another dimension by insisting on the importance of praxis—putting faith into action in solidarity with the poor. His understanding of Christology, grounded in the historical life of Jesus, aligns with Brueggemann's call for transformation through active engagement with the world. Sobrino's emphasis on praxis complements the larger conversation on the intersection of theology and social justice, reinforcing the idea that faith must be lived out in the pursuit of justice.

3.5.2. Theology and Justice in Modern Thought

This section examines the theological perspectives of several influential scholars, each of whom brings a unique approach to interpreting scripture and addressing contemporary social and theological issues. These scholars, including Herman Waetjen, Catherine Keller, John Caputo,

---

370. Yoder, *Politics of Jesus*, 210.

Mark C. Taylor, Peter Rollins, Serene Jones, and Richard Kearney, engage with a wide range of theological frameworks, from dialectical and poststructuralist methods to weak theology and feminist trauma theory. By focusing on the interplay between historical context, socio-political critique, and the need for theological engagement with modern realities, they offer ways to reconsider how theology interacts with societal challenges.

Central to their approaches is the rejection of rigid and static interpretations of faith. Waetjen's dialectical method, for instance, emphasizes the dynamic relationship between the biblical text and social justice, while Keller's apophatic theology highlights the importance of relationality and interconnectedness. Caputo and Rollins explore the concept of divine weakness and the problem of certainty, pushing for a more open and flexible understanding of faith. Meanwhile, Taylor and Kearney delve into the philosophical and postmodern dimensions of theology, arguing for new spiritualities that transcend traditional theistic frameworks.

As these thinkers challenge conventional theological models, their work invites a reconsideration of how religious thought can engage with pressing issues such as justice, power, trauma, and uncertainty. By deconstructing established structures and promoting relational, dynamic perspectives, they provide frameworks for addressing contemporary concerns while remaining rooted in theological tradition. This section will explore these approaches and their potential implications for modern theology and society.

Herman Waetjen's theological approach to interpreting the Bible is rooted in a dialectical method that emphasizes the dynamic interaction between historical context and contemporary relevance. His analysis often focuses on the socio-political dimensions of the biblical text, particularly highlighting the systemic injustices of the time. In his view, the exploitation of the lower classes by the governing aristocracy during Jesus' time serves as a crucial backdrop to understanding Jesus' public ministry and the transformative potential of the Kingdom of God.[371]

Waetjen also argues that the gospel narratives are shaped by specific rhetorical structures, designed to lead the reader toward a deeper understanding of both the historical setting and its implications for contemporary readers. The use of an omniscient narrator, as employed by the evangelist, serves as a key rhetorical tool in guiding the reader through

---

371. Waetjen, *Reordering of Power*, 12.

these layered meanings, presenting the text as a continuous unfolding of theological and political realities.[372]

The socio-political values that permeated Jesus' society were challenged and ultimately dismantled by his actions and teachings. Waetjen emphasizes that Jesus' submission to these social and moral orders was not passive but part of a broader redemptive process. Jesus' engagement with these systems represented a confrontation with the established structures of power, leading to the eventual establishment of God's rule, which is fundamentally different from the oppressive regimes of the time.[373]

In Waetjen's interpretation, the Kingdom of God is portrayed as a radical reordering of power and societal values, where the old order is abolished, and a new reality based on justice and compassion emerges. Jesus, as the New Human Being, precedes the establishment of this divine order, challenging Jewish millennial expectations and introducing a new understanding of divine rule that transcends traditional power structures.[374]

Through the lens of biblical narrative, Waetjen interprets Jesus' experience of nothingness and chaos as symbolic of the dismantling of oppressive power. This chaotic wilderness experience mirrors the confrontation with the old social order and signals the beginning of a new creation, rooted in justice and equality. The narrative of Jesus' life and ministry thus serves as a blueprint for the dismantling of unjust structures and the establishment of a new social reality grounded in the ethics of the Kingdom of God.[375]

Waetjen's work also highlights the role of John the Baptist in preparing the way for Jesus. He draws connections between John and Elijah, while pointing out the complex and sometimes ambiguous nature of their identities. This exploration of John's role further supports Waetjen's interpretation of the gospel narratives as deeply engaged with social and political critique, preparing the groundwork for Jesus' transformative ministry.[376]

In discussing Jesus' interactions with his disciples, Waetjen emphasizes the socio-economic realities of the time, noting the disciples' humble backgrounds as fishermen who lived on the margins of society.

372. Waetjen, *Reordering of Power*, 17.
373. Waetjen, *Reordering of Power*, 68.
374. Waetjen, *Reordering of Power*, 74, 71.
375. Waetjen, *Reordering of Power*, 74, 76.
376. Waetjen, *Reordering of Power*, 76, 77.

Their response to Jesus' call exemplifies the radical nature of the Kingdom of God, where those on the periphery are invited to participate in the dismantling of oppressive structures and the creation of a new social order.[377]

Through this framework, Waetjen invites readers to consider how the biblical text speaks to contemporary issues of justice and oppression. His dialectical method bridges the gap between the ancient context and the present, offering a compelling model for engaging with scripture as a source of inspiration for social and political change.[378]

Catherine Keller's exploration of apophatic theology centers on the concept of relationality and interconnectedness, proposing that theological inquiry is not about rigid boundaries but rather dynamic folds and entanglements that shape both divine and human realities. She describes these "folds" as spaces where relational dynamics replace traditional boundaries, leading to a more intricate understanding of reality. This relational aspect, according to Keller, underscores how creatures interact, influencing one another in ways that are not easily categorized but are instead continuously forming and reforming.[379]

Keller is aware of how apophatic theology, which embraces the idea of "not knowing," challenges conventional discourse, particularly in light of pressing issues like global warming. She argues that even as environmental crises become more urgent, they remain difficult to fully articulate, especially within the realm of theological discussion. This tension between what can and cannot be expressed is central to Keller's framework, as she emphasizes that theology must engage with these unspeakable challenges.[380]

Her understanding of apophatic theology also ties into the cosmos of relational ontology, where the unknown and unknowable aspects of existence are held in tension with the lived reality of human and non-human creatures. Keller suggests that this space of "not knowing" offers opportunities for new forms of expression and understanding, especially in theological contexts that are open to revisiting old ideas with fresh perspectives.[381]

---

377. Waetjen, *Reordering of Power*, 79, 23.
378. Waetjen, *Reordering of Power*, 30.
379. Keller, *Cloud of the Impossible*, 24.
380. Keller, *Cloud of the Impossible*, 25.
381. Keller, *Cloud of the Impossible*, 30–31.

Keller critiques the traditional reluctance to engage with apophatic mysticism or deconstruction, noting that in the late twentieth century, many theologians focusing on subjugated or marginalized knowledge systems overlooked the potential of apophatic approaches. However, Keller's approach emphasizes that embracing non-knowing can open up new avenues for theological and philosophical thought, especially in the context of relationality.[382]

Through her ecological and political theology, Keller highlights how creatures are intricately entangled with each other, not only on a physical level but also in the broader, relational web of existence. This idea of interconnectedness challenges individualistic or isolated views of creation, instead presenting a more integrated and holistic understanding of the universe.[383]

In Keller's framework, the theological concept of "not knowing" is not a barrier to understanding but a necessary space for allowing new relationalities and possibilities to emerge. She argues that by embracing uncertainty, theology can make room for a deeper engagement with the complexities of existence, particularly in the face of ecological and social challenges.[384] Through this approach, Keller calls for a reconsideration of traditional theological constructs, advocating for a theology that is fluid, relational, and continuously evolving in response to the world's changing realities.

John Caputo's work in The Weakness of God emphasizes the idea that weak theology does not diminish theological concepts but rather magnifies their full potential by releasing them from rigid structures. He describes weak theology as a "hyper-realism of the event," where the focus shifts from literal interpretations to a more dynamic understanding of divine action. This framework invites individuals to experience God not through overwhelming power but through a gentle, persistent call to justice.[385]

Caputo further explains that weak theology breaks down traditional distinctions, such as those between believers and non-believers or theists and atheists. He suggests that everyone is equally exposed to the call of God, regardless of their specific theological stance. In this context, he views theology as a collective experience in which people are invited

---

382. Keller, Cloud of the Impossible, 33.
383. Keller, Cloud of the Impossible, 24.
384. Keller, Cloud of the Impossible, 49.
385. Caputo, Weakness of God, 18.

to respond to the event of God, rather than being forced to adhere to dogmatic categories.[386]

In discussing the kingdom of God, Caputo portrays it as a kingdom without sovereignty or control, where the strong are made weak, and the weak are made strong. This vision stands in stark contrast to typical notions of divine rule. Rather than relying on power and might, the kingdom of God, as Caputo describes it, thrives on reversals and paradoxes, challenging conventional ideas of authority and strength.[387]

Caputo further develops the idea that the kingdom of God is ruled by "the weak and foolish," echoing Derrida's concept of sans—a form of being where weakness is maintained to prevent the full force of power from being unleashed. In this kingdom, the emphasis is on maintaining a weak force, one that does not overpower but instead sustains a form of radical openness and hospitality.[388]

Caputo's description of the kingdom highlights the provocative and transformative weakness of God. He clarifies that this is not a passive weakness but one capable of unsettling the powerful and uplifting the powerless. According to Caputo, the kingdom of God manifests whenever the mighty are brought low and the weak are elevated, demonstrating a divine reversal of worldly values.[389]

He also discusses the "power of powerlessness" as the true force of the kingdom. This power is not about domination or control but about softening hardened hearts and keeping hope alive in the face of despair. It is a power that sustains life when the world seems hopeless, offering a vision of something "otherwise" than the world's current state.[390]

Caputo presents the weakness of God as an ongoing theme, contrasting it with more traditional theological models, such as those offered by Thomas Aquinas. He argues that while Aquinas presents a stronger and more structured theology, his own focus on the weakness of God allows for a more fluid and open understanding of divine interaction with the world.[391]

In his exploration of forgiveness, Caputo returns to the theme of divine powerlessness, questioning what it means to be saved when the

386. Caputo, *Weakness of God*, 20.
387. Caputo, *Weakness of God*, 24.
388. Caputo, *Weakness of God*, 27.
389. Caputo, *Weakness of God*, 14.
390. Caputo, *Weakness of God*, 16.
391. Caputo, *Weakness of God*, 17.

concept of salvation is stripped of traditional notions of strength and control. He suggests that salvation in weak theology is more about embracing vulnerability and openness to transformation than adhering to rigid formulas of redemption.[392]

Through his discussion of powerlessness, Caputo challenges the idea that power must always be about force. Instead, he presents a theology where the power of powerlessness reigns, and the condition for true divine power is that it lacks the coercive force often associated with sovereignty.[393]

Finally, Caputo critiques the traditional narrative of power in theology, especially the notion of an omnipotent God who exerts control from on high. He argues that such narratives align too closely with imperial models of power and fail to capture the true nature of divine interaction, which he believes is marked by radical uncertainty and openness to risk.[394]

Mark C. Taylor engages deeply with the intersection of theology and poststructuralism, particularly focusing on how religion continues to shape culture and thought in ways that transcend traditional frameworks. In After God, Taylor observes that the study of religion has become entangled with broader theoretical movements, particularly structuralism and poststructuralism. These approaches have redefined how religion is understood across disciplines, expanding the lens through which scholars view theological structures and patterns.[395]

Taylor explains that poststructuralist thought, in particular, aims to reveal the instability and incompleteness of foundational structures. By destabilizing rigid categories, this mode of thinking opens up new possibilities for religious critique and reinterpretation. Taylor sees this as a critical task for theology in an era where old certainties no longer hold sway.[396]

While acknowledging the valuable contributions of structuralism and poststructuralism, Taylor critiques their limitations. He points out that structuralists, while adept at identifying patterns, struggle to explain how these structures evolve over time. Poststructuralists, on the other hand, challenge these fixed patterns but often leave the question of what

---

392. Caputo, *Weakness of God*, 19.
393. Caputo, *Weakness of God*, 26.
394. Caputo, *Weakness of God*, 59–60.
395. Taylor, *After God*, 7.
396. Taylor, *After God*, 10.

comes next unanswered. Taylor encourages moving beyond both paradigms to imagine new forms of religious and philosophical thought that engage with contemporary issues.[397]

In his exploration of modern philosophical and religious ideas, Taylor draws connections between historical figures such as Nietzsche, Kierkegaard, and Hegel, suggesting that these thinkers laid the groundwork for much of the postmodern critique of traditional religious structures. Taylor emphasizes how their work, particularly their rejection of essentialism and naturalism, continues to inform contemporary theological debate.[398]

Taylor's work is also situated in the context of revolutionary movements, such as the French Revolution, which he describes as a world-historical event that influenced modern thought. He highlights how philosophers like Hegel viewed such revolutions as catalysts for rethinking society, politics, and religion. This revolutionary spirit is reflected in Taylor's own call for a reimagining of religion that breaks from traditional theistic views.[399]

Throughout After God, Taylor is clear that his approach to religion is not about preserving the past but about reconfiguring spiritual thought in a way that addresses contemporary concerns. He critiques the focus on divine omnipotence in traditional Christianity and advocates for a new form of religious understanding that embraces uncertainty and fluidity, much like the poststructuralist frameworks he engages with.[400]

Taylor is careful to situate his arguments within a broader historical context, drawing connections between the theological shifts initiated by figures like Martin Luther and the broader cultural changes that followed. He argues that Luther's revolution extended beyond religion into politics and economics, and similarly, Taylor's vision for postmodern theology seeks to influence all areas of life by rethinking the role of religion in a rapidly changing world.[401]

Peter Rollins' theology critically examines how modern Christianity often turns the desire for certainty into a form of idolatry. He explains that much like the concept of Original Sin, this desire stems from a perceived gap or sense of separation, which leads people to create and cling

397. Taylor, *After God*, 12.
398. Taylor, *After God*, 60.
399. Taylor, *After God*, 85.
400. Taylor, *After God*, xviii.
401. Taylor, *After God*, xvi.

to idols—whether material or ideological—that they believe will fill that void.[402] Rollins emphasizes that idolatry is not based on the inherent qualities of an object but on the projected value individuals place upon it.[403]

Rollins goes further to argue that this idolatrous tendency affects how people view God. Rather than experiencing faith as an embrace of uncertainty, many reduce God to a product that promises to complete them, turning the divine into a mere tool for personal satisfaction. This, according to Rollins, distorts the original message of Christianity and turns it into a pursuit of an unattainable idol.[404]

For Rollins, the creation of an idol is not simply a result of human separation (as in Original Sin), but also requires the presence of a prohibition, like the law, which creates the idea of something forbidden that promises ultimate fulfillment. This dynamic begins at infancy, when humans first experience separation from their mothers, setting in motion the lifelong search for wholeness through idols.[405]

Rollins critiques this cycle, particularly how it manifests in religious practice, by discussing the symbolism of the crucifixion. He interprets the tearing of the Temple curtain at the moment of Jesus' death as a representation of the breaking down of barriers between people and God. In this sense, the crucifixion signifies the rejection of systems that promise fulfillment through idols, offering instead a life freed from such obsessions.[406]

Ultimately, Rollins frames the crucifixion as a sacrifice of sacrifice itself, challenging the conventional view of it as merely a transactional act of atonement. He suggests that the crucifixion breaks the human drive to find completeness through idols and invites people into a new form of life that embraces doubt and uncertainty.[407]

By engaging with these themes, Rollins provides a radical critique of contemporary faith practices, urging Christians to move away from idolizing certainty and instead embrace the uncertainties inherent in the human experience of faith. However, critics argue that his emphasis on

---

402. Rollins, *Idolatry of God*, 25.
403. Rollins, *Idolatry of God*, 26.
404. Rollins, *Idolatry of God*, 27.
405. Rollins, *Idolatry of God*, 30.
406. Rollins, *Idolatry of God*, 91.
407. Rollins, *Idolatry of God*, 94.

doubt and the deconstruction of traditional religious frameworks may lead to an overly negative or nihilistic outlook on faith.[408]

Serene Jones, in Trauma and Grace, brings together feminist trauma theory and systematic theology to address the often-silenced experiences of reproductive loss. She points out that this silence surrounding reproductive loss, a trauma shared by many women, reflects a broader societal discomfort with such experiences. By engaging feminist trauma theory, she seeks to better understand why this painful silence exists and to identify theological resources that can respond to the deep wounds it causes.[409]

Jones defines reproductive loss as a complex and deeply personal form of grief, particularly for women. She highlights that this loss includes miscarriage and stillbirth, and often affects women in ways shaped by both their embodied experiences and societal expectations. Her work emphasizes that the grief related to reproductive loss is not solely an individual experience but is always mediated by cultural contexts, which can both shape and amplify the pain.[410]

Within this framework, Jones turns to systematic theology to explore how these experiences might be addressed theologically. She contends that theology has the potential to provide a grace-filled response to trauma, particularly through the concept of prevenient grace. This form of grace, which is unearned and arrives unexpectedly, can break into moments of deep suffering, offering more than just comfort—it provides the possibility of renewal and transformation.[411]

Jones also draws connections between individual and collective trauma, weaving these themes throughout her analysis. She suggests that theology's role is to address not only grand narratives of redemption but also the more personal and imaginative aspects of healing. Rather than focusing solely on doctrinal resolutions, she argues that healing often comes through shifts in habits of heart and imagination, where individuals can reimagine their experiences in light of grace.[412]

Her work on reproductive loss, while offering a deep theological reflection on suffering and grace, has been critiqued for leaning heavily into psychological frameworks. Some argue that this focus might

408. Rollins, *Idolatry of God*, 97.
409. Jones, *Trauma and Grace*, 128–29.
410. Jones, *Trauma and Grace*, 130–32.
411. Jones, *Trauma and Grace*, 122–24.
412. Jones, *Trauma and Grace*, xii–xiv

overshadow more traditional theological approaches, raising questions about the balance between psychology and theology in addressing human suffering.[413] However, Jones continues to emphasize that theology's engagement with trauma can open up spaces for healing that might otherwise remain inaccessible.

Richard Kearney's work in Anatheism explores the complex interplay between atheism and theism, proposing a new framework that moves beyond both extremes. He introduces anatheism as a return to God after the death of God, one that rejects both the rigid certainties of theism and atheism. Kearney clarifies that anatheism differs from dogmatic atheism because it resists absolute positions regarding the divine, advocating instead for a more fluid understanding that welcomes doubt and uncertainty.[414]

Kearney underscores the importance of engaging with atheism critically, suggesting that only by acknowledging the potential dangers of religion—highlighted by atheistic critiques—can one truly embrace a more open form of faith. He describes atheism not as a final rejection of God, but as a moment of estrangement necessary for rediscovering faith. This approach encourages a kind of religious openness, where doubt becomes a productive force rather than a barrier to belief.[415]

At the heart of anatheism is the idea of an ongoing tension between faith and doubt, belief and unbelief. Kearney celebrates this tension, viewing it as a space for religious renewal. He uses the metaphor of "Siamese twins" to describe the relationship between theism and atheism, suggesting that both are intertwined in a way that makes it impossible to fully separate them. This relationship, for Kearney, is essential for fostering a faith that is dynamic and responsive to the complexities of human existence.[416]

In his discussion of the Holocaust, Kearney reflects on the deep anxieties that modernity has brought regarding belief and non-belief. Drawing on Hannah Arendt's concept of the "banality of evil," he argues that both belief and unbelief are grounded in doubt. This leads him to propose that anatheism, as a return to God through doubt, provides a

---

413. Jones, *Trauma and Grace*, 128–32.
414. Kearney, *Anatheism*, 16.
415. Kearney, *Anatheism*, 39.
416. Kearney, *Anatheism*, 56.

way to confront the uncertainties of modern existence without resorting to the absolutes of traditional theism or atheism.[417]

Kearney also engages with phenomenology, particularly through the works of Merleau-Ponty, to explore the embodied nature of religious experience. He discusses the "phenomenology of flesh" as a way to bridge the gap between the material and spiritual, arguing that the divine encounter happens through the everyday experiences of the body. This sacramental understanding of flesh helps to ground his concept of anatheism in the tangible realities of human life.[418]

Critics of Kearney's work often point out that his approach, while intellectually stimulating, risks alienating those who are not well-versed in the philosophical language he employs. The heavy reliance on postmodern theory and phenomenology can make his ideas seem distant from more traditional theological frameworks, which might make them less accessible to a broader audience.[419] Nonetheless, Kearney's anatheism offers a fresh way of thinking about the divine, one that embraces uncertainty and the unknown as essential aspects of faith.

Conclusively, the diverse theological frameworks discussed in this section reveal a consistent focus on challenging traditional structures of power, belief, and societal norms. Waetjen's dialectical approach to biblical interpretation emphasizes the socio-political dimensions of scripture, encouraging readers to engage with the text as a tool for understanding and addressing contemporary injustices. His view that the Kingdom of God represents a radical reordering of societal values highlights the relevance of scripture in critiquing oppressive systems and imagining new possibilities for justice and compassion.

Similarly, Keller and Caputo explore theological perspectives that challenge established norms, focusing on the relational and uncertain nature of divine encounters. Keller's emphasis on apophatic theology, with its focus on "not knowing" and relationality, provides a framework that moves beyond rigid boundaries and invites a dynamic engagement with the complexities of existence. Caputo's concept of weak theology further deconstructs traditional notions of divine power, proposing that true divine interaction lies in vulnerability and openness rather than in control and sovereignty. Both approaches encourage a reconsideration of how theology engages with issues of power and justice.

417. Kearney, *Anatheism*, 59.
418. Kearney, *Anatheism*, 87.
419. Kearney, *Anatheism*.

Finally, thinkers like Rollins and Kearney push the boundaries of traditional religious thought by advocating for a deeper engagement with doubt, uncertainty, and deconstruction. Rollins critiques the idolization of certainty within Christianity, while Kearney's concept of anatheism invites a return to God through doubt, suggesting that faith and uncertainty are inextricably linked. These perspectives offer valuable frameworks for understanding the evolving role of theology in addressing contemporary issues, particularly by embracing complexity and resisting simplistic or absolute answers.

3.6. APPROACHING HUMAN RIGHTS IN NORTH KOREA

The Kingdom of God serves as a meaningful framework for addressing human rights in North Korea by blending theological, political, and philosophical perspectives. This concept emphasizes that the Kingdom is not just a future promise but a present challenge to combat injustice, oppression, and inequality in all aspects of life. By adopting this approach, we can consider how theology informs the pursuit of justice within the context of North Korea's authoritarian regime.

Scholars like Cornel West, Judith Butler, and Slavoj Žižek offer relevant perspectives for understanding power dynamics, human rights, and the treatment of vulnerable populations. West critiques global systems that perpetuate inequality, while Butler highlights the importance of shared vulnerability in building a global solidarity that genuinely protects marginalized lives. Žižek, on the other hand, critiques traditional human rights frameworks, calling for more radical approaches that address the underlying power structures which sustain regimes like North Korea's.

Additionally, thinkers such as Amartya Sen, Martha Nussbaum, and Giorgio Agamben provide further depth to this conversation. Sen's focus on real freedoms and capabilities, rather than just legal rights, helps frame the human rights violations in North Korea in terms of denied opportunities and basic life conditions. Nussbaum extends this with a focus on essential human capabilities, while Agamben's analysis of how states manipulate legal frameworks to justify oppression is particularly useful for understanding the situation in North Korea. Together, these perspectives offer a more comprehensive approach to addressing human rights abuses through the lens of the Kingdom of God.

CHAPTER THREE

The concept of the Kingdom of God as a framework for addressing human rights issues in North Korea calls for an integration of theological, political, and philosophical approaches. Central to this theological vision is the understanding that the Kingdom of God is not just a future reality, but a present call to challenge injustice, oppression, and inequality in every social, political, and economic system. Scholars such as Cornel West, Judith Butler, Slavoj Žižek, Amartya Sen, Martha Nussbaum, and Giorgio Agamben provide crucial perspectives that engage the intersection of power, rights, and human dignity in contemporary discourse.[420]

Cornel West critiques neoliberal structures, highlighting their role in perpetuating poverty and racial inequality. West calls for a radical restructuring of both national and global systems that sustain inequality. His work is particularly relevant in the context of North Korea, where human rights violations are maintained through state-controlled mechanisms that suppress any form of dissent and limit the capacity of individuals to express their dignity.[421] By drawing attention to these oppressive systems, West advocates for a justice that prioritizes the marginalized and critiques the complicity of global powers in maintaining these injustices.

Judith Butler's exploration of vulnerability provides another significant lens through which to view the situation in North Korea. Butler contends that all human lives are interconnected, and that vulnerability should be the foundation of human rights discourses. By centering the recognition of shared vulnerability, Butler's approach calls for an ethical response that acknowledges the humanity of North Korea's marginalized populations, urging for international solidarity that is more than just a formal acknowledgment of rights but a genuine commitment to recognizing and protecting vulnerable lives.[422]

Slavoj Žižek challenges the liberal understanding of human rights, arguing that the traditional frameworks often reinforce the same structures of power they claim to dismantle. Žižek's critique is essential for understanding how state power in North Korea manipulates human rights narratives to justify its authoritarian control while maintaining the illusion of reform. His work calls for more radical approaches to dismantling these systems and creating a space for genuine liberation, which requires

---

420. Butler, *Precarious Life*; Sen, *Development as Freedom*; Nussbaum, *Creating Capabilities*; West, *Democracy Matters*; Žižek, *In Defense of Lost Causes*; Agamben, *State of Exception*.

421. West, *Democracy Matters*.

422. Butler, *Precarious Life*.

international efforts that go beyond superficial reforms and address the underlying power structures.[423]

Amartya Sen's capability approach is central to understanding human rights in North Korea. Sen argues that rights are not just legal entitlements but are tied to the real freedoms people have to live the lives they value. In North Korea, where basic capabilities such as access to education, healthcare, and freedom of expression are severely limited, Sen's framework highlights the urgency of addressing the structural conditions that deny individuals the ability to exercise their rights meaningfully.[424] This focus on capabilities rather than formal rights adds a crucial dimension to the theological discourse on justice and human dignity.

Martha Nussbaum builds on Sen's capability approach by outlining specific capabilities that are essential for human flourishing, such as bodily integrity, emotional health, and the ability to form meaningful relationships. These capabilities are systematically denied to large segments of the North Korean population through state control and repression. Nussbaum's work underscores the necessity of addressing not only political and civil rights but also the broader dimensions of human dignity that are neglected in authoritarian regimes.[425]

Giorgio Agamben's concept of the "state of exception" offers a powerful tool for analyzing the ways in which the North Korean government suspends normal legal protections to justify human rights abuses. Agamben's framework is especially pertinent in understanding how authoritarian regimes, including North Korea, manipulate legal norms to exclude certain populations from protection, thereby enabling gross violations of human rights under the guise of national security or state sovereignty.[426] This legal manipulation is a key area where international interventions must focus in advocating for systemic change in North Korea.

Beyond the immediate concerns of human rights, the theological conversation expands to include justice and care for creation, as seen in the works of Elisabeth Schüssler Fiorenza and Catherine Keller. Fiorenza's feminist theological critique, particularly her concept of kyriarchy, offers a way to analyze the multiple layers of oppression in North Korean society, including patriarchy, authoritarianism, and economic exploitation.

---

423. Žižek, *In Defense of Lost Causes*.
424. Sen, *Development as Freedom*.
425. Nussbaum, *Creating Capabilities*.
426. Agamben, *State of Exception*.

Her work invites a rethinking of liberation that considers the intersecting forms of domination that individuals in North Korea experience.[427]

Catherine Keller's process theology emphasizes relationality and the interconnectedness of all life, offering a broader ecological and social vision that challenges not only human exploitation but also environmental degradation. Keller's work is particularly relevant to North Korea, where environmental degradation exacerbates the suffering of the population. By framing justice in terms of relationality, Keller encourages a more comprehensive approach to addressing both human and environmental concerns.[428]

J. Kameron Carter's decolonial theology critiques the racial and national identities that authoritarian regimes manipulate to maintain power. In North Korea, where the regime constructs a rigid national identity to justify its control, Carter's framework offers a way to deconstruct these narratives and envision a more inclusive, liberating identity that transcends state-imposed categories.[429] This critique of nationalism is crucial for rethinking liberation theology in the context of North Korea.

In addition to addressing human and social justice, theologians like Birch and Cobb argue for an ecological model of justice that stresses the interdependence of all life forms. This model is particularly important in contexts like North Korea, where environmental degradation contributes to human suffering. Birch and Cobb's relational approach calls for a justice that integrates concern for both human and environmental well-being, a necessary component of any comprehensive liberation theology.[430]

Larry Rasmussen adds to this conversation by highlighting the ethical responsibility humans have toward the environment, particularly in the face of global ecological crises. Rasmussen's work emphasizes that ecological care is an integral part of justice, challenging both individuals and communities to rethink their role in contributing to environmental harm, especially in regions like North Korea where resource shortages and deforestation exacerbate human suffering.[431]

Stanley Hauerwas's focus on the Church as a countercultural community provides another dimension to the discussion of the Kingdom of God. Hauerwas argues that the Church must resist co-optation by the

---

427. Schüssler Fiorenza, *But She Said*.
428. Keller, *Face of the Deep*.
429. Carter, *Race*.
430. Birch and Cobb, *Liberation of Life*.
431. Rasmussen, *Earth-Honoring Faith*.

state and instead embody the values of the Kingdom through radical discipleship and communal solidarity with the poor. This call to countercultural living challenges Christians to critique systems of power, such as those present in North Korea, that perpetuate oppression and injustice.[432]

Shane Claiborne's advocacy for radical discipleship rooted in simplicity and solidarity with the poor resonates with the call for systemic change in North Korea. Claiborne's vision of the Kingdom of God as a space of resistance to empire and consumerism aligns with the need for both international solidarity and local transformation in addressing the root causes of human rights abuses.[433] His approach emphasizes the importance of living out the values of the Kingdom in everyday life, challenging believers to reject the complicity of consumerism and militarism.

Ched Myers frames the Kingdom of God as a force of resistance against imperial structures, offering a framework for understanding how liberation theology can confront the authoritarian regime in North Korea. Myers' emphasis on nonviolent resistance and grassroots movements is particularly relevant in contexts where state power seeks to suppress dissent and maintain control through violence and coercion.[434] His vision calls for a transformation that starts with local communities and expands outward, challenging both political and religious systems that perpetuate oppression.

Sallie McFague brings ecological responsibility into the conversation, emphasizing that the Kingdom of God must include care for creation. McFague's work challenges Christians to rethink their relationship with the environment, especially in contexts where environmental degradation directly affects human dignity, as in North Korea.[435] By integrating ecological concerns with social justice, McFague offers a holistic vision of the Kingdom that addresses both human and environmental needs.

John D. Caputo adds a postmodern theological perspective, inviting a reimagining of the Kingdom of God as an event that disrupts traditional norms and power structures. Caputo's emphasis on the openness and unpredictability of the Kingdom encourages a more flexible, dynamic approach to justice that can respond to the complexities of modern global

---

432. Hauerwas, *Community of Character*.
433. Claiborne, *Irresistible Revolution*.
434. Myers, *Binding the Strong Man*.
435. McFague, *New Climate for Theology*.

issues, including those in North Korea.[436] His postmodern framework challenges the rigidity of both state and religious systems, offering a new way of thinking about liberation.

Conclusively, the integration of theological, political, and philosophical frameworks offers a comprehensive approach to addressing human rights issues in North Korea. Scholars like Cornel West, Judith Butler, and Amartya Sen provide perspectives that critique the structures of power, vulnerability, and capability, encouraging a focus on human dignity in the face of authoritarian control. Their emphasis on justice and human rights brings attention to the need for systemic reform in North Korea's oppressive regime, urging a reevaluation of global complicity in sustaining these injustices.

Additionally, theological contributions from scholars such as Catherine Keller, J. Kameron Carter, and Birch and Cobb broaden the discourse to include ecological and social dimensions of justice. By focusing on relationality and interconnectedness, these thinkers offer a more inclusive understanding of justice that addresses not only human exploitation but also environmental degradation. This expanded framework is crucial for considering the full scope of suffering in North Korea and calls for a holistic response that includes both social and ecological reform.

Finally, the work of theologians like Stanley Hauerwas, Shane Claiborne, and Ched Myers highlights the role of the Church as a countercultural force resisting systems of power and imperial structures. Their focus on radical discipleship, nonviolent resistance, and solidarity with the marginalized provides a model for how religious communities can actively participate in global movements for justice. This vision of the Kingdom of God as a transformative force challenges both political and religious systems to promote liberation and dignity for all.

---

436. Caputo, *Weakness of God*.

CHAPTER FOUR

Conclusion:
A Framework for Sustainable Liberation

THIS SECTION EXPLORES A framework for sustainable liberation, integrating a diverse range of theological, ethical, and social perspectives to address contemporary forms of oppression and injustice. Liberation theology serves as the foundation for this approach, aiming to bridge theological reflection with active engagement in real-world issues. By focusing on liberation as both a personal and communal pursuit, this model offers a pathway to justice that is continually responsive to changing social, environmental, and political landscapes. Key thinkers across multiple disciplines contribute to this understanding, emphasizing that a truly liberative theology must be adaptable and grounded in practical application.

At the core of this framework is the collaborative nature of liberation. Figures like Franz Rosenzweig and Amartya Sen argue that liberation requires a combined commitment from both individuals and communities, underpinned by ethical responsibility and practical support systems. This perspective emphasizes that sustainable liberation cannot rely solely on personal transformation or isolated acts; rather, it demands structures that allow communities to thrive collectively. By incorporating social justice, ecological responsibility, and human rights, this approach ensures that liberation is both inclusive and comprehensive, addressing the interconnected needs of individuals and society as a whole.

Finally, this framework calls for an expanded view of theological education and religious engagement, encouraging communities to view their faith as a means to address systemic injustices. Liberation theology moves beyond doctrinal boundaries, advocating for a theology that actively confronts issues like economic inequality, environmental degradation, and racial injustice. By emphasizing education, community action, and an adaptable ethical framework, this approach equips future leaders with the tools to contribute meaningfully to social transformation, aligning their theological convictions with concrete efforts for justice. This comprehensive model presents liberation as an ongoing journey that incorporates spiritual values, practical commitments, and collective resilience.

4.1. FRANZ ROSENZWEIG AND THE COLLABORATIVE PATH TO LIBERATION

Franz Rosenzweig's approach to liberation envisions it as a collaborative journey, intertwining divine action with human responsibility. Rather than seeing liberation as a singular, historic event, he introduces the idea of an ongoing process that requires continuous human engagement and alignment with divine will. His concept of "Creation out of nothing" underscores this dynamic, suggesting that liberation must be regularly renewed, with communities adapting to evolving definitions of justice.[1] Rosenzweig's framework challenges static interpretations of doctrine and calls for a theology that remains responsive to real-world complexities, bridging the sacred and the secular in ways that unite belief with social action.

Scholars like Robert Gibbs and Steven Kepnes expand on Rosenzweig's vision, emphasizing that liberation emerges from shared efforts within communities rather than through isolated individual actions. This community-centered perspective frames ethical responsibility as collective, grounded in practices that create spaces for solidarity and shared values.[2] Benjamin Pollock, however, raises an important point of tension in Rosenzweig's model, questioning whether his emphasis on divine action might at times downplay the urgency of human agency in tackling pressing injustices.[3] This discussion invites readers to explore the balance between trusting in divine sovereignty and acting promptly in response to immediate needs for justice.

---

1. Ochs, *Another Reformation*.
2. Kepnes, *Jewish Liturgical Reasoning*; Gibbs, *Why Ethics?*
3. Pollock, *Franz Rosenzweig and the Systematic Task of Philosophy*.

Rosenzweig's model for liberation is deeply rooted in relational and social dimensions of justice, where historical memory and communal experiences are crucial. In seeing liberation as a journey, he highlights how traditions like Passover—a festival commemorating the Israelites' liberation from Egypt—anchor present-day struggles in a legacy of resilience and justice.[4] Such commemorative practices keep collective memory alive, reinforcing a commitment to justice that transcends generations and strengthens a community's identity and shared purpose. For Rosenzweig, this isn't just about individual responsibilities but about sustaining a cycle of collective renewal, where personal faith fuels broader communal transformation.

In Rosenzweig's theological view, he extends this collaborative vision to imagine a form of interfaith engagement that honors each community's unique identity. Rather than promoting supersessionism, or the belief that one tradition supersedes another, Rosenzweig advocates for mutual enrichment between faiths—particularly between Jewish and Christian traditions.[5] This commitment to interfaith solidarity allows diverse communities to join in the pursuit of justice without erasing their differences. Peter Ochs notes that Rosenzweig's stance on supersessionism opens doors for cooperative efforts across religious lines, where each tradition's unique values contribute to a shared goal of addressing social injustices.[6]

Leora Batnitzky delves into Rosenzweig's practical commitment to this collaborative vision. Following his publication of *The Star of Redemption*, Rosenzweig established the Freies Jüdisches Lehrhaus, a Jewish learning institute focused on making theological ideas accessible and actionable in everyday life.[7] For him, education was integral to liberation, equipping individuals with the knowledge and perspective to navigate both their spiritual heritage and contemporary socio-political challenges. This emphasis on education reflects Rosenzweig's belief in liberation as a process of personal growth and collective empowerment, where learning and adaptation are keys to meaningful engagement.

Steven Kepnes builds on this by highlighting the role of ritual and communal practices in Rosenzweig's vision of liberation. Observing the Sabbath, for example, or participating in shared liturgies, offers moments

---

4. Rosenzweig, *Star of Redemption*.
5. Ochs, *Another Reformation*.
6. Ochs, *Another Reformation*.
7. Batnitzky, *How Judaism Became a Religion*.

CHAPTER FOUR

of transcendence that reinforce community bonds and commitments to justice.[8] Rosenzweig viewed these rituals as not only spiritual practices but as expressions of an ethical framework, encouraging communities to maintain a focus on collective responsibility and continuous action against oppression. This communal focus adds a practical layer to his theological framework, connecting faith directly to lived experiences.

Gibbs further explores Rosenzweig's idea of ethical responsibility, describing it as an obligation that extends beyond the immediate community to encompass a universal commitment to justice. This broad ethical responsibility finds expression in Jewish practices like Yom Kippur, where accountability for the community's well-being is emphasized. Gibbs notes that Rosenzweig's view on ethics involves self-reflection, critical judgment, and an ongoing commitment to justice that transcends individual interest.[9] Here, Rosenzweig's model promotes a type of ethics that requires both personal and collective engagement in the fight against injustice.

Pollock's critique brings an important counterpoint to Rosenzweig's approach by questioning the potential limitations of emphasizing divine action in the liberation process. Pollock wonders whether this focus might inadvertently lessen the immediacy of human agency, especially in situations demanding swift responses to injustice.[10] This perspective invites a reexamination of Rosenzweig's balance between divine sovereignty and human responsibility, particularly when urgent action is needed to address systemic oppression. Pollock's critique adds a layer of complexity to the discussion, suggesting that while divine guidance is essential, human agency remains critical to affecting real change.

Ultimately, Rosenzweig's framework for liberation presents a comprehensive model that integrates divine action with human responsibility, historical memory with active engagement, and personal transformation with communal commitment. By encouraging continuous engagement with tradition, Rosenzweig promotes a theology that adapts to the evolving nature of justice. His vision positions liberation as a journey, where spiritual beliefs and practical actions come together in sustained efforts toward a more just world. Rosenzweig's collaborative model of liberation fosters a theological approach capable of addressing the systemic

8. Kepnes, *Jewish Liturgical Reasoning*.
9. Gibbs, Why Ethics?
10. Pollock, *Franz Rosenzweig and the Systematic Task of Philosophy*.

injustices of modern society while honoring the distinct contributions of each community involved in the journey.

4.2. EXPANDING LIBERATION THEOLOGY WITH INTERDISCIPLINARY INSIGHTS

Contemporary liberation theology has evolved, increasingly drawing on frameworks from ecological awareness, feminist critique, and postcolonial theory to address modern challenges that traditional theology often overlooks. This interdisciplinary approach opens new doors, enriching liberation theology's understanding of justice by recognizing connections across social, environmental, and economic issues. Figures like Miroslav Volf and Sarah Coakley emphasize the need to link action with reflection, advocating for a theology that directly responds to pressing social concerns.[11] Their approach sees the Kingdom of God not as a distant ideal but as a present, justice-driven effort that comes alive in community action and inclusive practices.

The theologians Stephen Graham and Willie James Jennings argue that theological inquiry should go beyond spiritual ideas to consider material realities, especially the community's role in promoting justice and equality.[12] By engaging with real-world issues, this broadened view encourages theologians to rethink traditional theological education, emphasizing a model grounded in praxis—where lived experience informs theological reflection and prioritizes marginalized voices.[13] In this way, liberation theology remains relevant, responding to the real-world challenges faced by marginalized groups.

Ecological justice has become a key component of liberation theology, especially through the work of Catherine Keller and M. Shawn Copeland. They argue that human liberation and ecological justice are intertwined and that recognizing and protecting the interconnectedness of life is essential to achieving true justice.[14] Their work challenges liberation theology to move beyond an anthropocentric view of liberation, instead advocating for a framework that includes all of creation. By expanding the concept of justice to include ecological health, liberation

---

11. Volf, *Public Faith;* Coakley, *God, Sexuality, and the Self.*
12. Graham, *Transforming Practice;* Jennings, *The Christian Imagination.*
13. Tanner, *Christ the Key.*
14. Keller, *Cloud of the Impossible;* Copeland, *Enfleshing Freedom.*

CHAPTER FOUR

theology supports sustainable practices that honor both human dignity and environmental integrity.

The contributions of feminist and postcolonial theologians, such as Kwok Pui-lan and Marcella Althaus-Reid, further shape liberation theology's inclusive framework. They highlight the intersections of oppression, particularly as experienced by marginalized groups, and call for a theology that embraces diverse voices historically excluded from theological discourse.[15] Recognizing these layers of oppression, liberation theology gains a broader perspective, addressing both systemic inequities and the specific, lived realities of marginalized communities. This approach brings a nuanced understanding of justice that tackles multiple forms of oppression and promotes inclusivity within the pursuit of liberation.

James Cone's contributions through Black liberation theology emphasize racial justice as central to the liberation movement. Cone critiques theological frameworks that ignore racial oppression, asserting that effective liberation theology must engage with the distinct experiences of racialized communities, particularly African Americans.[16] His work argues that a theology of liberation must include the unique histories and struggles of marginalized racial groups, placing their experiences at the core of theological reflection and activism. Cone's approach highlights the importance of centering racial justice within broader liberation efforts, affirming that racial equity is essential to any meaningful pursuit of justice.

John Cobb's eco-theological approach further enhances liberation theology's ecological focus, proposing that true liberation must address both environmental and human welfare.[17] He argues that environmental harm and social inequality are often linked, with marginalized communities disproportionately affected by ecological degradation. Cobb's framework expands the concept of liberation, advocating for sustainable practices that respect both human communities and the earth. This perspective aligns with liberation theology's mission by underscoring the inseparability of ecological and human justice.

Liberation theology also finds a practical ally in Paulo Freire's concept of praxis, which combines reflective thought with actionable change. Freire's educational model encourages communities to recognize

---

15. Kwok, *Postcolonial Imagination and Feminist Theology*; Althaus-Reid, *Indecent Theology*.

16. Cone, *Black Theology of Liberation*.

17. Cobb, *Process Theology as Political Theology*.

their power and challenge oppression through education and collective action.[18] This approach resonates with liberation theology's emphasis on active engagement, promoting a theology that not only reflects on injustice but also mobilizes communities to address it directly. Freire's model of praxis supports Rosenzweig's ideas of shared responsibility and the transformative potential of community-driven change.

Judith Butler's work on vulnerability and precarity adds another dimension to liberation theology by emphasizing the material conditions faced by marginalized groups. Butler highlights how precarious circumstances require urgent theological and social responses.[19] This perspective aligns with Freire's emphasis on praxis, suggesting that theological engagement should address immediate needs while also working toward lasting structural change. By focusing on vulnerability, Butler's approach reinforces the idea that liberation theology must be responsive to both survival needs and systemic injustices.

Amartya Sen's capabilities approach offers a practical lens through which liberation theology can redefine liberation in terms of real freedoms and the conditions that allow individuals and communities to thrive. Sen's model encourages liberation theology to move beyond abstract rights, advocating instead for tangible conditions that foster human flourishing.[20] This perspective dovetails with Rosenzweig's emphasis on communal responsibility, adding a pragmatic dimension to theological reflections on justice by prioritizing both spiritual and societal well-being.

Together, these interdisciplinary contributions expand liberation theology into a responsive model that addresses the complexities of contemporary oppression. By incorporating perspectives from ecology, feminism, and postcolonialism, liberation theology becomes a multifaceted framework capable of engaging with modern social, environmental, and economic issues. This interdisciplinary approach encourages a liberation theology that remains adaptable, addressing oppression in ways that support human dignity, social equity, and ecological sustainability. This inclusive model fosters a theology committed to holistic liberation—one that pursues personal growth, systemic justice, and communal well-being in a way that aligns with both divine and human values.

---

18. Freire, *Pedagogy of the Oppressed*.
19. Butler, *Precarious Life*.
20. Sen, *Development as Freedom*.

CHAPTER FOUR

4.3. A MULTIFACETED FRAMEWORK FOR ADDRESSING HUMAN RIGHTS ABUSES IN NORTH KOREA

Examining human rights abuses in North Korea requires a framework that goes beyond legal declarations, integrating ethical principles with the realities of authoritarian oppression. Thinkers like Cornel West, Judith Butler, Amartya Sen, Giorgio Agamben, Slavoj Žižek, Paulo Freire, Martha Nussbaum, and John Howard Yoder each offer perspectives that together form a powerful toolkit for addressing such complex abuses, where individual freedoms are crushed by state control.

Cornel West's work on justice critiques any system that sacrifices human dignity for institutional gain. In *Democracy Matters: Winning the Fight Against Imperialism*, West argues that justice must center human worth above institutional power. In North Korea, where the state prioritizes ideological loyalty over individual rights, his focus on dignity as the foundation of justice calls for frameworks that value people over authoritarian control.

Judith Butler's exploration of vulnerability in *Precarious Life: The Powers of Mourning and Violence* underscores the importance of protecting the most marginalized, particularly in repressive societies. In North Korea, where agency is limited and protections are scarce, her view on collective responsibility toward vulnerable populations is crucial. Butler's emphasis on interconnectedness suggests that a human rights framework in North Korea must actively defend those who cannot advocate for themselves.

Amartya Sen's *capabilities approach*, discussed in *Development as Freedom*, shifts the focus of human rights from legal entitlements to practical freedoms necessary for individuals to live meaningfully. In North Korea, where citizens lack access to education, healthcare, and personal choice, Sen's approach is a sharp reminder that justice demands real-life conditions that allow people to pursue autonomy and fulfillment, not just rights on paper.

Giorgio Agamben's idea of the "state of exception," laid out in *State of Exception*, explains how authoritarian regimes maintain control by manipulating legal norms to ensure absolute power. North Korea frequently suspends individual freedoms, using national security as justification for its oppressive actions. Agamben's concept underscores the need for a human rights framework that goes beyond legal protections, actively challenging systems that misuse laws to suppress freedoms.

Slavoj Žižek pushes this further, arguing that conventional human rights frameworks often address symptoms rather than underlying power dynamics. In *Violence: Six Sideways Reflections*, Žižek critiques frameworks that ignore the structural causes of oppression, suggesting that meaningful human rights work in North Korea must confront the authoritarian structures that enforce control. This perspective aligns with liberation theology's call to challenge oppressive systems head-on.

Paulo Freire's concept of praxis—combining thought and action—offers an educational model to empower oppressed groups. In *Pedagogy of the Oppressed*, Freire argues that awareness and agency, even under repressive regimes, are key to resistance. In North Korea, where ideological control is intense, a praxis-based approach could foster awareness of inherent dignity, even in small, underground communities, providing a pathway for resistance where open activism is impossible.

Martha Nussbaum's extension of the capabilities approach highlights specific conditions necessary for a dignified life. In *Creating Capabilities: The Human Development Approach*, she emphasizes essentials like safety, mental health, and meaningful relationships—all severely restricted in North Korea. Her framework supports a liberation theology that advocates for both basic rights and the broader conditions for fulfilling lives, underscoring the need to address human rights holistically.

John Howard Yoder introduces a faith-based response to oppression in *The Politics of Jesus*, proposing the church as a countercultural force. Yoder's vision of the church as a community of peace, justice, and solidarity positions religious communities as moral anchors, able to resist oppressive regimes nonviolently. In North Korea, where state ideology permeates life, Yoder's framework suggests that religious communities could provide ethical support and dignity for those deprived of freedom.

Combining these perspectives, liberation theology constructs a human rights model that integrates ethical ideals with practical strategies. This approach calls for immediate aid to alleviate suffering and structural reforms to challenge authoritarian power. By addressing both legal standards and daily realities, liberation theology offers a comprehensive framework for justice in North Korea, envisioning human rights as active commitments to freedom and dignity, not mere declarations. Through this inclusive model, liberation theology seeks a society where human rights aren't abstract ideals, but actionable, sustained practices rooted in compassion and justice.

CHAPTER FOUR

4.4. REIMAGINING THEOLOGICAL EDUCATION THROUGH PRAXIS

Liberation theology calls for a major reorientation in theological education, pushing it from theoretical study to a praxis-based model that merges reflection with active engagement in social justice. This shift envisions theological education as an immersive, experience-driven process where learning happens not only in the classroom but through direct involvement in the everyday struggles of people facing social, economic, and environmental injustices. Rather than keeping theology within academic walls, this approach challenges students to take their learning into communities, allowing theology to be tested, reshaped, and redefined through lived experience.[21]

This model expands theological education to encompass more than doctrinal study or ecclesial history. It calls for active participation in social issues, encouraging students to view their education as a toolkit for real-world transformation. Theological institutions, in this context, become centers of social awareness, advocacy, and active service, preparing future leaders to meet the needs of marginalized populations. Students learn not only from books but also through interaction with those most impacted by systemic injustices, building both intellectual understanding and a moral commitment to justice and equality.

Central to this praxis-based approach is the question: how can theological teachings be applied to tackle pressing social issues? This framework invites students and educators to explore how theology intersects with economic, social, and environmental systems, promoting a worldview that values human dignity and the interconnectedness of all life. Under this model, theology moves beyond theoretical reflection to become a resource for action. It's about preparing students to address real needs and contribute meaningfully to social change.

This reimagined approach brings the theological classroom out into the community, encouraging students to take part in community-based learning projects, collaborate with local organizations, and engage in direct service to vulnerable populations. These experiences allow students to witness firsthand the effects of systemic inequalities, deepening their understanding of justice and building a personal connection to the struggles they study.[22] Students learn to approach their theologi-

---

21. Tanner, *Christ the Key*.
22. Graham, *Transforming Practice*.

cal education not only as an academic journey but as a commitment to understanding and confronting societal issues.

In this model, educators become mentors rather than traditional lecturers, guiding students through the ethical and societal complexities they encounter. They facilitate discussions that tackle the real-world implications of theological ideas, helping students build frameworks for engaging with issues like poverty, environmental destruction, and systemic inequality. This mentorship approach connects students' theological studies with active social learning, pushing them to think critically about the relevance of theology in the face of contemporary issues.

A praxis-oriented theological education prepares students to serve as leaders within their communities, equipping them with practical tools and ethical frameworks necessary for addressing societal challenges. This preparation ensures that their future roles in ministry or social movements are grounded in both theological insight and real-world experience. By emphasizing active engagement, theological education remains responsive and relevant, enabling students to participate in and shape movements for justice, ecological stewardship, and economic equality.

Through this model, theological education becomes a practice of listening and responding to the needs of marginalized communities. Students are encouraged to view their training as a means to address these needs in practical ways, empowering them to apply their skills across a variety of contexts. This approach shapes graduates who are ready to contribute constructively to social movements, where their theological education can become a tool for justice and compassion. Rather than promoting passive contemplation, this model invites students to consider their role in creating equitable and sustainable communities.

By combining theological study with real-world application, this approach challenges the traditional structures of theological education. It creates a robust environment where students integrate their theological learning with a commitment to social responsibility. Aligning theological reflection with community needs, it encourages both educators and students to see theology as a dynamic discipline that evolves with the demands of the time, contributing to transformative social action. This shift repositions theological education as a catalyst for positive change, supporting a framework grounded in human dignity and committed to systemic justice.[23]

---

23. Tanner, *Christ the Key*; Graham, *Transforming Practice*.

CHAPTER FOUR

4.5. THE KINGDOM OF GOD AS A PRESENT REALITY: A CALL TO SOCIAL JUSTICE AND ACTIVE ENGAGEMENT

The concept of the Kingdom of God is increasingly being understood not as a distant future hope but as an active and immediate reality that calls for meaningful engagement in social justice and ethical responsibility. This interpretation encourages believers to embody divine values in their daily lives through practical and ethical actions, promoting a theology that emphasizes doing over mere believing. Theologians like Miroslav Volf and Gustavo Gutiérrez advocate for a vision of the Kingdom that actively confronts injustices, emphasizing principles of love, justice, and inclusion.[24] This shift moves theological focus from abstract expectations to tangible engagement with justice here and now, urging believers to express their faith through acts of compassion, advocacy, and service.

Building on this idea, theologians such as Jürgen Moltmann see the Kingdom of God as a transformative force in the present world. In *Theology of Hope*, Moltmann argues that Christian hope should inspire believers to participate actively in societal transformation, addressing issues like poverty, oppression, and environmental degradation.[25] This perspective asserts that faith and social action are intertwined, calling believers to contribute to justice and renewal in their communities as an essential expression of their faith.

Similarly, N.T. Wright emphasizes the Kingdom of God as a present reality that calls for active discipleship engaging with social and cultural needs. Wright suggests that Christians are invited to partner with God in renewing creation, committing themselves to efforts of justice, peace, and reconciliation.[26] This understanding broadens the mission of the church beyond spiritual concerns to include social engagement, highlighting the church's role in addressing contemporary issues from economic inequality to ecological challenges.

The Social Gospel movement, led by theologians like Walter Rauschenbusch, has historically connected the Kingdom of God with social reform. Rauschenbusch argued that the Kingdom involves transforming society to reflect God's justice and righteousness, challenging structures of exploitation and inequality.[27] His work lays a historical

---

24. Volf, *Public Faith*; Gutiérrez, *Power of the Poor in History*.
25. Moltmann, *Theology of Hope*.
26. Wright, *Surprised by Hope*.
27. Rauschenbusch, *A Theology for the Social Gospel*.

foundation for linking the Kingdom of God with social activism, establishing a model for modern theological approaches that prioritize justice as a central aspect of faith.

Liberation theologians expand this perspective by emphasizing the Kingdom of God's concern for marginalized and oppressed individuals. Leonardo Boff, for example, argues that the Kingdom requires a radical restructuring of society to eliminate injustice and uphold human dignity.[28] This view calls believers to solidarity with the poor and active involvement in struggles for liberation, presenting a theology that sees social justice as essential to realizing the Kingdom. Boff's approach underscores that the Kingdom of God is incomplete without efforts toward social and economic equity, pushing for changes that recognize and respond to the needs of the most vulnerable.

Sarah Coakley stresses that true discipleship involves both individual and communal responsibility. She advocates for a balance of spiritual practices that nurture personal faith while encouraging community collaboration, empowering believers to work collectively toward the Kingdom.[29] This perspective highlights the importance of integrating contemplation and action, demonstrating that the Kingdom of God can be realized through practices of justice, reconciliation, and communal service.

Stanley Hauerwas adds another dimension by emphasizing the church as a community that embodies the values of the Kingdom of God. He argues that the church should serve as a visible sign of God's reign, practicing peace, justice, and hospitality.[30] Hauerwas envisions the faith community as a collective witness to divine values, where believers actively live out the Kingdom through mutual support, ethical accountability, and service to others.

Furthermore, James Cone, a key figure in Black theology, connects the Kingdom of God to issues of racial justice and liberation. Cone's work highlights the Kingdom as a force against racial injustice, calling for the liberation of oppressed peoples and confronting systemic racism.[31] By linking the Kingdom to the struggle against racial inequality, Cone expands theological understanding to include a commitment to racial

---

28. Boff and Boff, *Introducing Liberation Theology*.
29. Coakley, *God, Sexuality, and the Self*.
30. Hauerwas, *Community of Character*.
31. Cone, *A Black Theology of Liberation*.

equity and social justice, advocating for transformation within societal structures.

Feminist theologians, including Rosemary Radford Ruether, further broaden the concept of the Kingdom by advocating for gender equality and challenging patriarchal systems. Ruether contends that the Kingdom of God must include justice for women and the dismantling of oppressive gender norms.[32] This perspective recognizes that the Kingdom requires justice in all human relationships, calling for an end to systemic inequalities based on gender.

Additionally, theologians like J. Kameron Carter explore the Kingdom of God in the context of postcolonial critique. Carter emphasizes that understanding the Kingdom involves addressing colonial legacies and their ongoing impact on marginalized communities.[33] This approach calls for a theology that is aware of historical injustices and committed to deconstructing oppressive narratives, promoting healing and reconciliation.

Environmental theologians like Sallie McFague contribute by integrating ecological concerns into the understanding of the Kingdom of God. McFague argues that the Kingdom involves caring for creation and addressing environmental issues as an integral part of faith.[34] This perspective emphasizes that stewardship of the earth is a component of living out the values of the Kingdom, linking ecological well-being with social justice.

These varied theological perspectives collectively support a vision of the Kingdom of God as an active force for justice in the present world, rather than a distant spiritual ideal. Each perspective underscores the need for believers to integrate their faith with actions that address social issues, embodying divine values in practical ways. By understanding the Kingdom as both a personal and communal responsibility, theological discourse moves toward a comprehensive framework that incorporates spirituality, community, and social activism.

Embracing this expanded interpretation of the Kingdom challenges believers to take an active role in creating a world that reflects the values of justice, peace, and love inherent in the divine vision of the Kingdom of God. This view calls for a lived faith that responds to contemporary

---

32. Ruether, *Sexism and God-Talk*.
33. Carter, *Race*.
34. McFague, *New Climate for Theology*.

injustices, engages with societal needs, and promotes a theology that actively contributes to building a more equitable and compassionate world.

4.6. ENVIRONMENTAL JUSTICE WITHIN LIBERATION THEOLOGY

Modern liberation theology has expanded its focus on justice to include ecological and environmental dimensions, recognizing that oppression impacts not only human communities but also the natural world. This shift challenges the traditional human-centered focus of theology, emphasizing the interconnectedness of all life. Theologians like Catherine Keller and M. Shawn Copeland advocate for a justice framework that integrates environmental concerns, urging a liberation that includes the well-being of both humanity and nature.[35] They call for a theology that directly addresses the ways in which environmental degradation and human suffering intersect, promoting a vision of liberation that recognizes the shared fate of people and the planet.

For Keller, environmental justice is central to liberation theology. She highlights those human activities—like pollution, resource depletion, and habitat destruction—often have the worst impact on marginalized communities who already face social and economic challenges. Keller argues that theological frameworks must account for these links between ecological harm and social inequality, as ignoring environmental issues only perpetuates cycles of oppression. Her perspective encourages a theology that advocates for sustainable practices and policies, recognizing that true justice cannot ignore the needs of the natural world alongside those of humanity.

M. Shawn Copeland builds on this view by underscoring the ethical responsibility humans have toward the planet. She points out that environmental crises, such as climate change and biodiversity loss, disproportionately affect vulnerable communities, exacerbating poverty, displacement, and health issues. Copeland's approach calls for theological reflection that includes protecting ecosystems essential for sustaining life. She urges believers to support environmental policies that safeguard marginalized communities, linking ecological stewardship with a commitment to human dignity and ethical responsibility.

Leonardo Boff's ecological liberation theology also stresses the necessity of environmental justice for true liberation. In *Cry of the Earth*,

---

35. Keller, *Cloud of the Impossible*; Copeland, *Enfleshing Freedom*.

CHAPTER FOUR

Cry of the Poor, Boff emphasizes that humans and nature are interconnected, arguing that ecological health is a critical component of justice. He presents environmental care as a moral obligation, advocating for sustainable practices that honor the environment as a sacred trust. Boff's vision promotes a theology where human liberation and ecological preservation are intertwined, insisting that both are essential to the overall well-being of creation.

Boff goes further by viewing environmental degradation as a symptom of deeper systemic injustices, including economic exploitation and disregard for marginalized communities. He contends that many environmental crises result from systems that prioritize profit over sustainability, harming both people and the earth. His theology calls for structural changes, pushing for economic models that respect ecological limits and prioritize community health. This perspective suggests that liberation theology should address the root causes of environmental harm, advocating for a fair and sustainable relationship between humanity and the natural world.

The inclusion of environmental justice within liberation theology also transforms theological education. Religious institutions are encouraged to teach sustainable practices and ecological ethics as part of theological training, helping future leaders understand their role in addressing environmental challenges. Courses in eco-theology and environmental ethics equip them to advocate for policies that align with values of ecological integrity and social responsibility, preparing them to confront environmental crises that disproportionately impact vulnerable populations.

Liberation theology's integration of ecological justice also calls for active participation in environmental and social movements. Many theologians urge believers to join initiatives that protect biodiversity, combat climate change, and ensure fair access to natural resources. This engagement offers a way to put faith into practice by serving the common good, demonstrating that environmental stewardship is an essential expression of justice. In doing so, liberation theology contributes to global efforts against environmental degradation, promoting sustainable development as a moral and ethical priority.

Moreover, the integration of ecological concerns in liberation theology resonates with indigenous and other traditional worldviews that regard the earth as a living entity deserving respect and care. By embracing these perspectives, liberation theology promotes a holistic view that honors the interconnectedness of all life. This approach respects diverse cultural traditions and ethical systems, fostering a theology that advocates for justice for both human and ecological communities.

Through this expanded framework, liberation theology calls on believers to see the earth not merely as a resource to be used, but as a community to which humans belong and for which they are responsible. Environmental justice, then, becomes a key part of a larger mission to create a just and equitable society. By uniting environmental and social concerns, liberation theology proposes a vision of justice that addresses both human and ecological needs, supporting a comprehensive approach to liberation that promotes harmony within creation.

4.7. REIMAGINING THE CHURCH AS A COUNTERCULTURAL FORCE

The Church's role in promoting justice increasingly calls for a countercultural approach—one that actively resists societal norms upholding inequality and oppression. This vision positions the Church as a distinct community, grounded in values of peace, justice, and solidarity, that stands apart from a culture of consumerism and self-interest. Theologian Stanley Hauerwas emphasizes this role, presenting the Church as a community rooted in the teachings of Jesus, where believers embody Kingdom values through radical discipleship. Hauerwas's framework rejects alliances with systems of power that perpetuate injustice, urging the Church to live out compassion and equity as visible signs of an alternative way of life.[36]

In Hauerwas's view, the Church's identity is tied to its commitment to justice, hospitality, and care for those who are marginalized. This countercultural stance fosters a community of accountability, where members encourage one another to resist materialism, individualism, and indifference. By choosing this path, the Church acts as a beacon of hope, advocating for the oppressed and offering a different vision for community—a place where love, respect, and mutual support take precedence.

Theologians Shane Claiborne and John Milbank expand on this vision by advocating for a Church that distances itself from consumerism and militarism. Claiborne calls for a lifestyle of simplicity, resisting the relentless pursuit of material wealth and consumption that shapes much

---

36. Hauerwas, *Work of Theology*.

of contemporary society.[37] Milbank echoes this, urging the Church to serve as a moral counterpoint to militaristic and consumer-driven cultures, focusing instead on relationships, compassion, and sustainable practices.[38] Together, they argue that by rejecting consumerism and militarism, the Church can model a way of life that respects both people and the environment.

At the heart of this approach are the values of simplicity and solidarity with the poor. Claiborne and Milbank's perspectives call on the Church to live humbly and responsibly, recognizing the social and environmental impacts of its choices. For Claiborne, this lifestyle is a direct response to Jesus's teachings, which call followers to care for those in need and live without attachment to wealth or status. Milbank emphasizes that the Church's role in fostering compassionate, community-centered relationships is essential, encouraging a shift from self-centeredness to collective well-being.

This reimagined role for the Church also involves a commitment to social transformation. Standing as a countercultural community gives the Church the potential to influence society by promoting human dignity, equality, and peace. In practice, this means actively opposing systemic injustices such as poverty, discrimination, and violence and advocating for policies that support marginalized populations. Through participation in social justice movements and partnerships with organizations working for the common good, the Church amplifies its impact, demonstrating the meaningful role faith communities can play in shaping a more just world.

Furthermore, this countercultural vision expands the Church's mission to include pressing global issues like environmental justice, human rights, and economic inequality. Through advocacy, education, and service, the Church can address these challenges by aligning its practices with values that promote the welfare of all people and the earth. This approach positions the Church as a model of the Kingdom in action, embodying love and justice in practical ways that resonate with those it serves.

Hauerwas's vision also suggests that the Church should champion nonviolence and peacebuilding, countering the violence and divisiveness that permeate society. By modeling peaceful conflict resolution,

---

37. Claiborne, *Irresistible Revolution*.
38. Milbank, *Theology and Social Theory*.

advocating for reconciliation, and bridging divides within communities, the Church can offer an example of harmony rooted in compassion and understanding. This aligns with the teachings of Jesus, who called his followers to love their neighbors and even their enemies, challenging the Church to embody forgiveness and reconciliation as core to its mission.

In this reimagined role, the Church becomes more than a place of worship—it becomes a community of action and transformation. It is a space where believers are equipped to challenge oppressive systems, stand with the vulnerable, and advocate for justice. This vision calls for an active, relational faith that is attuned to the needs of the world, reminding believers that their commitment to God also means a commitment to human dignity and social healing.

By embodying these countercultural values, the Church presents an alternative model of community life, one that rejects the isolating effects of individualism and the exploitation inherent in consumerism. Instead, it offers a framework based on interdependence, mutual support, and shared purpose. In this way, the Church inspires others to seek lives centered on compassion, equity, and care for creation, becoming a living example of the Kingdom's values in a world often driven by self-interest and inequality.

4.8. HISTORICAL MEMORY AND LIBERATION

Liberation theology places historical memory at the center of its framework for justice, seeing it as more than a recollection of events—it's a foundation of identity and resilience. For communities that have faced generational oppression, memory connects present-day struggles to past victories, creating a powerful narrative that fuels current movements. This connection is visible in practices like Jewish festivals, where commemorations of liberation remind communities of their shared commitment to justice and resilience.[39] These traditions enable communities to tap into their heritage, drawing on the experiences and endurance of their ancestors to face present challenges with a sense of strength and unity.

Within liberation theology, historical memory is not only encouragement but a guiding force, one that shapes identities and informs strategies for justice. Instead of viewing justice as isolated, present-day

---

39. Rosenzweig, *Star of Redemption*.

CHAPTER FOUR

actions, this approach integrates memory as a long-term framework, helping communities build on past achievements and adapt them to new challenges. By remembering victories and lessons from previous struggles, communities can better sustain resistance against oppression. Memory, in this sense, is a resource for justice that emphasizes liberation as a continuous journey, rooted in historical experience but responsive to contemporary realities.

Liberation theologians argue that memory serves as more than inspiration—it's a practical foundation for resilience. Remembering past strategies, principles, and successful actions provides a blueprint that communities can adapt for modern struggles. For example, the legacies of social justice movements reinforce the idea of shared commitment, showing individuals that their actions are part of a larger, enduring struggle. This historical continuity supports communities in avoiding past mistakes, drawing on proven strategies to confront current injustices with greater efficacy.

Storytelling, oral traditions, and cultural rituals further preserve a community's collective identity, keeping histories of resistance alive and fostering a strong sense of purpose. Engaging in these practices allows communities to remember and honor their struggles for liberation, creating a shared identity that transcends generations. For individuals, these collective memories provide belonging and purpose, framing present struggles as part of a larger narrative of resilience. This continuity anchors the pursuit of justice, making it a natural extension of their heritage rather than a disconnected goal.

Liberation theology's emphasis on historical memory also challenges communities to see the injustices of the past as ongoing issues that require action today. Remembering the oppression faced by previous generations reinforces the need for vigilance and solidarity in confronting modern forms of injustice. Memory becomes a call to action, urging communities to carry forward the legacy of liberation by opposing today's oppression. This perspective instills a responsibility to honor past struggles by working toward a just future, inspired by the endurance and sacrifices of those who came before.

Importantly, memory within liberation theology isn't static—it's dynamic and adaptable, allowing communities to reinterpret their histories in response to contemporary challenges. This adaptability ensures that memory remains relevant, offering insights that resonate with each generation's unique context. By blending historical events with current experiences, communities create a "living memory" that evolves alongside their journey toward liberation. This approach fosters a justice framework that is both grounded in tradition and responsive to current needs, ensuring liberation efforts remain rooted in heritage while adapting to the present.

Practically, liberation theologians advocate for educational initiatives and community gatherings that sustain an awareness of historical memory. These efforts include teaching younger generations about cultural heritage and the importance of past struggles, ensuring that history's lessons remain accessible and actionable. Such educational programs promote a commitment to justice informed by the sacrifices and achievements of earlier generations, encouraging younger members to embrace the cause of liberation with a grounded understanding of their community's history. This emphasis on memory as a source of resilience helps communities persist in their efforts for justice, even in the face of adversity.

Ultimately, valuing historical memory as part of liberation reinforces that justice is a long-term commitment spanning generations. Liberation isn't a single event but an ongoing process, requiring sustained effort and a commitment to learning from the past. This perspective encourages communities to see themselves as part of a larger movement for justice, one that began long before and will continue. Memory, then, becomes a source of unity, providing continuity that strengthens collective action and reinforces the shared commitment to liberation.

4.9. INTEGRATING THEOLOGY AND PRACTICAL JUSTICE

Liberation theology pushes for a strong integration between theological reflection and practical justice, making sure that religious teachings actively address social issues and drive real change. This approach doesn't just stop at spiritual ideals; it connects those principles to concrete ethical actions, framing faith and justice as inseparable partners. Gustavo Gutiérrez, a key figure in liberation theology, insists that theology must be rooted in the actual experiences of people facing oppression. He advocates for a theology informed by reality and directed toward action.[40] This approach challenges theologians to go beyond abstract teachings, urging them to engage with the struggles of marginalized communities.

40. Gutiérrez, *Theology of Liberation*.

CHAPTER FOUR

By embedding theology in real-world contexts, liberation theology promotes a model where religious reflection is always grounded in social realities.

Liberation theology insists that theology cannot stay confined to seminaries or churches but must engage with issues like economic inequality, social injustice, and environmental degradation. By focusing on the everyday lives of marginalized people, liberation theology aims to make religious teachings relevant to current social challenges. This is a praxis-oriented theology, where faith is expressed through actions that uplift human dignity, equity, and respect for creation. It calls for theology to act as a tool for societal change, promoting justice that embodies both divine values and community needs.

Amartya Sen's *capability approach* complements liberation theology by defining liberation as the ability for people and communities to live lives they value. Sen highlights the need for social conditions that enable individuals to thrive, advocating for justice that fosters human flourishing at all levels.[41] This aligns with liberation theology's focus on justice by underscoring practical conditions necessary for true liberation, such as access to resources, freedom from discrimination, and opportunities for growth. By merging these frameworks, liberation theology builds a comprehensive model that unites spiritual values with tangible goals, supporting both individual well-being and community empowerment.

This model of integration calls for religious engagement that moves beyond doctrine to include active social involvement. Liberation theology encourages faith communities to participate in social change movements, addressing issues like poverty, racial injustice, and environmental destruction. Here, theology becomes a living discipline, one that responds to the challenges of modern life. The focus on practical justice challenges believers to view their faith as a moral compass that leads them to advocate for policies and practices promoting social equity.

Liberation theology also expands the vision of theological education, prompting religious institutions to teach students not only traditional doctrine but also how to apply faith in social and political arenas. This approach equips future leaders with tools to tackle systemic injustices, fostering a theology rooted in compassion, empathy, and a commitment to human dignity. It emphasizes a holistic understanding of justice, where students learn to integrate faith with actions addressing local and

---

41. Sen, *Development as Freedom*.

global issues. By encouraging this model, liberation theology prepares leaders who can contribute to community development and social movements, embodying a faith actively engaged in the work of justice.

Liberation theology's embrace of diverse perspectives—like human rights and ecological justice—creates a flexible model that addresses individual and systemic needs alike. This perspective calls on theologians and communities to view justice as a layered commitment, requiring personal dedication and structural reform. For example, liberation theology highlights humanity's connection to the natural world, advocating for sustainable practices that protect the environment. It sees environmental stewardship as essential for liberating oppressed communities, recognizing that environmental degradation often harms those already living in poverty.

The focus on practical justice within liberation theology builds an ongoing commitment to address contemporary challenges with flexibility and responsiveness. This adaptability is essential in a world where social, economic, and environmental issues are increasingly interconnected. By promoting a framework that merges theological reflection with real-world engagement, liberation theology equips communities to respond to changing circumstances, fostering a faith that is both resilient and capable of inspiring transformation.

This expanded view of theology emphasizes that liberation is not just a personal journey but a shared mission to reform social structures for equity and dignity. By encouraging a collaborative approach to justice, liberation theology inspires communities to work together on shared challenges, fostering mutual respect and solidarity. This perspective reinforces the idea that liberation is a comprehensive, ongoing process, combining spiritual and practical dimensions and demanding sustained effort from individuals, communities, and institutions.

In conclusion, liberation theology presents a holistic model that combines theological reflection with practical action, showing that justice requires both ethical commitment and an understanding of modern life's complexities. This integrated framework supports a theology that remains relevant, advancing a justice-oriented faith that responds to issues like poverty, human rights, and ecological sustainability. By engaging diverse perspectives and adapting to each generation's needs, liberation theology envisions a justice aligned with both divine and human values, fostering a future where liberation is realized in all areas of life.

EPILOGUE

THE EPILOGUE: THE KINGDOM of God and Korean Reunification Theology explores the concept of the Kingdom of God by integrating perspectives from theology, philosophy, sociology, and political science. This interdisciplinary approach frames the Kingdom not merely as a theological abstraction but as a dynamic, relational construct deeply influenced by the lived experiences and collective aspirations of the Korean people. By considering real-world examples and societal contexts, the Kingdom is re-envisioned as an evolving reality that interacts with the everyday lives of Korean Christians. Rather than viewing the Kingdom solely as a distant, eschatological promise, this interpretation presents it as an adaptable reality continuously shaped by believers actively engaging with the socio-political tensions on the Korean Peninsula.

Building upon this foundation, the discussion draws an analogy with Einstein's theory of relativity, particularly the concept of space-time being influenced by gravitational forces. In this analogy, the Kingdom of God is likened to a responsive "field" that is molded by Korea's historical and social context. Just as massive objects cause a curvature in space-time, the collective efforts and aspirations of the Korean people create a "gravitational pull" within the Kingdom field. This pull is directed toward peace, reconciliation, and unity, suggesting that the Kingdom is not merely a static destination but a transformative journey that is constantly evolving. By engaging in communal actions and fostering reconciliation, Korean Christians contribute to shaping this Kingdom field, actively participating in its development. The use of scientific concepts to illustrate theological ideas bridges the gap between faith and reason, offering a tangible framework for understanding the Kingdom's dynamic nature.

Immanuel Kant's transcendental idealism further enriches this perspective by positioning the Kingdom of God as an essential framework through which believers perceive and interpret their efforts toward

EPILOGUE

reunification. According to Kant, space and time are not external realities but necessary conditions of human perception.[1] Similarly, the Kingdom is conceptualized as a perceptual and ethical framework that shapes how Korean Christians understand and engage with issues of justice, reconciliation, and unity. This means that the Kingdom is not an external realm to be entered after death but an intrinsic part of how believers experience and interact with the world. By adopting this framework, the Kingdom becomes an active, present-day reality that informs and guides Christian engagement with societal divisions, transforming abstract ideals into tangible actions.

Philosophical contributions from Friedrich Nietzsche and Martin Heidegger further enhance this vision. Nietzsche's philosophy emphasizes the concept of "becoming" over a static "being," advocating for continuous self-overcoming and transformation.[2] This idea supports an adaptable approach to reunification, aligning with the fluid and ever-changing socio-political landscape of Korea. It suggests that reunification is not a fixed goal but an ongoing process requiring constant effort and adaptation. Heidegger's concept of existential spatiality proposes that space is shaped by relationships and interactions among people.[3] This perspective informs a communal understanding of the Kingdom as a "gathering place" where individuals enact values such as peace, mutual understanding, and unity. The Kingdom becomes a lived experience created through communal actions and relationships rather than a distant realm.

Rudolf Bultmann's existential theology shifts the focus from physical spaces to relational encounters. Bultmann argues that authentic existence is realized through relationships and personal engagements rather than adherence to doctrinal structures.[4] In the context of Korean reunification theology, this perspective aligns with the emphasis on relationships over mere territorial reunification. It suggests that the essence of reunification lies in restoring relationships, mutual recognition, and solidarity between people of North and South Korea. This approach encourages Korean Christians to prioritize building genuine relational bonds, viewing reunification not just as a political or geographical merger but as an ethical commitment to healing divisions and fostering understanding.

1. Kant, *Critique of Pure Reason*.
2. Nietzsche, *Thus Spoke Zarathustra*.
3. Heidegger, *Being and Time*.
4. Bultmann, *Essays*.

EPILOGUE

Adding to the interdisciplinary framework, Eugen Rosenstock-Huessy's fourfold concept of space introduces individual, social, historical, and cosmic dimensions into understanding the Kingdom.[5] This comprehensive approach supports a holistic vision of the Kingdom as an active, participatory space shaped by diverse human interactions across multiple levels of existence. By integrating these dimensions, the Kingdom becomes a collaborative effort transcending individual actions and involving collective participation in various life aspects. This multi-dimensional perspective emphasizes that realizing the Kingdom is intertwined with all facets of human existence, not confined to spiritual activities alone.

In reimagining the Kingdom, there is a strong emphasis on inclusivity and an ecumenical outlook that embraces Korea's religious diversity. Recognizing that reunification and peacebuilding challenges require collective efforts, this perspective encourages collaboration across different faiths and ideologies. Interfaith dialogues and cooperative initiatives become vital in promoting understanding and unity among various religious communities. By fostering partnerships with Buddhist, Confucian, and other religious traditions present in Korea, Christians can contribute to a more cohesive society. This inclusivity not only strengthens the Kingdom's relevance within Korea but also enhances its global significance, serving as a model for interreligious cooperation in addressing common human concerns.

From a political standpoint, this understanding of the Kingdom balances divine sovereignty with human agency, encouraging ethical involvement in governance structures without advocating for theocracy. The Kingdom serves as a guiding principle that informs political actions and policies, promoting values such as justice, peace, and respect for human rights. Korean Christians are encouraged to participate in political processes, advocate for policies upholding human dignity, and work toward the common good on the Korean Peninsula. This involves addressing issues like human rights violations, economic disparities, and social injustices, emphasizing the responsibility of Christians to influence governance through moral contributions.

Practically, this theological model calls upon the church to actively engage with Korea's social, economic, and political challenges. The church is urged to adopt a prophetic stance, speaking out against injustices and advocating for the marginalized. This involves aligning its mission with grassroots movements working toward justice and peace,

5. Rosenstock-Huessy, *The Christian Future*.

such as organizations addressing poverty and human rights. By collaborating with non-governmental organizations and civil society groups, the church can amplify its impact and contribute to meaningful change. This approach positions the church not just as a spiritual institution but as a transformative force in society, actively working to bring about the Kingdom's values in tangible ways.

In theological education, this vision necessitates a reorientation of curricula to include a stronger focus on public theology and social ethics. Seminaries and theological institutions are encouraged to equip future leaders with knowledge and skills to address societal challenges from a Kingdom-centered perspective. This may involve introducing courses on social justice, conflict resolution, and community organizing. Practical training opportunities, such as internships with social service agencies, can provide hands-on experience in applying theological principles to real-world situations. By integrating these elements into theological education, future church leaders will be better prepared to engage with modern society's complexities and lead their congregations in meaningful action.

Finally, narrative theology plays a crucial role in bridging this theological vision with individuals' lived realities affected by division. By grounding the Kingdom concept in personal stories and testimonies, theology becomes connected to everyday experiences. These narratives of resilience, hope, and overcoming provide tangible examples of how the Kingdom's values manifest in real life. Sharing stories of families separated by division or communities fostering unity amidst conflict can inspire others to engage in reunification efforts. This focus on lived experiences ensures that the Kingdom remains relevant and accessible, encouraging believers to see reunification as a present reality. By emphasizing the power of personal stories, theology serves as a practical framework that unites faith with action, inviting all members of society to participate in the collective journey toward building a peaceful and unified Korea.

Through this transformative journey, the theology presented becomes a practical tool for uniting faith with tangible actions. It invites believers and the broader community to participate in building a peaceful and unified Korea actively. By integrating interdisciplinary insights and focusing on relational and ethical commitments, this vision of the Kingdom of God offers a comprehensive framework for addressing the complex challenges of reunification on the Korean Peninsula.

ABOUT THE AUTHOR

DR. DONG IN BAEK is a thoughtful scholar whose work bridges diverse intellectual and cultural worlds. His journey has taken him across continents, where he has cultivated an approach that integrates philosophy, theology, and social responsibility. Born in Korea, Dr. Baek's academic and spiritual pursuits reflect a commitment to understanding and connecting the philosophical and theological traditions of East and West.

Dr. Baek earned his Ph.D. in philosophy from Johann Wolfgang Goethe University in Frankfurt, Germany, immersing himself in Western philosophical frameworks. His further studies in political science at L'École des Hautes Études Politiques in Paris and St. Petersburg State University enriched his understanding of global political dynamics and the intersections of ideology and power. His career in academia, including significant roles at Keimyung University in Korea, St. Petersburg State University in Russia, and the University of Vienna in Austria, highlights his dedication to cross-cultural and interdisciplinary dialogue. As co-Chancellor of the Institute of Eastern and Western Societies at St. Petersburg State University, Dr. Baek continues to foster discussions that bridge geographical and intellectual divides.

An ordained minister with the Seoul North Presbytery of the Presbyterian Church (Tonghap) in Korea and a member of the Cascade Presbytery of the Presbyterian Church (U.S.A.), Dr. Baek approaches his theological work as an intersection of belief and social practice. His faith informs his scholarship, particularly his exploration of themes like nature, time, and justice as active forces in human history. His recent book, *Nature and Time (Vol. II): Paths to Justice and Transformation*, reframes nature and time as participants in the divine process of reconciliation, inspired by natural rhythms and the complexity of theological constructs.

Guided by the perspectives of thinkers like Franz Rosenzweig, Eugen Rosenstock-Huessy, Robert Cox, and Fernand Braudel, Dr. Baek's

ABOUT THE AUTHOR

work offers a comprehensive framework for peacebuilding that transcends traditional social boundaries. His interdisciplinary approach reimagines theology to address contemporary needs for justice, ecological responsibility, and human solidarity. Through his writings, teachings, and mentorship, he encourages readers and students alike to question established narratives and engage actively with the pressing ethical and spiritual challenges of our time.

BIBLIOGRAPHY

Agamben, Giorgio. *State of Exception*. University of Chicago Press, 2005.
Althaus-Reid, Marcella. *Indecent Theology: Theological Perversions in Sex, Gender, and Politics*. Psychology Press, 2000.
Appiah, Kwame A. *Cosmopolitanism: Ethics in a World of Strangers (Issues of Our Time)*. W. W. Norton & Company, 2010.
Arendt, Hannah. *Eichmann in Jerusalem: A Report on the Banality of Evil*. Viking Press, 1963.
———. *The Origins of Totalitarianism*. HarperCollins, 1973.
Badiou, Alain. *Being and Event*. A&C Black, 2007.
Bantum, Brian. *Redeeming Mulatto: A Theology of Race and Christian Hybridity*. Baylor University Press, 2010.
Barth, Karl. *Church Dogmatics: The Doctrine of Creation, Volume 3, Part 4: The Command of God the Creator*. Edited by G. W. Bromiley and T. F. Torrance. A&C Black, 2004. Originally published 1958.
———. *Religion and Science*. SCM Press, 1990.
Batnitzky, Leora. *How Judaism Became a Religion: An Introduction to Modern Jewish Thought*. Princeton University Press, 2011.
Bauckham, Richard. *The Theology of Jürgen Moltmann*. Bloomsbury Publishing, 1995.
Bell, Daniel M. *Liberation Theology After the End of History: The Refusal to Cease Suffering*. Psychology Press, 2001.
Benhabib, Seyla. *The Claims of Culture: Equality and Diversity in the Global Era*. Princeton University Press, 2002.
Benjamin, Walter. *Illuminations*. Schocken Books, 1986.
Berman, Nadav S. "Franz Rosenzweig on Divine Love and on the Love of Enemies: Complications of Agape in the Secularized World." *Religions* 15.7 (2024).
Bhabha, Homi K. *The Location of Culture*. Routledge, 2012.
Birch, Charles, and John B. Cobb. *The Liberation of Life: From the Cell to the Community*. CUP Archive, 1985.
Boff, Clodovis. *Theology and Praxis: Epistemological Foundations*. Orbis Books, 1987.
———. *Trinity and Society*. Orbis Books, 1988.
Boff, Leonardo. *Church, Charism and Power: Liberation Theology and the Institutional Church*. Crossroad, 1985.
———. *Cry of the Earth, Cry of the Poor*. Translated by P. Berryman. Orbis Books, 1997. Originally published 1995.
Boff, Leonardo, and Clovodis Boff. *Introducing Liberation Theology*. Burns & Oates, 1987.

Boesak, Allan Aubrey. *Comfort and Protest: The Apocalypse of John from a South African Perspective*. Wipf and Stock, 2015.
Bonhoeffer, Dietrich. *Ethics*. Simon & Schuster, 1995.
Bonino, Jose Míguez. *Doing Theology in a Revolutionary Situation*. Fortress Press, 1975.
Brown, Wendy. *Undoing the Demos: Neoliberalism's Stealth Revolution*. MIT Press, 2015.
Brueggemann, Walter. *A Social Reading of the Old Testament: Prophetic Approaches to Israel's Communal Life*. Fortress Press, 1994.
———. *Journey to the Common Good*. Westminster John Knox Press, 2010.
———. *The Prophetic Imagination: 40th Anniversary Edition*. Fortress Press, 2018.
Bultmann, Rudolf Karl. *Essays: Philosophical and Theological*. The Library of Philosophy and Theology. Macmillan, 1955.
Butler, Judith. *Gender Trouble: Feminism and the Subversion of Identity*. Routledge, 2011.
———. *Precarious Life: The Powers of Mourning and Violence*. Verso, 2006.
Caputo, John D. *The Weakness of God: A Theology of the Event*. Indiana University Press, 2006.
———. *What Would Jesus Deconstruct? The Good News of Postmodernism for the Church*. Baker, 2007.
Carter, J. Kameron. *Race: A Theological Account*. Oxford University Press, 2008.
Cavanaugh, William T. *Migrations of the Holy: God, State, and the Political Meaning of the Church*. Eerdmans, 2011.
Chen, Jiji. "Views on the Ecological Crisis." *International Journal of Public Theology*, 2024.
Claiborne, Shane. *The Irresistible Revolution: Living as an Ordinary Radical*. Harper Collins, 2006.
Coakley, Sarah. *God, Sexuality, and the Self*. Cambridge University Press, 2013.
Cobb, John B. *Process Theology as Political Theology*. Wipf and Stock, 2016.
Cone, James H. *A Black Theology of Liberation*. Orbis Books, 2010.
———. *The Cross and the Lynching Tree*. Orbis Books, 2011.
Copeland, M. Shawn. *Enfleshing Freedom: Body, Race, and Being*. 2nd ed. Fortress Press, 2023.
Cornille, Catherine. *The Im-Possibility of Interreligious Dialogue*. Crossroad, 2008.
Cox, H. *The Secular City: Secularization and Urbanization in Theological Perspective*. Princeton University Press, 2013.
Creswell, John W. *Research Design: Qualitative, Quantitative, and Mixed Methods Approaches*. SAGE, 2013.
De La Torre, Miguel A. *Reading the Bible from the Margins*. Orbis Books, 2002.
Derrida, Jacques. *Of Grammatology*. Johns Hopkins University Press, 1976.
Dussel, Enrique. *Ethics of Liberation: In the Age of Globalization and Exclusion*. Duke University Press, 2013.
Einstein, Albert. *Relativity: The Special and General Theory*. Barnes & Noble Publishing, 2004. Originally published 1916.
Ellul, Jacques. *The Technological Society*. Knopf Doubleday, 1964.
Edwards, Denis. *Ecology at the Heart of Faith*. Orbis Books, 2006.
Fanon, Frantz. *The Wretched of the Earth*. Grove Press, 1963.
———. *The Wretched of the Earth*. Grove/Atlantic, Inc., 2007.
Fisher, Cass. "Divine Perfections at the Center of the Star: Reassessing Rosenzweig's Theological Language." *Modern Judaism* 31.2 (2011) 188–212.

Foucault, Michel. *Discipline and Punish: The Birth of the Prison.* Knopf Doubleday, 1995.
Fraser, Nancy. *Justice Interruptus: Critical Reflections on the "Postsocialist" Condition.* Psychology Press, 1997.
Freire, Paulo. *Pedagogy of the Oppressed.* Seabury Press, 1970.
Fretheim, Terence E. *Exodus: Interpretation: A Bible Commentary for Teaching and Preaching.* Presbyterian Publishing Corporation, 2010.
Gadamer, Hans-Georg. *Philosophical Hermeneutics.* University of California Press, 1977.
———. *Truth and Method.* 2nd rev. ed. A&C Black, 2013.
Galli, Beatrice E., and Franz Rosenzweig. *Franz Rosenzweig and Jehuda Halevi.* McGill-Queen's Press—MQUP, 1995.
Gebara, Ivone. *Out of the Depths: Women's Experience of Evil and Salvation.* Fortress Press, 2002.
Gibbs, Robert. *Why Ethics? Signs of Responsibilities.* Princeton University Press, 2000.
Giroux, Henry A. *Theory and Resistance in Education: A Pedagogy for the Opposition.* Bloomsbury Academic, 1983.
Graham, Elaine. *Transforming Practice: Pastoral Theology in an Age of Uncertainty.* Wipf and Stock, 2002.
Grenz, Stanley J. *The Moral Quest: Foundations of Christian Ethics.* InterVarsity Press, 2000.
Gutiérrez, Gustavo. *A Theology of Liberation: History, Politics, and Salvation.* Orbis Books, 1988.
———. *The Power of the Poor in History.* Wipf and Stock, 2004.
———. *We Drink from Our Own Wells: The Spiritual Journey of a People.* Orbis Books, 1984.
Habermas, Jürgen. *The Theory of Communicative Action: Volume 2: Lifeworld and System: A Critique of Functionalist Reason.* Beacon Press, 1985.
Hall, Douglas John. *Professing the Faith: Christian Theology in a North American Context.* Fortress Press, 1993.
Hauerwas, Stanley. *A Community of Character: Toward a Constructive Christian Social Ethic.* University of Notre Dame Press, 1981.
———. *The Work of Theology.* Eerdmans, 2015.
Heidegger, Martin. *Being and Time* (J. MacQuarrie & E. S. Robinson, Trans.). Harper. (Original work published 1927), 1962.
Herskowitz, D. M. "Franz Rosenzweig's Account of Revelation in Light of Its Protestant Background." *Harvard Theological Review* 117.3 (2024) 583–606.
Hessel, Dieter T., and Rosemary Radford Ruether, eds. *Christianity and Ecology.* Harvard University Press, 2000.
Higgins, J. August. "Spirit and Truth: Gadamer's Fusion of Horizons and Contemporary Spirituality Studies." *Philosophy and Theology* 28.2 (2016) 469–90.
hooks, bell. *Teaching to Transgress.* Routledge, 2014.
Hughes, Aaron W. *The Invention of Jewish Identity: Bible, Philosophy, and the Art of Translation.* Indiana University Press, 2010.
Jennings, Willie James. *The Christian Imagination: Theology and the Origins of Race.* Yale University Press, 2010.
Johnson, Elizabeth A. *Ask the Beasts: Darwin and the God of Love.* A&C Black, 2014.
Jones, Serene. *Trauma and Grace: Theology in a Ruptured World.* Presbyterian Publishing Corp, 2009.

Joo, Sang Rak. *Re-imagining Peace and Reconciliation Between South and North Korea in the Missiological Perspective*. Theology and Praxis, 70. 2020.

Kang, Wi Jo. "A Korean Theology and Praxis of Reconciliation for the Reunification of Korea." *Journal of Asian and Asian American Theology* 9 (2009) 82–100.

Kant, Immanuel. *Critique of Pure Reason* (P. Guyer & A. W. Wood, Trans.). Cambridge University Press, 1998.

Kearney, Richard. *Anatheism: Returning to God after God*. Columbia University Press, 2010.

Keller, Catherine. *Cloud of the Impossible: Negative Theology and Planetary Entanglement*. Columbia University Press, 2014.

———. *The Face of the Deep: A Theology of Becoming*. Routledge, 2003.

Knotts, Matthew W. "Readers, Texts, and the Fusion of Horizons: Theology and Gadamer's Hermeneutics." *AUC Theologica* 4.2 (2014) 233–46.

Kohler, George Y. *Reading Maimonides' Philosophy in 19th Century Germany: The Guide to Religious Reform*. Springer Science & Business Media, 2012.

Kwok, Pui-lan. *Postcolonial Imagination and Feminist Theology*. Westminster John Knox Press, 2005.

LaDuke, W. *All Our Relations: Native Struggles for Land and Life*. South End Press, 1999.

Levinas, Emmanuel. *Totality and Infinity: An Essay on Exteriority*. Springer Science & Business Media, 1979.

Löwith, K. *Meaning in History: The Theological Implications of the Philosophy of History*. University of Chicago Press, 1949.

Marcuse, Herbert. *One-Dimensional Man: Studies in the Ideology of Advanced Industrial Society*. 2nd ed. Beacon Press, 2012.

Mbiti, J. S. *Introduction to African Religion*. 2nd ed. Heinemann. 1991.

McFague, Sally. *A New Climate for Theology: God, the World, and Global Warming*. Fortress Press, 2008.

Meiring, P. G. J. "Forgiveness, Reconciliation, and Justice á la Desmond Tutu." *Verbum et Ecclesia* 43.2 (2022).

Mendes-Flohr, Paul R. *From Mysticism to Dialogue: Martin Buber's Transformation of German Social Thought*. Wayne State University Press, 1989.

Merleau-Ponty, Maurice. *Phenomenology of Perception*. Routledge & Kegan Paul, 1962.

Milbank, John. *Theology and Social Theory: Beyond Secular Reason*. John Wiley & Sons, 2008.

Mohanty, Chandra Talpade. *Feminism Without Borders: Decolonizing Theory, Practicing Solidarity*. Duke University Press, 2003.

Moltmann, Jürgen. *Ethics of Hope*. SCM Press, 2013.

———. *The Coming of God: Christian Eschatology*. Fortress Press, 1996.

Mootz, F. J. III, and G. H. Taylor, eds. *Gadamer and Ricoeur: Critical Horizons for Contemporary Hermeneutics* A&C Black, 2011.

Moyn, Samuel. *Origins of the Other: Emmanuel Levinas Between Revelation and Ethics*. Cornell University Press, 2005.

Myers, Ched. *Binding the Strong Man: A Political Reading of Mark's Story of Jesus*. Orbis Books, 1988.

Niebuhr, Reinhold. *Moral Man and Immoral Society: A Study in Ethics and Politics*. Westminster John Knox Press, 2013.

Nietzsche, Friedrich. *Thus Spoke Zarathustra: A Book for All and None* (Based on the Thomas Common translation, extensively modified by B. Chapko). Penguin UK. (Original work published 1883), 1974.

Northcott, Michael S. *A Moral Climate: The Ethics of Global Warming*. Orbis Books, 2007.

Novak, David. *The Jewish Social Contract: An Essay in Political Theology*. Princeton University Press, 2005.

Nussbaum, Martha C. *Creating Capabilities: The Human Development Approach*. Harvard University Press, 2011.

———. *Frontiers of Justice: Disability, Nationality, Species Membership*. Harvard University Press, 2006.

Ochs, P. *Another Reformation: Postliberal Christianity and the Jews*. Baker Academic, 2011.

Park, Sam-kyung. "The Notion of Reconciliation in Sangsaeng Theology for Korean Reunification." *Madang: Journal of Contextual Theology* 18 (2012) 95–114.

Patel, Eboo. *Sacred Ground: Pluralism, Prejudice, and the Promise of America*. Beacon Press, 2012.

Pollock, Benjamin. *Franz Rosenzweig and the Systematic Task of Philosophy*. Cambridge University Press, 2009.

Raschke, Carl A. *Fire and Roses: Postmodernity and the Thought of the Body*. SUNY Press, 1996.

Rasmussen, Larry L. *Earth-Honoring Faith: Religious Ethics in a New Key*. Oxford University Press, 2013.

Rauschenbusch, Walter. *A Theology for the Social Gospel*. Macmillan, 1917.

Rawls, John. *A Theory of Justice*. Harvard University Press, 2009.

Riach, G. *An Analysis of Gayatri Chakravorty Spivak's Can the Subaltern Speak?* CRC Press, 2017.

Ricoeur, Paul. *Time and Narrative: Volume I*. University of Chicago Press, 2012.

Rieger, Joerg, and Priscila Silva. "Liberation Theologies and Their Future: Rethinking Categories and Popular Participation in Liberation." *Religions* 14.7 (2023) 925.

Rollins, Peter. *The Idolatry of God: Breaking Our Addiction to Certainty and Satisfaction*. Simon & Schuster, 2013.

Rorty, Richard. *Contingency, Irony, and Solidarity*. Cambridge University Press, 1989.

Rosenstock-Huessy, Eugene. *Out of Revolution: Autobiography of Western Man*. Jarrolds, 1938.

———. *The Christian Future: Or the Modern Mind Outrun*. Harper, 1966.

Rosenzweig, Franz. *Speech and Reality*. Argo Books, 2013.

———. *The Star of Redemption*. University of Wisconsin Press, 2005.

Ruether, Rosemary Radford. *Sexism and God-Talk: Toward a Feminist Theology*. Beacon Press, 1983.

Said, Edward W. *Culture and Imperialism*. Knopf Doubleday, 2012.

Sang-Rak, Joo. "Re-imagining Peace and Reconciliation between South and North Korea in the Missiological Perspective." *Theology and Praxis* 70 (2020) 435–59. https://doi.org/10.14387/jkspth.2020.70.435.

Schüssler Fiorenza, Elisabeth. *But She Said: Feminist Practices of Biblical Interpretation*. Beacon Press, 1992.

———. *Transforming Vision: Explorations in Feminist Theology*. Fortress Press, 2011.

Segundo, Juan Luis. *Liberation of Theology*. Wipf and Stock, 2002.

Sen, Amartya. *Development as Freedom*. Oxford University Press, 1999.
Sennett, Richard. *The Corrosion of Character: The Personal Consequences of Work in the New Capitalism*. Norton, 2011.
Smith, James K. A. *Desiring the Kingdom: Worship, Worldview, and Cultural Formation*. Baker Academic, 2009.
Smith, Jane I. *Muslims, Christians, and the Challenge of Interfaith Dialogue*. Oxford University Press, 2007.
Sobrino, Jon. *Christology at the Crossroads: A Latin American Approach*. Wipf and Stock Publishers, 2002.
———. *Christ the Liberator: A View from the Victims*. Orbis Books, 2001.
———. *Jesus the Liberator: A Historical Theological Reading of Jesus of Nazareth*. A&C Black, 1994.
———. *No Salvation Outside the Poor: Prophetic-Utopian Essays*. Orbis Books, 2008.
Sölle, Dorothee. *Suffering*. Fortress Press, 1975.
———. *Thinking About God: An Introduction to Theology*. Wipf and Stock, 2016.
Sugirtharajah, R. S. *The Bible and the Third World: Precolonial, Colonial, and Postcolonial Encounters*. Cambridge University Press, 2001.
Tanner, Kathryn. *Christ the Key*. Cambridge University Press, 2010.
———. *Christianity and the New Spirit of Capitalism*. Yale University Press, 2019.
Tarrow, S. G. *Power in Movement: Social Movements and Contentious Politics*. Cambridge University Press, 2011.
Taylor, Charles. *The Ethics of Authenticity*. Harvard University Press, 1992.
———. *After God*. University of Chicago Press, 2008.
Taylor, M. C. *After God*. University of Chicago Press, 2008.
Tutu, Desmond. *No Future Without Forgiveness*. Doubleday, 1999.
Unger, Roberto M. *The Self Awakened: Pragmatism Unbound*. Harvard University Press, 2007.
Volf, Miroslav. *A Public Faith: How Followers of Christ Should Serve the Common Good*. Brazos Press, 2011.
Waetjen, H. C. *A Reordering of Power: A Socio-Political Reading of Mark's Gospel*. Wipf and Stock, 2014.
Walzer, Michael. *Exodus & Revolution*. Basic Books, 1985.
West, Cornel. *Democracy Matters: Winning the Fight Against Imperialism*. Penguin, 2005.
———. *The Cornel West Reader*. Basic Books, 2000.
———. *Race Matters*. Vintage Books, 1994.
West, Gerald O. *The Stolen Bible: From Tool of Imperialism to African Icon*. Brill, 2016.
Wright, Christopher J. H. *The Mission of God: Unlocking the Bible's Grand Narrative*. InterVarsity Press, 2013.
Wright, Nicholas Thomas. *Surprised by Hope: Rethinking Heaven, the Resurrection, and the Mission of the Church*. HarperOne, 2007.
Yong, Amos. *In the Days of Caesar: Pentecostalism and Political Theology*. Eerdmans, 2010.
———. *The Spirit Poured Out on All Flesh: Pentecostalism and the Possibility of Global Theology*. Baker Academic, 2005.
Yoder, John H. *The Politics of Jesus*. Eerdmans, 1994.
Žižek, Slavoj. *In Defense of Lost Causes*. Verso, 2009.
———. *The Sublime Object of Ideology*. Verso, 1989.
———. *Welcome to the Desert of the Real! Five Essays on September 11 and Related Dates*. Verso, 2002.

www.ingramcontent.com/pod-product-compliance
Lightning Source LLC
Chambersburg PA
CBHW050614300426
44112CB00012B/1499